I0817540

The *Illustrated* Tudor Dictionary

The *Illustrated* Tudor Dictionary

An A to Z of notable characters, themes and events from 1485 to 1603.

Simon Sandys-Winsch

First published in Great Britain in 2024 by
Pen & Sword History
An imprint of Pen & Sword Books Limited
Yorkshire – Philadelphia

ISBN 978 1 03610 198 5

A CIP catalogue record for this book is available from the British Library

Typeset by Mac Style
Printed in the UK by CPI Group (UK) Ltd, Croydon, CR0 4YY.

Pen & Sword Books Limited incorporates the imprints of After the Battle, Atlas, Archaeology, Aviation, Discovery, Family History, Fiction, History, Maritime, Military, Military Classics, Politics, Select, Transport, True Crime, Air World, Frontline Publishing, Leo Cooper, Remember When, Seaforth Publishing, The Praetorian Press, Wharncliffe Local History, Wharncliffe Transport, Wharncliffe True Crime and White Owl.

For a complete list of Pen & Sword titles please contact

PEN & SWORD BOOKS LIMITED
47 Church Street, Barnsley, South Yorkshire, S70 2AS, England
E-mail: enquiries@pen-and-sword.co.uk
Website: www.pen-and-sword.co.uk
or
PEN AND SWORD BOOKS
1950 Lawrence Rd, Havertown, PA 19083, USA
E-mail: uspen-and-sword@casematepublishers.com
Website: www.penandswordbooks.com

To Penny,
for everything.

In memory of
Dave Roberts
(1965–2023)

Contents

SCOTLAND
Edinburgh
Langside
Pinkie
Ancrum Moor
Flodden
Solway Moss
Durham
Route of the Spanish Armada
DONEGAL
ULSTER
Yellow Ford
CUMBERLAND
THE PALE
IRELAND
Dublin
YORKSHIRE
York
Doncaster
LINCOLNSHIRE
Stoke
MUNSTER
Waterford
Cork
Kinsale
Bosworth
Norwich
NORFOLK
Ludlow
Milford Haven
WALES
Cambridge
Oxford
Tilbury
Bristol
London
Henry Tudor's route to Bosworth
Canterbury
Gravelines
DEVON
KENT
Portsmouth
Exeter
Calais
CORNWALL
Plymouth
The Solent
Boulogne
The Lizard
Honfleur
FRANCE

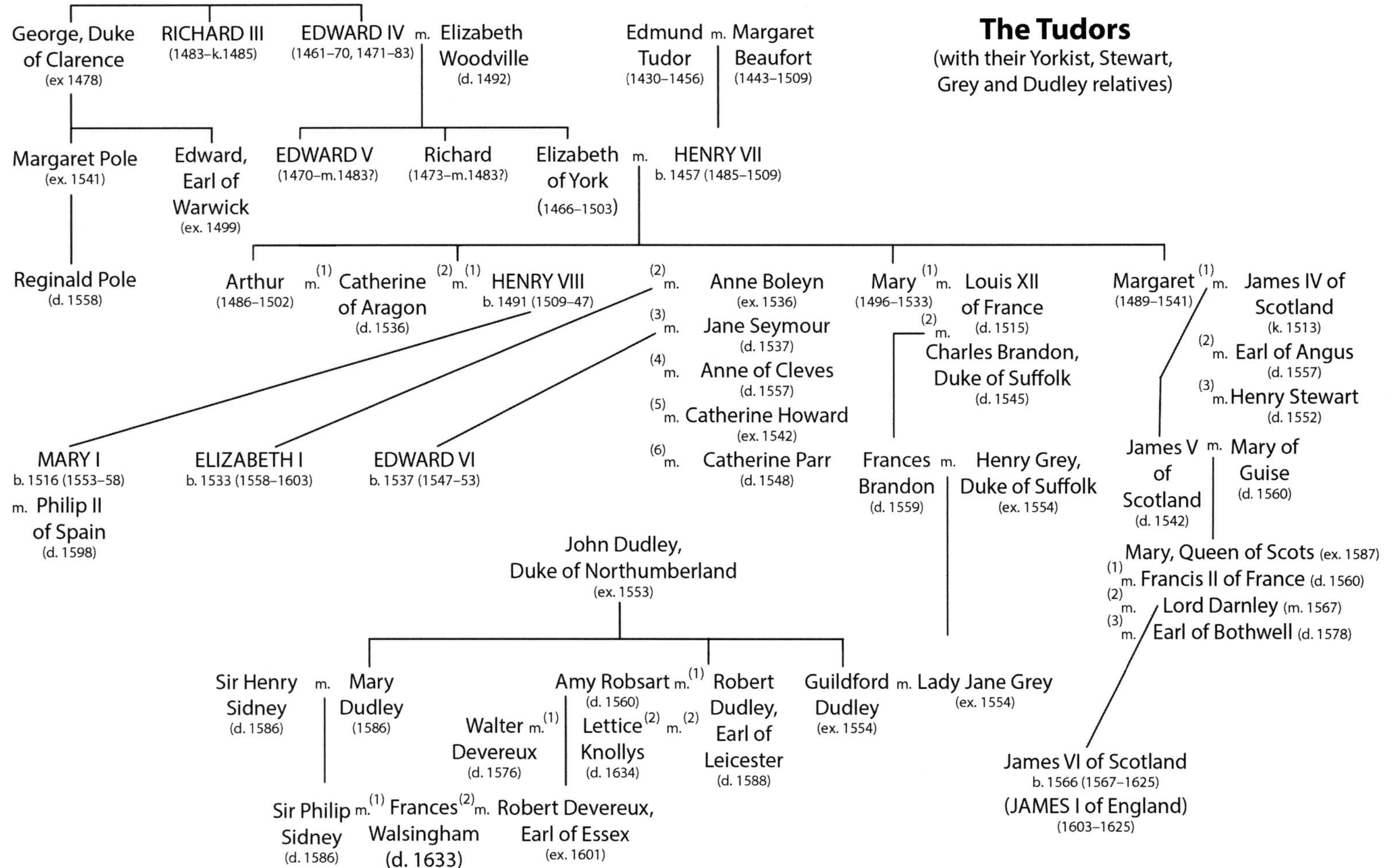
The Tudors
(with their Yorkist, Stewart, Grey and Dudley relatives)
George, Duke of Clarence (ex 1478)
RICHARD III (1483–k.1485)
EDWARD IV (1461–70, 1471–83) m. Elizabeth Woodville (d. 1492)
Edmund Tudor (1430–1456) m. Margaret Beaufort (1443–1509)
Margaret Pole (ex. 1541)
Edward, Earl of Warwick (ex. 1499)
EDWARD V (1470–m.1483?)
Richard (1473–m.1483?)
Elizabeth of York (1466–1503) m. HENRY VII b. 1457 (1485–1509)
Reginald Pole (d. 1558)
Arthur (1486–1502) m.(1) Catherine of Aragon (d. 1536) (2) m. (1) HENRY VIII b. 1491 (1509–47)
(2) m. Anne Boleyn (ex. 1536)
(3) m. Jane Seymour (d. 1537)
(4) m. Anne of Cleves (d. 1557)
(5) m. Catherine Howard (ex. 1542)
(6) m. Catherine Parr (d. 1548)
Mary (1496–1533) (1) m. Louis XII of France (d. 1515)
(2) m. Charles Brandon, Duke of Suffolk (d. 1545)
Margaret (1489–1541) (1) m. James IV of Scotland (k. 1513)
(2) m. Earl of Angus (d. 1557)
(3) m. Henry Stewart (d. 1552)
MARY I b. 1516 (1553–58) m. Philip II of Spain (d. 1598)
ELIZABETH I b. 1533 (1558–1603)
EDWARD VI b. 1537 (1547–53)
Frances Brandon (d. 1559) m. Henry Grey, Duke of Suffolk (ex. 1554)
James V of Scotland (d. 1542) m. Mary of Guise (d. 1560)
Mary, Queen of Scots (ex. 1587)
(1) m. Francis II of France (d. 1560)
(2) m. Lord Darnley (m. 1567)
(3) m. Earl of Bothwell (d. 1578)
John Dudley, Duke of Northumberland (ex. 1553)
Sir Henry Sidney (d. 1586) m. Mary Dudley (1586)
Amy Robsart (d. 1560) m.(1) Robert Dudley, Earl of Leicester (d. 1588)
Walter Devereux (d. 1576) m.(1) Lettice Knollys (d. 1634) (2) m.(2)
Guildford Dudley (ex. 1554) m. Lady Jane Grey (ex. 1554)
Sir Philip Sidney (d. 1586) m.(1) Frances Walsingham (d. 1633) (2) m. Robert Devereux, Earl of Essex (ex. 1601)
James VI of Scotland b. 1566 (1567–1625) (JAMES I of England) (1603–1625)

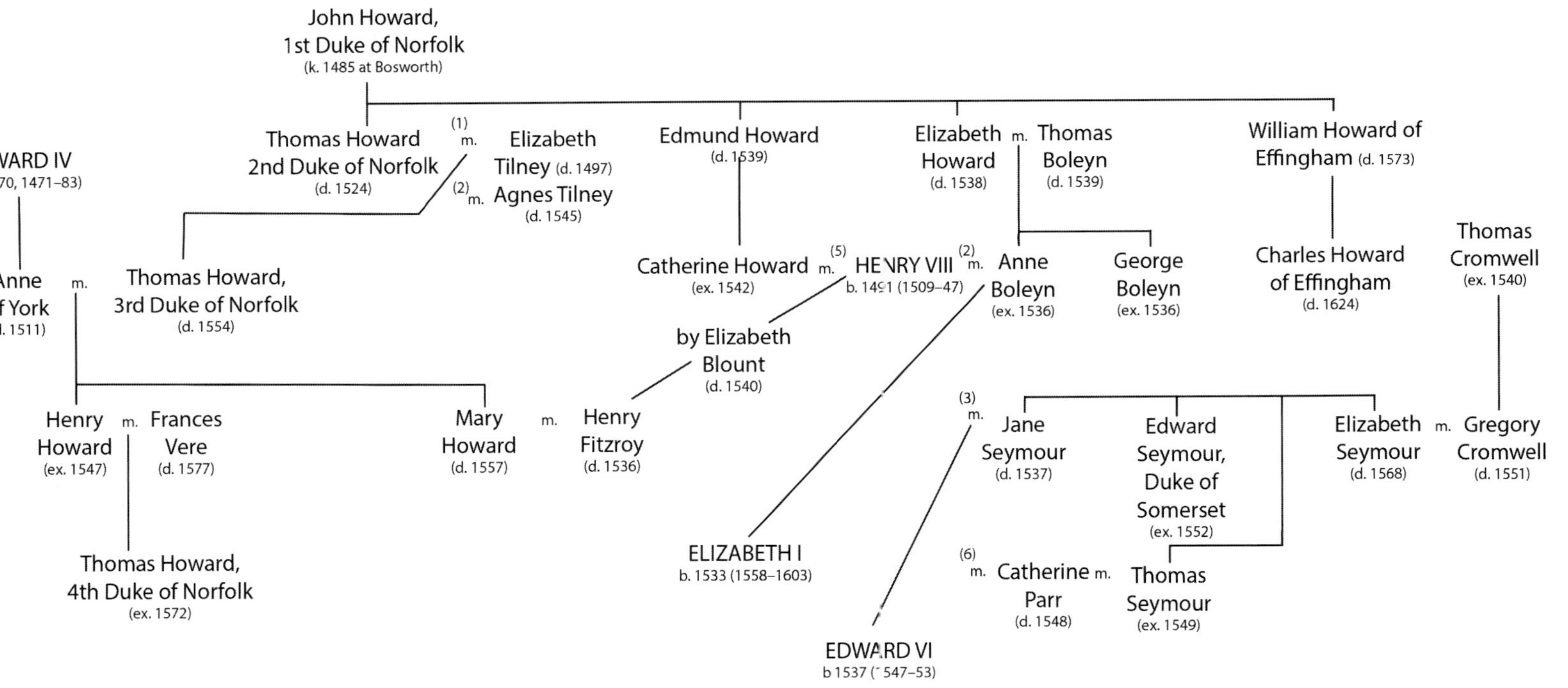

The Howard and Seymour Families

Preface

This is not so much a book but more of an intricate signpost. One that is designed to help anyone with even a passing interest in the Tudors to navigate their way around sixteenth century England. A signpost that will lead to discoveries of heroes and villains, glories and disasters, piety and bigotry. Moreover, just as signposts have a habit of leading to others, one may simply dip into it at any page and begin a journey that will, hopefully, be enlightening and fascinating.

There is a wealth of information to be found on the Tudor period and I confess that, sometimes, I found it overwhelming. Therefore, the largest challenge was to write concisely and yet retain the important facts in a way that can be easily understood. There were also two other important objectives. When I taught history in schools I always aimed to make my lessons interesting (with variable success, I am certain!) and ensure that I provided balance. I can only hope that, within these pages, I have overcome these challenges. Balance, in particular, can be hard to achieve when writing about characters such as Richard Rich and Bishop Bonner, especially when contemporary evidence is lacking or biased.

Some of you may wonder why I excluded certain characters, events or themes. The answer, inevitably, is that I had to draw the line somewhere. Difficult decisions had to be made and I can only apologise for all of my omissions. I am also painfully aware of the gender inequality within these pages – a reflection of the fact that women were treated as second-class citizens in the Tudor Age. Nevertheless, I hope that the likes of Margaret Beaufort, Catherine of Aragon and Bess of Hardwick will be more inspiring than any of their male contemporaries.

This period is undoubtedly one of the most important in England's history; when the country subtly shifted from medieval to modern. A time when the 'new men' of ability replaced the nobility. A time when a growing, educated middle class began to assert itself. A time when government became more centralised. A time when a sense of nationalism developed based on a new religion and growing cultural and military achievements. A time when the country started to turn away from the European continent and seek wealth and power beyond the Atlantic.

Whether this is a book or a signpost, welcome to the Tudor Age.

Timeline

HENRY VII

1485	Battle of Bosworth. Accession of Henry VII and start of the Tudor dynasty. First outbreak of the sweating sickness.
1486	Henry marries Elizabeth of York. First recorded use of the word 'football'.
1487	Battle of Stoke. Law against livery and maintenance.
1491	Appearance of the pretender, Perkin Warbeck.
1492	Treaty of Etaples between England and France.
1495	World's first dry dock at Portsmouth.
1496	James IV of Scotland invades northern England.
1497	Cornish Rebellion. J Cabot sails to America. Capture of Warbeck.
1499	Marriage, by proxy, of Prince Arthur to Catherine of Aragon. Executions of Warbeck and Earl of Warwick.
1500	First English cook book. Plague kills a third of Londoners.
1502	Death of Prince Arthur. Population stands at approx. 2.2 million.
1503	Death of Elizabeth of York. Margaret marries James IV of Scotland.
1505	Margaret Beaufort founds Christ's College, Cambridge.
1508	S Cabot searches for NW Passage.

HENRY VIII

1509	Death of Henry VII and accession of Henry VIII who marries Catherine of Aragon.
1511	Launch of the *Mary Rose*.
1512–14	First Anglo-French War.
1512	*On Copia* by Erasmus. Boys aged 7 upwards have to practise archery.
1513	Battle of Flodden. First edition of *Anglia Historia* by Vergil.
1514	Mary Tudor marries Louis XII of France.
1515	Wolsey becomes cardinal and Chancellor. Rebuilding of Hampton Court Palace begins.
1516	*Utopia* by T More. Birth of Princess Mary.
1517	Evil May Day. Luther initiates the Reformation.
1520	Field of Cloth of Gold.
1521	Henry attacks the teachings of Luther.

1522–25 Second Anglo-French War.
1525 Failure of The Amicable Grant. Hops first cultivated in Kent.
1526 Translation of a work by Erasmus by Margaret 'Meg' More.
1527 Start of the king's 'Great Matter'.
1529–36 Reformation Parliament
1529 Wolsey falls from power.
1530 *Practice of Prelates* by W Tyndale.
1532 Submission of the Clergy. More resigns as Chancellor. Holbein settles in England.
1533 Henry marries Anne Boleyn. Annulment of his marriage to Catherine of Aragon. Anne gives birth to Princess Elizabeth.
1534 Acts of Succession and Supremacy. Execution of Elizabeth Barton.
1535 Executions of Fisher and More. Welsh Act.
1536 Pilgrimage of Grace. Executions of Anne Boleyn and Tyndale. 10 Articles.
1536–40 Dissolution of the monasteries.
1537 Birth of Prince Edward.
1539 The Great Bible is distributed. First horse race is held (at Chester). 6 Articles. Statute of Proclamations.
1540 Execution of Cromwell.
1542 Execution of Catherine Howard. Battle of Solway Moss.
1543–46 Third Anglo-French War.
1543–50 The War of the Rough Wooing.
1544–51 The Great Debasement
1545 Battle of Ancrum Moor. Sinking of the *Mary Rose.*
1546 Execution of Anne Askew.
1547 Execution of Henry Howard. Death of Henry VIII and accession of Edward VI. Somerset becomes regent. Battle of Pinkie.

EDWARD VI

1549 Book of Common Prayer introduced. Kett's Rebellion. Prayer Book. Rebellion. Somerset replaced by J Dudley.
1550 England's population reaches approx. 3 million.
1551 Last outbreak of the sweating sickness.
1552 Execution of Somerset. 42 Articles. 35 grammar schools founded.
1553 Death of Edward VI. Lady Jane Grey coup. Accession of Mary I.

MARY I

1553 Execution of Northumberland.
1554 Wyatt's Rebellion. Marriage of Mary to Philip of Spain. Chancellor meets Ivan the Terrible. Heresy laws revived. England rejoins Catholic Church.

1555	Executions of Latimer and Ridley.
1556	Execution of Cranmer. Pole becomes Archbishop of Canterbury. Rapid inflation.
1557	Influenza epidemic.
1557–59	Fourth Anglo-French War
1558	Loss of Calais. Death of Mary I and accession of Elizabeth I.

ELIZABETH I

1559	Church Settlement.
1561	Reversal of debasement begins.
1562	Hawkins's first slave voyage. Smallpox almost kills Elizabeth. French civil wars begin (to 1598).
1563	39 Articles. *Book of Martyrs* by J Foxe. Plague kills 20,000 in London.
1565	First human dissection allowed in England. Hawkins brings tobacco to England.
1568	Mary, Queen of Scots flees to England. Douai Jesuit College opens. Battle of San Juan de Ulua.
1569	Northern Rebellion. First public lottery in England (outside St Paul's)
1569–73	First Desmond Uprising.
1570	Pope excommunicates Elizabeth.
1571	Royal Exchange opens. Ridolfi Plot.
1572	St Bartholomew Day's Massacre. Fourth Duke of Norfolk executed.
1574	All remaining serfs in England are formally emancipated.
1575	Byrd and Tallis granted a monopoly in music production.
1576	First imprisonment of Wentworth. Frobisher searches for NW Passage.
1577–80	Drake's circumnavigation.
1579–83	Second Desmond Uprising
1581	Execution of Campion.
1583	Throckmorton Plot.
1584	Bond of Association. Jesuits banned.
1585–1604	Anglo-Spanish War
1586	Babington Plot. Potatoes introduced to England.
1587	Execution of Mary, Queen of Scots. Raid on Cadiz. Davis's third voyage to the NW Passage. Roanoke colony re-established. Burghley House completed.
1588	Spanish Armada. Death of Leicester.
1589	English 'counter-armada'.
1590	*The Faerie Queene* by Spenser. *Arcadia* by Sidney. Death of Walsingham.

1591	Capture of the *Revenge* and death of Grenville. Probable first performance of Shakespeare's first play – *Henry VI*.
1592	Plague kills over 19,000 in London.
1593	*Venus and Adonis* by Shakespeare. Murder of Marlowe. Executions of dissident Puritans.
1594–1603	Tyrone's Rebellion.
1595	Spanish raid Penzance and Mousehole. Death of Hawkins.
1596	Death of Drake. Raid on Cadiz. Harrington's first flushing toilet, the 'Ajax' or 'Jakes', is described.
1597	Gresham College opens. *Essays* by Bacon. Father Gerard escapes from Tower of London.
1598	Death of Burghley. Battle of Yellow Ford.
1599	Opening of the Globe theatre. Essex returns from Ireland.
1600	Population reaches approx. 4 million.
1601	Essex's Rebellion and execution. Possible first performance of *Hamlet*. Poor Relief Act.
1602	Battle of Kinsale.
1603	Death of Elizabeth I. End of the Tudor Age.

A

Allen, William

(1532–94)

A leading proponent of the Counter-**Reformation** against Elizabethan England.

Cardinal Allen. (*Artist: Unknown. BM de Reims via Wikimedia Commons*)

After graduating from Oxford University, Allen sought an ecclesiastical career. However, Queen **Elizabeth I**'s Church of England ran counter to his strong **Catholic** beliefs and, in 1561, he felt compelled to emigrate to the Netherlands in order to avoid persecution. In the following year, though, he returned in order to preach Catholicism and campaign against the newly established Church. Four years later, he was forced to leave the country again, this time never to return.

After visiting Rome, Allen came up with the idea of establishing a seminary for English Catholic exiles. This would provide a supply of trained priests who would be ready to return to England in order to bring its people back into the Catholic fold. With the help of local monasteries, he founded such a college at Douai, in the Spanish Netherlands, in 1568. The college expanded rapidly under his leadership and its press produced a stream of Catholic literature. Allen received papal funding for this enterprise and was invited by the Pope to establish a similar seminary in Rome. However, in 1576, the Douai college was forced to relocate to the safety of Rheims due to the threats of Dutch **Protestants** who considered its students to be collaborators of their Spanish enemies.

Soon after this, he started a working relationship with a **Jesuit** priest called Robert Parsons and, as result, his activities became more radical. In 1580 they started to send priests, such as **Edmund Campion**, to England in order to preach Catholicism and undermine the Protestant state. In time, over 160 Douai priests were caught, tortured and executed but Allen had instilled such confidence and fanaticism in his students that they celebrated each martyrdom with a special Mass of thanksgiving.

Under the influence of Parsons, Allen adopted more political methods in his attempts to save the souls of the English. He corresponded with **Mary, Queen of Scots** and, after her execution, he supported King Philip of Spain's plan to invade England and remove Elizabeth, '…this woman, hated by God and man.' In 1587, Philip secured Allen's promotion to cardinal of England. As such, if the **Spanish Armada** had succeeded, he would probably have become Archbishop of Canterbury.

Allen further angered the English government by publishing letters and pamphlets in which he attempted to stir up trouble amongst the English Catholics. In these, he attacked the queen and encouraged all Englishmen to surrender to the Spanish. The failure of the Armada, however, dealt a severe blow to his hopes and his influence declined. However, he continued to believe that England would soon become Catholic again and he helped to establish another English seminary at Valladolid in Spain. After living the rest of his life in near-poverty he died, in debt, in Rome in 1594.

Allen was clearly an intelligent man with an unshakeable religious faith and the present-day college at Douai is a monument to his work and beliefs. He possessed great powers of persuasion, too, and was extremely generous with whatever money he had. On the other hand, his faith seemed to cloud his judgement of the English Catholics, the majority of whom had actually celebrated the failure of the Armada and, as a result of his activities, they only suffered further persecution.

Ancrum Moor, Battle of

(1545)

A battle in the **War of the Rough Wooing**.

In 1544, English troops had already committed much destruction in southern Scotland. Early in the following year, another force set out across the border to pillage more properties in order to compel the Scottish government to the negotiating table. Led by Sir Ralph Euer and Sir Brian Laiton, it numbered around 5,000 men. The majority were German and Spanish mercenaries and included 700 Scottish 'borderers' who had declared their support for the English.

On 27 January, having plundered the town and abbey at Melrose, they were on their return journey when a group of Scottish cavalry was spotted on a hill near Ancrum village named Peniel Haugh. The Scots feigned a retreat and the English cavalry gave chase only to run into the long Scottish pikes waiting on the other side. With their opponents' horsemen badly mauled the Scots then attacked down the hill towards the English infantrymen who, due to the marsh, were struggling to get into battle formation. As their pikes were considerably longer than the English bills, the Scots were able to force the English vanguard into their rear-guard, thereby causing further confusion. At this point, the Scottish 'borderers', renowned for their fickle character, switched sides and the confusion turned into a rout as the English attempted to flee.

The Scottish forces had been outnumbered 2:1 but suffered very few casualties. About 800 English were killed, including both Euer and Laiton, and 1,000 were captured. An unusually large border raid, especially for the middle of winter, had suffered a humiliating defeat but the Scottish regent, the Earl of Arran, was reluctant to follow up this victory for fear of provoking further English retaliation. In fact, **Henry VIII** was provoked into escalating military action anyway and so the battle had little political significance.

As an interesting aside, contemporaries dated the battle as 27 January 1544. This is because the Tudor calendar started on Lady Day (25 March) although 1 January was still celebrated to remember the Roman New Year. It was not until 1752 that England finally brought its calendar into line with the rest of Europe and started its year on 1 January.

First Anglo-French War

(1512–14)

A sideshow of the War of the League of Cambrai whose major players were France, Spain, the Holy Roman Empire and the Papacy.

After ascending to the throne, **Henry VIII** was keen to assert himself on the international stage, gain military glory and restate English claims to the French throne. He finally got his chance when the Holy League of Spain, the Holy Roman Empire and the Papacy formed an alliance with the aim of driving France out of northern Italy. Henry allied with the League and sent 12,000 men to Aquitaine in 1512. The plan was to combine with Spanish forces and reconquer former English possessions in south-west France. However, King Ferdinand of Spain simply abandoned his allies and invaded Navarre for himself. The idle English army suffered from dysentery, poor supplies and mutiny and the survivors had to beat an ignominious retreat.

Undeterred, Henry personally led an invasion of northern France the following year, aiming to coordinate with the Emperor Maximilian. This time, **Thomas Wolsey** ensured that the army was well supplied and equipped. The English captured the towns of Tournai and Therouanne and won a minor victory at Guinegate (known as the Battle of the Spurs due to the speed of the French

Battle of the Spurs. A minor battle but glorified by the English. The French town of Therouanne, in the background, was captured afterwards. French knights can be seen fleeing on the right. The original painting depicted Henry VIII fighting on horseback in the centre but, in truth, he was a spectator. (*Artist: Unknown. From* The Pictorial History of England *by George Craik and based on a 1513 Flemish painting*)

retreat). In the same year, the Scots supported their French allies by invading England but were routed at the Battle of **Flodden**.

However, Henry was once again abandoned by his allies who made separate peace treaties with France. He had to follow suit and in the ensuing treaty England kept Tournai and received annual pensions. Also, Henry's sister, **Mary**, was married to the French king, Louis XII.

The war was costly though (it depleted the treasury that **Henry VII** had so carefully built up) and confirmed England's junior status in European politics. At the same time, Wolsey's organisational skills were brought to Henry's attention and his rise to power accelerated. Perhaps the most important consequence of this conflict was the establishment of a standing royal navy. Henry had recognised the importance of controlling the English Channel and so built larger warships, enlarged his fleet and maintained it during times of peace.

Second Anglo-French War

(1522–25)

A part of the Italian War of 1521–26 in which Francis I of France fought Charles V of Spain and the Holy Roman Empire.

This war provided another opportunity for **Henry VIII** to gain military glory and for Cardinal **Wolsey** to extend English influence as well as his own.

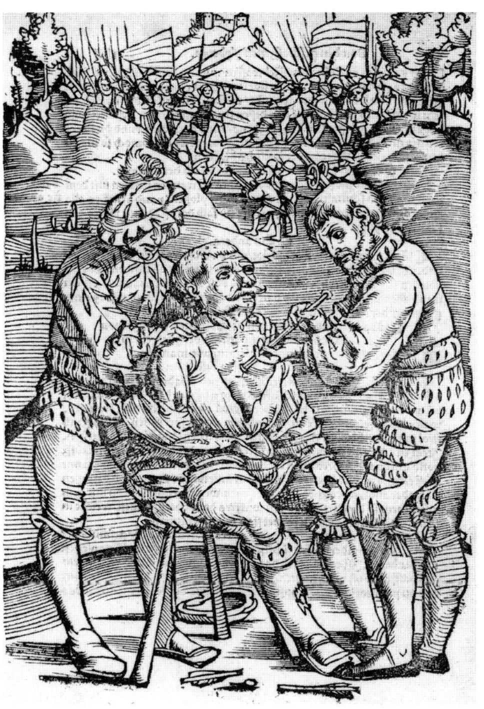

Treatment of a battlefield injury. (*Author: from* Fieldbook of Surgery *by Hans von Gersdorf, 1517. Wellcome Images*)

The pretext was English anger with France's interference in Scottish politics and so Henry and Charles V signed the Treaty of Windsor in June 1522 in which a joint attack on France was outlined. Charles also agreed to compensate for England's lost pensions from France and to marry Henry's daughter **Mary**. The following month the English navy, led by the **Earl of Surrey**, looted and burned its way along the coasts of Picardy and Normandy but achieved little else.

In 1523, the **Duke of Suffolk** led a large army from Calais with the aim of taking Boulogne and strengthening the English position in Picardy. However, Wolsey diverted it towards Paris. This was probably due to the Pope's death and the subsequent belief that an English capture of the French capital would encourage Charles V's support for Wolsey's candidature to the Papacy. The stretched French forces could offer little resistance and Suffolk marched to within fifty miles of Paris, causing panic within the city. However, freezing temperatures, an outbreak of smallpox in the army and the failure of imperial forces to offer support forced him to withdraw to Calais. He also suffered a shortage of supplies due to a chronic lack of finances. In fact, Wolsey had had difficulty in raising money from **Parliament** and a system of forced loans had caused such a degree of civil unrest that it had had to be abandoned.

In February 1525, Charles achieved outright victory at the Battle of Pavia in northern Italy. This meant that he did not need English support anymore and refused to back another invasion of northern France. He also demanded a huge dowry for his planned marriage to Mary.

Wolsey, therefore, changed tack and arranged a rapprochement with France at the Treaty of the More. In return for giving up territorial claims in France, England would receive annual pensions and the promise of French non-interference in Scotland. Wolsey hoped that an Anglo-French alliance would redress the European balance of power and maybe force Charles to accept Wolsey as the new Pope.

Third Anglo-French War

(1543–46)

Henry VIII's third and final war with France
and also his most costly and unsuccessful.

The background to this conflict was the renewal of hostilities between Francis I of France and Charles V of the Holy Roman Empire. Angered by French interference in Scottish politics, Henry allied with Charles in late 1543 with both leaders agreeing to invade France. The alliance was never a secure one though. Charles had misgivings about cooperating with the Head of the heretical Church of England and they squabbled about the goals of the campaign.

Battle Scene. Well-drilled rows of pikemen, as seen on the right, were very effective against cavalry assaults. (*Artist: Sebastian Munster, 1550–1628. Wikimedia Commons*)

In 1544, the **Duke of Suffolk** laid siege to Boulogne despite Charles's insistence upon an attack on Paris. The city finally fell after two months but soon after, Charles made a separate peace with Francis due to a lack of funds and domestic problems within Germany.

Henry, however, decided to carry on alone against France but his main army, led by the **Third Duke of Norfolk,** had to retreat to Calais leaving 4,000 men to defend Boulogne against a lengthy siege. Henry refused to surrender the city and demanded the withdrawal of French support for the Scots who were campaigning against the English in the **War of the Rough Wooing**.

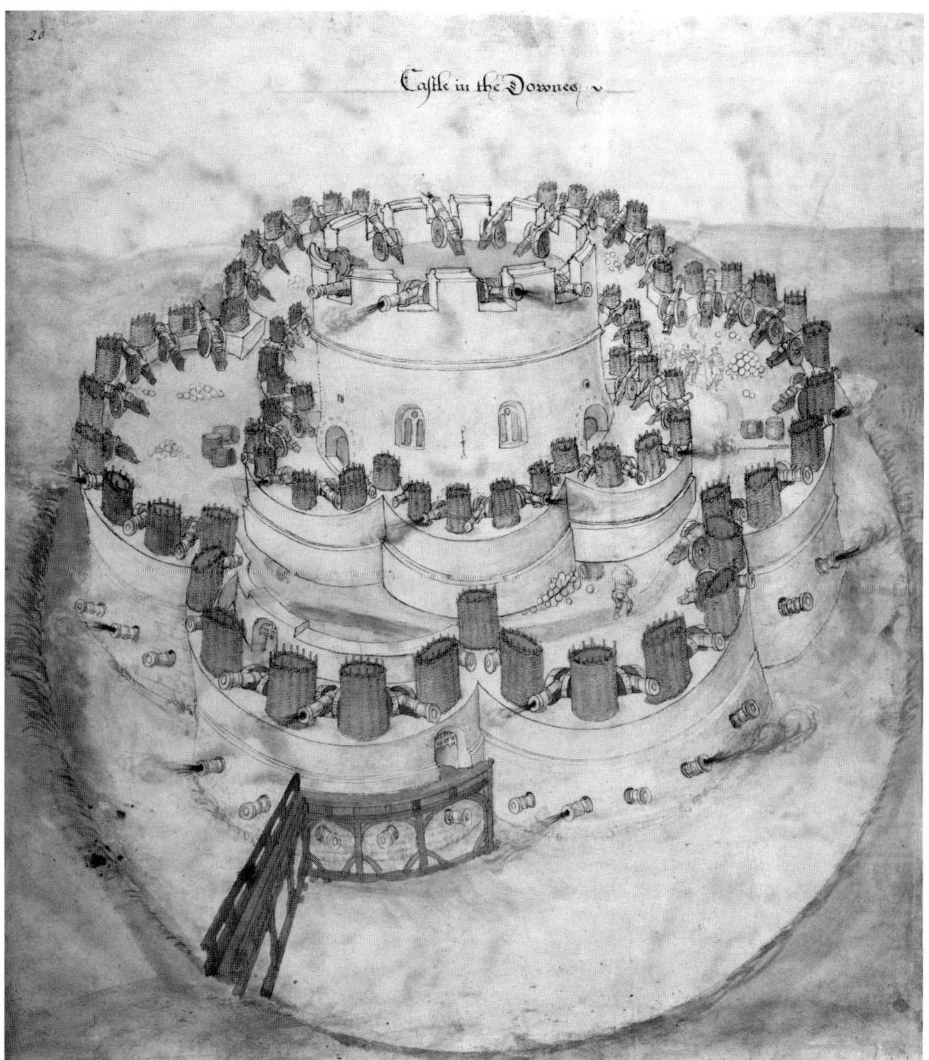

Deal Castle. Part of Henry VIII's coastal defenses. Probably a draft plan presented to King Henry. (*Artist: unknown, 1539. British Library*)

In 1545, Francis made an ambitious assault on England with 400 ships and 30,000 men. The fleet was hampered by bad weather, though, and a series of accidents. It only managed a brief skirmish with the English fleet in the Solent in which the latter's ***Mary Rose*** sank accidentally. The French also made some abortive landings on the mainland and the Isle of Wight before returning to the blockade of Boulogne.

Eventually, the adversaries, both short of funds, recognised the stalemate and agreed to the Treaty of Camp in 1546. England was allowed to keep Boulogne until 1554 and France would resume its annual pensions to Henry. In fact, four year later, after renewed hostilities, England was forced to return the city anyway at the Treaty of Boulogne. The war was ruinously expensive for both sides and caused a drastic **debasement** of the English coinage.

Fourth Anglo-French War

(1557–59)

Part of the Italian War of 1551–59, which pitted Henry II of France against his traditional Habsburg foes in Spain and the Holy Roman Empire.

In 1556 Queen **Mary I** was persuaded by her husband, Philip II of Spain, to provide him with military support despite her lack of finances and preparations for such an enterprise.

In August 1557 the English and Spanish forces combined to rout the French army at St Quentin. However, Philip failed to press home his advantage and indeed withdrew to the Netherlands. This left the English force in Calais exposed to a French counter-attack. Unfortunately for them, the city's defences had become neglected and security measures had been relaxed. This allowed French forces to enter the city in January 1558 and take over England's last foothold on the continent.

Calais had been in English hands since 1347 and the humiliation at its loss was felt deeply throughout the nation. Mary and her Spanish marriage were widely blamed and she herself felt such remorse that she is supposed to have uttered, 'When I am dead and opened, you will find Calais engraved on my heart.'

Enough money was raised to fund a counter-attack in Brittany. Little was achieved though and Mary died soon afterwards. At the Treaty of Cateau-Cambresis (1559) French ownership of Calais was formally recognised. Ultimately, though, the loss of Calais may have benefitted England as it forced her to focus her efforts beyond the oceans rather than on the continent, which had limited potential for gain.

Anglo-Spanish War

(1585–1604)

A long, draining conflict between England and Spain, which was never formally declared, at the end of the Tudor period.

An unofficial war had already been waged in the Atlantic and Spanish Main since 1568. Spanish attempts to exert its trading monopoly in the West Indies had led to a campaign of privateering by English 'sea-dogs' such as **Francis Drake** and **John Hawkins**. Many Spanish treasure ships were being hijacked with Queen **Elizabeth I**'s tacit consent, which had had a damaging effect on the Spanish treasury. Insult was added to injury in 1581 when Elizabeth knighted Drake. He had just returned from a circumnavigation of the world in which he had raided and looted several Spanish ships and colonies around South America.

Capture of Cagafuego. Cagafuego ('Fireshitter') was the nickname of the huge Spanish treasure galleon captured by Drake after he entered the Pacific in 1579. (*Artist: Friedrich van Hulsen, 1626. The Kraus Collection of Francis Drake*)

Interwoven in this was the religious polarisation within Europe. Philip II of Spain saw himself as the leader of the **Catholic** counter-**reformation** and Elizabeth as the leading **Protestant** heretic who needed to be replaced with the Catholic **Mary, Queen of Scots**. This view was compounded by the growing English support for the Dutch Protestants in the Netherlands who had, since 1566, embarked upon a course of rebellion against their Spanish overlords. As a counterweight to this, Philip would later provide aid for the Irish in their struggle against English overlordship.

From Elizabeth's point of view, it was vital that Protestant forces on the continent survived in order to prevent England's isolation. For this reason, she had also been supporting the French Huguenots in their civil war against the French Catholic League (started 1562). The Treaty of Joinville (1584) between Spain and the League alarmed her so much that she finally agreed, at the Treaty of Nonsuch (1585), to provide military assistance to the Dutch despite her personal dislike of aiding rebels.

This treaty, in effect, amounted to an unofficial declaration of war and Philip ordered an ambitious invasion of England. Despite the destruction of many supply ships at Cadiz by Drake in 1587, the **Spanish Armada** set sail the following year. Its defeat, however, put Spain on the back foot and England sent a 'counter-armada' of its own in 1589. Its aims were to destroy the Spanish Atlantic fleet, capture its treasure ships, stir up rebellion in Portugal and establish a base in the Azores but it failed, at a huge cost, and Elizabeth refused to countenance such an ambitiously offensive campaign again.

In the Netherlands, meanwhile, the **Earl of Leicester** was sent over with 6,000 troops to bolster the Dutch Revolt. He was a poor commander, though, and ill-supplied and his clumsy and high-handed leadership forced his early return to England. However, thousands of English troops remained in the Netherlands for the war's duration.

The 1590s was a generally disappointing decade for England after its initial successes. A much-improved Spanish convoy system thwarted the 'sea-dogs' and the talismanic Drake and Hawkins died at sea. An Anglo-Huguenot force was defeated in Brittany and, in 1595, Spanish troops landed in Cornwall and sacked Penzance. The next year saw an Anglo-Dutch fleet succeed in destroying Cadiz but Spain still managed to launch two further armadas (1596 and 1597) although both were defeated by adverse weather conditions. However, a final armada in 1601 successfully landed 3,000 troops in southern **Ireland** to support **Tyrone's Rebellion**. The rebels' defeat forced the Spanish to surrender, though, and return home.

The conflict had become a war of attrition with England very much on the back foot; its finances, resources and trade were draining away. In 1604 the two countries' new leaders, James I of England and Philip III of Spain, were keen to make peace. The terms of the Treaty of London (1604) were mostly favourable to Spain, which caused a good deal of resentment towards the new English king at home. England agreed to stop supporting the Dutch Revolt and the raiding of Spanish shipping. In return, the Spanish signatories, in effect, acknowledged the Protestant state in England.

Aragon, Catherine of

(1485–1536)

First wife of **Henry VIII** and Queen of England from 1509 to 1533.

The youngest child of King Ferdinand and Queen Isabella of Spain, Catalina was betrothed at the age of three to Prince **Arthur**, aged two, the son of **Henry VII** of England. She received an excellent, broad **education** and was brought up as a devout **Catholic**.

In 1501, she finally travelled to England and married Arthur although they had difficulties communicating as they had learnt different pronunciations of Latin. However, within five months they both contracted **sweating sickness**, which killed him. Catherine, as she was now known, survived and wanted to return to Spain but obeyed her father's wishes to remain. Henry VII now betrothed her to his second son, Henry, in order to maintain the Spanish alliance and keep the huge **marriage** dowry. However, he treated her very poorly, providing her with very little money and few servants. He even threatened to break the betrothal when he considered allying with alternative countries. In 1507 she served as Spanish ambassador to England (the first female ambassador in European history).

In 1509, upon Henry VIII's accession, the Pope granted him permission to marry his brother's widow because Catherine testified that her marriage to Arthur had not been consummated. It was an openly loving relationship; Henry was a devoted husband and had surprisingly few mistresses. Catherine had at least six pregnancies but only **Mary** (1516) survived. Whilst away fighting in France in 1513 Henry appointed Catherine Regent of England. After the Scots invaded she addressed the army in full armour before the Battle of **Flodden** despite being pregnant. Afterwards, she sent her husband the king of Scotland's blood-stained cloak to announce the English victory. As well as being unswervingly loyal to her husband, Catherine was also a devoted mother to Mary. In addition, she encouraged the education of women, donated money to colleges and started a programme of poor relief. Few other queens have been as popular with the English as she was.

However, by 1526 Catherine was considered too old to have any more children and Henry was desperate to have a male heir in order to secure the succession. At the same time, he had fallen in love with one of her ladies-in-waiting, **Anne Boleyn**. So Henry petitioned Pope Clement VII to annul their marriage, arguing that he should never have married Catherine in the first place due to the Bible forbidding marriage to a brother's widow. Catherine, too, appealed to the Pope, reiterating that her marriage to Arthur had never been consummated.

She refused to enter a nunnery – which would have annulled their marriage – and made impassioned pleas to Henry to change his course of action. He was determined though and so he removed her from court and, in 1531, installed Anne into her rooms. However, it was becoming increasingly clear that an annulment might be impossible to obtain. The Pope was a virtual prisoner of Catherine's nephew – King Charles of Spain – and so he simply procrastinated.

Anne's pregnancy in early 1533 brought matters to a head. Henry's only option now was to marry Anne and break from Rome by making himself Head of the English Church. This allowed Archbishop **Cranmer** to annul the marriage to Catherine later that year. Throughout, Catherine professed her loyalty to the king and refused to accept Anne as queen. She had widespread support throughout England and Europe including that of **Thomas More**, Martin Luther and Henry's own sister, **Mary**. Even her enemy, **Thomas Cromwell**, stated that, 'If not for her sex, she could have defied all the heroes of history'.

Catherine was exiled to various castles in England and was refused permission to even see her daughter. She spent most her time finding solace in prayer and fasting and would confine herself to a single room. She died, probably of cancer, in 1536 amid rumours that she had been poisoned by Henry and/or Anne. The king did not go to the funeral and also refused permission for Mary to attend. Catherine's last letter to Henry had been a love letter and signed, 'Katherine the Queen'. She had remained loyal and steadfast to the very end.

Arthur, Prince of Wales

(1486–1502)

Eldest son of King **Henry VII** and **Elizabeth of York**.

Henry VII believed that his first-born son would usher in a new golden era for England and so christened him Arthur in honour of his supposed ancestor. In order to strengthen his position against the joint threats of France and **Yorkist** pretenders, Henry sought an alliance with Isabella of Castile and Ferdinand of Aragon in which Arthur would marry their youngest daughter, **Catherine of Aragon**, aged three. This was agreed at the Treaty of Medina del Campo in 1488.

Arthur was well educated, being familiar with the best Latin and Greek authors, and was known to be thoughtful, studious and reserved. He probably had little to do with his siblings as he was sent, at the age of six, to Ludlow Castle to begin his proper training for kingship.

He finally met his bride-to-be after she landed in England in 1501. Apparently, he was very pleased at meeting his 'lovely bride' and, ten days later, they were married at St Paul's Cathedral in London. The couple then travelled to Ludlow Castle whereupon Arthur suddenly died at the mere age of fifteen.

The cause of death is unknown but was probably tuberculosis, diabetes or the mysterious **sweating sickness**. Conspiracy theorists argue that he was murdered upon royal orders due to concerns that he was too unhealthy to be able to rule the country strongly, unlike his more robust younger brother, **Henry**. However, there is no evidence of this or indeed that he was even a sickly child. The king did not attend Arthur's funeral, possibly because he was too grief-stricken, and Prince Henry became heir to the throne.

Articles (of Religion)

(1536, 1539, 1552, 1563)

Official written declarations that attempted to define the faith of the new Church of England.

Ten Articles of 1536

These were probably compiled by Archbishop **Cranmer** and were the first statement of the Church of England's theology, which remained largely **Catholic** but with some **Protestant** leanings. For instance, it asserted the importance of only three of the seven sacraments.

Many Protestants, especially those on the continent who had sought England as an ally after its break from Rome, were disappointed that the Articles did not go far enough. At the same time, they caused displeasure amongst conservatives in England and contributed to the **Pilgrimage of Grace** in the north.

Six Articles of 1539

King **Henry VIII**, always a Catholic himself, had become concerned with the pace of radical reform in his Church and with the degree of disaffection that it had caused. He also wanted better relations with France and Spain whom he feared might launch a joint attack on 'heretical' England.

The Act of Six Articles, therefore, reasserted the full traditional Catholic doctrine and prescribed severe punishments upon those who refused to follow them. It was a setback for the reformers such as **Thomas Cromwell**, Archbishop Cranmer (who felt compelled to send his family back to the safety of Germany) and Bishop **Latimer** (who resigned his see). Protestants referred to it as 'the bloody whip with six strings' and it remained in force for the rest of Henry's reign.

Forty-Two Articles of 1552

The reign of the Protestant **Edward VI** permitted the introduction of radical reform of the Church of England. This culminated in the Forty-Two Articles, written by Cranmer and issued by royal decree. These articles represent the zenith of Protestantism in England. They included the repudiation of most of the Catholic tenets, including transubstantiation, and endorsed the view that faith alone, rather than the sacraments and good works, was the key to salvation.

However, these articles were never enforced as Edward died soon after and the Catholic Queen **Mary** suppressed them.

Thirty-Nine Articles of 1563

After the accession of Queen **Elizabeth** and the re-establishment of the Church of England it was necessary to redefine the country's faith. Convocation (meeting of the leading clergy), led by Archbishop **Parker**, drew up the Thirty-Nine Articles which were based on Cranmer's Forty-Two Articles. Elizabeth wanted a national Church that would appeal to the broadest domestic opinion; one that steered a middle path between Catholicism and **Puritan**ism, of which the moderate reformers of Henry VIII's reign may have approved. As a result, the Articles were deliberately phrased loosely to allow a degree of interpretation.

They shared the same platform as Catholicism such as the belief in the Holy Trinity and Jesus dying for the redemption of human sins. However, they also asserted some key Protestant principles such as the denial of transubstantiation and all but two of the sacraments. They also stated the importance of faith rather than good works, the supremacy of the scriptures over Church traditions, the belief in predestination, the necessity to preach sermons in English and gave permission for priests to marry.

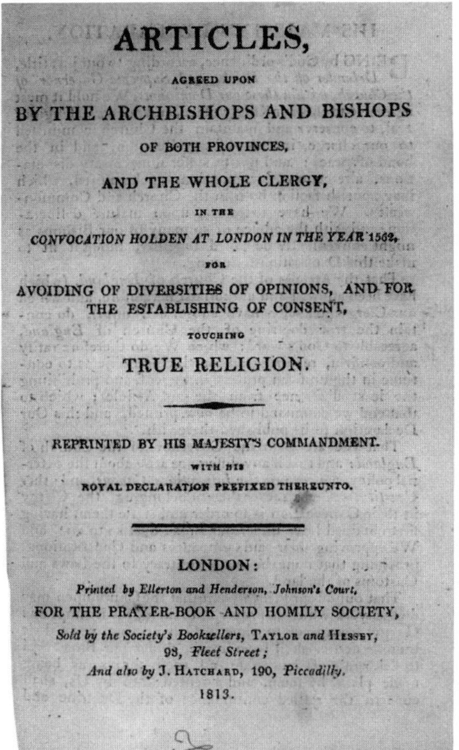

ARTICLES,
AGREED UPON
BY THE ARCHBISHOPS AND BISHOPS
OF BOTH PROVINCES,
AND THE WHOLE CLERGY,
IN THE
CONVOCATION HOLDEN AT LONDON IN THE YEAR 1562,
FOR
AVOIDING OF DIVERSITIES OF OPINIONS, AND FOR THE ESTABLISHING OF CONSENT,
TOUCHING
TRUE RELIGION.

REPRINTED BY HIS MAJESTY'S COMMANDMENT.
WITH HIS
ROYAL DECLARATION PREFIXED THEREUNTO.

LONDON:
Printed by Ellerton and Henderson, Johnson's Court,
FOR THE PRAYER-BOOK AND HOMILY SOCIETY,
Sold by the Society's Booksellers, TAYLOR *and* HESSEY,
93, *Fleet Street;*
And also by J. HATCHARD, 190, *Piccadilly.*
1813.

39 Articles of 1563. An 1813 reprint of the 39 Articles. After 250 years, the government was still guarding the 'true' religion. (*Author: Unknown. From Cleveland Public Library*)

At first, Elizabeth refused to allow the Thirty-Nine Articles to go through **Parliament** for fear of upsetting the Catholic powers. However, after the Pope excommunicated her in 1570 she felt that she had nothing to lose and so they were enacted in law two years later and, to this day, are the bases of the Anglican faith.

Askew, Anne

(1520–46)

A notable **Protestant** martyr in the reign of **Henry VIII**.

Born into a wealthy Lincolnshire family, Anne Askew developed strong Protestant beliefs. When forced into **marriage** with a **Catholic** at the age of fifteen she refused to adopt her husband's name and she soon left him to preach against transubstantiation (a cornerstone of the Catholic faith) in London.

After being arrested and sent back to her husband she again returned to preaching in the capital. Rumours about her connections to **Catherine Parr**, via the queen's ladies-in-waiting, brought her the unwelcome attention of the Catholic party at court. These included Lord Chancellor, Thomas Wriothesley, **Sir Richard Rich** and the **Third Duke of Norfolk**. With King Henry VIII clearly having little time to live they feared Catherine Parr, a suspected Protestant, would use her influence to undermine their positions of power after the king's death. If they could prove that she was a heretic, then Henry would have to get rid of her.

Askew was therefore arrested and sent to the **Tower of London**. There, she was tortured on the rack to force her admission of connections to the queen. The racking of a gentlewoman shocked many people but this did not prevent Wriothesley and Rich from personally torturing her. However, she refused either to speak or to recant her faith in order to save her life.

The Rack. The instrument upon which Anne Askew was tortured. Here, it is the Protestant heretic, Cuthbert Simpson, suffering in 1558. (*Artist: John Foxe from his* Book of Martyrs, *1563 via Wikimedia Commons*)

Subsequently, in July 1546, she had to be carried in a chair to Smithfield Market where she was slowly burned alive. A large crowd was impressed by her fearlessness in the face of such cruelty and her death was later written into Foxe's ***Book of Martyrs***. In this way, she became a prominent martyr for the Protestant cause.

B

Babington Plot

(1586)

A **Catholic** conspiracy aimed at replacing Queen **Elizabeth** with **Mary, Queen of Scots**.

Anthony Babington was born in 1562 into a wealthy Catholic family in Nottinghamshire although, publicly, they were **Protestants**. His maternal grandfather was one of the executed leaders of the **Pilgrimage of Grace**. At the age of fifteen he became a page to the Earl of Shrewsbury, gaoler to Mary, Queen of Scots. At this point, the impressionable young man must have become devoted to her and her cause. In the 1580s he joined an inner circle of Catholics in London whose aim was to protect priests and **Jesuit** missionaries such as **Edmund Campion**. Even so, he became a member of the royal court and gained access to Queen Elizabeth.

Mary's emissaries made contact with Babington on one of his visits abroad and persuaded him to become embroiled in a plot to assassinate Elizabeth, rescue the Queen of Scots and put her on the English throne. At this point in the plan, the ensuing Catholic uprising would be supported by a Spanish invasion force.

However, the conspiracy was very quickly discovered by Sir **Francis Walsingham**, Elizabeth's Secretary of State, through the use of his extensive spy network and the employment of a double agent. Coded correspondence between Babington and Mary was allowed via watertight containers hidden inside beer barrels that entered and left Chartley Hall (the place of her confinement). All letters were intercepted and decyphered by Walsingham's spies until their master finally had the evidence he sought: a letter by Mary approving of the planned assassination of Elizabeth. A postscript was added, which compounded her guilt.

Babington and thirteen other conspirators were arrested and hanged, drawn and quartered. Mary herself was tried at Fotheringhay Castle but denied any role in the plot.

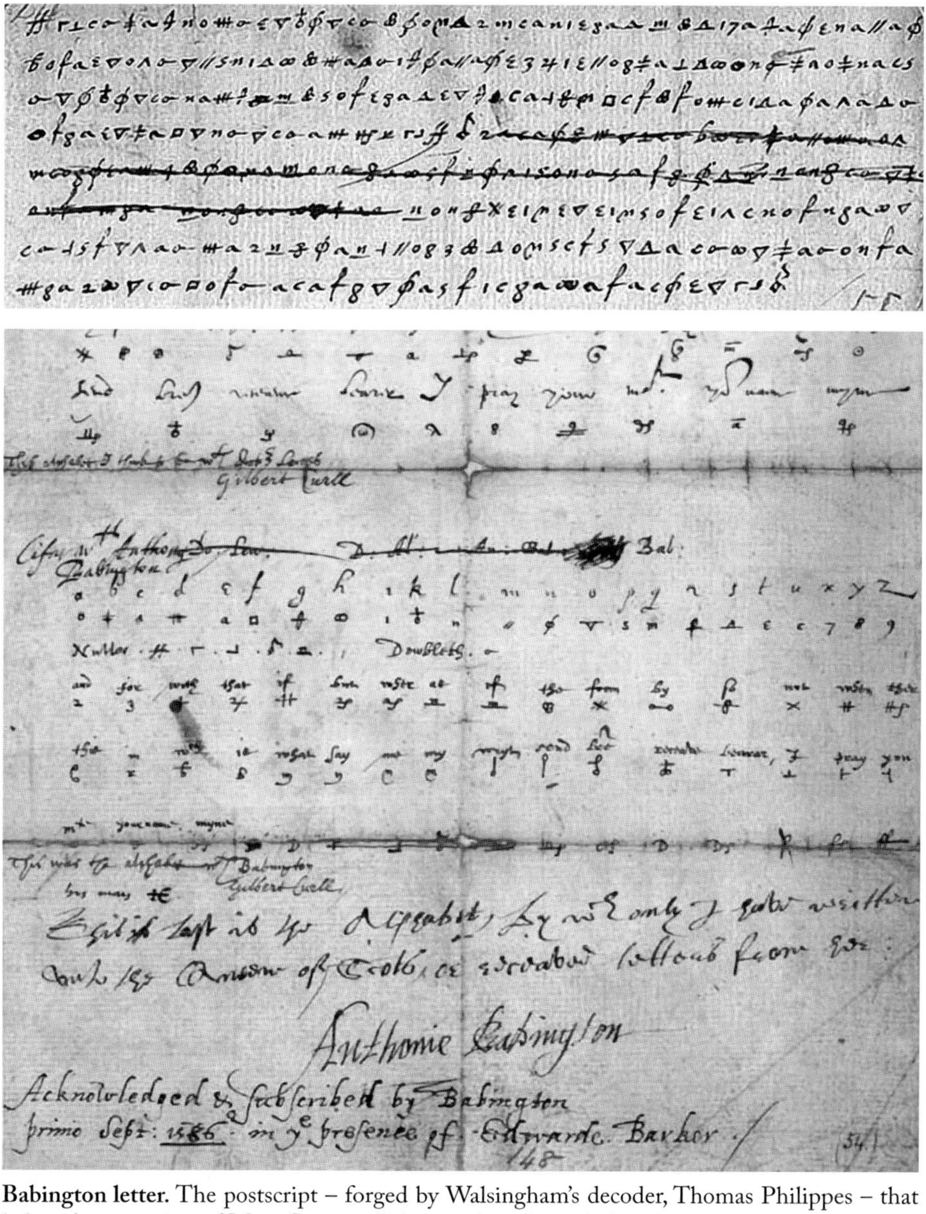

Babington letter. The postscript – forged by Walsingham's decoder, Thomas Philippes – that led to the execution of Mary Stewart. Babington's cipher is below. (*Author: Anthony Babington and Thomas Philippes, 1586. The National Archives of UK*)

The letters were used as proof however and, subsequently, she was beheaded in February 1587 but to this day many claim that her 'letters' were mere forgeries.

Barton, Elizabeth

(c. 1506–1534)

A **Catholic** nun who was thrust into the limelight by her mystical prophecies.

Elizabeth Barton was initially a servant girl who worked on an estate belonging to **William Warham**, the Archbishop of Canterbury. In 1525, she became ill and started to have fits in which she made prophecies and exhorted people to refrain from sin. After she had recovered, Warham sent two of his monks to investigate her. One of them, Dr Edward Bocking, concluded that Barton was genuinely in contact with the Virgin Mary and installed her as a nun at St Sepulchre's convent in Canterbury.

Elizabeth Barton. A late-18th-century engraving depicting Barton having a 'death-like trance' in which she had her visions. (*Artist: probably Thomas Holloway based on a painting by Henry Tresham, late 18th century. Wikimedia Commons*)

Further trances, fits and prophecies brought her much fame and national attention. She attracted many pilgrims and was even recognised as a true mystic by those in power including Warham, Cardinal **Wolsey**, Sir **Thomas More** and King **Henry VIII** himself, with whom she had two meetings. Their association with the popular 'Nun of Kent' probably arose from their genuine respect for her. Female mystics were not uncommon in the Catholic Church.

However, matters changed considerably in 1532 when Barton started prophesying that the king would quickly die '…a villain's death' if he married **Anne Boleyn**. Henry ignored her at first but, after his **marriage** to Anne, Barton started to proclaim that he was no longer the rightful king of England. Such treasonable announcements by a well-known public figure could not be ignored any longer. Barton constituted a very real threat to Henry who was well aware of the unpopularity of the annulment of his marriage to **Catherine of Aragon**.

He ordered **Thomas Cranmer**, Warham's successor, to cross-examine Barton. At this point, she confessed to being a fraud and being part of a conspiracy that included Bocking, More, Bishop **Fisher** (who had been in frequent communication with her) and ten others. An Act of Attainder was brought against them although the charges against More were soon dropped and Fisher escaped with a £300 fine. The others were further examined before the **Star Chamber** and made to read out public confessions at St Paul's Cross. The 'Nun of Kent' and seven others were then hanged at Tyburn.

Depending upon one's views, Barton is also known as the 'Holy Maid of Kent' or the 'Mad Maid of Kent' and it is, of course, impossible to prove her guilt or innocence. Equally, she may or may not have been manipulated by those who opposed the king's annulment. We do know, however, that many contemporaries believed her 'confession' to be a forgery, possibly created by **Thomas Cromwell**, and that she was allowed no trial at which to defend herself. The case remains open.

Beaufort, Margaret

(1443–1509)

Mother of King **Henry VII**, politician and cultural benefactor.

Margaret was born in Bedfordshire and her father was the Duke of Somerset, a great-grandson of King Edward III. He died when she was only one, seemingly by suicide, and so she inherited his vast wealth. Being a rich, young heiress with a potential claim to the throne, she soon became a pawn in the political power struggle between the families of York and Lancaster in the **Wars of the Roses**.

At the age of twelve, she married the Lancastrian Edmund Tudor, a match designed to improve his own weak claim to the throne. However, within a year, he had been captured by his Yorkist enemies and died of the plague whilst in captivity. This was not before he had made Margaret pregnant though and, at the age of thirteen, she produced Henry. The pain and probable complications of giving birth at such a young age possibly explain why she never had any more children.

A year later, she was married to another Lancastrian nobleman, Sir Henry Stafford. This seems to have been a harmonious **marriage** but he died from wounds received at the Battle of Barnet (1471). After this Lancastrian defeat, she urged her teenage son to flee the country and, subsequently, she did not see him for the next fourteen years. Margaret was now keen to rehabilitate herself in the royal court so she married Thomas Stanley, an ally of the Yorkist king, Edward IV. She was gradually able to acquire influence and favours in the royal household, which she hoped would facilitate the return of her son. She was even chosen to be a godmother to one of the king's daughters.

When Edward IV unexpectedly died in 1483, the throne was seized by his brother, Richard III. Rumours soon circulated that the new king had murdered Edward's two sons, the Princes in the **Tower**. This led to a clandestine alliance between Margaret and Elizabeth Woodville, Edward's widow and the mother of the two boys. They plotted to replace King Richard with Henry and, in order to gather support from both Yorkists and Lancastrians, they agreed to betroth Henry to Elizabeth's daughter, **Elizabeth of York**. The ensuing rebellion, however, was crushed and Margaret was lucky to escape with house arrest and the loss of all her estates. She was banned from communication with the outside world, too, but her husband turned a blind eye to this. As a result, through secret correspondence, she was able to drum up support for her son's imminent invasion.

Henry Tudor eventually landed in 1485 and defeated Richard at the **Battle of Bosworth Field**. Soon afterwards, he married Elizabeth of York, just as their mothers had planned. Henry VII displayed much gratitude and love towards his mother for all her support during his exile and his first **Parliament** declared her a *feme sole*. This gave her permission to own her property – rather than her husband doing so – and to sue in court, two rights that no other women had.

During her son's reign, Margaret wielded much influence and was referred to as 'My Lady, The King's Mother'. Determined to display her high status, she wore the same quality garments as the new queen and was allowed to walk a mere single pace behind her. Nothing is known of how Elizabeth of York felt about her mother-in-law; one can only surmise. When she died in 1503, Margaret assumed her role as leading lady of the court.

In 1499, she swore a vow of chastity and decided to live alone near Stamford. At the same time, she involved herself in many projects. These included the commissioning of several works printed by William Caxton, a drainage scheme in the Fens, the building of chapels in Wales and the construction of a free school for the general public in Dorset. Margaret also funded a lectureship in divinity at Oxford University and, guided by her chaplain, **John Fisher**, she founded two new university colleges at Cambridge – St John's and Christ's.

She took a great interest in her grandchildren too. When **Arthur** died, she ensured that the new heir, Prince Henry, received an appropriate **education** and she prevented her favourite, Princess **Margaret**, from being married to the Scottish king at too early an age. She had clearly resolved not to allow her granddaughter to share the same fate that she had suffered. When her son died in 1509, Margaret helped organise his funeral and prepare for the new king's coronation. **Henry VIII** was then guided by her in choosing the members of his first privy council. On 29 June, two months after her son's death, she passed away in Westminster Abbey where she was later buried.

In the past, some historians have criticised Margaret for being domineering and unscrupulous. A few have even suggested that she may have ordered the murder of the Princes in the Tower in order to smooth the way for her son's succession. There is no evidence for this though. Despite the probable bias of the Tudor propagandists who wrote about her, it is clear that Margaret Beaufort was a pious and loving woman who ushered in a period of royal patronage of the arts, education and religion. Even more important is this astonishing fact: in a period when women were considered to be the mere property of their husbands, she displayed enough resilience and single-mindedness to establish a whole new dynasty.

Bess of Hardwick

(1521/22 or 1527–1608)

Noblewoman, businesswoman and builder.

Elizabeth, or 'Bess', was born into minor gentry on Hardwick Manor, Derbyshire but details of her youth are sketchy. The early death of her father brought financial hardship to the family and she was forced to serve on the estate of wealthy neighbours where, it seems, she met and married her first husband – Robert Barlow – a boy in his early teens. He died within two years and Bess was initially prevented from receiving her widow's income from his estate but, in an early sign of her strong character, she fought for her rights in court and won.

Her next **marriage**, in 1547, propelled her into the higher echelons of society where she was to remain. Sir William Cavendish was Treasurer of the King's Chamber and had amassed much wealth from the **Dissolution of the Monasteries**. It seems that the two had a loving relationship and went on to have eight children within ten years. The list of their godparents includes such illustrious names as **Lady Jane Grey**, Lady Elizabeth, the future **Duke of Northumberland** and Queen **Mary I**. Much was spent on parties, gambling and public celebrations such as the Lord of Misrule when a local peasant would be randomly chosen to arrange drunken revelries at Christmas. Bess also persuaded William to buy land at Chatsworth where she oversaw the first of her building projects (only the Hunting Tower remains today).

Cavendish's death in 1557 left her with huge debts but her third marriage, to William St Loe, rescued her. In his position as **Elizabeth I**'s Captain of the Queen's Guard, he managed to remove most of the debt although he, himself, was locked in a land dispute with his brother who probably poisoned him in

1565. Again, Bess had to fight for her widow's inheritance in the courts and she successfully ended up with an annual income of £60,000 (over £20 million in 2024), making her the second-richest woman in the country. Furthermore, being the queen's Lady of the Bedchamber, she had enormous influence too.

Her fourth wedding, to the rich and powerful Earl of Shrewsbury in 1567, elevated her status even further to the Countess of Shrewsbury. At first, their marriage was harmonious but the arrival of an unexpected visitor created unprecedented strains. After **Mary, Queen of Scots**, had escaped from her rebellious lords, Elizabeth asked Shrewsbury to be her gaoler in his various country houses. The expense of guarding Mary and looking after her and her entourage was enormous whilst, at the same time, Bess was still pouring money into Chatsworth. At first, Mary and Bess were friends and spent much time embroidering together (their combined efforts can be seen today in the huge tapestries hanging in Oxburgh Hall, Norfolk). Divisive comments by Mary, however, widened the cracks in the marriage but the final straw may have been when Bess arranged a clandestine marriage between her daughter and Charles Lennox - Mary's brother-in-law and a potential heir to both the Scottish and English thrones. Such a union without the queen's permission could be seen as treasonable and, although Elizabeth forgave Bess, Shrewsbury was much embarrassed. Soon after, his irrational behaviour caused by gout and mental stress caused the couple to permanently separate.

Shrewsbury died in 1590 and, again, Bess had to fight for her widow's income. She then threw her energy into the building of a new mansion near to her childhood home. The resulting Hardwick Hall, designed by one of England's first architects – Robert Smythson – is an impressive example of **Renaissance** architecture with so much glass that people would say, 'Hardwick Hall, more glass than wall'. Now into her seventies, she also showed much business acumen by becoming a money lender (normally a reserve of Jews, not Christians) and investing in local iron mines and glass workshops.

Bess eventually died in her eighties but this remarkable woman had managed to achieve an unprecedented degree of female power and independence in a strongly parochial society. She had successfully played the 'game of marriage' to rise through the ranks but she also displayed huge degrees of determination and vigour to further her family's interests as well as her own whilst skilfully avoiding the deadly minefields of sixteenth century politics and religion.

Blount, Charles (Lord Mountjoy)

1563–1606

Soldier and Lord Lieutenant of **Ireland**.

Blount was born into a noble family that had fallen on hard times but, on becoming Lord Mountjoy after his elder brother's death, he determined to restore his family's fortunes. He spent several years fighting the Spanish in the Low Countries where he made a name for himself and later took part in the **Earl of Essex**'s expedition against the Azores in 1597. His youthful good looks, military prowess and outstanding horsemanship brought him to Queen **Elizabeth**'s attention and she often called upon him to share his military advice. Jealousy between Mountjoy and Essex led to a duel in which Essex was wounded but, remarkably, they became good friends thereafter.

Charles Blount. (*Artist: Nicholas Hilliard c. 1587 via Wikimedia Commons*)

After Essex's failure to subdue **Tyrone's Rebellion** in 1600, Mountjoy was appointed Lord Deputy of Ireland with instructions to quell the revolt which had been going on since 1593. Provided with able commanders and more resources than Essex had been, Mountjoy achieved considerable success. He showed himself to be a master tactician and effectively made use of fortifications to contain pockets of rebellion. He also weakened Tyrone by making deals with some of his allies and through the use of scorched earth tactics which caused the deaths of many civilians. In 1601, Mountjoy defeated an Irish/Spanish force at the Battle of Kinsale and by 1603, he had worn Tyrone down to the point of surrender and imposed relatively lenient peace terms a mere six days after the death of Elizabeth.

Mountjoy returned to a hero's welcome and King James granted him the earldom of Devonshire. In 1605 he married Lady Penelope Rich, sister of Essex and former wife of Lord Rich. Penelope and Mountjoy had been long-term lovers for many years and she had borne him five illegitimate children. However, Rich had only divorced her on the grounds that she could not remarry. The king's advisor, **Robert Cecil**, who regarded Mountjoy as a member of the opposing 'Essex faction', was now able to persuade James to ban the couple from court. The following year, Mountjoy, who had become a tobacco addict, died from lung cancer.

Boleyn, Anne

(1501/7–36)

Second wife of **Henry VIII** and Queen of England from 1533 to 1536.

Daughter of Thomas Boleyn and niece of the **Third Duke of Norfolk**, Anne was educated in the Netherlands and France. On her return to England she became a maid of honour to **Catherine of Aragon**. Her elegant style, charming wit and beautiful dark eyes brought her much attention at Henry's court and she fell in love with Henry Percy, heir to the Duke of Northumberland, and became betrothed to him.

At the same time, though, Henry sought her for himself and ordered Cardinal **Wolsey** to break the betrothal and banish Percy from court. However, Anne refused to be just another mistress to the king, like her sister Mary had been. Possibly encouraged by her ambitious father, Anne insisted on **marriage** or nothing. Henry's infatuation was made clear by his many love letters to her despite his loathing of writing. From 1527 he stepped up his demands for an annulment of his marriage to Catherine as his desire for a son was now entwined with his desire for Anne. Possibly as an act of revenge for his expulsion of Percy, Anne blamed Wolsey for his failure to obtain the papal annulment and, along with others, brought about his downfall. Meanwhile, her position and influence at court rose and, in 1531, she occupied the rooms of the banished Queen Catherine.

Eventually, Anne submitted to Henry's amorous advances and became pregnant in late 1532. The two secretly married in haste (January, 1533) to ensure that the 'boy' would be legitimate. In May, Archbishop **Cranmer** annulled Henry's marriage to Catherine and Anne was crowned queen the following month. Thus began the schism between the English Church and Rome. Public opinion, however, was very much on Catherine's side and rumours abounded that Anne had bewitched their king. An extra nail on her little finger and a large mole on her neck provided the 'evidence' that she was indeed a sorceress.

The heavy expectations for a male heir were dealt a blow in September when **Elizabeth** was born. However, Henry did not seem to have been too undeterred and, at Anne's request, Catherine's daughter, **Mary**, was declared illegitimate. Within a year, though, Anne's star was rapidly fading. Her sharp tongue and high-handed treatment of lords and ministers gained her many enemies. She also appeared to favour religious reform, which antagonised the conservative party at court. Furthermore, later pregnancies resulted in stillborn children and a miscarried son (possibly caused by Anne's shock upon hearing about Henry suffering a serious jousting accident). The king himself began to believe that she had bewitched him and started to take a fancy to one of the queen's attendants, **Jane Seymour**. Anne's position further worsened in early 1536 when Catherine died. Henry would now be able to marry again with fewer complications.

In order to rid himself of an unpopular queen who clearly was not going to provide him with a son Henry ordered **Thomas Cromwell** to create a legal case against Anne. Subsequently, her friend and musician, Mark Smeaton was arrested and probably tortured. In his 'confession' he admitted to being the queen's lover and incriminated four other men, too, including her own brother George. Their executions were soon followed by trumped-up charges of adultery, incest and treason against Anne herself. On 19 May 1536 she was beheaded in the **Tower of London** by a swordsman from Calais but not before Cranmer had annulled her marriage to the king. Eleven days later, Henry married Jane Seymour.

Bonner, Edmund

(c. 1500–69)

Controversial Bishop of London from 1540 to 1549 and from 1554 to 1559.

Bonner studied canon and civil law at Oxford University, entered the service of Cardinal **Wolsey** and became his chaplain. After Wolsey's fall in 1529 he loyally remained by his master's side and was with him when he died. Possibly due to **Thomas Cromwell**'s influence, Bonner entered **Henry VIII**'s service and, from 1532, represented the king abroad. He worked hard to gain support for Henry on the question of the king's 'Great Matter' and, in 1539, he encouraged the printing of **Coverdale**'s 'Great Bible' in Paris. As a reward, he was given the see of London in the same year.

The appointment probably came as a surprise to many people as, up to this point, he had been regarded as a rather coarse lackey of Cromwell's, had shown no interest in theology and had upset many with his arrogant manner. Indeed, he soon became unpopular in London where he faithfully enforced the Act of Six **Articles** by prosecuting heretics and his enemies accused him of excessive cruelty.

Bonner was very much a conservative and, despite his ardent support for the break with Rome, disliked **Protestant**ism and reformists. Therefore, after Henry VIII's death in 1547, he opposed the religious changes proposed by the **Duke of Somerset** and Archbishop **Cranmer**. He even questioned the legality of the royal supremacy during the reign of a minor, i.e. **Edward VI**. In

Edmund Bonner. (*Artist: unknown, c. 1800. Engraving based on a 16th-century portrait via Wikimedia Commons*)

1549 he refused to enforce the new Book of Common Prayer and so was deprived of his bishopric and thrown into Marshalsea Prison.

Upon **Mary**'s accession he was released and restored to his see. He now accepted papal supremacy and set about restoring **Catholic**ism in his diocese. It is due to his subsequent persecution of Protestants in London that he has been vilified in history under the nickname of 'Bloody Bonner'. John Foxe in his ***Book of Martyrs*** wrote of him, 'This cannibal in three years space three hundred martyrs slew. They were his food, he loved so blood, he spared none he knew.' He further alienated the reformers with his brutal jeering of Cranmer when asked to degrade his former superior.

However, Bonner's apologists argue that he always tried to persuade heretics to recant in order to avoid the stake and that his diocese was by far the most violently anti-Catholic in England. Indeed, at one point, the Queen's Council told him that he was not being severe enough (in fact, over 40 per cent of those who were burned lived in London).

On balance, it seems that the new regime employed him as a useful instrument with which to carry out unpleasant work and that he had little choice but to carry out orders in the toughest part of the country. However, he certainly must take a large part of the blame and, upon **Elizabeth**'s accession in 1558, it is no surprise that the new queen refused to allow him to kiss her hand. Bonner faithfully adhered to his religion though and refused to remove the service of the Mass from his diocese when ordered to do so. He would not take the new oath of supremacy either and so he was sent, again, to Marshalsea Prison (1560). He died nine years later but had to be secretly buried at midnight to avoid the risk of violent demonstrations.

Book of Martyrs
(1563)

A hugely influential book, written by John Foxe, which depicts **Protestant** martyrdom.

John Foxe (1517–1587) distinguished himself at Oxford University and turned to Protestantism during the 1540s. In 1547, he became the tutor of the children of the executed **Earl of Surrey**. These included **Thomas Howard**, later the Fourth Duke of Norfolk, and **Charles Howard** who later commanded the English fleet against the **Spanish Armada**. His circle of friends at this time included **Nicholas Ridley**, **John Hooper** and **William Cecil**. After the **Catholic** Queen **Mary**'s accession Foxe just managed to evade capture by the authorities and fled to the continent. He lived in near-poverty as a proof reader in Basle before returning to England after Mary's death in 1558.

Foxe started writing his *Actes and Monuments of these Latter and Perilous Days, Touching Matters of the Church*, commonly known as *The Book of Martyrs* in 1552. Later, he added a chapter to include the Marian persecutions so that the first edition was not published until 1563. It is an account of Christian martyrdom since the death of Christ but it focuses on the suffering of fourteenth- and fifteenth-century religious dissidents and sixteenth-century Protestants. Its 1800 pages are illustrated with woodcuts graphically depicting the burnings of such 'martyrs' as **William Tyndale**, **Anne Askew**, **Hugh Latimer**, **Nicholas Ridley** and **Thomas Cranmer**. The most shocking image is that of a baby being thrown into the flames straight after her mother had given birth during her execution.

After its publication Foxe soon became famous but he remained poor, despite the fact that each book sold for the equivalent of three weeks' pay for a skilled labourer, as there were no royalties then. The book was popular with the Church of England, which ordered copies be installed in each church, and it even outsold the Bible for a while. In response to accusations of inaccuracies and exaggerations Foxe wrote three more editions but leading Catholics continued to denounce it, one calling it '…that huge dunghill of your stinking martyrs, full of a thousand lies.'

There has been much debate regarding the reliability of the *Book of Martyrs.* It is accurate in the sense that Foxe based his later chapters on written primary evidence and eyewitness accounts. However, he wrote it in order to demonise Catholics and identify their Church with tyranny. As a result, it is biased and its language often lacks neutrality with words such as '…Mark the apish pageants of these popelings…' Trustworthy or not, the *Book of Martyrs* was a huge influence on English Protestant thinking right up to the nineteenth century and contributed to the strong anti-Catholic sentiment of the seventeenth century.

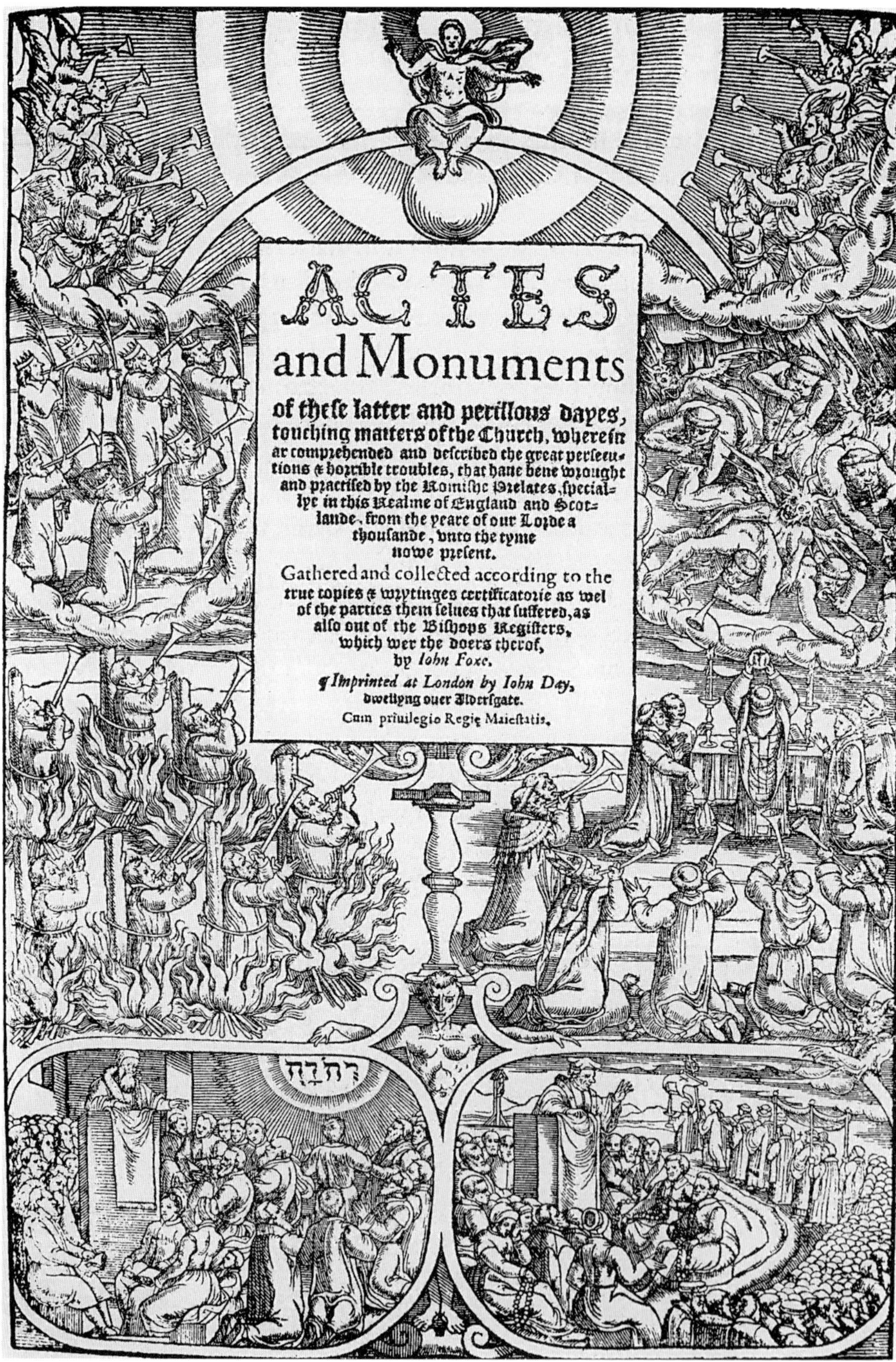

ACTES
and Monuments
of these latter and perillous dayes, touching matters of the Church, wherein ar comprehended and described the great persecutions & horrible troubles, that haue bene wrought and practised by the Romishe Prelates, speciallye in this Realme of England and Scotlande, from the yeare of our Lorde a thousande, vnto the tyme nowe present.
Gathered and collected according to the true copies & wrytinges certificatorie as wel of the parties them selues that suffered, as also out of the Bishops Registers, which wer the doers therof, by *Iohn Foxe*.
Imprinted at London by Iohn Day, dwellyng ouer Aldersgate.
Cum priuilegio Regię Maiestatis.

Book of Martyrs. The cover page of one of the most influential books in English history. (*Author: John Foxe, 1563. The Horizon Book of the Elizabethan World (which credits the Folger Shakespeare Library), American Heritage / Houghton Mifflin*)

Bosworth Field, Battle of

(1485)

A landmark battle in English history which signalled the end of the medieval period and the start of the Tudor dynasty.

For thirty years the noble families of York and Lancaster had been waging a civil war for the throne of England, known as the **Wars of the Roses**. In 1485 the Yorkist king, Richard III, was in power but was unpopular due to rumours that he had murdered his two nephews. The Princes in the **Tower** had been the rightful heirs to the throne after the death of their father, Edward IV.

His leading Lancastrian opponent was Henry Tudor who had previously taken refuge in Brittany and France. In 1485 Henry landed a small force in south-west Wales and slowly marched east, picking up recruits on his way. Richard's army gathered at Leicester, headed west and the two armies clashed near Bosworth on 22 August.

Henry had no military experience and so gave command of his 5,000 troops to the capable Earl of Oxford. Richard had twice as many men divided into three 'battles' led by himself, the Duke of Norfolk and the Earl of

19th-century depiction of Lord Stanley bringing the crown to Henry Tudor on Bosworth Field. (*Author: John Cassell, 1865. Internet Archive*)

Northumberland. Nearby, to the south, lay 6,000 men under the command of Lord Thomas Stanley and his brother, Sir William Stanley. Their allegiance was uncertain and, for this reason, Richard had taken Lord Thomas's son as hostage to guarantee his loyalty.

The battle began when Oxford moved against Norfolk and an unclear melee ensued. Both Richard and Henry signalled for the Stanleys' assistance but none came but the subsequent order for the execution of Stanley's son was never carried out. Richard's position deteriorated sharply when Northumberland refused to commit his 4,000 reserves to the struggle. Whether this was due to treason or practical difficulties in manoeuvring his troops is not clear. News also reached Richard that Norfolk had been slain.

The king, however, saw a golden opportunity to win the battle quickly. He had spotted Henry's banner moving towards the Stanleys and bravely decided to charge at his enemy's leader with 800 men and slay him. In the attack he killed William Brandon, Henry's standard bearer, and closed in on Henry himself. At this juncture, though, William Stanley decided to intervene on the Lancastrian side. As a result, Richard soon found himself surrounded before being cut down and news of his death caused the Yorkist troops and Northumberland to flee the battlefield. Richard's crown was found on the field and placed by Lord Stanley on the head of Henry Tudor, now **Henry VII**. The Tudor Age had begun.

Brandon, Charles (First Duke of Suffolk)

(1484–1545)

Statesman, soldier and advisor to **Henry VIII**.

Whilst only a baby, his father, William Brandon was killed by Richard III at the **Battle of Bosworth Field**. To repay the debt, **Henry VII** took him under his own wing and educated him; Prince **Arthur** and he were probably playmates. Later on, his athleticism and love of sport made him very popular with Prince Henry and a long-standing friendship was formed.

After Henry's accession to the throne, Brandon rose in prominence and influence despite a few embarrassing amorous dalliances which included upsetting the daughter of the Holy Roman Emperor. He distinguished himself in the **First Anglo-French War** and soon after, the king elevated his friend to the peerage of the Duke of Suffolk. Alongside Cardinal **Wolsey**, he had become one of the most powerful men in England.

However, he almost wrecked his career the following year by secretly marrying Henry's younger sister, **Mary**. Mary had suffered an arranged **marriage** to the elderly Louis XII of France but he died within five months and Suffolk was sent to bring Mary back from Paris. However, the two had been in love for a long time and, out of fear that Henry would arrange another marriage for his sister, they quickly wed. Henry's anger was assuaged partly by Wolsey and partly out of his own love he bore for his friend and sister and the couple were allowed to return to England. Their punishment was to pay Henry back the costs of Mary's wedding to Louis as well as his wedding gifts to her.

After a few years of retirement Suffolk returned to prominence when he attended the **Field of the Cloth of Gold** in 1520. In 1523, he led an English army into France in the **Second Anglo-French War** and earned some military success before circumstances forced him to retreat. He sided with the king in 1529 by speaking out against his erstwhile friend, Wolsey. He attended the trials of **Thomas More** and **Anne Boleyn**, supported Henry's break with Rome and led his forces against the **Pilgrimage of Grace** in 1536. Suffolk always had an eye for profit though and managed to acquire much land during the **Dissolution of the Monasteries**. After Mary's death in 1533 he even married his son's fiancée for financial gain. In 1544, he led an army against France again but died the following year. His grand funeral was paid for by the king himself in recognition of his truest friend's long and loyal service.

Burbage, Richard

(1567–1619)

Actor

Burbage was the son of James Burbage, a joiner, actor and entrepreneur who built the first permanent theatre in London since the Romans, known as The Theatre. The younger Burbage was greatly influenced by his father, who gave him a head start in the world of acting. Like most performers, he probably began his career by taking the parts of women and, by his early twenties, had already become a popular actor.

He acquired his greatest fame and fortune after 1594 when he joined the Lord Chamberlain's Men – a group of actors under the patronage of Henry Carey, Lord Chamberlain of the queen's household. By this time, he would have met the playwright, **William Shakespeare**. The two became lifelong friends and established an incredibly successful working partnership. Burbage always took the lead role in Shakespeare's plays such as *Hamlet*, *Macbeth*, *Othello* and *King Lear* and there is one anecdote that reveals their great friendship. After one performance, an infatuated female member of the audience sent a note backstage asking for Burbage's attentions. Shakespeare intercepted the note and went off to meet her himself, saying, "William the Conqueror was before Richard III."

Burbage and Shakespeare starting working together at The Theatre but had problems renewing the lease with its landowner so they tore it down, rebuilt it on the south side of the Thames and renamed it The Globe (1599). Burbage and his older brother, Cuthbert, owned half the shares in the new theatre whilst Shakespeare and other actors in the company owned the other half. The following year, Burbage married Winifred Turner and the couple had eight children although only one survived infancy.

Burbage had a prolific career and continued acting right up to his death. He took on huge roles too. In the 1580–1610 period, there were only twenty parts that had more than 800 lines and Burbage had thirteen of them. His acting showed great versatility although he was particularly good in tragedies. It was his convincing performances, however, that really drew the crowds. He could so easily slip into character that audiences were able to suspend disbelief. Shakespeare's writing undoubtedly made a contribution but such was the demand to see Burbage that Shakespeare had to write some of his plays 'around' his lead actor.

Richard Burbage was considered the best actor of his time and would perform for other playwrights, too, such as Ben Jonson and John Marston. When he died, there was a general outpouring of grief that threatened to overshadow the official mourning period for King James I's wife, Queen Anne, who had died ten days previously. He was buried in Shoreditch although his gravestone has become lost. Apparently, the epitaph simply read 'Exit Burbage'.

Burghley, Lord

(See Cecil, Sir William)

Butts, Sir William

(c. 1486–1545)

Personal physician to King **Henry VIII**.

Butts was born in Norwich, studied medicine at Cambridge University and by the mid-1520s had become the chief physician in the royal household. His patients also included Princess **Mary**, Cardinal **Wolsey** and members of the nobility such as the **Third Duke of Norfolk**. In 1528, Henry sent him to

Hever Castle to treat Anne **Boleyn**, whom he feared had the **sweating sickness**, as well as deliver a love letter. From 1536, he increasingly had to treat the king himself, who was a notoriously bad-tempered patient, for a chronically ulcerous leg. In 1540, it was Butts who reassured Henry that his inability to consummate his marriage to **Anne of Cleves** was not a result of his impotence but rather her failure to attract him.

William Butts. (*Artist: Hans Holbein, c. 1543. Isabella Stewart Gardner Museum*)

Paid over £100 per year and knighted in 1544 for his services, Butts stood high in Henry's confidence and, due to his intimate contact with the king, was able to help people in need of royal ſavour. In 1529, he tried to reconcile Henry with Cardinal Wolsey. He himself had reformist views and used his influence to further the cause of religious reform. He helped advance the career of **Hugh Latimer**, recommended Sir **John Cheke** as Prince **Edward**'s tutor and he intervened on behalf of Archbishop **Cranmer** several times.

Much to the ailing king's grief, Butts died in 1545 after suffering from a form of malaria.

Byrd, William

(1540/43–1623)

One of the leading composers of the late Renaissance period.

Born in Lincolnshire, Byrd became an organist and then choirmaster at Lincoln Cathedral. Under the influence of Thomas Tallis, one of the leading composers of the day, Byrd quickly developed a reputation for creating fine music and became a gentleman of Queen **Elizabeth**'s Chapel Royal. The queen also granted both him and Tallis a monopoly to publish music for twenty-one years.

As a **Catholic**, Byrd had to practise his religion discreetly. However, he did get into trouble in 1583 due to his association with Lord Paget, a suspect in the **Throckmorton Plot**. Byrd was temporarily expelled from the Chapel Royal, his house was searched and his movements restricted. After his name was cleared though, his loyalty to the Crown was never again questioned and his religion, thereafter, was tolerated.

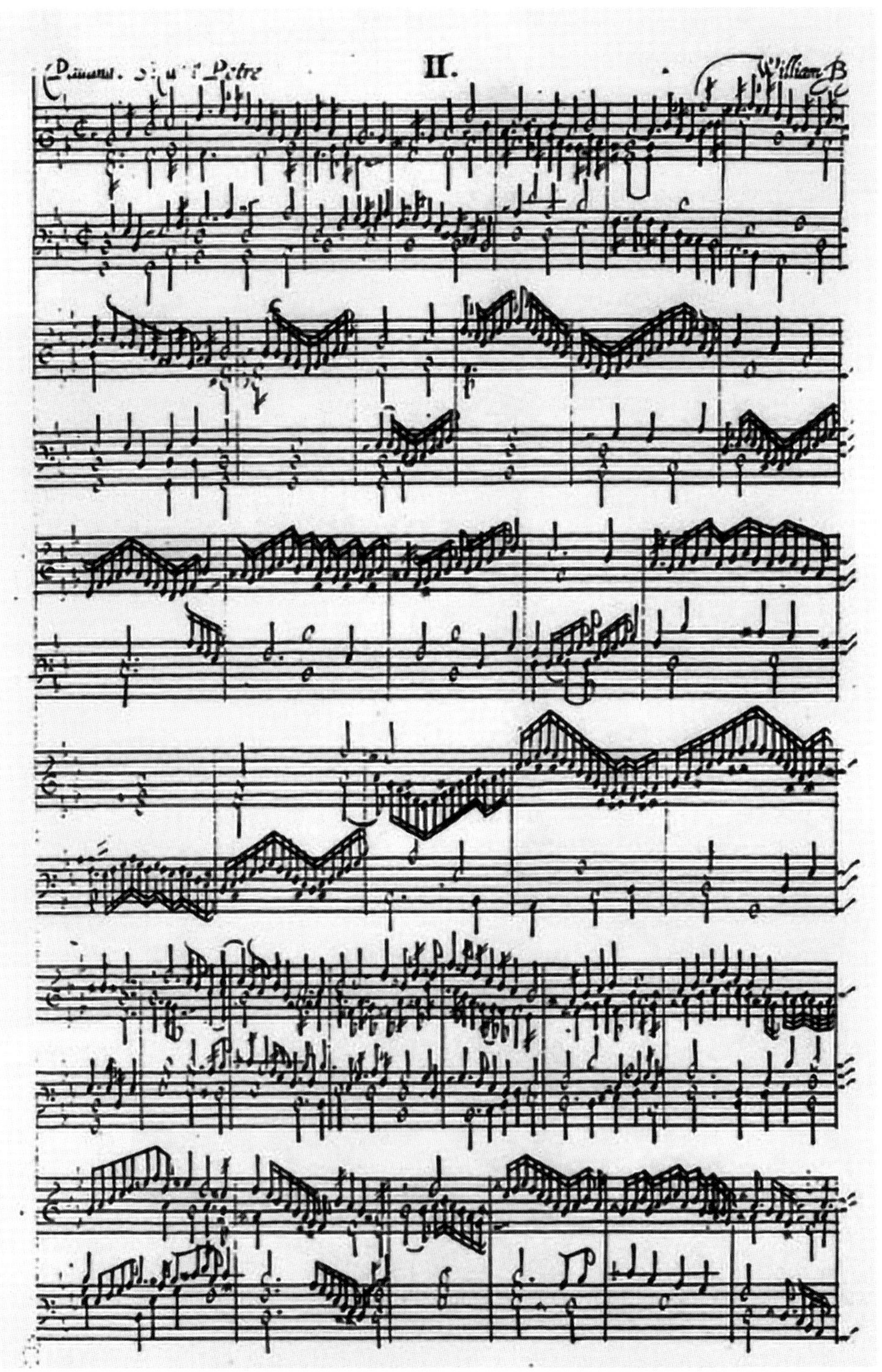

Parthenia – II – Pavan. Composed for the virginals and harpsichord. The pavan was a slow processional dance. (*Author: William Byrd, 1611*)

William Byrd. Presumably a copy but no contemporary portrait has been discovered. (*Artist: Gerard van der Guch, 18th century. British Museum*)

Byrd's strong religious beliefs led him to compose some of his finest work for Catholic services in private homes. The Latin songs in *Cantiones Sacrae* (1575) are of uniformly high quality and later compositions included *Latin Masses* (1593-95) and two large volumes of *Gradualia* (1605 and 1607) that consisted of liturgical music, which, technically, were an immense achievement. He also composed music for the Church of England such as the *Great Service*, many shorter anthems such as *Sing joyfully* and several psalm settings.

In addition, Byrd produced a substantial amount of consort music, usually for viols, for more secular occasions. These included pavans (slow processional dances) and galliards (athletic dances featuring much leaping and hopping, much favoured by Elizabeth). He produced consort pieces for songs too. These varied widely in character, ranging from plaintive lullabies to dramatic elegies for the popular boy-plays of London.

Byrd was also well known as a keyboard player and composed much music for virginals and harpsichords with *My Ladye Nevells Book* (1591) being a collection of some of his finest keyboard music. His compositions included all the major genres of the time, including the austere fantasia as well as the pavan and galliard. Such was the originality and volume of his work that it can almost be said that he invented keyboard music.

The sheer quantity (470 compositions), quality and variety of his work make Byrd one of the greatest composers of the late sixteenth and early seventeenth centuries. Along with Tallis, with whom he worked on some of his earlier pieces, he modernised music and put England at the forefront of the European classical scene for the only time in its history. He was a major influence on contemporary composers in Germany and Holland in particular. For several centuries, his work became largely neglected until it was rediscovered in the twentieth century when the full range of his genius became evident and accessible to music lovers.

His death in 1623 was noted in the Chapel Royal Check Book in an entry describing Byrd as 'a Father of Musick'.

C

Cabot, John

(c. 1450–c. 99)

An Italian explorer who sailed in the service of **Henry VII** of England and discovered mainland America.

Giovanni Caboto was born in either Genoa or Venice and became a trader in the Mediterranean. There, he learnt the skills of cartography and navigation. After getting into financial trouble in the late 1480s he fled from Venice to Spain where he was inspired by stories of Christopher Columbus's Atlantic voyage to 'Asia' in 1492. Cabot believed that he could find a much shorter route by sailing along a more northerly latitude. His plan was rejected by both Spain and Portugal and so, in around 1495, he went to England to seek patronage from Henry VII.

In 1496, Henry gave him permission to sail under the English flag and discover new lands. With merchant sponsorship he sailed west out of Bristol but poor weather and a lack of supplies forced his single ship to return.

In the following year he tried again in the fifty-ton *Matthew*, which had a crew of about twenty men and supplies for around seven months. After a voyage of five to six weeks he made landfall, probably in Newfoundland (the exact location is debated) on 24 June 1497. It seems that his crew were the first Europeans to land in North America since the Vikings 500 years previously. Cabot met no natives, claimed the land for the King of England and, after exploring the coast and noting the huge quantities of codfish, returned to Bristol.

He received a hero's welcome for finding the 'Land of Spices' and Henry rewarded him with £10, the equivalent of two years' pay for an ordinary craftsman. Later, he increased this to a pension of £20 per year. In 1498 he loaned Cabot money for another, larger expedition consisting of five ships laden with trading goods. However, the fate of this expedition is rather vague. It appears that it reached the coast of Greenland but further progress was hampered by the cold and icebergs. Cabot himself either died on the voyage home or soon after his return in 1499 or 1500.

His voyages are of major importance as they laid the basis for England's future colonisation of North America.

Cabot, Sebastian

(?–c. 1557)

Maritime explorer and cartographer.

Sebastian Cabot. (*Artist: Samuel Rawle. 19th century engraving and probable copy of a Hans Holbein painting. Library of Congress*)

Sebastian was the son of the famous **John Cabot** who discovered mainland America in 1497. However, the details of his life and achievements are hard to prove; his own accounts were lost and those of people who later interviewed him tend to contradict each other. He was born some time before 1484 in either Venice or Bristol and we cannot even be totally certain of the year in which he died.

He may have been present on his father's voyages of 1497 and 1498 and gained early experience of navigation and cartography. It seems likely that he sailed to the area of Newfoundland in 1504, returning with a large quantity of salted fish, as he began receiving an annuity from King **Henry VII** the following year. In 1508, he led an expedition to seek the north-east passage to China and it is reckoned that he may have been the first European to reach the entrance to Hudson Bay. His sole surviving map of 1544 shows the beginning of a wide northerly passage in this area. After ice forced him back, he sailed down the east coast of North America as far as south as Chesapeake Bay.

Upon his return to England, he discovered that the king had died and that the new king, **Henry VIII**, was far more interested in European ventures than voyages of discovery. He was employed, instead, to make maps of south-west France for the English army during the **First Anglo-French War** but then offered his services to the Spanish court.

A mission to the New World was planned and then abandoned and, for several years, Cabot sought funding for a voyage from England and Venice as well as Spain. At one point, in 1521, he was offered support by Cardinal **Wolsey**. However, the investing merchant company refused to back a voyage led by a 'foreigner' whom they could not trust.

At last, in 1524, a Spanish company, with royal backing, appointed Cabot to lead an expedition around South America to the Indies. The survivors of

Magellan's voyage had just returned from their global circumnavigation and it was clear that the 1494 demarcation of the world between Spain and Portugal needed updating.

The expedition, however, was deemed a fiasco. One ship ran aground off Brazil and was lost after which Cabot quarrelled with his officers and marooned them on an island. Later, instead of aiming for the Magellan Straits (as instructed), he was lured up the River Plate estuary by stories of gold. Nothing was achieved, however, and eighteen of his men were killed in a native Indian ambush. He then returned to Spain where he was found guilty of disobeying orders and causing the deaths of his own men. He was sentenced to a heavy fine and banishment to north Africa. It seems, though, that King Charles V was impressed with his maps of the River Plate region and overrode the court's decision to exile him. He was even retained as Spain's Pilot-Major.

In 1547 or 1548, much to Charles's annoyance, he returned to England. In 1553, he became governor of the Muscovy Company and helped to prepare Willoughby and **Chancellor**'s mission to seek a north-east passage. He died around four years later. Very little is known of his private life other than he was married twice and had at least one daughter. As such, no one can prove their descent from him.

Campion, Edmund

(1540–81)

A **Jesuit** priest who symbolised the Counter-**Reformation** in England.

Born in London to a **Catholic** bookseller, Edmund Campion showed a sharp intellect during his **education** and became a Fellow at Oxford University. He took the oath of supremacy and when Queen **Elizabeth** visited the university in 1569 she was impressed by his wit and charm. He also earned the patronage of the **Earl of Leicester** and **Sir William Cecil** who later referred to him as 'a diamond of England'. At this point he was tipped as a future Archbishop of Canterbury or even as a potential husband for the queen.

However, he started to have a theological change of heart and, during a visit to Dublin, his increasingly Catholic views forced him into hiding. In 1571 he escaped to Douai in the Netherlands and converted to Catholicism. Later, he made a pilgrimage to Rome where he became a Jesuit priest. He then spent several years teaching and writing in Prague.

In 1580 he joined a Jesuit mission to England despite realising the great risks involved. After entering the country as a jewel merchant he began to secretly preach to English Catholics and hear their confessions. He even wrote a pamphlet inviting the queen's Privy Council to a public debate. The authorities hunted him through several counties but Campion always managed to elude capture despite taking many risks.

Edmund Campion. The knife in his chest and the gallows in the background signify his martyrdom. (*Artist: Johann Martin Lerch, 1670s. British Museum*)

During this time, he wrote *Ten Reasons*, which denounced the Church of England. It was printed on a secret press and its distribution further alarmed the government. Finally, thirteen months after landing in England, one of **Walsingham**'s spies captured him in Oxfordshire and he was taken to London.

In the **Tower**, Campion was offered his freedom in return for recanting his faith but he refused and was tortured on the rack. Later, he was summoned to several public debates in an attempt to discredit him but, despite his weak state, he acquitted himself very well. The exasperated authorities finally decided to convict him on a charge of treason and sentenced him to death along with several of his fellow priests. After hearing the sentence, Campion famously replied, 'In condemning us, you condemn all your own ancestors, all our ancient bishops and kings, all that was once the glory of England.'

He was hanged, drawn and quartered on 1 December 1581 and beatified in 1886. The ropes used for his execution are kept in a glass cabinet at Stonyhurst College, Lancashire, where there is a holiday every year on his feast day – 1 December.

Carew, Sir Peter

(c. 1514–75)

English soldier and adventurer.

Carew was the third son of a Devonshire gentleman and, it seems, had a difficult childhood. After playing truant from school many times he threatened to jump off a turret on Exeter's city wall. Afterwards, his father leashed him and tied him to one of his hounds for a while. Out of despair, he later gave him to a friend in France where he was treated badly and rescued by a passing relative. Afterwards, he had several adventures amongst soldiers in Italy but, in 1530, returned to England to seek service with the Crown.

Peter Carew. (*Artist: JJ Chant, copy of a portrait c. 1550. From The Western Rebellion of 1549 by F Rose-Troup, 1913. Robarts Library University of Toronto*)

Henry VIII was impressed with his athleticism, riding skills and fluency in French and so employed him, initially, as a mere henchman. Carew spent most of the next ten years at court and, in 1540, travelled to Constantinople disguised as an alum merchant. In the **Third Anglo-French War** he led a company of soldiers, dressed in black, at his own expense and was knighted by the king for his services. It was his brother, George, who commanded the **Mary Rose** when it sank.

Carew became a Member of **Parliament** in 1545 and was one of the commanders sent to suppress the **Prayer Book Rebellion** (1549). The severity of his reprisals against the rebels earned him a reprimand however. In 1553, Carew supported **Mary**'s accession to the throne but, in the following year, he joined **Wyatt's Rebellion** against her marriage to Philip of Spain. However, his attempts to raise rebellion in the West Country failed and he just managed to escape to the continent. Carew did not give up though; he agitated for French military intervention and led a piratical operation against Spanish shipping in the Channel. Later, English assassins almost murdered him in Venice so he fled north again. However, he was abducted near Antwerp whilst travelling with **Sir**

John Cheke and both were sent, blindfolded, back to England. Carew was kept in the **Tower** but released after the payment of an old debt of his grandfather's to the Crown. There is a suspicion, although unproven, that he had earlier betrayed Cheke and that this gained him his surprise release.

Carew returned to royal service after **Elizabeth**'s accession but in 1568 he set sail for southern **Ireland**. It had been brought to his attention that one of his ancestors had owned land in Munster so he intended to claim his inheritance. His land acquisitions, however, eventually led to warfare with the Butler family, an old Anglo-Norman dynasty. He had some military success and, in 1569, was given permission to colonise confiscated lands in Munster with English settlers and thereby extend his own dominions. The ensuing Irish revolt was violent and bloody and, due to his part in the affair, Elizabeth summoned him home. However, he refused the queen's request that he return to parliamentary duties and, after the revolt had died down, he returned to Ireland in 1574. There, he died of an illness on his way to Cork.

Catholic

A follower of Roman Catholicism, the major religion of western Europe in the sixteenth century.

The subject of one's individual and national faith became an issue of major importance and divisiveness during the Tudor period, not only in England but the whole of western Europe. At the start of this period, western Europe, including the British Isles, was predominantly Roman Catholic, just as it had been for several centuries.

Beliefs and practices of the Catholic Church in the sixteenth century included:

1. The belief that the Church is the one true source of all Christian teachings.
2. The infallibility of the Pope, who was the successor to St Peter, disciple of Jesus and the first Bishop of Rome.
3. The sacred authority of ordained bishops and priests.
4. The importance of the seven sacraments in order to receive salvation. These included baptism and penance for one's sins.
5. Transubstantiation: the belief that the bread and wine really do turn into the Body and Blood of Christ during the Eucharist.
6. The use of images, crucifixes, candles, music and vestments during services.

7. The belief that, upon death, judgement by God is based upon an individual's deeds in life. In between Heaven and Hell is purgatory where the dead can be purified of all their sins.
8. Devotion to the Virgin Mary and sites of pilgrimage and prayers to saints and the dead.
9. The belief that the Bible, prayer books and church services should be in Latin, the original language of the first Bishops of Rome.
10. Clergy were not allowed to marry in order to allow them to give their undivided attention to serving God.

However, by the sixteenth century, various abuses had become endemic within the Church such as simony (buying and selling of Church positions), ignorance of the clergy, sinful behaviour of the leaders of the Church and the selling of indulgences to buy forgiveness from God.

These abuses sparked the **Reformation** and the start of **Protestant**ism. This, in turn, led to the Counter-Reformation and attempts to reform the Roman Catholic Church.

Cavendish, Sir Thomas

(1560–1592)

Elizabethan explorer and privateer and only the second Englishman to circumnavigate the world.

Cavendish inherited a large fortune at the age of twelve but, after leaving school, he managed to squander his money on an extravagant lifestyle and so he decided to seek a new fortune overseas. In his first voyage, led by **Sir Richard Grenville**, he commanded his own ship in the 1585 expedition to Virginia, which planted a colony at **Roanoke** Island. The scheme was a costly failure but Cavendish gained some valuable experience and yearned for success elsewhere.

It is his second voyage that was to earn him fame and glory. Inspired by **Sir Francis Drake**'s successful circumnavigation, Cavendish determined to follow in his footsteps and capture as much Spanish booty as possible. Subsequently, he became the first person to *intentionally* circumnavigate the world.

In July 1586, he led 126 men and three ships out of Plymouth: the 120-ton *Desire*, the 60-ton *Content* and the 40-ton *Hugh Gallant*. By Christmas, this small fleet was anchored off Patagonia where they studied the lifestyle of the native Indians. During a forty-nine-day passage through the Magellan Straits they lived off shellfish and birds and discovered the starving survivors of a Spanish garrison that had been left there to guard the Straits.

After entering the Pacific on 24 February, Cavendish spent the next few months raiding Spanish ships and towns along the coasts of Chile and Peru. His task was made less easy by the fact that, after Drake's expedition, the Spanish were much more alert and had developed a system which allowed them to send quick warning messages to towns further up the coast. In fact, losses in combat forced him to sink the *Hugh Gallant* in order to man his other ships properly.

Thomas Cavendish. A print based on a 1588 portrait. (*Artist: Unknown, 1590–92 via Wikimedia Commons*)

However, Cavendish's big chance came when a captured Spanish pilot informed him of the approach of the *Santa Ana*, a huge and undefended treasure ship laden with gold, spices and silk, that had set sail from the Philippines. Cavendish intercepted her off the south coast of California and, after a six-hour battle, finally succeeded in capturing his prize. After loading his ships with as much loot as possible, he landed the Spanish crew on the shore and burnt the *Santa Ana*.

They then headed west but, for unknown reasons, the *Content* held back and disappeared, never to be seen again. It had either encountered difficulties, heavily laden as it was, or its crew, dissatisfied with their share of the plunder, had mutinied. The *Desire* reached Guam in January 1588 and sailed on to the Far East where Cavendish collected important information about the coasts of China and Japan. He then rounded the Cape of Good Hope and eventually reached Plymouth in September 1588 with a crew of just forty-eight men. The **Spanish Armada** had just been defeated, and Cavendish was feted as a hero and knighted by the queen. The expedition had been a huge financial success, too.

Cavendish attempted to repeat his success in 1591. This time he had five ships and the added aim of opening up trade with China. He was also accompanied by the explorer, **John Davis**, who planned to investigate the North-West Passage from the Pacific side. This expedition, however, was a disaster and revealed dangerous flaws in Cavendish's character and leadership skills. Unusually severe storms, separations of ships within the fleet and a shortage of supplies prevented him from attempting the Magellan Straits. It seems that these setbacks put him under so much stress that he quarrelled with his officers and Davis who tried to reason with him calmly. He then abandoned his fleet in a single ship and set off across the Atlantic before dying of unknown causes, possibly near Ascension Island, but not before accusing Davis of being a traitor in his last letter home.

Cavendish was known as 'The Navigator' and, for a while, was as popular and famous as Drake himself. He clearly lacked Drake's strength of character, though, and is a typical example of one of the many Tudor glory-seekers who pushed themselves beyond their capabilities or resources.

Cecil, Sir Robert (First Earl of Salisbury)

(1563–1612)

An important statesman who oversaw the transition from the House of Tudor to the House of Stuart.

The son of **Sir William Cecil**, Robert was short and born with a slight hunchback of which he became highly sensitive when he was older. He was educated at Cambridge University and groomed by his father in the art of statecraft. He became an MP in 1584 and, in 1591, Secretary of State after the death of **Sir Francis Walsingham**. He was knighted by Queen **Elizabeth** who would refer to him as 'my pygmy' or 'my elf' and then became the youngest ever member of the Privy Council, aged twenty-eight. He succeeded his father as First Secretary in 1598.

Cecil dominated the government at a difficult time for England. The **Anglo-Spanish War** was dragging on accompanied by **Tyrone's Rebellion** in **Ireland** and a series of bad harvests. At the same time, he fought a political power struggle with the **Earl of Essex**. One of their many areas of contention was the choice of successor to the old queen. Essex openly favoured James VI of Scotland whilst Cecil seemed to prefer the Archduchess Isabella of Spain. Later, Cecil expediently changed his support to James and repudiated Essex's accusations that he was opposed to the Stuarts.

He cleverly persuaded Essex to accept the job of dealing with the rebellion in Ireland in 1600. His rival's disastrous performance brought about his downfall and allowed Cecil to completely dominate both court and Crown. After Elizabeth's death, he ensured the smooth and peaceful succession of James VI to the

English throne and James rewarded him with various titles culminating in the earldom of Salisbury in 1605.

Cecil managed to build up a considerable network of spies with which to protect the **Protestant** monarchy and he took the credit for uncovering the Gunpowder Plot (1605) for which he was richly rewarded. More recently there have been claims, unproven, that he manipulated or even devised the plot in order to discredit the **Catholic**s and strengthen his own position.

Robert Cecil. (*Artist: attributed to John de Critz the Elder, 1599. Dickinson Gallery*)

Cecil's foreign policy was in favour of peace in order to stabilise domestic finances. For this reason, he was instrumental in agreeing to the unpopular terms of the peace treaty with Spain in 1604. Above all, though, he aimed to maintain the balance of power between Spain and France and preserve the independence of the Netherlands.

Cecil had some success in reducing the huge government debt. One of his methods was the granting of monopolies, which were very unpopular. Indeed, he became a widespread figure of dislike and his numerous enemies accused him of greed, corruption and duplicity. It is hard to say how much truth there was in these accusations but he was certainly a skilled and effective administrator who worked tirelessly for the Crown.

In 1611, he rapidly fell ill with stomach cancer which produced painful tumours. His death the following year spawned a huge amount of libellous epitaphs, which shocked many observers.

Cecil, Sir William (Lord Burghley)

(1521–98)

Chief advisor to Queen **Elizabeth I** from 1558 to 1598.

Born into a family noted for its loyalty to the Tudors, Cecil was educated at Cambridge University where he was influenced by **Protestant**ism and the foremost academics of the day. He started his career in the service of the **Duke of Somerset** in 1547 and became noted for his administrative skills and industrious work ethic. He also impressed people with his ability to remember vast amounts of detail. He accompanied Somerset to the **Battle of Pinkie Cleugh** (1549) where, apparently, he nearly lost his life.

When Somerset was toppled by the **Duke of Northumberland** Cecil was briefly imprisoned in the Tower. However, he managed to ingratiate himself with the new Lord Protector who recognised his usefulness. Indeed, he was appointed Secretary of State in 1550 and knighted the following year. In 1553, he was apparently forced into recognising **Lady Jane Grey** as the new queen but he plotted against Northumberland as soon as the duke left London to confront Princess **Mary**. This probably saved his life along with the fact that he accepted the new **Catholic** faith. He lost his offices, though, and kept a fairly low profile throughout Mary's reign.

Northumberland had previously asked Cecil to administer Lady Elizabeth's lands and she had noted his skills and intelligence. Cecil, for his part, kept in touch with the princess and was in secret communication with her before Mary died. Upon her accession in 1558 Elizabeth appointed Cecil, or her 'spirit' as she called him, as her Secretary of State. She realised that he was the safe pair of hands that she needed and whom she could completely trust with the affairs of state. She said, 'This judgement I have of you, that you will not be corrupted by any manner of gifts, and that you will be faithful to the state.' He was not an innovator or creative thinker; caution and discretion were his watch words. Moreover, he was a born survivor and she probably hoped that he could use this ability to ensure the survival of her monarchy.

The queen elevated Cecil to Lord Burghley in 1571 and Lord Treasurer in 1572 and he influenced every aspect of Elizabethan policy. In religion, he helped to frame the religious settlement and although he was opposed to other faiths publicly he did tolerate the English Catholics as long as they were loyal to the Crown. Although he became increasingly Protestant with time, he was prepared to act against **Puritan**s as well as Catholics if he perceived them to be a threat. Burghley was the driving force behind the execution of **Mary, Queen of Scots** in 1587. Elizabeth had been reluctant to act so boldly but he saw the need to remove the Catholic figurehead. Upon hearing of the execution, Elizabeth was so shocked that she temporarily dismissed him from court.

Burghley was capable of acting boldly in his foreign policy too. It was he who pushed for the military interventions in Scotland (1559) and the Netherlands (1585). Such actions he considered to be a last resort though. His ambition was to create a united British Isles, which could be easily protected by a powerful navy. His aims were thwarted in **Ireland** but he did achieve a lasting peace with Scotland and he strengthened the navy. In addition, he recognised both Spain and France as major threats and, for this reason, he provided just enough support for the Dutch and Huguenot rebels to keep them going.

Burghley constantly had to deal with Elizabeth's various favourites, such as **Leicester**, **Ralegh** and **Essex**, who pampered the queen's vanity and tried to exert their own influence over her. He also made enemies of the more established nobility, such as the **Fourth Duke of Norfolk**, who perceived him as a lowly upstart. He handled them all with his customary tact and caution but, ultimately, Elizabeth understood that he, unlike the others, was indispensable.

If any criticisms can be levelled at Burghley it is that he was very ambitious to further his son, **Robert Cecil**'s, career and that he lacked any real personal convictions and scruples. He himself, however, would have argued that this was necessary for the interests of the state, which he put above all else.

In 1598 he suffered a heart attack or stroke and Elizabeth herself nursed him in his illness during his final days. Later, she broke down in mourning because the steady shoulder that she had leaned upon for the past forty years had just passed away.

Chancellor, Richard

(c. 1521–56)

An English explorer who sought the North-East Passage.

Chancellor learned his navigational skills from the explorer **Sebastian Cabot**. He was particularly interested in finding a north-east passage to China, which would by-pass the Portuguese and Spanish-controlled routes further south, and open up a trade route for English merchants. In 1553, he organised the Company of Merchant Adventurers, under the patronage of the **Duke of Northumberland**, to finance such an expedition. Under the leadership of Sir Hugh Willoughby, with Chancellor as second-in-command and Pilot-General, the small fleet of three ships left London in May of that year.

Richard Chancellor meeting Ivan the Terrible. (*Artist: unknown, no later than 18th century. Via Wikimedia Commons*)

However, Chancellor's ship, the *Edward Bonaventure*, was separated from the others in a storm off northern Norway. Willoughby continued as far as Novaya Zemlya but on his return he became trapped in ice near Murmansk. There, he and his crew froze to death; their bodies and ships were recovered by fishermen the following year.

Chancellor, in the meantime, sailed into the White Sea where the native Russians were astounded by the size of his ship. The Russian Tsar, Ivan the Terrible, heard of his arrival and invited him to Moscow. After a journey of 600 miles through snow and ice Chancellor finally reached the Russian capital, which he found to be larger than London, primitively built but with an impressive palace. The Tsar was keen to open a direct trade route that would by-pass the monopoly of the Hanseatic League in the Baltic Sea so he gave Chancellor letters offering trading privileges to English merchants.

Chancellor returned to England overland in mid-1554 to find a new monarch, Queen **Mary**, who had beheaded Northumberland. However, the Muscovy Company, as it was now called, was allowed to send Chancellor on another expedition to Moscow in the following year. At the court of the Tsar he organised further trade links and tried to learn about a northern route to China.

On his return voyage in 1556, with Russia's first ambassador to England, his ship foundered off the coast of Scotland. Chancellor was drowned (although the ambassador survived) but despite his premature death he had succeeded in opening up the only direct trade route with Russia.

Cheke, Sir John

(1514–57)

English classical scholar and tutor to **Edward VI**.

After being admitted to Cambridge University, Cheke developed an expertise in linguistics, especially ancient Greek for which he discovered the true pronunciation. Indeed, he gained a reputation as being one of the most learned men of Europe and, upon the recommendation of his friend, **Sir William Butts** (the royal physician), **Henry VIII** granted him a scholarship to encourage his studies.

Whilst at Cambridge, Cheke privately studied the works of Martin Luther and adopted reformist doctrines. He promoted **Protestant**ism and urged scholars to question the traditions of the **Catholic** Church. He also embraced the ideals of **humanism**, which he endeavoured to pass on to his students.

Amongst his pupils were **William Cecil** (who married Cheke's sister, Mary) and Roger Ascham (who later tutored Princess **Elizabeth**) and, in 1544, he was confirmed as tutor to Prince Edward. He occasionally tutored Elizabeth too and, no doubt, was a major influence on both of these future monarchs.

John Cheke. (*Artist: Joseph Nutting, 1705. Engraving based on an earlier painting from Life of Sir John Cheke by John Strype*)

In 1547 Cheke became a Member of **Parliament** and was knighted in 1551. His fervent Protestantism led him to follow the **Duke of Northumberland** who appointed him to the Privy Council and made him Secretary of State during the brief reign of **Lady Jane Grey**.

Upon Queen **Mary**'s accession, though, he was thrown into the **Tower** and his properties confiscated. Thirteen months later he was released and given a licence to travel abroad. He eventually settled in Strasbourg where he taught Greek for a living. However, in early 1556, upon the orders of Philip II of Spain, he was abducted whilst travelling back from seeing his wife in Brussels. Along with his travelling companion, **Sir Peter Carew**, Cheke was bound and blindfolded, bundled into a fishing boat and returned to England. He was then confined to the Tower of London ostensibly for not returning to England by the time specified on his licence.

There, he was urged to recant his faith. At first, he refused but fear of the stake finally induced him to embrace Catholicism. His public recantation left him humiliated and, filled with shame and regret, he died within a year.

Cleves, Anne of

(1515–57)

Fourth wife of King **Henry VIII** and queen of England from January to July 1540.

After England's break from Rome the country felt isolated and threatened by a plausible-looking alliance between France and the Holy Roman Empire. To counter this threat Henry's chancellor, **Thomas Cromwell**, urged a **marriage** union with the **Protestant** Duchy of Cleves, which was an opponent of Emperor Charles V and supporter of the **Reformation**.

So Henry ordered the court painter, **Hans Holbein**, to produce honest paintings of the duke's sisters, Amalia and Anne. Upon seeing them he consented to marry the younger sister by proxy (January 1540) and allowed marriage negotiations to proceed. Although Anne had had no formal **education**, could only read and write in German and showed no ability in music, which was Henry's passion, she was considered virtuous and docile enough to gain the king's heart.

After her landing at Dover, Henry rushed to meet his new wife at Rochester. The encounter, however, was a disaster. It would seem that he was put off by her looks, apparently referring to her as a 'Flanders mare' and having 'evil smells'. At the same time, the political scene had changed. The emperor and the French king were at loggerheads again and so the alliance with Cleves was no longer necessary. He immediately demanded an annulment of the marriage on the grounds of non-consummation and her earlier wedding contract to Duke Francis of Lorraine when she was only ten years old.

Anne readily agreed, probably remembering how Henry had treated previous wives who had angered him, and received a very generous settlement. This amounted to £3,000 per year and several properties, including some belonging to Cromwell who had fallen from power due to the fiasco. This made her one of the richest women in England.

Anne never left England as this would have broken the terms of the settlement. Besides, it appears that she enjoyed a freedom that she had never had in Cleves and was most fond of English ale and gambling. She was often invited to court as a sign of Henry's gratitude for not contesting the annulment and she took the young Lady **Elizabeth** under her wing. After **Catherine Howard**'s execution, she offered to marry Henry again but he politely refused. However, he did regard Anne as a friend, often sought her advice and bestowed upon her the title of 'The King's Beloved Sister'.

At Queen **Mary**'s coronation Anne rode alongside Elizabeth. She then converted to Catholicism (her original faith) and later praised Mary for marrying Philip of Spain. She died (probably of cancer) in July 1557, having outlived all of Henry's other wives, and is the only one of them to be buried at Westminster Abbey.

Colet, John

(1467–1519)

Scholar, theologian and **Renaissance** humanist.

Colet was born to a very wealthy family and his father was twice Lord Mayor of London. His mother bore eleven sons and eleven daughters but only John survived infancy.

After graduating in mathematics and philosophy at Oxford, he travelled to Italy and France. Whilst abroad, he met several important renaissance philosophers, such as Marcilio Ficino, and started his friendship with Erasmus, the leading exponent of **humanism** in northern Europe. Upon his return, he took holy orders, settled in Oxford and gave many lectures which attracted much attention. His teachings placed much importance on study of the Bible as the only route to holiness and he would interpret the words of Jesus and St Paul so that ordinary people could better understand the Bible. He also brought characters, such as St Paul, to life by discussing their personalities and historical surroundings. He simultaneously encouraged the learning of the ancient Greek and Roman texts as a path to intellectual enlightenment. Erasmus himself stated that listening to Colet was like listening to Plato.

John Colet. (*Artist: Hans Holbein c. 1535, based on a bust by the sculptor Pietro Torrigiano. Royal Collection*)

In 1505, he was appointed Dean of St Paul's and from that cathedral he attacked abuses within the Church, the worship of idols and large revenues of the bishops and demanded reform of the institution. He would often deliver his sermons in English rather than the traditional Latin so that the ordinary masses could understand what was written in the Bible. As a result, St Paul's became so crowded that many had to wait outside to hear what he had said. His criticisms of the established order, however, lay him open to accusations of heresy and the Bishop of London, Richard FitzJames, tried to bring him to trial. The Archbishop of Canterbury, **William Warham**, would have none of it though.

In around 1509, his father died and his inheritance made Colet very wealthy enabling him to found Saint Paul's School for boys in London. Interestingly, he appointed the company of mercers to be its trustees, the first example of non-clerical management of a school.

In 1512, he gave a sermon before **Henry VIII** who was about to go to war against France. He had the audacity to preach against war but the king bore him no grudge and had amicable meetings with him afterwards. Indeed, Colet even became the King's Chaplain.

In 1519, he died from the **sweating sickness**. There has been much conjecture about which side Colet would have taken during the **Reformation**. However, like his great friend, Erasmus, he would probably have refused to be drawn into favouring one camp or the other. Although he railed against abuses of the clergy and wanted Church reform, he was always a devout **Catholic** and would probably have detested the ensuing schism within Christianity.

Cornish Rebellion, The

(1497)

A revolt against **Henry VII** caused by a tax levy.

In 1497, King Henry VII anticipated a war with Scotland due to the agitating presence there of **Perkin Warbeck**, pretender to his throne, so he ordered a general tax levy to fund the campaign. However, this angered the people of Cornwall, partly because they regarded the distant war as an English matter (most Cornish could not speak English then) that did not concern them and partly because they had been promised a degree of tax exemption in the reign of Edward I.

Led by Michael Joseph, a blacksmith, and Thomas Flamank, a lawyer, 15,000 Cornishmen marched east and picked up further support in Devon. At Wells they were joined by Baron Audley, a poor noble with some military experience. Remarkably, they marched unopposed across southern England to Kent, a hotbed of previous rebellions, where they hoped to attract more support. In actual fact, though, they were met with resistance and some disillusioned rebels started to drift back home.

In the meantime, Henry had been surprised by the sheer scale and speed of the revolt. He recalled his northbound army and ordered his forces which were already in the north to conduct a defensive campaign against the Scots. There was a degree of panic inside London as the rebels approached. Citizens were ordered to man the defences whilst the royal family and the Archbishop of Canterbury were moved to the safety of the **Tower**.

After a brief skirmish near Guildford, the Cornishmen moved to Blackheath and set up camp looking down onto the City of London. Somehow, Joseph, the chosen military commander, had managed to hold his forces together although further desertions had reduced his army to around 9,500 men. The royal forces, led by Lord Daubeney, numbered 25,000 and also possessed the advantages of cavalry, artillery and an experienced leadership. The rebels therefore had little chance of success despite their formidable archers. On 17 June, they were attacked and surrounded. In the fierce fighting, in which Daubeney himself

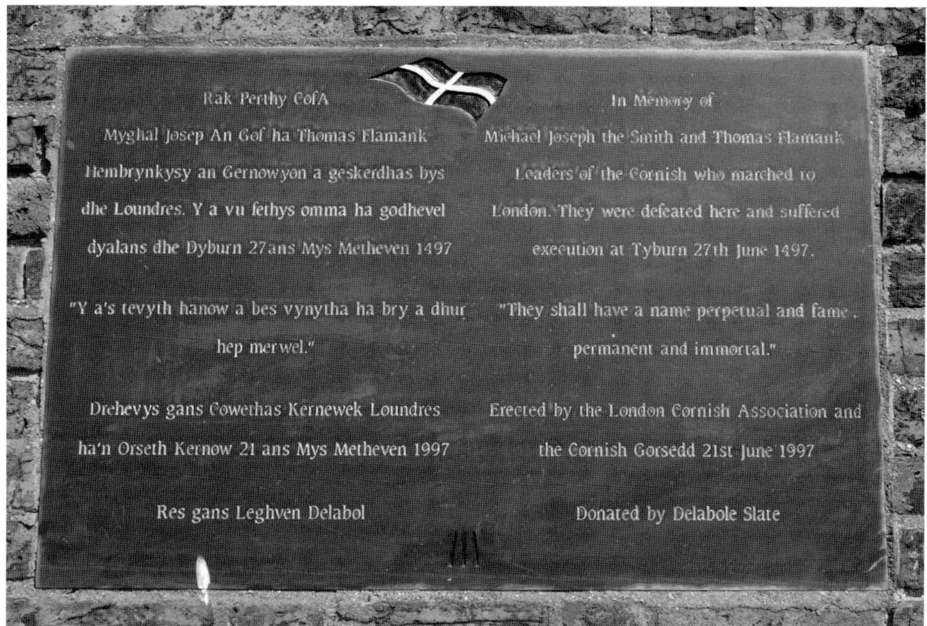

Blackheath plaque, half in Cornish, marking the Cornish Rebellion of 1497. (*Author: Ethan Doyle White, 2020 via Wikimedia Commons*)

was captured and then strangely released, 200 to 2,000 rebels were slaughtered and their leaders were captured.

Joseph and Flamank were hanged until dead then drawn and quartered whilst Audley was beheaded. Some prisoners were sold into slavery, several estates were confiscated and severe fines were imposed on various sections of Cornish society. This relatively bloodless retribution probably reflected Henry's need for money rather than revenge.

Coverdale, Miles

(c. 1488–1568/69)

A key figure in the English **Reformation** who helped translate the Bible into English.

Coverdale was born in Yorkshire and studied theology and philosophy at Cambridge University. He became a priest in 1514 and entered an Augustinian monastery whose prior was Robert Barnes, an early follower of Martin Luther. Barnes probably started Coverdale's conversion to **Protestant**ism and during the 1520s, Coverdale regularly met with other like-minded reformers, including

Thomas Cranmer and **Hugh Latimer**, at Cambridge's White Horse Inn, which they nicknamed 'Little Germany'.

After leaving the monastery Coverdale devoted his time to preaching against the practices and abuses of the **Catholic** Church. Subsequent persecution by the authorities forced him to emigrate to Germany where he met **William Tyndale** who had already translated the New Testament into English. Coverdale firmly believed that the Bible in its original, pure form (rather than its Catholic interpretation) should be understood by all and so started work on its full translation into English. Work was completed and published in Hamburg in 1535 and copies were smuggled into England.

Under the influence of Archbishop Cranmer and Coverdale's friend, **Thomas Cromwell**, King **Henry VIII** accepted the new Bible. Indeed, he ordered the revised edition of 1539, the 'Great Bible', to be installed in every church and Coverdale returned to England that same year. However, Cromwell's execution in 1540 and the danger of renewed persecution of Protestants forced him to flee once again.

Between 1543 and 1547 Coverdale worked as a poorly paid pastor and school teacher in Germany. After the death of Henry, he returned again to England where he was very well received at the court of **Edward VI** and was made the King's Chaplain. In 1551 he was appointed Bishop of Exeter and worked tirelessly in an area that was predominantly Catholic.

Upon the accession of Queen **Mary**, Coverdale was imprisoned for his beliefs. The intervention of the Danish king on his behalf saved him from the stake,

Tyndale and Coverdale Bible. (*Authors: William Tyndale and Miles Coverdale, 1549. Huntington Library via E Polk*)

though, and Mary allowed him to join the host of other English Protestant exiles living abroad. On the continent he carried out further work on the Bible and returned to England for the last time in 1559, after **Elizabeth**'s accession to the throne. However, the authorities viewed him as a **Puritan** due to his opposition to the clergy being required to wear colourful vestments. Classified as a non-conformist, Coverdale had to relent from full-time preaching and lived the remainder of his life in relative poverty. He eventually died in London, aged eighty-one.

Coverdale was described by a contemporary as a '…pious, conscientious, laborious, generous and a thoroughly honest and good man'. Certainly he was a very popular preacher and this, allied to the sheer volume of his work, makes him an important figure of the Reformation.

Cranmer, Thomas

(1489–1556)

Archbishop of Canterbury from 1532 to 1553 and an architect of the English **Reformation**.

Born to a non-aristocratic family in Nottinghamshire, Cranmer was sent to Cambridge University at the age of fourteen. There, he studied philosophy, classical literature, logic and **humanism** before studying theology and being ordained as a preacher of the university. During the 1520s he allegedly frequented 'Little Germany' (the White Horse Inn in Cambridge) to discuss theological issues with future reformers and conservatives such as **Hugh Latimer**, **Miles Coverdale, William Tyndale** and **Stephen Gardiner**.

In 1529, it was Cranmer who offered a solution to King **Henry VIII**'s 'Great Matter' by suggesting that the universities of Europe could decide if the king's marriage to **Catherine of Aragon** was illegal or not rather than the Pope. This immediately brought him to the king's attention and propelled him into the limelight. Henry ordered him to join the mission to Europe's universities and it was probably during his visit to Germany that Cranmer started to lean towards the **Protestant** faith.

In 1532, whilst in Italy, Cranmer was informed that he had been appointed Archbishop of Canterbury. He was probably no less surprised than anyone else as he had previously only held minor clerical positions. However, he had little choice but to accept and was immediately set to work on creating a legal context for Henry's desired annulment of his marriage. The matter became particularly urgent after the king's mistress, **Anne Boleyn,** became pregnant. Presiding at a court at Dunstable Priory in May 1533, which Catherine refused to attend,

Cranmer declared Henry's **marriage** null and void. Five days later, he proclaimed the marriage of Henry and Anne, who had already secretly wedded in January. He then crowned Anne as Queen of England and became a godparent of the baby **Elizabeth**.

Three years later, he had to annul the king's marriage to Anne, even though he expressed doubts about the accusations laid against her, and it was he who informed Henry of the infidelity of **Catherine Howard** in 1541.

As Archbishop of Canterbury, Cranmer slowly and quietly worked on establishing the principles of Protestantism in England. He compiled the Ten **Articles** of 1536, which had reformist tendencies and, along with **Thomas Cromwell**, promoted the use of **Coverdale**'s 'Great Bible' for which he wrote the preface. In 1545 he wrote the Litany (processional prayer) in English, which revealed his mastery of the language and still survives to this day albeit with minor alterations. He also promoted fellow reformers such as Hugh Latimer.

Cranmer constantly had to deal with challenges from the conservative bishops who objected to his power and argued that his role was not defined by the Act of Supremacy (1534). He seemed to lack the political ability to deal with them and so it was that Henry appointed Cromwell as his vicegerent in spiritual affairs. In this position, Cromwell superseded Cranmer in matters of faith and was able to protect him from his enemies.

At times, though, the conservatives seemed to hold sway over the king. In 1539 they succeeded in passing the Act of Six Articles, which blocked any further reforms, and in the following year, they conspired to bring about the execution of Cromwell. From this point on the archbishop was particularly vulnerable. However, Cranmer always had the personal support and protection of the king who valued his loyalty and so he survived. Cranmer was present at Henry's death in 1547 and grew a beard to show his grief. However, the beard was also a symbol of rejection of the **Catholic** Church and may have represented his confidence in being able to push ahead the pace of reform. The dead king's trust in him had been reflected in his will, which made him an executor and instated him on the Council of Regency. Moreover, the new king, **Edward VI**, and the Lord Protector, the **Duke of Somerset**, both supported him.

The archbishop was, indeed, now free to stimulate the growth of Protestantism in England and he invited leading reformers from the continent to help him. He himself wrote several sermons to be read aloud in churches, which promoted the new faith, and he was primarily responsible for the Book of Common Prayer which was enforced by the Act of Uniformity (1549). He also revised the canon law, which stated how the Church of England should be run, and drafted the 42 Articles which asserted its new Protestant nature.

Upon Edward's death in 1553, Cranmer was persuaded to accept **Lady Jane Grey** as the new queen. His reluctance was simply due to the illegality of her claim despite knowing what would happen if the rightful heir, the Catholic, Princess **Mary**, was crowned. Indeed, upon Mary's accession, Cranmer's religious reforms were rapidly reversed. He refused to follow his friends' advice and flee the country and subsequently was imprisoned in the **Tower** for his heretical views and then transferred to a prison in Oxford.

There, he was forced to watch his friends, Latimer and **Nicholas Ridley**, being burned at the stake. Afterwards, he was persuaded to recant his faith several times, confess his past sins and accept Catholicism. Possibly this was the sign of a broken man who feared the stake but it may also have been a reflection of his strong belief in the divine right of monarchs. If a monarch declared Catholicism to be the true faith, then who was he to argue?

It was not to save him though. Mary could never forgive the man who had annulled her mother's marriage and made her illegitimate and so Cranmer's execution was ordered to go ahead, in Oxford, on 21 March 1556. However, the manner of his death was a triumph for the Protestant cause. That very same day he publicly reversed his recantations and declared the Pope to be the Antichrist. Afterwards, as the fire lapped around him, he thrust the hand that had signed the recantations into the flames.

At times, Cranmer appears to be an unprincipled opportunist who was simply a tool of the reigning monarch. It should be remembered, though, that he had a strong belief in the ecclesiastical authority of the Crown. To him, the monarch had the final say in both politics and religion. However, there can be no doubt that he was a committed scholar whose written work is a major contribution to English literature and has been a huge influence on the Anglican Church.

Crime and Punishment

In Tudor England, divine authority filtered down from the monarch and through the nobles. The sense of the monarch being the font of all justice increased when **Henry VIII** became Head of the Church in the 1530s. Penalties usually took the form of corporal and capital punishments which were often brutal. With there being no police force, deterrence was seen as the main way to prevent crime. Many of the punishments were designed to be humiliating and were a form of entertainment. Executions, in particular, attracted large crowds; many people even brought their children along with a picnic.

Prisons were not seen as a form of punishment; they were merely holding areas for suspects awaiting justice. By Queen **Elizabeth**'s reign there were eighteen prisons in and around London and they tended to specialise in types of criminal. For instance, the infamous Newgate Prison held felons, debtors and those awaiting execution, Ludgate was used for debtors and bankrupts and Fleet

PILLORY WHIPPING

From the Bagford Ballads

A VAGRANT

From the Roxburghe Ballads

Pillory, whipping and a vagrant. (*Late 17th century images from the 'Bagford Ballads'. Later included in* Travel in England in the Seventeenth Century *by Joan Parkes (1925). Department of Commerce. Bureau of Public Roads. National Archives at College Park*) held those convicted by the **Star Chamber**. Conditions inside were predictably shocking and relatives were expected to provide food whilst wealthier inmates could pay to improve their quarters.

The Tudor legal system was quite fractured, as it had been for several centuries. There was not a single, hierarchical system and different courts would deal with different types of crimes. Generally, the royal courts dealt with political and financial cases, Church courts handled religious and moral crimes and the manor courts dealt with more local, secular cases. A jury of twelve freemen would decide on the defendant's guilt and the punishment. Justice could often be subverted, however, when the jury and court officials were intimidated by powerful gentry. The Statute of Livery and Maintenance (1487) attempted to remedy this problem.

As a general rule, crimes committed by the poor were usually out of a desperation to escape poverty. Those committed by nobles were usually linked to furthering political aims. The following table is a list of Tudor crimes along with their usual punishments:

Begging	Three days in the stocks or whipping or branding with a 'V', for Vagrant. Repeat offenders would be hanged. The **Poor Law** of 1601 started a more compassionate approach to vagrancy.
Stealing	Whipping, usually, but amputation of hand or branding with a 'T', for Thief, could happen. Hanged if stolen item was valued above 5p.
Gossiping/ Scolding a Husband	Wearing a brank's bridle. The husband could lead her around with a rope attached to the bridle to humiliate her.
Drunkenness	Stocks (for sitting in), pillory (for standing in) or placed in a 'drunkard's cloak' for humiliation.
Brawling/ Swearing	Stocks or pillory.
Failure to pay debt.	Pillory and an ear removed.
Poaching	Hanged if caught at night. Otherwise whipped.
Witchcraft	Ducking stool possibly followed by hanging. Attitudes to 'witches' were more lenient than on the continent. Some even became respected members of their communities.

Murder	Hanged. Boiled alive if murder was by poisoning. Nobility were beheaded.
Heresy (holding the 'wrong' religious views)	Burned at the stake.
Petty Treason (murder or betrayal of a master or husband).	Beheaded or burned at the stake.
High Treason (crime against the monarch or country)	Hanged, drawn and quartered. This meant being dragged through the cobbled streets on a wooden board, hanged until almost dead then being disembowelled and chopped into four pieces. Not for women due to the nudity involved.
Suicide	Wooden stake driven through the body which was then buried in unconsecrated ground.

In Tudor times, torture became much more common due to the perceived threats to Henry VIII and Elizabeth caused by the political and religious upheavals of the time. It was a way of gaining information, was conducted in the **Tower of London** and required royal assent as well as the attendance of a royal official.

Brank's bridle and drunkard's cloak. (*Artist: William Andrews, 1890.* Old-time punishments *by William Andrews*)

Most people considered it abhorrent though and the case of **Anne Askew** shocked many people.

Around 80,000 people were executed in the Tudor period, the vast majority in Henry VIII's reign. Did this and the threat of other brutal punishments keep the crime rate down? If homicide can be taken as a benchmark, the rate in the late sixteenth century was around 150 per million per year. This represented a sharp increase on previous decades due to economic depression, crop failures and soldiers frequently demobilising from the long war with Spain. The domestic homicide rate was considerably lower at 6.8 per million. Today, the homicide and domestic homicide rates in the UK are 11.7 and 0.00023 respectively although it should be noted that modern day medical care would have saved the lives of many of the sixteenth-century victims.

Cromwell, Thomas (First Earl of Essex)

(c. 1485–1540)

Chief advisor to **Henry VIII** who engineered England's break from Rome.

Cromwell was born in Putney, the son of a blacksmith, cloth merchant and brewer. His father was prone to violent drunkenness and, after a quarrel, Thomas fled to the continent. There, he served as a mercenary in the French army and then became involved in banking in Italy and the cloth trade in the Netherlands.

Upon his return to England he trained as a lawyer and entered the service of Cardinal **Wolsey**. Wolsey recognised a man of great ability and Cromwell became his most confidential servant and the manager of his affairs. In 1525, he assisted Wolsey in dissolving several small monasteries in order to finance two of the Cardinal's schools although the vigour and ruthlessness with which he carried this out earned him several enemies.

The downfall of his master in 1529, therefore, left him critically exposed and, at one point, reduced him to tears. However, the subsequent courage and loyalty that he showed whilst defending Wolsey impressed many. Above all, though, he owed his survival to the Boleyn faction at court. Cromwell had previously persuaded Wolsey to pay bribes to members of the Boleyn family for which they were grateful but they also wanted to use his administrative and political skills to further their own ambitions at the expense of the conservative faction. This alliance worked well as both the Boleyns and Cromwell prospered. However, when **Anne Boleyn** fell from favour in 1536, Cromwell showed his ruthless streak by prosecuting a case of adultery against her. This led to her execution and the downfall of her family, his erstwhile allies.

By 1532, Cromwell was one of Henry VIII's closest advisors and the king's representative in **Parliament** although it was only in 1534 that Henry formally appointed him as his chief minister. His first task was to pave the way for a possible break with Rome in order to allow for the annulment of the king's **marriage** to **Catherine of Aragon**. In order to do this, he set about discrediting the clergy as well as the Papacy.

His main tool for this was Parliament, which was already anti-clerical in mood and would legitimise the king's actions. Through the use of manipulation and persuasion Cromwell succeeded in getting Parliament to pass a raft of laws, that he himself drafted, which progressively severed the English Church from Rome. Such laws included the Act in Restraint of Appeals (1533), which forbade all appeals to Rome and made the king the final legal authority in all religious matters. The following year saw the Act of Annates which withheld all church taxes to Rome, the Act for the Submission of the Clergy which deprived the Church of the right to make Church laws without royal assent and, finally, the Act of Supremacy which declared Henry the Supreme Head of the English Church.

Cromwell also conducted a propaganda campaign at grassroots level. He encouraged anti-papal sermons and plays and was the first English politician to recognise the power of the newly invented printing press by ordering the publication of numerous biased pamphlets.

Cromwell believed in a strongly centralised sovereign state with a powerful and solvent monarch at its centre. For this purpose, he initiated a set of administrative and financial reforms that revolutionised the government. By directing the **Dissolution of the Monasteries** (1536–40) he removed the papal power base in England and filled the royal treasury with much-needed cash. He also set up six new financial departments, such as the Court of Augmentations, to collect specific royal revenues.

He replaced the old, medieval forms of government too with a more structured and modern bureaucracy staffed by capable men who worked to a series of rules and procedures and whose loyalty lay with the state rather than in seeking personal advancement. He incorporated Wales and the Welsh Marches into the English county system (1536) and established the Council of the North (1537) to replace the semi-feudal lordships in northern England. He also attempted to strengthen the Crown's control over **Ireland** through a combination of force and direct control from London via an English deputy in Dublin.

Cromwell displayed a social conscience, too, by drafting a revolutionary law that would have helped the poor. The final **Poor Law** Act of 1535 was a watered-down version of what he wanted but it still ordered the giving of alms to the elderly, sick and impotent poor, the provision of public works and the apprenticing of children of the poor.

In religion, Cromwell was as secular as anyone could be in those times. Judging by his actions, though, he clearly leaned towards **Protestant**ism like his friend the Archbishop of Canterbury, **Thomas Cranmer**. He valued the Protestants because of their anti-papal stance and, subsequently, the Act of Ten **Articles** (1536) was a compromise between the old and new faiths in its definition of the new Church of England. As Henry's vicegerent (deputy) in spiritual affairs, he also ordered **Coverdale**'s English Bible to be placed in every church and, later, he campaigned against statues, images and centres of pilgrimage. At the same time, he was destroying English monasticism.

However, Henry, who never renounced his own **Catholic** faith, was becoming unhappy with the pace of religious reform and was concerned about further popular reaction after the **Pilgrimage of Grace** (1536). This was reflected in the reactionary Act of Six Articles (1539), which embodied the full Catholic doctrine, and the growing influence of Cromwell's many enemies led by the **Third Duke of Norfolk** and Bishop **Gardiner**. The former saw him as a political rival and a common upstart; the latter, a heretic.

The ground, therefore, was already prepared for Cromwell's downfall, when he erred in the realm of foreign policy. Fearful of a Franco-Spanish attack against England he persuaded the king to accept a marriage union with the Protestant Duchy of Cleves in 1540. The marriage to the duke's sister, **Anne of Cleves**, was a disaster though and the conservative faction's hand was further strengthened by Norfolk's introduction of his beautiful young niece, **Catherine Howard**, to the king. Cromwell's demise was stunningly rapid. In April, he had been elevated to the earldom of Essex; in June, he was arrested and a bill of attainder accused him of treason, heresy, corruption and plotting to marry Princess **Mary**. He was condemned to death without a trial and so was unable to defend himself or attack his enemies. On 28 July, after stating that he would die as a Catholic, he was beheaded on **Tower** Hill following several blows of the axe. On the same day, Henry married Catherine Howard. Soon after, though, the king was filled with regret and raged against those whom he thought had tricked him into executing his ablest and most faithful servant.

Cromwell sometimes comes across as an ambitious, cold and ruthless bureaucrat who lacked principles. However, the same could largely be said of any politician of that time. Little is known of his private life. In character, he seems to have been free from personal vice and was a kind master and loyal friend. He was also modest and disliked flattery. His wife and two daughters died of the **sweating sickness** and he married his son to **Jane Seymour**'s sister. In terms of his career, Cromwell had a profound effect upon England. He was an administrative genius with an eye for detail who modernised the English state and worked tirelessly in the interests of his king and country. Above all, he engineered a largely peaceful revolution in the 1530s which changed the course of English history.

D

Davis, John

(1543–1605)

English explorer who sought the North-West Passage.

A childhood neighbour of **Humphrey Gilbert** and **Walter Ralegh** in Devon, Davis is first mentioned in the diary of his friend, **John Dee**.

In 1585, Davis was involved in a successful plot to entrap a Catholic priest called Thomas Aulfield by offering him ships to aid the Spanish cause against England. Possibly in return for this, the Secretary of State, **Sir Francis**

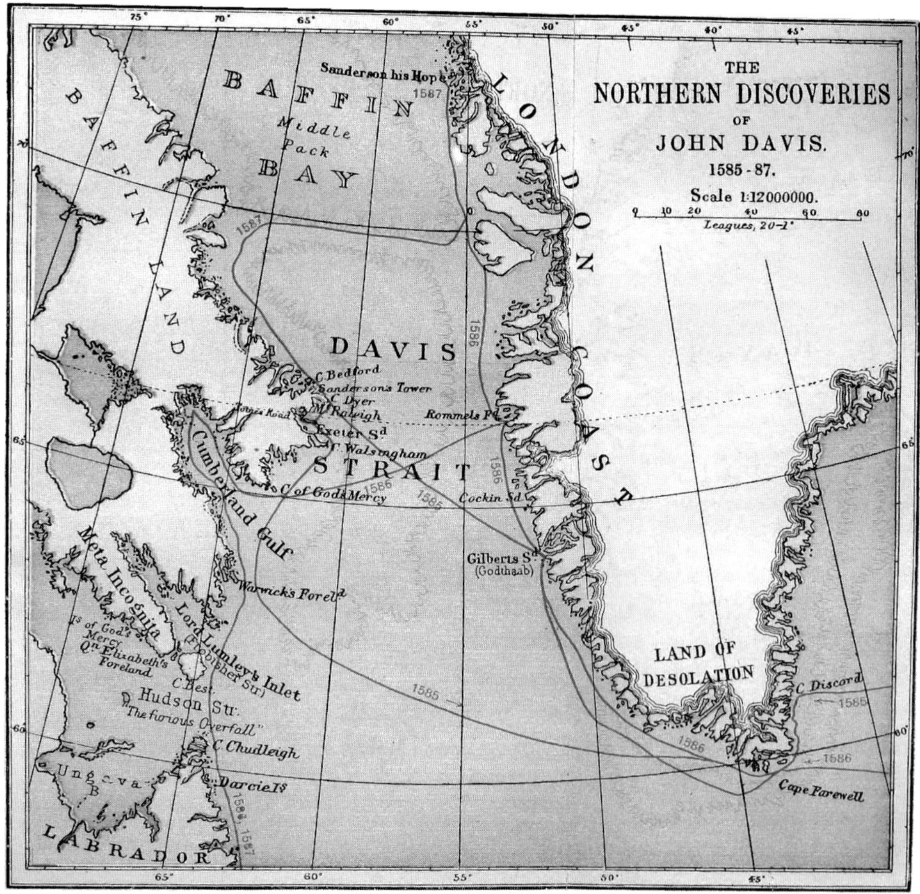

Voyages of John Davis. (*Author: Clements Markham, 1889. https://archive.org/details/lifeofjohndavisn01mark/page/n53*)

Walsingham agreed to fund a voyage to discover a passage around the north of the American continent which, if successful, would open up a quicker trade route to China and the Spice Islands than that controlled by the Spanish around South America. Davis sailed along the strait between Greenland and Baffin Island that now bears his name before ice forced him back. He made two further attempts and managed to reach 72° north along the west coast of Greenland. Despite criticism of his failures, Davis had shown excellent navigational skills and his 1587 log book became the model for all future log books. His achievements also prepared the way for Henry Hudson to reach the Hudson Strait twenty-three years later. Davis also showed forward thinking by trying to build friendly relations with the local Inuit. This relationship, however, was soured when an anchor was stolen, probably during a religious ceremony.

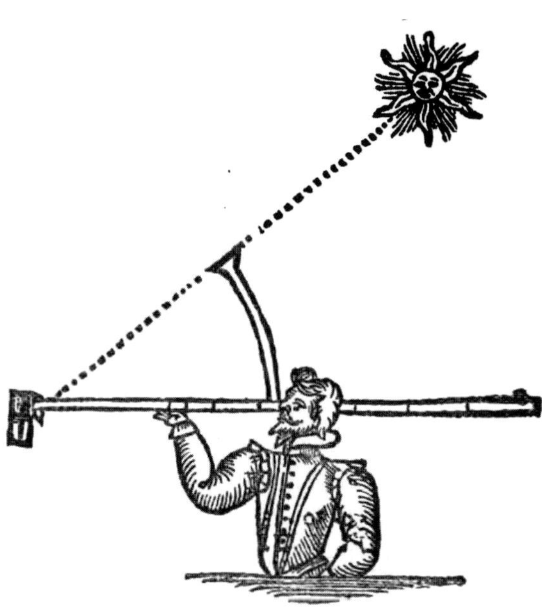

Backstaff. The upper vane cast a shadow onto the horizon vane from which a degree of latitude could be measured. (*Author: John Davis, 1594. From* The Seaman's Secrets *published in 1633. https://archive.org/details/voyagesandworks00wriggoog/page/n458*)

In 1588, it seems he commanded a ship against the **Spanish Armada** and in the following year he took part in **Cavendish**'s expedition to open up the North-West Passage from the Pacific Ocean. This expedition, however, faltered in the Magellan Straits and although he discovered the Falkland Islands in 1593, only fifteen of his seventy-six men returned home alive. After his return he produced his *Seaman's Secrets*, a navigational guide for sailors and he invented the backstaff, an improved instrument for measuring latitude.

In the 1590s and early 1600s Davis joined various Dutch and English expeditions to the Far East in order to open up trade routes to the Spice Islands. It was during one of these that he was murdered by Japanese pirates who, pretending to be friendly, had accepted English hospitality.

Debasement

Also known as The Great Debasement of 1544–51.

In the Tudor period the coinage was debased several times. This means that the government ordered the reduction of the amount of gold and silver within the coins but, at the same time, maintaining their face value; the deficit was largely made up of cheaper copper. The need for this partly came about because of the recent influx of gold and silver from South America, which reduced the value of the Crown's treasury and partly because **Henry VIII** desperately needed more money to fund the **Third Anglo-French War**. So debasement was an attempt to increase the amount of money available to the monarch without having to use more precious metal.

Cardinal **Wolsey** carried out the first debasement in 1526 but it was not until 1544 that a series of debasements had a profound economic effect on the country. Despite the increased revenue from the **Dissolution of the Monasteries** more money was needed to fund Henry VIII's lavish lifestyle and wars with France and Scotland. With **Parliament** being reluctant to raise further taxes for the king, it was probably the idea of the king's Secretary, Thomas Wriothesley, to initiate a series of debasements. The following shows the effects on Tudor coins:

One penny – eighty per cent less silver.
One groat (fourpence) – sixty per cent less silver.
One testoon (twelve pence and forerunner of the shilling) – introduced in 1542 and only had a thin layer of silver.
One angel (roughly ten testoons) – no change in gold purity.
One sovereign (twenty testoons) – thirteen per cent less gold.

Inevitably, there were negative consequences. Despite the attempted secrecy, traders soon noticed the decreased values, charged more for their goods and inflation rose dramatically. Also, people would hoard the more valuable, older coins which further fuelled inflation. A law forbade these practices but was largely ignored. Also, overseas, the diminished English coins meant that the cost of foreign

Henry VIII testoon. The thin layer of silver on Henry VIII's raised nose soon rubbed off to reveal the underlying copper. F.D. only began to appear on British coins in George I's reign. (*1509–47. Metropolitan Museum of Art*)

imports rose and the country's financial reputation suffered. With wear and tear, the silver on the king's protruding nose would wear off and his nickname, 'Old Coppernose', came into usage. The debasements were undoubtedly a major contributory factor leading to the economic hardship of the 1540s and the rebellions at the end of the decade.

The policy continued in the reign of **Edward VI** until 1551. However, it was not until 1560 that Queen **Elizabeth** ordered all inferior coins to be melted down and newly minted ones to be restored to their pre-debasement quality.

Dee, Dr John

(1527–1608)

Mathematician, astronomer and alchemist.

Dr John Dee. (*Artist: Thomas Pennant, 1781. The National Library of Wales*)

A grandson of a Welsh courtier to **Henry VII**, Dee also claimed descent from Rhodri the Great, a ninth-century ruler of Gwynedd. He was educated at Cambridge University and became one of the original fellows of Trinity College when it was founded in 1546. Whilst there, he produced a classical play whose stage effects so astonished the audience that it was believed he must have used magic. Thus began his reputation as a sorcerer which remained with him for the rest of his life.

In the late 1540s and early 1550s, Dee spent much time in the Low Countries where he befriended renowned mathematicians and geographers such as Mercator. He returned with a large collection of mathematical and astronomical instruments and two globes constructed by Mercator which he donated to Trinity College. He was soon to create the largest private library in England at his home in Mortlake near London and was generous in making it accessible to other scholars. He later became technical advisor to England's greatest seamen such as **Chancellor**, **Frobisher**, **Ralegh** and **Drake** and was probably the first to coin the term 'British Empire'.

Dee's burgeoning reputation allowed him to meet many European scholars and rulers and he was also invited to give a series of lectures which attracted huge audiences of people, some of whom had to listen through open windows. His greatest wish, however, was to acquire an official position in the English court but in 1555 he was accused of attempting to murder Queen **Mary** through the use of magic. For this he was briefly imprisoned and interrogated by Bishop **Bonner** but the **Star Chamber**, under Mary's influence, later acquitted him.

When **Elizabeth** ascended the throne in 1558 Dee became her astrological and scientific advisor and used the stars to select her coronation date. He even converted to **Protestant**ism but, to his increasing frustration, she never handed him the official position that he craved.

In the 1560s and 1570s he wrote several scientific, astrological and mathematical treatises including *Steganographia*, which discussed the making of cyphers as well as the summoning and employment of demons, and *Monas Hieroglyphica* in which he explained a glyph he had designed that he claimed to express the mystical unity of nature. At the same time, he was visiting several courts of Europe in the continual hope of acquiring a patronage. The Catholic monarchs, although they admired his knowledge, mistrusted him as a Protestant and possible English spy. Several times, however, he was requested to speak before Queen Elizabeth both at court and his own home. On one occasion she listened for three days about a comet that had terrified her court. Later, he was requested to calculate the effects of adopting the Gregorian calendar and discovered that eleven days would have to be omitted. The Protestant hierarchy, however, refused to accept any associations with the Papacy and it was not until 1752 that Dee's eleven days were subtracted.

In the 1580s, Dee fell in with a dubious character called Edward Kelly and was convinced that he was able to communicate with angels. Together, they toured eastern Europe in hope of patronage but were met with cynicism. Kelly later told Dee that an angel had ordered them to share their possessions including their wives. It appears that Dee initially went along with this but it probably caused him to return to England soon after. On his return, he discovered that

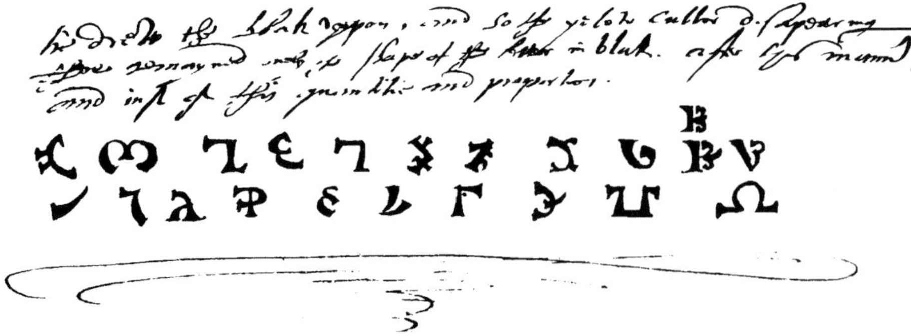

Enochian letters. The divine language transmitted to Dee and Kelly by angels and used to practise their magic. (*Author: Dr John Dee and Edward Kelly, 1583. British Library*)

a mob, believing him to be a sorcerer, had broken into his house and destroyed many of his books and instruments. Nine months later, his wife gave birth to a son, whom he raised as his own.

By the 1590s, interest in the occult had waned and Dee was always short of money, often having to sell off various possessions. The queen finally appointed him as Warden of Manchester College but he resigned in 1604 due to bad **health** and returned to London. He spent his final years in poverty, looked after by his daughter Katherine, until his death at the age of eighty-one. It seems almost certain that, in 1611, **William Shakespeare** modelled his character Prospero in *The Tempest*, on Dee.

It is hard not to find much sympathy with John Dee. Although many of his interests in alchemy and the supernatural may seem absurd to us he can be considered a true intellectual pioneer who was constantly searching for answers to many of the most profound questions of the day; a **renaissance** man who became widely respected throughout Europe for his expertise in many scientific spheres. Despite this, he was dogged throughout his life by a lack of official recognition and financial reward.

Devereux, Robert (Second Earl of Essex)

(1567–1601)

Soldier, courtier and a favourite of Queen **Elizabeth**.

Devereux was the great-grandson of Mary Boleyn, **Anne Boleyn**'s sister, and therefore a cousin, twice-removed, of Queen Elizabeth. Upon his father's early death Devereux inherited the earldom of Essex and was adopted by **William Cecil**, the queen's chief advisor. In addition, he became the stepson of the queen's great favourite, the **Earl of Leicester** when his mother married him in 1578. With such advantages, combined with his eloquence, wit and showmanship, it was inevitable that his star would rise rapidly.

In 1586, Essex showed great courage fighting the Spanish at the Battle of Zutphen in the Netherlands and upon his return home was appointed the prestigious title of Master of the Horse. When Leicester died in 1588, he became a chief advisor to the queen and a member of the Privy Council. He was also handed his step-father's monopoly in sweet wines which provided a lucrative income. In the same year it was he who raised the army that gathered at Tilbury to await a Spanish invasion force.

At court, however, he constantly seemed to be at loggerheads with Elizabeth's other advisors as he sought to increase his influence and power. On many occasions, he also angered the queen by disobeying her orders. In 1589, for example, he joined an expedition to Spain against her wishes and in the following year he secretly married **Walsingham**'s daughter, Frances, without Elizabeth's permission. After each occasion, though, the queen forgave him and brought him back into her fold.

During the 1590s, Essex consolidated his power as various members of Elizabeth's old guard died including **Hatton**, Walsingham and Cecil. His popularity and influence reached a zenith in 1596 after his heroic role in the spectacular capture of Cadiz. Warnings not to underestimate Elizabeth fell on deaf ears however. In 1597, his attempts to capture Spanish treasure ships and the Azores ended in failure. In the following year, during a row in council, Essex turned his back on the queen who promptly slapped him causing him to half draw his sword before being forcibly escorted out of the room.

After yet another reconciliation, Essex was appointed Lord Lieutenant of **Ireland** in 1599 and sent with an army of 17,000 men to crush **Tyrone's Rebellion**. This appointment, along with the lack of sufficient resources to go with it, was probably manufactured by his political rival, **Robert Cecil**, in the hope that he would fail. After some fruitless campaigning, he disobeyed his orders and concluded a truce with Tyrone, which many regarded as humiliating. Possibly fearing loss of influence to Cecil, he then deserted his army without permission and returned home in order to vindicate his actions in Ireland. After further outraging Elizabeth by storming into her bedroom before she was fully dressed he was confined to his home, York House, on the Strand. From there, it is quite conceivable that he sent messages to James VI of Scotland along the lines of supporting his accession to the English throne. Nothing came of this though.

In June 1600, a trial found him guilty of desertion and he was deprived of his offices and his wine monopoly and returned to house arrest. Out of desperation, he fortified his home and gathered around him loyal friends and various malcontents. One of these, in order to stir up the local populace, organised a showing of **Shakespeare**'s *Richard II* including the previously banned deposition scene. Finally, on 8 February, he broke out of his home and with over 200 of his supporters marched towards the City with the aim of rousing the Londoners and forcing the queen to at least grant him an audience. The ill-thought-out rebellion shocked Elizabeth but was a complete failure; no one came to his support and, after being forced to retreat, he surrendered. After a court found him guilty of treason, Essex became the last person to be executed inside the **Tower of London**, purportedly after three blows of the axe. Ironically, the man who beheaded him had previously been pardoned by Essex, after being convicted of rape, on the condition that he became the state executioner.

Essex represented the last of the old noble families to seek self-aggrandisement at the expense of the Crown. He had pushed against the new order of rising, talented 'new men' such as the Cecils and Walsingham and then, through his arrogance and poor political acumen, he lost the support of the queen, the very source of his power.

Diet

The people of Tudor England had a much less rich and varied diet than people are accustomed to today. There was also little in the way of imported food as the country was self-sufficient. This did expose the country to famines, however, if there were poor harvests and, as far as we know, there were two major famines in the Tudor period: in the mid-1550s and mid-1590s. Given that there was no refrigeration or canning then, meat tended to be salted, smoked or dried in order to prolong its edibility.

The majority of people ate relatively little meat and this would usually have been bacon along with fish, rabbit and birds such as pigeon and pheasant. The most common vegetables were onions and cabbages but towards the end of the century tomatoes, potatoes and purple carrots were introduced from America. The staple food was bread. The poorest people ate Carter's bread, made from rye and wheat and, for those who could afford it, bread made from wholemeal flour was preferred. The most common meal was pottage, a stew which was chiefly made of cabbage with barley or oats and occasional bacon.

The wealthiest in society ate manchet, made of white wheat flour, a bread that was softer on the teeth. They could also afford a wider range of fruit, such as oranges and watermelons and a greater variety of meat which included venison and turkey. They tended to finish a meal with sweets such as heavy custards, pastries and puddings packed with eggs, butter, honey and cream. Later in the Tudor period, sugar was imported and often replaced honey. This explains why the very wealthy, including Queen **Elizabeth**, developed blackened teeth. The richest could also flavour their food with herbs and imported spices, the most popular being ginger, cinnamon and saffron.

This was a very fattening diet which partly explains why **Henry VIII**'s waist expanded from thirty-two inches in 1522 to fifty-two inches at the time of his death. Individual royals had a penchant for certain foods: **Catherine of Aragon** liked seal and porpoise, **Jane Seymour** had a craving for Cornish pasties and cherries and **Mary I** had a weakness for pears. It has been estimated that the Tudor nobility's diet was eighty per cent protein and each feast contained thousands of more calories than we would eat today. However, colder homes and more physical lifestyles would also have burned many of these calories.

The banquet course became very fashionable for the rich during this time. After the main feast, guests were invited to a warmer, smaller and more private room where there were no servants. Popular banquet food included comfits, sweetmeats, sugar-coated seeds, marzipan and wet and dry suckets, similar to marmalade, made out of quince. This banqueting course was deemed to improve well-being and digestion and act as an aphrodisiac.

Over time, the wealthier middle classes were to adopt these fashionable foods although attempts were made to keep people within their social classes. The Sumptuary Law of 1517, for example, dictated the number of dishes that could be served per meal depending on rank. For example, a cardinal could serve nine dishes whilst lower-ranking gentry with an income of £40-100 per year could only serve three.

The most common beverage for all was ale as water was considered too unhealthy due to sewage contamination. This ale was brewed without hops and so was not alcoholic. The wealthiest could also drink imported wine from France from expensive wine glasses; the majority used wooden goblets or cups. Tea and coffee only arrived in England in the 1650s.

Dissolution of the Monasteries

(1536–40)

This has been described as one of the most revolutionary events in English history due its huge impact on the social and spiritual lives of a great many people.

The groundwork for the closure of England's 800 monasteries had been laid earlier in the 1530s through a series of parliamentary acts which had destroyed papal power within the country. At the same time, King **Henry VIII**'s wars with France, costly fleet and fort-building programmes and extravagant lifestyle meant that the Crown had become desperately short of money. It was inevitable, therefore, that the wealthy religious houses, which owned a quarter of the country, would be targeted by the state. Attacks on monastic lands had already happened in the Protestant states of Europe. However, these had largely been driven by the general **population**s who had resented the monks' and nuns' wealth and abuses. In England, the monasteries were still generally quite popular so the drive for dissolution came largely from the top.

The project was overseen by the Vicar-General, **Thomas Cromwell**, who in 1535 sent out hand-picked commissioners to visit the monasteries, convents and friaries. The intention was clearly to create justification for their imminent closures. It seems certain that within some there were financial and sexual abuses going on and that many occupants had become lax in their religious vows. The commissioners, however, exaggerated these and largely ignored the

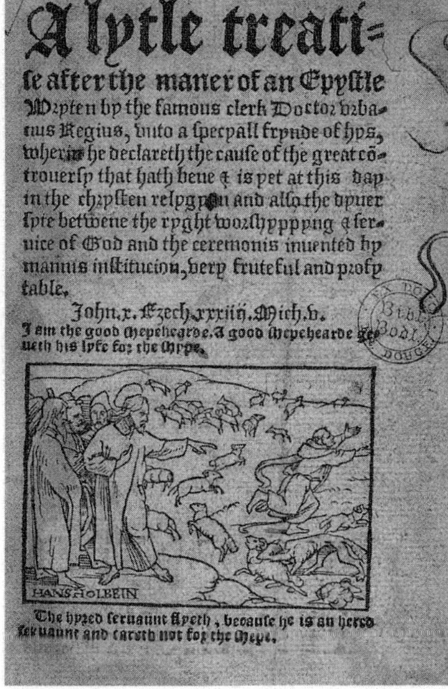

A lytle treati=
se after the maner of an Epystle
Wryten by the famous clerk Doctor Vrba=
nus Regius, vnto a specyall frynde of hys,
wherin he declareth the cause of the great cõ=
trouersy that hath bene & is yet at this day
in the chrysten relygyon and also the dyuer
syte betwene the ryght worshyppyng & ser=
uice of God and the ceremonis inuented by
mannis institucion, very fruteful and profy
table.
John.x. Ezech.xxxiiii. Mich.v.
I am the good shepehearde. A good shepehearde ge
ueth his lyfe for the shepe.

HANS HOLBEIN

The hyred seruaunt flyeth, because he is an hered seruaunt and careth not for the shepe.

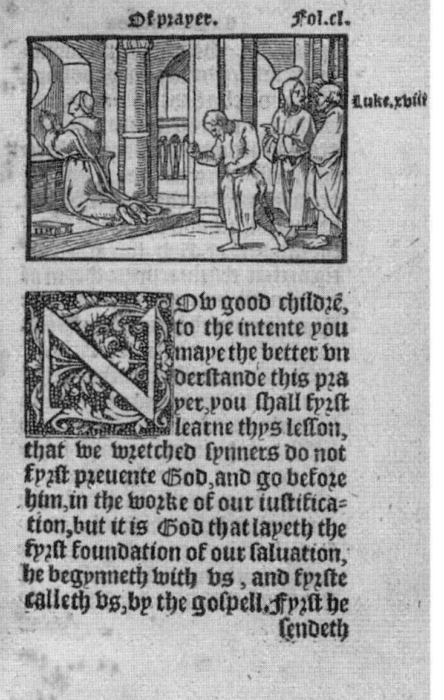

Of prayer. Fol.cl.

Luke.xviii

Now good chyldre, to the intente you maye the better vnderstande this prayer, you shall fyrst learne thys lesson, that we wretched synners do not fyrst preuente God, and go before hym, in the worke of our iustification, but it is God that layeth the fyrst foundation of our saluation, he begynneth with vs, and fyrste calleth vs, by the gospell. Fyrst he sendeth

Anti-monastic woodcuts. A series of pictures that satirised monastic life. Thomas Cromwell used Holbein as a tool for anti-clerical propaganda. (*Artist: Hans Holbein, 1530s. From* Holbein in England *by Susan Foister, 2006*)

considerable good work that was going on such as the provision of spiritual comfort and giving of alms to the poor. Indeed, the early sixteenth century had seen a revival in monasticism.

Armed with the required evidence, **Parliament** passed an Act of Suppression in 1536 which ordered the closure of all religious house with an income of less than £200 per year. This first round of closures caused widespread resentment especially in Yorkshire and Lincolnshire where a large scale uprising, known as the **Pilgrimage of Grace,** occurred. The revolt was crushed and probably added to Henry's suspicions that the monks owed more loyalty to the Pope than the Crown.

Pressure on the monasteries continued. Many abbots and priors surrendered voluntarily in order to benefit from Cromwell's offer of more generous pensions. Others resisted in the hope that internal monastic reform would save them despite the risk that such defiance could be construed as treason. These were sent warnings against asset-stripping or concealment of valuables.

Finally, the second Suppression Act of 1539 ordered the closure of all remaining religious houses. Those leaders that resisted were punished; the abbots of Colchester, Glastonbury and Reading were hanged, drawn and quartered for treason as an example to others and their monks would only receive the basic pension of £4 per year (£1,700 in 2024).

In terms of its effects, the dissolution benefitted the monarchy to the tune of around £150,000 per year (£100 million in 2024). This was before the deduction of pensions, though, and another war with France in the 1540s caused much land to be sold off to local lords and gentry so that by 1547 income from the old monastic lands had fallen to £90,000. It can be argued that the costs were far greater. The monasteries had provided employment, alms, hospitality and medical care for their local communities as well as being centres of learning with valuable libraries. All of these were lost and the buildings and their precious contents were looted over the following decades.

Drake, Sir Francis

(c. 1541–96)

Sailor, explorer and privateer

Drake was born in Devon but his family fled to Kent during the reprisals that followed the 1549 **Prayer Book Rebellion**. Near the mouth of the Medway he learned to sail and adopted his father's strong **Protestant** beliefs.

In the 1560s he took part in his first voyages into the Atlantic Ocean. Led by his cousin, **John Hawkins**, attempts were made to profit from the trans-Atlantic African slave trade which, up until then, was dominated by the Spanish and Portuguese. Although English law actually forbade the capture of people it was deemed legal if they were already captives, non-Protestants or criminals. During one such expedition, they were forced into the harbour of Vera Cruz in modern-day Mexico in order to make repairs. A surprise Spanish attack, however, led to the loss of many ships and men. Both Hawkins and Drake just managed to escape but, apparently, from that day Drake became a sworn enemy of Spain.

In the early 1570s, Drake led three expeditions against the Spanish Main in northern South America and Panama with the intention of strangling the gold and silver trade routes that were financing Spain. The final voyage proved particularly lucrative and although Queen **Elizabeth** could never approve of this piracy in public she acknowledged Drake's usefulness as a weapon for weakening the power of Spain and for filling the English coffers. During the same expedition, Drake became the first Englishman to see the Pacific Ocean when he climbed a tree in the Panama isthmus.

Possibly inspired by this view, Drake led a voyage in 1577 with the intention of raiding Spanish settlements and treasure ships in the Pacific. To maintain secrecy, Drake had assured his men that the purpose was to seek trade with Egypt. A mutiny, however, broke out in Patagonia but was suppressed through a combination of violence and clemency. The leader and former friend, Thomas Doughty, was beheaded whilst his co-conspirators were forgiven.

Later, only Drake's ship, *The Pelican*, was able to make the hazardous passage through the Magellan Straits. After being forced south, Drake discovered the channel south of Tierra del Fuego that still bears his name and he renamed his ship *The Golden Hind* (named after the coat of arms of **Christopher Hatton**, a chief financier of the expedition). The unsuspecting Spanish were vulnerable to attack as Drake successfully raided his way north, filling his holds with treasure.

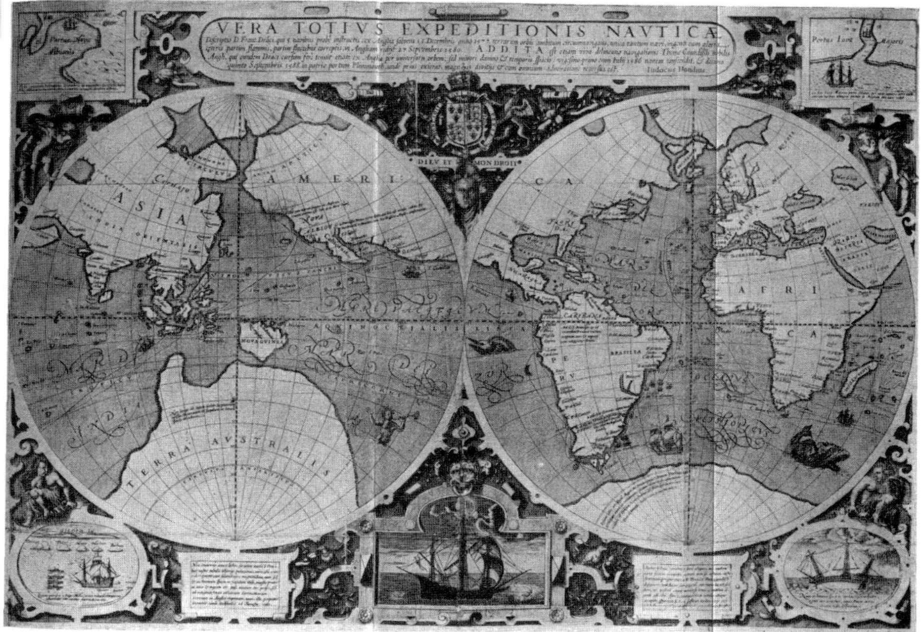

Drake's circumnavigation of the world. Based on Mercator's 1569 world map but showing Drake's 1577–80 voyage. 'Terra Australis' is deliberately vague as are the possibilities of the north-west and north-east passages. (*Artist: Jodocus Hondius, 1595, The Kraus Collection of Francis Drake*)

He paused somewhere on the coast of modern-day Oregon and claimed the land of New Albion for the queen. Returning the way that they had come was considered too risky so Drake took his crew west across the vast Pacific. Over a year later, they finally returned to Plymouth with a cargo that paid a dividend of 1,400 per cent on the initial outlay of the expedition. Elizabeth herself boarded *The Golden Hind* after it docked in London and, at her behest, the French ambassador knighted Drake on the spot.

Drake's actions accelerated the moves towards the **Anglo-Spanish War** which finally broke out in 1585 and one of the queen's first actions in this conflict was to send him to the Spanish Main to inflict maximum damage. Although the expedition was not profitable Drake ransacked Cartagena and stole many valuable cannons. On his return, he rescued the starving colonists of **Roanoke** Island, in modern-day North Carolina, and the settlement was abandoned.

In 1587, Drake led a mission to thwart Spanish plans to launch an invasion fleet destined for England. A daring raid into Cadiz harbour resulted in the loss of around thirty Spanish ships; this was followed by the capture of various stores including a year's supply of seasoned staves for making barrels. Consequently, when the **Spanish Armada** eventually did sail the casks were made of unseasoned wood and so leaked badly. This was followed by the capture of another treasure ship off the Azores. This 'Singeing of the King of Spain's Beard' delayed the Armada for a year and catapulted Drake to the height of his fame. In Spain, he was feared and loathed and often referred to as 'El Draque' – The Dragon – with many believing that he owned a magic mirror which gave him the locations of Spanish ships.

In the following year, Drake commanded a squadron of the English fleet that saw off the Spanish Armada and, in 1589, he was given command of an English fleet. This had three objectives: 1) to destroy the Spanish ships being repaired in Spain's northern ports, 2) to capture Lisbon, raise a rebellion and put the Portuguese pretender, Dom Antonio, on the throne, 3) to capture the Azores so that it could be used as a base against Spanish shipping. Due to better Spanish defences and the confused and overly-ambitious plans, the mission failed on all three fronts and over 12,000 lives and twenty ships were lost. Drake was blamed by his fellow officers and, although an enquiry acquitted him, he fell out of royal favour and was demoted to organising Plymouth's naval defences.

In 1595, Elizabeth finally agreed to allow him joint command, with Hawkins, of a punitive expedition to the Caribbean. The mission, however, was beset by disease and military defeats and Drake himself succumbed to dysentery in January 1596. He was buried at sea near Panama and to this day, divers continue to search for his lead-lined coffin.

Of all the Tudors, Sir Francis Drake is possibly the one whose heroic reputation has been the most burnished over time. He has been credited with numerous

Francis Drake. The favour tied to Drake's left sleeve indicates the royal patronage of Queen Elizabeth. (*Artist: Jodocus Hondius, 1583. www.raremaps.com/gallery/detail/55344/sir-francis-drake-franciscus-draeck-nobilissimus-eques-a-hondius*)

feats of sang froid, tenacity, fair play and unflappability. He was undoubtedly a brave and skilful leader who commanded the respect of his men. On the other hand, he can also be considered a dangerous fanatic who was hasty, difficult to work with and could show cruelty to others.

Dudley, John (Duke of Northumberland)

(1504–53)

Soldier, admiral and statesman

John Dudley was the son of Edmund Dudley, the financial minister of **Henry VII** who was executed by **Henry VIII**. In the 1520s he gained attention through his military prowess during the **Second Anglo-French War** as well as his skills in horsemanship, archery and wrestling. By 1534 he was responsible for the king's body armour, had befriended **Thomas Cromwell** and was becoming a regular member of the royal entourage.

Duke of Northumberland. (*Artist: Unknown, 16th century. Panel painting from Penshurst Place*)

His star rose further in the 1540s. After becoming a member of the House of Commons in **Parliament** he later joined the Lords and became Lord Admiral of the Navy. In that position he introduced much-needed administrative reforms and, in 1544, he commanded the fleet which helped to destroy Edinburgh in the **War of the Rough Wooing**. In the same year, he became Governor of Boulogne, the siege of which had cost his son's life. In the following year, he was conducting naval operations in the inconclusive Battle of the Solent and entertaining the king on his ship.

He and his friend, Prince Edward's uncle, **Edward Seymour**, became the leaders of the **Protestant** faction within the court and two of the executors of the king's will. By the time of Henry's death, in 1547, they had manoeuvred themselves into a predominant position. Seymour became the Duke of Somerset and was recognised as the leader of the Regency Council that was to rule until **Edward VI** came of age. Dudley, by now the Earl of Warwick, was considered Somerset's right-hand man who controlled the army. Together, they invaded Scotland and won the **Battle of Pinkie Cleugh** (1547) and two years later, Dudley put down **Kett's Rebellion** in Norfolk.

Somerset's policies, however, had made him unpopular and Dudley, possibly out of self-preservation, turned on his erstwhile friend. By joining forces with the dissatisfied propertied classes and leading **Catholics** he imprisoned Somerset and took control of the Council. A few months later the two men appear to have been reconciled although Somerset always remained a threat to Dudley's power. Later, after trumped-up charges of conspiracy, he had Somerset executed.

From 1550 to 1553, Dudley was, in effect, the sole ruler of the country and in 1551 appointed himself Duke of Northumberland. An increasingly Protestant king allowed him and Archbishop **Cranmer** to carry out sweeping religious reforms. These included the Forty-Two **Articles** and a new English Prayer Book in 1552 which was enforced by an Act of Uniformity. To improve the economy, he made peace with France and Scotland, stopped the practice of coin **debasement** and hired the financial expert, **Thomas Gresham** who managed to raise the value of English currency on the Antwerp stock exchange. Dudley also tried to fix the prices of foodstuffs and was successful in prosecuting those landlords guilty of illegal **enclosures**. He also brought the young king more into the political field and ensured that his **education** became more practical.

Edward was beginning to take an increasing control of affairs when he became seriously ill with tuberculosis in early 1553. It is not clear how much Dudley influenced the king but Edward's will was altered to exclude his half-sisters (**Mary** and **Elizabeth**) and stated that the throne should, instead, go to Edward's Protestant cousin, **Lady Jane Grey**. At around the same time, Dudley arranged for his second son, Guildford, to marry Lady Jane. People were quick to draw their own conclusions and Princess Mary saw the danger. The morning after Edward died in July, Dudley sent 300 soldiers to 'secure' Mary but she had already fled to Norfolk to raise an army. It seems that Dudley had been unprepared for this situation and her popularity took him by surprise. Jane was proclaimed queen but Dudley had become outnumbered and battered by demands from all quarters for him to disband his small army so he surrendered himself at Cambridge. Amidst widespread hatred and rumours that he had poisoned the king, he was put on trial and found guilty of high treason. Weeks later, he was beheaded on **Tower** Hill but not before declaring that he had always been a Catholic.

John Dudley has always had a bad press and understandably so. It is hard not to conclude that he was a self-serving autocrat who would do anything to acquire power and then maintain it. Even his religious views, whatever they were, were subservient to political gain. On the other hand, several historians argue that he was an excellent and hard-working administrator who merely wanted to serve the Crown and point out that his financial reward was far less than that of his predecessor, Somerset. They argue that his final actions were not driven by survival instinct but had merely been to enforce the dead king's will. In his own words, Dudley lamented that he was to share 'my poor father's fate who, after his master was gone, suffered death for doing his master's commandments'.

Dudley, Robert (Earl of Leicester)

(1532–88)

Soldier, courtier and favourite of Queen **Elizabeth I**.

Robert Dudley was the fifth son of **John Dudley**, the Earl of Northumberland, who was executed in 1553. Being the son of the Lord Protector, he counted amongst his tutors the likes of **John Dee** and Roger Ascham, who also taught Lady Elizabeth. He was raised a **Protestant** and attended his father during his suppression of **Kett's Rebellion**. A year later, in 1550, he married Amy Robsart, the daughter of a Norfolk gentleman farmer. Subsequently, he became the MP for Norfolk.

His fortunes took a turn for the worse when he supported his father's attempt to exclude Princess **Mary** from the throne in 1553. Dudley was imprisoned and sentenced to death. However, maybe because Mary's new husband, King Philip of Spain, wanted to ingratiate himself with the English nobility, he was pardoned and released a year later. His rehabilitation into royal favour was aided by his mother who had befriended the incoming Spanish nobility and in 1557 he was able to prove his loyalty by fighting for the Spanish at the Battle of St Quentin against France.

Within days of her accession to the throne in 1558, Queen Elizabeth promoted her childhood friend to Master of the Horse and made him her Knight of the Garter. The athletic and handsome Dudley was constantly by her side and she called him her 'eyes' which explains why he signed off his letters to her with 0 0. Rumours abounded that she was going to marry him, despite his current **marriage**, and that they even had an illegitimate child. It was in this atmosphere that the story emerged of Amy Robsart's death in 1560. Found at the bottom of her stairs with a broken neck it was suspected that she had been murdered so that Dudley could marry the queen. The rumours were impossible to quash despite Dudley's call for an impartial enquiry. On balance, however, modern historians tend to believe that it was an accidental fall caused by a symptom of her breast cancer or possibly suicide.

His relationship with the queen had to be kept more clandestine for the time being but he still occupied apartments next to hers at court. In 1562, when Elizabeth fell seriously ill with smallpox, she named Dudley as Lord Protector-in-waiting but to everyone's relief, the queen recovered. Dudley's arrogance and closeness to the monarch had aroused much jealousy and dislike amongst the nobility especially the older families such as the **Duke of Norfolk**. To many, he was simply the son of a convicted traitor so he took to wearing protective mail under his clothes whenever he was about.

In the following year, Elizabeth showed that her love of her country came before that of any man when she proposed that Dudley marry **Mary, Queen of Scots**. This was the condition for naming Mary as her heir; Elizabeth clearly hoped to bring Scotland firmly under English influence and away from the French. She also granted Dudley the earldom of Leicester to make him more acceptable to the Scottish queen. It seems that Mary was interested but Dudley refused the offer; perhaps he still entertained hopes for the English throne.

By the mid-1560s it was becoming clear to Dudley that Elizabeth would never marry him. At the same time, she demanded his continual company and on ceremonial occasions he acted as an unofficial consort. When he was away for a few weeks the queen was apparently beside her herself with anxiety. Not surprisingly, perhaps, he had secretive affairs with other women such as Douglas Sheffield who bore him an illegitimate son, Robert, in 1574. Then, four years later, Elizabeth was both hurt and furious when she discovered that Dudley had secretly married Lettice Knollys, the Countess of Essex and widowed mother of **Robert Devereux**. The couple had a child who died in its infancy but Dudley proved to be a loving father to his stepchildren. The queen forgave Dudley but forever harboured a hatred of 'that she-wolf' and 'flouting wench', Lettice.

Politically, Dudley favoured a hard-line approach against Spain which dovetailed with his increasingly **Puritan** stand on religion. Throughout the 1580s he was one of those who advocated the execution of Mary, Queen of Scots. He often clashed with the queen's more cautious chief advisor, **William Cecil**, but the two generally had a good working relationship and their counter-balancing views must have greatly aided Elizabeth's decision-making. Dudley also forged an alliance with the Secretary of State, **Walsingham**, who, like him, favoured a more militant Protestant foreign policy.

Dudley took a great interest in other affairs too. As well as being a principal patron of various sailors such as **Drake** and **Frobisher** he invested in overseas trading ventures such as the Muscovy Company. He also made efforts to relieve poverty and regularly donated money to improve prison conditions. He showed tremendous interest in the arts too. He collected paintings, encouraged poetry and the translation of foreign books and he founded his own company of actors (Lord Leicester's Men, which included **James Burbage**), which was given royal permission to tour in 1574.

Throughout this period tensions with **Catholic** Spain were increasing and, in 1585, Elizabeth reluctantly agreed to send an expeditionary force to the Netherlands to aid the Dutch in their fight for independence against the Spanish. She put Dudley in charge but, against her explicit wishes, he accepted the Dutch offer to be governor of their provinces. Later, his arrogance and military inability upset his fellow Dutch commanders and very little was achieved and at great cost. This was not entirely Dudley's fault, however; he was partly stymied by a lack of funding and Elizabeth's orders to be militarily cautious. After returning home in 1587 he was once again in the queen's favour.

In 1588, with the **Spanish Armada** approaching, Dudley was put in charge of the army that waited at Tilbury and he stood beside the queen when she delivered her famous speech to the waiting troops. Later that year, on his way to take the waters at Buxton, he unexpectedly died. The cause remains unclear but it was probably either stomach cancer or malaria contracted whilst in the Low Countries. Elizabeth was beside herself with grief and locked herself in her rooms for several days until Cecil finally ordered her door to be broken open. She kept Dudley's last letter to her in a treasure box by her bed until the day she died.

Leicester as Governor-General. Engraving commemorating Leicester as Governor-General of the Dutch provinces. (*Author: Hendrik Goltzius, 1586. British Museum*)

It is easy to dismiss Dudley as an arrogant, preening, overly-ambitious courtier. More recent historians, however, conclude that he was as important a statesman as Cecil. Certainly there can be no doubting his loyalty to family, Crown and country and one may even sympathise with his position as being the man who came closest to marrying the queen.

E

Education

The majority of children in Tudor England received no education at all and would do manual work to help their parents instead. Boys who were lucky enough would receive an apprenticeship at the age of seven or eight. Subsequently, there were very low literacy rates in the sixteenth century – about thirty per cent of men and ten per cent of women. Reading and writing were made more difficult by the lack of dictionaries and standardised English. Spellings and punctuation varied according to different regions and customs. An added complication was the fact that the letters i and j were often considered interchangeable (with j usually used as the capital). The same with u and v, with the latter only being used at the start of words.

Unsurprisingly, perhaps, Tudor education was generally the reserve of upper and middle class boys who would start learning the basics of literacy, mathematics and religion at a 'Petty School' (also known as a 'Dame School'). These were usually run in the home of a local, educated housewife.

From seven to fourteen, boys could then attend grammar schools. At the start of the Tudor period these were known as chantry schools which were usually run by monasteries with the specific purpose of drumming Latin into children. By the 1540s these had largely disappeared due to the **Dissolution of the Monasteries**. Around twenty of them were replaced with a semi-secular version by **Edward VI** and hence known as Edward VI Grammar Schools. In **Elizabeth I**'s reign, seventy-two new grammar schools were established, usually by wealthy trading guilds such as the Merchant Taylors and Haberdashers. The **Reformation** facilitated the broadening of the curriculum; boys were taught mathematics, history, oratory, logic, Ancient Greek and philosophy in addition to Latin and the scriptures. Non-academic activities included running, wrestling, archery and chess.

There were just three two-week holidays in the year and the school day was a long one: from 6.00am to 5.00pm (shorter in the winter) and the boys were only free on Sundays and Thursday and Saturday afternoons. Lessons were dull as learning was done by rote and classes were large, with varied ages and a wide degree of abilities. Discipline was therefore very strict, with teachers often dishing out beatings with a birch cane. The wealthier families could afford a special friend for their child called a 'whipping boy'. When their son was naughty, the 'whipping boy' would receive the punishment. Classroom equipment was quite basic. The richer schools had a greater supply of reading and writing books but most children learned to read with a hornbook. This was a sheet of paper with, for example, the Lord's Prayer on it, which was attached to a wooden board and protected by a thin slice of cow horn. Writing was done with a goose or hen quill, sharpened by a knife and dipped into an ink pot. Technically, grammar schools were free but those who could afford to paid a few pennies per day which added up to about £20 a year. In 1560, this could have bought you four horses or sixteen cows and was around twice the annual salary of a skilled labourer.

The only universities were at Oxford and Cambridge and there was no fixed age for entry. Boys usually started between the ages of fifteen and eighteen and their original purpose had been to prepare them for careers in the Church but after the Reformation they struggled to attract students. They recovered in Elizabeth I's reign when the growing middle classes wanted their sons to

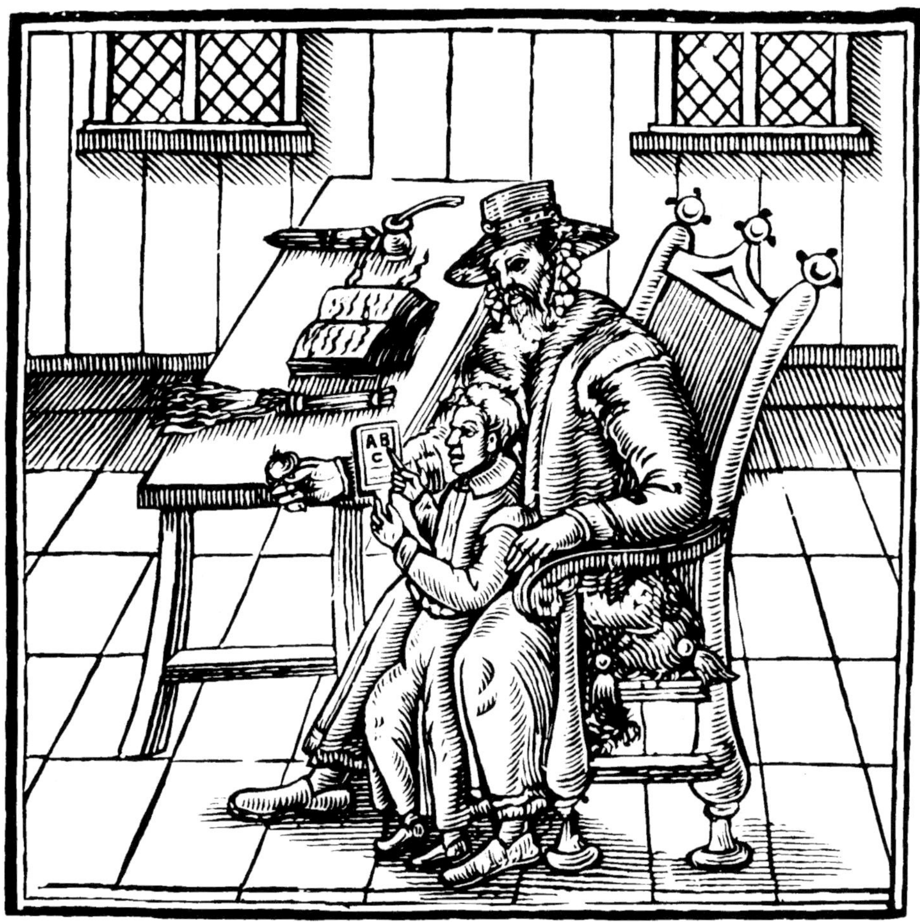

Learning from a hornbook. (*Artist: unknown. From* Hornbye's Horn-book, *1622 via Wikimedia Commons*)

have a higher education in order to further their future careers. A degree course lasted four years (seven years for a master's) and whilst some colleges were still devoted to divinity there was now a much greater range of subjects on offer, such as geography, rhetoric, astronomy and trade. The **Renaissance** also meant that the ideas of **humanism** became popular and ancient knowledge was taught through the mediums of Latin and Ancient Greek. By 1600, each university was receiving 500–600 students per year.

The final part of a wealthy Tudor's education could include a tour of European cities. However, travelling to other countries required the monarch's permission so only the sons of the nobility usually had this opportunity. A popular alternative was to study law at the Inns of Court in London.

For most girls, education was seen as unnecessary as all they needed to learn was how to run a household and prepare for **marriage**. In poorer families they were sent out to work to bring in extra money or carried out the household chores. There were some petty schools and even a few grammar schools that allowed girls to enter but these were few and far between and girls would usually leave long before the boys. By the 1530s, however, it was becoming more fashionable for the wealthier families to educate their daughters. The humanist, **Thomas More**, set the example by educating his three daughters to a high standard. Girls were taught practical skills at home such as embroidery, music and dancing as well as some literacy and divinity. Their parents could usually afford a tutor for this.

The daughters of the nobility and royal family tended to be educated to a very high standard. Amongst other subjects, they would learn hunting, archery, French and various musical instruments and they were usually taught by a university-educated scholar. Elizabeth I had the good fortune to be tutored by the humanist, Roger Ascham, who was far more forward-thinking than most as one of his guiding principles was that children should be taught to think.

There is no doubt that the provision of education improved in the Tudor period. The curriculum became much broader and an increase in the number of free schools and the relatively cheap grammar schools meant that literacy rates rose. There was a steady increase in printed material and more girls became educated too. However, by 1600, the vast majority of girls and the poor were still deprived of a proper start in life. In addition, education was still seen as a means to an end as opposed to the pursuit of knowledge for its own sake. At the same time, the methodology of teaching left much to be desired as too much emphasis was placed on results and it was considered more important to teach the subject than the child.

Edward VI

(1537–53)

King of England from 1547 to 1553.

Son of **Henry VIII** and **Jane Seymour**, Edward lost his mother to the effects of childbirth twelve days after he was born. Despite poor eyesight he was a healthy child and was lovingly looked after by the many ladies of the court, particularly **Catherine Parr**, the king's last wife. He was shown affection by his older half-sisters, **Mary** and **Elizabeth**. The **humanist**, **Sir John Cheke**, was put in charge of his **education** and he developed a great proficiency for languages, music and astronomy. Edward was much devoted to Cheke, the only person on whose behalf he is known to have revealed any emotion but he could also show an awful temper. It was said that, in a fit of rage, he once tore a falcon apart in front of his tutors.

After defeating the Scots at the **Battle of Solway Moss**, Henry forced his northern neighbours to agree to the Treaty of Greenwich in 1543. This included the betrothal of the six-year-old Edward to the seven-month old **Mary, Queen of Scots**. The Scots later reneged on the agreement and, despite the **War of the Rough Wooing**, the **marriage** never came about.

Edward was only nine when his father died and so a Regency Council was appointed to rule the country. This was first led by his uncle, the **Duke of Somerset**, then **the Duke of Northumberland**. The old king's will had never requested that a single person should be Lord Protector; rather it had envisaged a collective leadership that reflected the two main faiths. Soon after his death, however, the majority of the council agreed to Somerset's leadership.

Edward was brought up to become a fervent **Protestant** and he liked to make notes after listening to sermons and read twelve chapters of scriptures each day. John Foxe described him as 'a godly imp'. Therefore, the religious reforms of Archbishop **Cranmer** and Bishops **Latimer** and **Ridley** accelerated with the new king's approval. Such changes included the offering of communion to laity as well as clergy, the introduction of the 1552 Common Prayer Book and culminated in Cranmer's Forty-Two **Articles**. Following on from Henry's **Dissolution of the Monasteries**, Cranmer also ordered the closure of chantries (private chapels) which raised much money for the Crown.

Early in his reign, attempts were made by Somerset's brother, **Thomas Seymour**, to ingratiate himself with the king with a view to increasing his own power. Edward, however, seems to have ignored Seymour's attempts to undermine his brother. Matters came to a head in early 1549 when it appears that Seymour killed Edward's dog in a botched attempt to abduct the king. Soon after, Edward signed his death warrant.

In the same year, serious uprisings broke out – the **Prayer Book Rebellion** in Devon and Cornwall and **Kett's Rebellion** in Norfolk. The former was sparked by the Protestant reforms, the latter largely by encroaching **enclosures**. Somerset was blamed, ejected from power and, later, Edward signed his death warrant too.

Under Northumberland's leadership, Edward became more involved in the affairs of state but it is impossible to know how much he was included in the decision-making process of government. It seems Northumberland certainly promoted the idea that Edward was, in effect, a ruling monarch. This gave his power more legitimacy and enabled him to thwart his rivals' attempts to undermine him.

In early 1553, Edward became seriously ill with tuberculosis. He seemed to recover but by June his condition became serious. Henry VIII's Succession Act of 1543 had finally acknowledged the rights of his daughters to the throne after that of his son but Edward overturned this with his Device for the Succession. This disinherited his half-sisters and gave priority to his Protestant cousin-once-removed, **Lady Jane Grey** and any sons she may have. Jane had just been married to Northumberland's son but we cannot be sure how much influence Northumberland had on the Device. Certainly, he stood to benefit especially as the **Catholic** Mary would have brought about his ruin. However, it is also doubtful if Edward would have wanted a Catholic successor to reverse all the religious changes of his reign. The young king finally died on the 6 July, aged fifteen.

Although his reign was brief, Edward VI oversaw the zenith of the English **Reformation** and the country's lurch towards the Protestant faith. His sister, Mary, attempted to reverse this process but ultimately failed and it was left to Queen Elizabeth to complete England's religious revolution.

Effingham, Lord Howard of

(see Howard, Charles)

Elizabeth I

(1533–1603)

Queen of England from 1558 to 1603

Elizabeth was born at Greenwich Palace and named after both of her grandmothers but she was possibly the biggest disappointment in her father's life. **Henry VIII** had broken from Rome, fallen out with friends and made many enemies in order to annul his marriage to **Catherine of Aragon**, wed Elizabeth's mother, **Anne Boleyn**, and thereby have the son that he craved. So when Anne's later pregnancies ended in miscarriages not only did he appear foolish but it seemed that God was punishing him. So, on trumped-up charges of adultery, he had Anne beheaded in 1536 and then married **Jane Seymour**. Elizabeth, along with her older sister **Mary**, was declared illegitimate and barred from succession to the throne. Instead of Princess Elizabeth, she suddenly became Lady Elizabeth although Henry did reinstate her in the succession in 1543.

Educated by the leading scholars of the day, including Roger Ascham and **John Cheke**, Elizabeth excelled at languages and soon became fluent in Italian, French, Greek and Latin. Later in her life, she could even speak several Gaelic languages. She was also fond of music and dancing. During this time, she formed a close attachment to her brother, **Edward**, and she was shown much kindness by a later stepmother, **Catherine Howard**. The latter's execution when Elizabeth was eight shocked her and it was at this age that she apparently told her friend, **Robert Dudley**, that she would never marry.

Henry's sixth wife, **Catherine Parr**, took great care of her stepchildren but when Henry died in 1547 she married **Thomas Seymour**, the Lord Protector's brother. Seymour took an unhealthy interest in Elizabeth who may have developed a crush on him. After Parr's death the following year, Seymour plotted to overthrow his brother, marry Elizabeth and wed her brother, Edward VI, to his cousin **Lady Jane Grey**. The plot failed, Seymour was executed and Elizabeth was interrogated to ascertain her involvement. No evidence could be found, however, and it was unlikely that she would have got herself involved in such a hair-brained scheme.

In 1553, Edward VI fell seriously ill. Neither he nor the new Lord Protector, the **Duke of Northumberland**, wanted the **Catholic** Mary to become queen so Elizabeth and Mary were again excluded from the throne and the succession was handed to the **Protestant** Lady Jane Grey. Due to Mary's popularity, however, this plot failed and later that year, Elizabeth rode into London alongside the new queen. Mary never trusted her Protestant sister though and, in the following year, Elizabeth was imprisoned in the **Tower of London**, accused of being involved in the abortive **Wyatt's Rebellion**. This uprising had aimed to dethrone Mary and place Elizabeth on the throne. Elizabeth pleaded her innocence but Mary's advisors, including her Lord Chancellor, **Stephen Gardiner**, urged the queen to put her on trial. However, due to the lack of evidence and her growing popularity, Elizabeth was released and spent a year under house arrest in Woodstock.

By 1558, Mary was seriously ill and still with no child to succeed her. With great reluctance, she finally announced her sister as her heir on 6 November. Eleven days later she died and, against all the odds, Elizabeth had become queen.

Religion

The new monarch's priority was to becalm the religious storms of the last decade. The 1559 Church Settlement gave Elizabeth the title of 'Supreme Governor of the English Church' rather than the more contentious 'Head' used by her father and brother. A more modified version of **Cranmer**'s 1552 Prayer Book was enforced and punishments for non-attendance at church became more lenient. Then in 1563, the doctrines of Elizabeth's new Church were laid down in the Thirty-Nine **Articles** which aimed to appeal to the majority of Protestants and Catholics. This is the basis of today's Church of England.

Elizabeth herself was a Protestant but, for her day, she had a remarkably tolerant view and none of her sister's bigotry. This was evident when she said, '…there is only one Jesus Christ and all the rest is a dispute over trifles.' This middle path, however, did not appeal to the more extreme Catholics and **Puritans** but the queen refused to budge. All she demanded was loyalty and she was quite prepared to execute those of either faith if they betrayed her.

Succession

The question of who would succeed Elizabeth was a dilemma that dogged the queen and her government for the entire reign. She was the last of her dynasty and the fear was that, should she die childless, the country could descend into a civil war between its nobles. Elizabeth understood this and allowed a stream of suitors to approach in order to gain her hand in **marriage**. These included princes of France, Sweden, Austria and Saxony as well as several English nobles. Her advisors, particularly **Lord Burghley**, favoured a foreign match which would strengthen England's hand against the Catholic threat from Spain. Elizabeth, however, rejected all. For one thing, she did not want to be dominated by a foreign ruler like her sister had been. For another, she probably realised that the possibility of marriage gave her a powerful negotiating weapon. The man she came closest to marrying was probably her childhood friend, the **Earl of Leicester**. Her love for him was clear to all but firstly, he was scandalised by the suspicious death of his wife and secondly, Burghley warned that marriage to an English lord could provoke trouble with other, rival noblemen. This advice seemed particularly prescient when news came of the problems facing **Mary, Queen of Scots** caused by her marriages in the 1560s.

Elizabeth's refusal to name a successor, let alone marry, provoked two crises. In 1562 she almost died of smallpox; her life was only saved by a young German physician who happened to be present when all the other doctors had given up on her. Panic had ensued and **Parliament** made repeated appeals for her to

People dancing a galliard. The galliard was an athletic dance involving many leaps and hops. Elizabeth's favourite dance, she is said to have practised it as her morning exercise at least until 1589. (*Artist: unknown. Copy of 16th century woodcut from* Manners, Custom and Dress During the Middle Ages and During the Renaissance Period *by Paul Lacroix, 1874*)

marry in case she was not so lucky again. The MP, **Peter Wentworth**, made particularly strident demands for which he was imprisoned in the Tower.

The second crisis was more serious and prolonged. In 1568, Mary, Queen of Scots, fled a civil war in Scotland and asked for Elizabeth's protection. Mary was Elizabeth's closest living relative and, therefore, technically the heir to the English throne. However, she was also a Catholic and ally of the French and her sudden appearance in England made her a potential focal point for Catholic plots and rebellions. Indeed, in the **Northern Rebellion** the following year, several nobles planned to replace Elizabeth with Mary. The revolt was crushed but, in 1570, the Pope excommunicated Elizabeth, thereby giving any Catholic permission to oust her. Further plots were uncovered and the queen was exhorted to execute Mary and thereby remove the Catholic figurehead. Elizabeth refused to set the precedent of murdering a fellow monarch though. After the **Babington Plot** of 1586 she finally relented and signed Mary's death warrant. Even then, she was furious with those advisors who delivered the warrant without her permission.

The plots subsequently fizzled out but the burning question of her successor remained. It became assumed that Mary's Protestant son, James VI of Scotland, would succeed but it was only by way of a gesture on her deathbed that she finally acknowledged this.

Foreign Affairs

Elizabeth pursued a generally defensive foreign policy. She inherited the disastrous **Fourth Anglo-French War** and readily agreed to the Peace of Cateau-Cambresis within a few months of her accession. In one sense, she was fortunate because her powerful southern neighbour became engulfed in a series of religious civil wars between1562 and 1598 and so was unable to threaten England. At the same time, the Franco-Scottish alliance, which had plagued her father and siblings, was weakened by the expulsion of **Mary, Queen of Scots** from Scotland and the **Protestant**ism of her successor, James VI. However, Elizabeth was keen to support the Huguenots (French Protestants) and her most aggressive act was to seize the port of Le Havre in 1562. However, its expensive loss the following year discouraged her from further overseas ventures.

Spain was a far more dangerous enemy. Its king, Philip II, had had a temporary grasp on England when he had married Queen Mary and he saw it as his God-given duty to restore England to the **Catholic** faith. He also had a powerful military backed up by huge supplies of gold and silver from the New World. Again, Elizabeth can be considered fortunate. The Protestant Dutch Revolt broke out in the 1560s and Spain's armies and resources became heavily bogged down in the Netherlands for the next eighty years.

The outbreak of the **Anglo-Spanish War** in 1585 was, however, inevitable. For many years, English privateers such as **Hawkins** and **Drake** had been conducting an unofficial war by raiding Spanish treasure ships and New World colonies. Elizabeth was privately pleased with these lucrative expeditions but outwardly feigned disapproval for fear of provoking Philip. Matters became far more serious, though, in 1584 when it seemed that the Spanish army would finally conquer the whole of the Netherlands. Elizabeth, as leader of the Protestant world, could not stand by quietly and ignore the Dutch pleas for help. If Spain took control of all the ports in the Netherlands, the risk to England would have been enormous. Reluctantly, she agreed to the dispatch of an English army in 1585, led by the Earl of Leicester and the official war finally broke out. A combination of Leicester's inability to command, overly defensive instructions from the queen and her parsimonious control of the purse strings meant the expedition was a costly failure. Fortunately, however, the Dutch were saved when the Spanish army was later ordered to intervene in the French civil war.

The greatest danger to England came in the shape of the **Spanish Armada** of 1588. Elizabeth bravely inspired her waiting army at Tilbury with a famous speech that included the words, 'I know I have the body of a weak and feeble woman but I have the heart and stomach of a king, and a king of England too…', which has resonated over the centuries. A combination of the English fleet and adverse weather conditions defeated the Armada and, feeling encouraged, Elizabeth ordered an English armada to Spain and Portugal but it failed in all its objectives.

The war continued for the rest of Elizabeth's reign and became a huge drain on England's resources. Spain sent more armadas, all of which were defeated by the weather, and assisted **Tyrone's Rebellion** in **Ireland**. Despite the **Earl of Essex** managing to sack Cadiz in 1596, English successes at sea became less common due to the Spanish adoption of a convoy system to protect their treasure ships. Ironically, perhaps, it was the English army which achieved greater feats of arms in the Netherlands.

Later Years

Government propaganda and her annual processions around the country had endeared 'Good Queen Bess' to the public but her popularity declined in her later years. By the mid-1590s, her heroic 'seadogs', such as Drake, and most of her key advisors, such as **Walsingham**, **Burghley** and Leicester, were dead. Elizabeth became more isolated, tired and paranoid and appeared to allow rivalry between the factions of **Robert Cecil** and the **Earl of Essex** to dominate the court whilst she increasingly withdrew from public affairs. The dual burdens of the Anglo-Spanish War and rebellion in Ireland, combined with a series of poor harvests, increased repression of Catholics and rows with **Parliament** and the Puritans added to the pervasive gloom. This was worsened by Elizabeth's granting of monopolies to courtiers as a way of raising money but this only had the effect of raising the prices of various goods.

She remained in fairly good health until 1602 when the deaths of a few friends sent her into a depression from which she never recovered. Unable to speak, Elizabeth finally died on 24 March 1603 to the shock of much of the nation. The reign of Queen Elizabeth has been considered a golden age in English history and a large part of this can be attributed to the queen herself. She attempted to adopt a cautious approach in all that she did and walk a middle path between the extremisms that were prevalent in the sixteenth century. She also put much trust in a handful of capable and loyal advisors, none more so than **Lord Burghley**, possibly the ablest lieutenant in English governmental history. These men acted as a foil to her own often temperamental personality. As a result, England went through a period of prolonged stability in which English nationalism thrived. It was also the age of great English **Renaissance** literature as headlined by **Spenser**, **Marlowe** and **Shakespeare**. These writers were partly responsible for the cult of the 'Virgin Queen' and 'Gloriana' that has echoed down the ages and, due to much skill and a little luck perhaps, Elizabeth has been very favourably remembered.

Elizabeth of York

(1466–1503)

Wife of **Henry VII** and mother of **Henry VIII**.

Elizabeth was born at Westminster Palace, the eldest child of King Edward IV and Elizabeth Woodville. As a young child, she was twice betrothed – to the sons of an English lord and a French king – but neither arrangement came to fruition. She grew up during the turbulence of the **Wars of the Roses** between the families of York and Lancaster but it seems that she was largely insulated from the troubles. Elizabeth's father taught her history and alchemy and, along with her sisters, she learned literacy, mathematics, household management, needlework, music, French and dancing from her ladies-in-waiting.

After her father unexpectedly died, her uncle seized the throne and was crowned Richard III in 1483. Soon after, her two younger brothers – Edward and Richard – disappeared whilst in his care in the **Tower of London** and were presumed murdered. Elizabeth and her sisters were taken by their mother into Westminster Abbey to claim sanctuary and Richard declared his brother's **marriage** invalid and thereby bastardised Elizabeth. Rumours then circulated, paradoxically perhaps, that he planned to marry her. Richard denied this and instead aimed to marry her into the Portuguese royal family.

In 1485, the Lancastrian, Henry Tudor, invaded England and King Richard was defeated and killed at the **Battle of Bosworth Field**. Elizabeth's mother had previously agreed with Henry's mother, **Margaret Beaufort**, that Elizabeth would marry Henry should he become king. Henry claimed right of conquest but had agreed to the union in order to strengthen his own dynastic claim to the throne. Nevertheless, he was crowned alone in order to show that he was king in his own right and it was not until 1487 that Elizabeth was finally crowned as Queen Consort.

Despite it being a **marriage** of convenience, it appears that Elizabeth and Henry developed a close and caring relationship and that the first Tudor king drew much strength from her. She produced seven children, four of whom survived childbirth – **Arthur**, **Margaret**, Henry and **Mary**. They both enjoyed family occasions, he bought her lavish gifts and they liked to gamble with dice and cards together. When Arthur died in 1502, they provided much comfort for each other and, after her own death, the story goes that Henry ordered the Queen of Hearts card to be modelled on his dead wife as a way of commemorating her.

Elizabeth never wielded much political power; her formidable mother-in-law took her place in that sense. She was not without some influence though. She helped to arrange political marriages for her sisters and would intervene when she received appeals in judicial cases. Elizabeth was better known as a generous benefactor to various monastic orders, a provider of alms to the poor and a patron of the printer, William Caxton. Such was her generosity that she would sometimes fall into debt.

In February 1502, Elizabeth gave birth to another child – a baby girl who died a few days later. Unfortunately, she herself passed away from an infection a week afterwards, on her thirty-seventh birthday. Her husband and children were devastated by the loss; Henry himself fell into a depression. Elizabeth of York had, however, carried out the primary duty of a queen – the provision of heirs to secure the dynasty – and her reddish-gold hair was to become a trait shared by all the Tudor monarchs.

Enclosures

In pre-Tudor times, the majority of village land had been common: in return for rent, villagers could grow crops and rear cattle on the lord's land. Sheep tended to only graze in the hillier north and west of the country.

However, from the mid-fifteenth century, English wool became much sought after by Flemish cloth merchants due to its high quality. Therefore, English landowners started to enclose some of the common land with fences in order to graze sheep and make more profit. This would sometimes involve the pulling down of villagers' houses in order to make more room. In 1489, **Parliament** passed a law to prevent more enclosures as the government feared an increase in vagrancy and starvation due to less wheat being produced. This law was largely ignored, however, as its enforcers were the very people who were gaining from the enclosures.

Further attempts were made to limit the degree of sheep grazing but the enclosing of land continued. Some of these enclosures were lawful and agreed to by all parties but many were not. Poverty increased as villagers were forced off their lands, many had to move to towns in order to seek a living and localised riots, which involved the tearing down of enclosure fences, became increasingly common.

The situation became exacerbated by **debasement**s of the coinage in the 1540s which led to inflation. In **Kett's Rebellion** of 1549, the single biggest grievance of the rebels was that of illegal enclosures. The uprising failed and enclosures continued but matters generally improved due to the end of coinage debasement and the increase of corn prices in the second half of the sixteenth century. Instead of enclosures, people now sought ways to make arable farming more profitable.

Essex, Earl of

(see Devereux, Robert)

Etiquette

There was a strict code of manners amongst the Tudor wealthy especially during feasts. The most important guests would enter the hall first and sit at the high table with the hosts. This table was usually raised on a dais with the other tables arranged at right angles on either side. As a general rule, the most honoured guests would sit to the right of the lord whilst the lowliest sat to the left and the left-hand tables. Etiquette demanded that hands were washed before the meal and guests would bring their own knives and spoons (forks were considered foreign and unnecessary). The wealthiest hosts would provide their own cutlery. People would also drape their napkins over their left shoulders or wrists and it was important to make sure that your spoon only touched the food you were about to eat and not be left in a communal dish. In addition, it was considered rude to talk with one's mouth full or to lean on the table with one's elbows (the latter could, after all, upset the board resting on the trestle legs). Food was eaten off trenchers made of bread which would either be eaten afterwards or given as alms to the poor. Later in the sixteenth century, the wealthier used trenchers made of pewter or even silver.

With regards to personal hygiene, bathing was considered unnecessary as the Tudors believed that diseases entered through the pores of the skin. To keep breath fresh, mouths were rinsed first thing in the morning and a cloth was used to rub salt and charcoal onto the teeth. Unpleasant smells were masked with perfumed oils using herbs such as rosemary, lavender and thyme.

When meeting each other, hats could only be worn by the higher-ranking men. Tudor women tended to keep their hair long but had it covered by a headpiece. It was only acceptable for a woman to wear her hair down during her wedding as a sign of her virginity.

When addressing each other it was considered a sign of foolishness to cross one's arms. This may be why **Henry VIII**'s court fool, **Will Somer**, is shown this way in the famous painting of the king with his family. Forms of address were taken very seriously. 'Thee' and 'thou' were the informal second person used when speaking to friends, children, social inferiors and animals whilst 'you' was more formal and used for strangers. 'Master' and 'Mistress' were respectful forms of address reserved for talking to social superiors and 'Your Honour' and 'Sir/Madame' for people of even higher status. 'My Lord/Lady' was used for nobles, 'Your Grace' for dukes and 'Your Highness' for any member of the royal family. The only form of address for the monarch was 'Your Majesty'. 'Sirrah' and 'wench' could be used when disrespectfully talking to people of very low rank; more polite superiors would use 'Goodman' or 'Goodwife'.

Evil May Day
(1517)

By the early sixteenth century, about six per cent of London's 50,000 inhabitants came from abroad. Most of these were Flemish and Dutch cloth workers who had come to England partly due to warfare in the Low Countries and partly because of royal invitations and promises of protection from the king. The Crown had been keen to boost the English cloth industry by encouraging the immigration of skilled workers. There were also groups of wealthier French, Italians and Germans who tended to be merchants, diplomats, courtiers and bankers.

These 'strangers', as they were called, tended to live in 'liberties'. These were small communities within areas of the city where they lived and worked and could operate outside civic jurisdiction. The types of 'liberty' granted varied widely but a common dispensation was not having to follow the rules regarding the manufacture and trading of goods. Some 'liberties' had even been known to harbour debtors and criminals from the law. Naturally enough, this caused much resentment amongst Londoners who felt that they were at an unfair disadvantage and that royal favour had gone too far.

On 30 April 1517, a broker named John Lincoln persuaded a preacher named Dr Beal to whip up a crowd outside St Paul's Cathedral with an inflammatory speech that railed against the 'strangers'. He accused them of stealing English jobs, abducting wives and daughters and 'eating the bread from poor fatherless children'. Instigators planned to cause trouble on May Day, a traditionally boisterous public holiday, in order to drive out the foreigners and send a strong message to the government. News of this reached the authorities and the Lord Mayor ordered a 9.00pm curfew. The under-sheriff of London, **Thomas More**, and his men tried to disperse a small crowd breaking the curfew but this provoked greater trouble and the crowd soon swelled to over a thousand, mostly made up of young male apprentices and servants.

The mob first stormed Newgate Prison where they released several men who had previously been jailed for attacking foreigners. Then they aimed their anger at various 'liberties' around the city. Both rich and poor immigrants were attacked; although none were killed, many of their houses, belongings and goods were damaged or destroyed. Soldiers from outside the city, led by the **Second Duke of Norfolk**, were summoned to restore order and by 3.00am the riot had died down.

Hundreds of rioters were arrested over the next few days. Lincoln and thirteen others were hanged, drawn and quartered. The rest, after an appeal for clemency from either **Catherine of Aragon** or the Lord Chancellor, **Thomas Wolsey**, were granted a pardon by **Henry VIII**. His mercy was probably also an attempt to quash the rumours that he favoured the 'strangers'. Tensions, however, went on simmering, the 'liberties' continued and other outbreaks of violence against foreigners occasionally flared up in the sixteenth century. None, however, matched the scale of Evil May Day.

F

Field of the Cloth of Gold

(1520)

An extravagant summit meeting between **Henry VIII** and Francis I of France.

The background to this meeting was the intense political rivalry between King Francis and Charles V, King of Spain and Holy Roman Emperor. Both sought to dominate the continent and, as recently as 1516, had been fighting for hegemony in northern Italy. England was a relatively minor player but was seen by both sides as a useful ally who could tip the balance in their favour. As a result, Henry had already been drawn into the **First Anglo-French War**.

The awful brutality of the conflict in Italy motivated several **humanists**, such as Desiderius Erasmus and **Thomas More**, to call upon monarchs to enhance their reputations through the search for peaceful resolution. Simultaneously, Pope Leo X appealed for a united Christian front to push back the Muslim Ottoman advances in Hungary. Subsequently, Henry's chief advisor and papal legate, **Thomas Wolsey**, was able to initiate the Universal Peace in London in 1518. Representatives from France, Spain, England and the Pope all showed their countries' commitments to peace and it was agreed that the kings of France and England would meet to cement their new-found friendship.

It was decided that the meeting would take place over two weeks in June 1520 near Guînes, six miles south of Calais and just inside England's last remaining territory in France. Both Henry and Francis had succeeded to their thrones relatively recently and were keen to give the impression of being young, important and wealthy **Renaissance** princes. As a result, both parties poured a huge amount of time, effort and money into the most lavish display of the century. The entire event was planned by Wolsey who was determined to portray his master in the most favourable light as well as impress him with his organisational prowess.

The centrepiece was Henry's 'palace' which was built by 6,000 men. On a brick foundation a wooden framework and canvas were erected with windows of real glass and the canvas was painted to make the whole structure look like a real castle. Just outside were two fountains which provided wine and beer for the guests. Many of the tents were made of a fabric woven with silk and gold and thereby gave their name to the occasion.

There were as many as 12,000 people present and English accounts reveal that the provisions included 200,000 litres of wine, 66,000 litres of beer, 98,000 eggs, over 2,000 sheep, 13 swans and 3 porpoises. The estimated cost to the Crown, including the lavish gifts that were presented to Francis and his retinue, was around £35,000 (about £20 million in 2024).

As well as the constant banquets, there were various competitions such as tournaments, archery and wrestling which gave opportunities for both sides to express their rivalry. One account mentions Henry even challenged Francis to a wrestling match which was unwise as the experienced French king easily overcame him. Henry then challenged him at archery but, apparently, Francis was unable to draw the heavy longbow. On the final Sunday, Wolsey gave Mass to the assembled crowd and then the festivities were finally brought to an end by a spectacular dragon kite powered by fireworks.

The intended aim of the Field of the Cloth of Gold was laudable but every detail was planned with the intention of each side outdoing the other. Both kings and their retinues wore highly fashionable and jewelled clothes. Henry included in his party two monkeys covered in gold leaf, which greatly amused Francis who, in turn, presented a musical performance which included the finest choir in Europe. If anything, it would appear that the event merely accentuated the rivalries of two traditional enemies. Soon after, Henry met Charles in Burgundy and, in August the following year, they made a secret agreement to invade France which led to the **Second Anglo-French War**. The Field of the Cloth of Gold raised Wolsey's prestige and probably Henry VIII's but, politically, it achieved little.

Fisher, John

(1469–1535)

Bishop, theologian and **Catholic** martyr.

Fisher was born in Selby, Yorkshire, and entered Cambridge University at the age of fourteen. Whilst there, he steadily rose through the ranks so that by 1504 he had become its chancellor. In 1491 he had also been ordained as a priest and subsequently dedicated himself to improving the provision of theological **education** at Cambridge. He is credited with bringing **Renaissance humanism** to the university, encouraging a much greater study of the Ancient Greek and Roman writers and lecturing on the importance of pastoral work by the clergy. At the same time, he decried the abuses within the Church and called for its self-purification. A dour and serious character, he was known to place a human skull on the altar during his sermons and on his table during meals. The great humanist, Erasmus, visited Cambridge and described Fisher as being, 'the one man at this time who is incomparable for uprightness of life, for learning and for greatness of soul'.

In 1495, he met **Margaret Beaufort**, the mother of **Henry VII**, and they formed a strong attachment. Within a few years he had become her chaplain and personal confessor and he persuaded her to found St John's and Christ's Colleges at Cambridge. It is also likely that he tutored the young Prince Henry at around this time. In 1504 he was made Bishop of Rochester. This was viewed as the poorest see in the country and merely a stepping stone to more lucrative bishoprics. However, Fisher preferred to stay at Rochester and carry out duties which most bishops would have delegated to others such as visiting the poor and the sick. In 1509, his reputation was so great that he was appointed to preach the funeral ovation at the funerals of both Henry VII and Margaret Beaufort.

Despite their obvious differences in character and Fisher's dislike for pomp and politics, the new king, **Henry VIII**, found him to be a useful ally in his attacks against Martin Luther at the start of the **Reformation**. Fisher launched many oral attacks against 'heretical' **Protestants** and encouraged the burning of all their literature. It is even possible that Fisher wrote Henry's treatise against Luther which won the king the title of 'Defender of the Faith' from the Pope in 1521.

Bishop Fisher. (*Artist: Hans Holbein, c. 1532–35. Royal Collection*)

However, relations between the two rapidly deteriorated during the king's 'Great Matter' – his prolonged attempts to annul his **marriage** to **Catherine of Aragon** and marry **Anne Boleyn**. In the late 1520s, Fisher almost single-handedly dared to defy the king by publicly defending Catherine and declaring his willingness to die for the sanctity of marriage. Henry was furious but Fisher's fame and reputation made him a difficult thorn to remove. The bishop then went on to accuse **Parliament** of heresy by allowing royal encroachments on the Church's power.

When it became clear to Fisher that the English Catholic Church was in severe danger he made the mistake of secretly appealing to Emperor Charles V to invade England and protect the 'true' faith. His position further weakened after his involvement in the **Elizabeth Barton** affair for which he escaped with a large fine. In 1531, he survived a poisoning attempt on his life and a cannon ball being fired at his home. It is quite possible that the Boleyn family were involved or, equally, both could have been accidents. Nevertheless, these events encouraged Fisher to leave London.

In early 1534 he denounced the annulment of Henry's marriage to Catherine and then refused to swear the Oath of Succession, which recognised Anne Boleyn's children as heirs to the throne. For this, he was thrown into the **Tower of London**, along with his friend **Thomas More**, and made to endure the direst conditions for over a year. Throughout his captivity he refused to swear the oath or recognise Henry as Supreme Head of the English Church. In May 1535, the Pope made Fisher a cardinal thinking that it may improve the bishop's conditions. However, this only further enraged the king who said he would rather send the bishop's head to Rome than receive the cardinal's hat.

In June, Fisher was found guilty of treason in Westminster Hall and sentenced to be hanged, drawn and quartered though this was commuted to beheading. As expected, he met his death on Tower Hill with great dignity but his naked body was thrown into a rough grave with no funeral prayer and his head was stuck on a pole on London Bridge. However, its appearance appeared to grow more ruddy and lifelike each day and drew much attention from crowds. So it was thrown into the Thames and replaced by that of More, who was executed two weeks after Fisher.

It is possible to argue that Fisher, through his outspoken and stubborn defence of papal supremacy and undermining of Henry's succession plans, actually hastened the downfall of the English Catholic Church by angering his opponents. However, there can be little doubt that he was a man who worked hard for the unity and purity of the Church and whose genuine faith gave him the courage to stand up to a powerful king. Even a highly respected theologian was not safe from royal anger though and so he died a martyr. In 1935, Fisher was made a saint by the Pope and his feast day is 22 June (the date of his execution).

Fitzroy, Henry (Duke of Richmond)

(c. 1519–36)

Illegitimate son of **Henry VIII**.

In around 1518, Henry VIII took as his mistress, Elizabeth Blount, a lady-in-waiting to **Catherine of Aragon**. Blount became pregnant and was spirited away to a priory in Essex to avoid embarrassment. Apparently, Henry was overjoyed by the news of the birth of his son and visited him several times. The boy became the only illegitimate child that Henry publicly acknowledged. Indeed, **Thomas Wolsey** was appointed as his godfather and, at his christening, he was given the surname 'Fitzroy', which was derived from the Norman French for 'son of the king'.

The king often presented him on public occasions and was perhaps trying to prove to everyone that he was capable of producing a son, something that his wife had, as yet, failed to do. When he was only six, Fitzroy was showered with titles including the Duke of Richmond, Earl of Nottingham, Lord High Admiral of England and Warden of the Marches. Within a few years, he was also Lord Lieutenant of **Ireland**. By a clear distance, he was the second richest person in England.

For most of his youth he was raised at Sheriff Hutton Castle, near York, and tutored by Richard Croke, a relative of Blount, who took a liking to the boy. Fitzroy appears to have been a reluctant learner of Latin and Greek but he enjoyed hunting and was able to sing and play the virginals. He also impressed the French ambassador who described him as a 'well-mannered, handsome and learned young gentleman'.

By 1527, King Henry was debating how to provide a male heir. He sent Croke to the Vatican to look into the possibility of having Fitzroy 'legitimized'. Whilst he was there, however, the king changed tack and ordered him to see if he could annul his **marriage** to Catherine and thereby have a son with another wife. Negotiations dragged on with little success, however, and a break with Rome looked inevitable. To avoid this, it was even suggested that Fitzroy marry his elder half-sister, Princess Mary, in order to strengthen the boy's claim to the throne.

The plan was rejected though and, in 1533, he was married to Lady Mary Howard, daughter of the **Third Duke of Norfolk** and cousin of the new queen, **Anne Boleyn**. As both husband and wife were only fourteen, they never lived together and so the marriage was never consummated. In 1536, Fitzroy suddenly became very ill. One of his last public appearances was at the attendance of Anne Boleyn's execution before he was to die of tuberculosis. He was buried at Thetford Priory but, during the **Dissolution of the Monasteries**, his remains were removed to Framlingham Church in Suffolk.

Whilst he was dying, **Parliament** was in the process of passing an Act which would have allowed Henry to nominate anyone, legitimate or not, to be his heir. One will never know how close Fitzroy came to becoming King Henry IX had he not been slain by a virus.

Flodden, Battle of

(1513)

The largest battle fought between England and Scotland.

Henry VIII had already initiated the **First Anglo-French War** as part of a wider European conflict. The Scottish king, James IV, despite being married to Henry's sister, **Margaret**, decided to invoke the Auld Alliance. This was an agreement signed by France and Scotland in 1295 stating that if either country was attacked by England then the other would come to its aid. Henry was with his main army in northern France when he received a note from James demanding his withdrawal from French territory. Henry refused and James chivalrously gave the English one month to prepare for war. Henry had anticipated an attack from the north so he had only recruited his force from the southern and central counties and appointed the seventy-year-old **Thomas Howard**, Earl of Surrey, to defend the north. Surrey was a trusted commander who had gained military experience in the **Wars of the Roses**, including the **Battle of Bosworth Field**.

On 22 August 1513, King James crossed the border with around 42,000 men who promptly raided many properties and captured some border castles. At the same time, Surrey gathered a force of around of 26,000 which was augmented by cannons brought up on ships by his son, the Lord Admiral **Thomas Howard**.

On 4 September, James, hearing of Surrey's approach, gathered his army on a hill called Flodden Edge. By now, his army was of a similar size to that of the English due to the garrisoning of troops in captured castles and desertions of booty-laden followers. His position was strong, though, as Surrey was reluctant to attack up the steep slopes and the Scottish king refused his offer of a fair fight on flat ground. The English commander was now in a difficult position: retreat would have brought disgrace, attack would surely bring defeat and his army was running low on supplies. A commander with local knowledge, however, offered an alternative which Surrey accepted.

Following a six-mile detour, he swung his army around to the east, then north, then west so that it was now positioned between James's forces and the Scottish border. Surrey clearly hoped that having his lines of retreat and supply cut off would force the Scottish king to attack. James, however, upon seeing the manoeuvre marched a mile north and set his forces upon Branxton Hill to prevent the English from capturing the high ground.

At 4pm on 9 September, the battle began with an exchange of artillery fire. The larger Scottish guns were more unwieldy and slower to reload and, firing downhill, they appeared to frequently miss their mark. The English cannons were smaller but more numerous and quicker to fire and, subsequently, inflicted more damage. Then, for some unknown reason, the Scots started to advance downhill. Possibly, they were provoked by the damage wrought by the English cannon balls or maybe it was a lack of discipline that led to the Highlanders and Borderers on the Scottish left making a wild charge. This initial assault was actually successful and the English right wing almost collapsed. Encouraged by this success, James ordered his centre forward.

Before manoeuvring to Branxton Hill, however, the Scots had not reconnoitred the surrounding terrain. The main strength in James's army lay in his formidable echelons of pikemen. These soldiers carried eighteen-foot-long pikes, supplied by their French allies, that represented the new style of warfare on the continent. Well-drilled blocks of pikemen operating on flat ground were a very dangerous proposition for both enemy infantry and cavalry. However, as these men marched down the slope they encountered wet, boggy terrain that caused their formations to disintegrate as some units were forced to slow down. The English had a large number of longbowmen. These were able to inflict casualties on the rearmost ranks but did little to the well-armoured pikemen at the front. What was decisive

19th-century depiction of the Battle of Flodden. Note the bill hooks on the right, which proved decisive. (*From* British Battles on Land and Sea, *volume 1, 1873 by James Grant. British Library via Flickr*)

for the English, however, was their use of the bill – a six-foot agricultural tool that could be used for stabbing and cutting. The Scots, seeing the futility of wielding their heavy pikes on the marshy ground, resorted to swords but they were easily picked off at a safe distance by the lighter bills.

Matters were made worse for the Scots when James and his nobles dismounted and joined the fray. This instantly meant that there was no commander at the rear who could oversee the strategic situation. At the same time, English forces arriving late were able to drive off the Scottish right wing through use of their archers and then came behind the Scottish centre. Simultaneously, the successful Scottish earls on the left decided that they had done enough and took no more part in the fighting. This allowed remnants of the English right to also attack the Scottish centre.

By around 7pm it was all over and the result was carnage. Estimates vary but it seems that the Scots lost 10,000–12,000 men, including James IV himself, the last British king to die in battle, and a host of the Scottish nobility. English casualties amounted to about 1,500 men. The disaster was widely felt north of the border with nearly all sections of society being affected. Harvests were temporarily abandoned, many lands had to be sold due to the deaths of so many landowners and a political struggle for control of James's seventeen-month-old son ensued. Such was the damage that Scotland posed no threat to the English for over three decades. James had been a popular king and, for many years, rumours abounded that he had survived the battle and perhaps gone on pilgrimage to the Holy Land.

His body was, in fact, kept in a lead coffin and stored in a wood shed in Sheen Priory, south-west of London. It could not be buried on consecrated ground as the Pope had excommunicated him for supporting his enemy, the French. Over the next few decades it was forgotten about until some workmen discovered it, lopped off the head and used it as a football. Since then, the whereabouts of his remains is unknown. His blood-stained cloak, however, was sent by Queen **Catherine of Aragon** to her husband who kept it as a memento. The grateful king also rewarded Surrey by restoring him to the title of Duke of Norfolk, which had previously been lost due to his father's support for the Yorkists at Bosworth.

Foxe, Richard

(c. 1448–1528)

Politician and churchman.

Little is known of the first thirty-six years of Foxe's life other than that he was born in Lincolnshire to yeoman parents and studied law at Oxford University. He first surfaces in Paris where, in 1484, he met the exiled **Henry** Tudor; possibly he had fallen out with King Richard III himself and had fled the country too. Foxe was taken into Henry's service, travelled with him to England and was with him at the **Battle of Bosworth Field**. Afterwards, it was Foxe who wrote to the English lords notifying them of their new king.

Henry VII rewarded him with the bishopric of Exeter and made him his principal secretary. He was always subordinate to Cardinal **Morton** but when Morton died in 1500 he became Henry's chief advisor. Foxe's most important work during the first Tudor king's reign was as a diplomat. He was the king's chief negotiator in the **marriage** treaties with Spain, Scotland and the Holy Roman Empire, an important trade deal with Flanders and, in 1492, he helped to conclude the peace treaty with France at Etaples.

Foxe appears to have been involved in helping Henry to become financially solvent too. According to **Thomas More**, it was he, not Morton, who came up with the instrument known as Morton's Fork, which extorted fines and taxes from rich and poor alike. Foxe's zealous approach to serving his master led to accusations that 'he would sacrifice his father to save his king'. Nevertheless,

Henry rewarded him with the bishoprics of Durham and, later, Winchester – the richest see in the kingdom.

In 1509, the new king, **Henry VIII** put much trust in him and Foxe's power increased. It was he who persuaded Henry to carry out his father's wish that he should marry **Catherine of Aragon**. One ambassador even referred to him as the 'alter rex' – the other king.

From about 1512, however, his influence declined as the king relied more on **Thomas Wolsey** to execute his demands. This may have been due to Foxe's failing health but, more likely, because the two disagreed over the king's bellicose policy towards France that led to the **First Anglo-French War**. Henry still held him in high regard, though, and referred to him as 'a foxe indeed'.

Foxe now devoted himself to his religious duties, which he had long neglected. He deplored the clerical abuses which he now witnessed and sought Church reform. However, disagreements with **William Warham**, the Archbishop of Canterbury, meant that he could not alter anything. His most long-lasting achievement, possibly, was the foundation of Corpus Christi College in Oxford in 1517. This became a centre of **Renaissance** learning and the great **humanist** Erasmus himself stated that its library was, 'among the chief beauties of Britain'.

By 1518, Foxe was becoming quite blind but he continued to work in his role as Bishop of Winchester. Just before he died ten years later, he announced his huge regret that he had spent too much time in politics and not enough working for the Church.

Frobisher, Sir Martin

(1536–94)

Sailor, explorer and privateer.

Born in Yorkshire, Frobisher was sent to live with his uncle – a wealthy and influential trader – in London in order to seek his fortune. In 1553, he accompanied the first English expedition to West Africa. They plundered some Portuguese ships near Madeira before trading for gold and pepper on the Gold Coast and with the Kingdom of Benin. Disease, however, decimated the crew and only a quarter of the seamen, including Frobisher, made it home. Undeterred, he joined a second expedition the following year; he even offered himself up as a hostage with an African king to facilitate trade in pepper. Once ashore, though, the Portuguese attacked the English ships which fled, leaving Frobisher behind. The Africans handed him over to the Portuguese who imprisoned him in a castle on the Gold Coast. They later sent him to Portugal and, from there, he eventually made his way home in 1558.

The following year, he married a widow named Isobel Richard who provided two children and all her wealth to finance his future expeditions. It appears that he abandoned his family in the 1570s, though, and Isobel died in a poorhouse in 1588.

During the 1560s, Frobisher preyed on French **Catholic** ships but he had a habit of going beyond his brief and would attack Spanish and French **Protestant** ships too. This landed him in prison on several occasions and it was only through the intervention of the Secretary of State, **William Cecil**, that he was released and his life took a new direction. Details are sketchy but it looks like Frobisher was working directly for the government in the early 1570s and may even have been a double-agent in the Crown's dealings with rebels in **Ireland**.

In 1576, he came into the employ of the Muscovy Company in order to fulfil his ambition of discovering a north-west passage around North America and thence to the riches of the Indies. In 1508, **Sebastian Cabot** had voyaged as far as Hudson Bay but no serious attempts had been made since then. With three ships he reached the coast of Labrador and from there to Frobisher Bay on Baffin Island (which he believed was a strait). Whilst there, five of his crew were kidnapped by the local Inuit and, after failing to retrieve them, Frobisher returned home. Inuit oral tradition later claimed that the men had chosen to live with them and, after several years, had drowned whilst trying to leave Baffin Island in a self-made boat.

Inuit hunting. (*Artist: unknown, 1580. From a description by Martin Frobisher.* Populär historia *magazine*)

Frobisher brought back a black rock found on a beach and an Italian alchemist living in London claimed that it contained gold. The ensuing excitement about possible riches led to the creation of the Cathay Company which financed a second, larger expedition in 1577. This time, he was instructed to merely search for precious metals rather than explore and was given lessons on the mathematics of navigation by the famous scholar, **John Dee**. Some 200 tons of rock samples were collected but several Inuit were killed during skirmishing in which Frobisher himself received an arrow in his behind. Three natives were captured– a man, a woman and a child – but they all died soon after the expedition's return to England.

Queen **Elizabeth I** was delighted with the new rocks and contributed ships and money for the Cathay Company's next expedition in 1578. With a large fleet of fifteen ships, Frobisher was again commanded to search for more gold-bearing ore but this time he was also to establish a permanent mining colony. Stormy weather temporarily forced the squadron into the Hudson Strait, the true route for the north-west passage, but Frobisher named it the 'Mistaken Strait' and returned to pick up more ore. Unfortunately, the ship carrying the prefabricated huts for the colony had been sunk by an iceberg and so there was little else to do but return home. After much testing, all the rock samples were considered worthless and were put into the construction of roads and walls. The Cathay Company, subsequently, went bankrupt and folded.

Frobisher spent the next few years rebuilding his reputation and, in 1585, was vice-admiral in **Francis Drake**'s expedition to the West Indies. Three years later he was a commander of one of the squadrons that fought the **Spanish Armada** and, for his courage and leadership in that campaign he was knighted by **Lord Howard of Effingham**.

He then attempted to settle down as one of the landed gentry in his native Yorkshire and remarried. However, boredom soon overcame him and he jumped at the offer of leading a small fleet charged with harassing Spanish shipping off the coasts of Portugal and France. In 1594, he led a seaborne assault on a Spanish fort near Brest. The fort was eventually captured but not before Frobisher had been shot in the thigh. Unfortunately, the surgeon who removed the musket ball left the wadding behind and the wound became infected. He made it back to Plymouth but, soon after, died of gangrene.

Frobisher was a typical example of an Elizabethan adventurer: driven, courageous, reckless and sometimes cruel and dishonest. He was only one of a group of talented seamen whose jealous rivalry with each other spurred them on to seek further glory.

G

Gardiner, Stephen

(1483/93–1555)

Bishop and politician.

Gardiner was born in Bury St Edmunds but it is currently impossible to identify when. It is not even certain who his parents were either. Some say it was William Gardiner, a mercenary during the **Wars of the Roses** and the man who killed Richard III with a poleaxe at the **Battle of Bosworth Field**. Less likely was the claim that his mother was Helen Tudor, the illegitimate daughter of Jasper Tudor, **Henry VII**'s uncle.

At Cambridge University he studied law. He was such an able student that he became secretary to Cardinal **Thomas Wolsey** in 1524 and a legal advisor to **Henry VIII**. It was as an expert in ecclesiastical law that he was sent to Rome to argue Henry's case in the king's 'Great Matter' – his attempts to annul his **marriage** to **Catherine of Aragon**. Gardiner argued with much skill and eloquence in front of the Pope and his cardinals but, ultimately, he failed because the Pope would not dare upset Catherine's nephew, the Emperor Charles V.

Although Wolsey was to subsequently fall from power, Gardiner's efforts were appreciated by the king who appointed him as his secretary in 1529. A year later, he managed to persuade Cambridge University to agree that it had been illegal for Henry to marry his brother's widow, an important pretext for the king's desired annulment. He was rewarded with the bishopric of Winchester (vacant after Wolsey's death). In 1533, he assisted Archbishop **Cranmer** in making the official declaration that Henry's marriage to Catherine was null and void and that their daughter, **Mary**, was illegitimate.

However, it gradually dawned on Gardiner that the break with Rome was endangering the Catholic Church in England. As a result, he and Henry sometimes came to blows. For instance, he publicly defended the Church's right to make its own laws. The king was furious because he saw this as undermining his own powers and so, in 1534, appointed **Thomas Cromwell** as his secretary instead. In attempting to regain royal favour, Gardiner wrote *'De vera obedienta'* – an essay that supported the king's new supremacy over the Church by stating that it was God's wish that kings should be obeyed without question. After supporting the execution of **John Fisher**, the appeased king appointed him as his ambassador to France. For the rest of the 1530s he spent most of his time on the continent, usually seeking support for Henry after the controversial annulment.

In 1539, the English king was persuaded that the new **Protestant** religion was gaining too much ground and so condoned the Six **Articles** which reaffirmed the Catholic faith. Gardiner helped to draw these up and then attempted to remove those who represented the Protestant reformers. He tried to have Cranmer convicted of heresy but the archbishop always had the king's support. Later, he attempted to have Henry's wife, **Catherine Parr**, arrested for making reformist comments. He even ordered the shocking torture of **Anne Askew** in order to provide evidence of Parr's guilt. Askew said nothing, however, and Catherine pleaded her way back into the king's favour.

Gardiner had much influence with the king but, by 1547, the reform party possibly had more because Henry did not include his name in the sixteen-man council that was to rule in his son's name. After **Edward VI**'s accession, the council enacted a series of radical, Protestant reforms which Gardiner publicly defied. As a result, he was deprived of his see and spent the last two years of the reign in the **Tower of London**.

Mary became queen in 1553 and immediately released Gardiner, restored him to his bishopric and appointed him as her Lord Chancellor. It was Gardiner who placed the crown upon the new queen's head, he who opened her first **Parliament** and he who spearheaded the reversal of King Edward's reforms. Ironically, he had to recant what he had earlier written about royal supremacy over the Church and the bastardisation of the queen. He also led the negotiations for the queen's marriage to Prince Philip of Spain of which he disapproved and so ensured that the terms of the treaty were as favourable for England as possible.

It is not clear just how responsible Gardiner was for the religious persecutions of Mary's reign. He participated in the trials of various Protestant notables, approved of the threat of burning to force their recantations and advocated the arrest and execution of the queen's sister, **Elizabeth**. However, he may have worried that the burnings would create the opposite of the desired effect for, in his own diocese, no one was executed while he was alive. In 1555, after a short illness, he died at Westminster.

Over the years, Gardiner has received a largely negative press and has been accused of being an inconsistent, bloodthirsty and ambitious opportunist. His detractors have claimed that both Henry VIII and Queen Mary thoroughly disliked him and simply used him as a tool to achieve their ends. This unfair criticism smacks of Protestant bias though. Gardiner was always a staunch believer in the Catholic faith, Henry and Mary both respected him for his intelligence, hard work and honesty and he was capable of showing compassion. The difficulty comes when comparing him to martyrs like Fisher and **Thomas More**. For them, the supremacy of the Catholic Church always overrode that of the monarch. Judging by his final words – 'Like Peter, I have erred; unlike Peter, I have not wept' – it is doubtful that Gardiner was able to die with the same clear conscience.

Anti-Catholic propaganda. From a book printed by Protestant exiles in Germany. Gardiner, with a wolf's head, is biting the neck of the lamb (Christ). At his feet lie six more 'lambs' representing martyrs such as Cranmer and Ridley. The Pope appears as the Devil in the top-right corner. (*Author: unknown.* The Lambe Speaketh, *1555. British Museum*)

Margaret Beaufort. Wewyck, a Dutchman, was Henry VII's preferred court painter. Large scale paintings of women on their own were very rare and this is the earliest of its kind. A reflection, probably, of Beaufort's power and importance. (*Artist: Meynnart Wewyck c.1510. St John's College, Cambridge*)

The Matthew. A replica of the first European ship, captained by John Cabot, to reach mainland America. The nearby dinghies reveal its diminutive size (24m). (*Author: Hugh Llewelyn, 2010*)

Elizabeth of York. The much-loved queen whose marriage and children allowed the Tudor dynasty to survive and prosper. (*Artist: unknown, c.1530. Probably a copy of a Meynnart Wewyck painting. Cultural Heritage Agency of the Netherlands Art Collection*)

Thomas Howard, 3rd Duke of Norfolk. Norfolk holds the gold baton of Earl Marshal and the white staff of Lord High Treasurer, and wears the Order of the Garter. An imposing presence, Norfolk led the conservative faction against the reformists in Henry VIII's court. It was his own son, however, who brought about his downfall. (*Artist: Hans Holbein, c.1539. Royal Collection*)

Prince Arthur. The only contemporary portrait of Henry VII's eldest son. (*Artist: Anglo-Flemish School, c. 1500. Private collection, Hever Castle*)

Henry VIII. The most famous portrait of Henry VIII, copied from a sketch used for the original mural destroyed by fire at Whitehall Palace in 1698. His pose, direct gaze, exaggerated width and hand near his dagger all reflect his reputation as the most powerful monarch in England's history. (*Based on a copy of 1537 Hans Holbein mural, post-1537. Walker Art Gallery*)

Field of the Cloth of Gold. Centre-left: King Henry arrives on horseback with his entourage. Centre-right: the canvas castle with fountains of beer and wine in front of it. Centre-distant: Henry and Francis embrace in a golden tent. (*Artist: unknown. Possibly copy of Hans Holbein painting, 1545. Royal Collection*)

Catherine of Aragon with a monkey. A miniature painted on vellum. Horenbout taught the renowned Hans Holbein how to paint miniatures. (*Artist: Lucas Horenbout, 1525*)

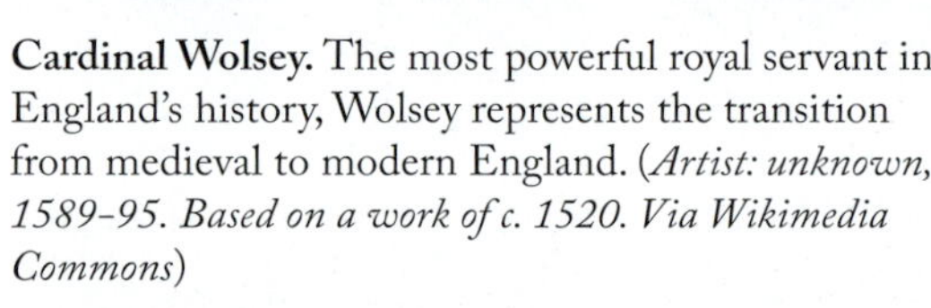

Cardinal Wolsey. The most powerful royal servant in England's history, Wolsey represents the transition from medieval to modern England. (*Artist: unknown, 1589–95. Based on a work of c. 1520. Via Wikimedia Commons*)

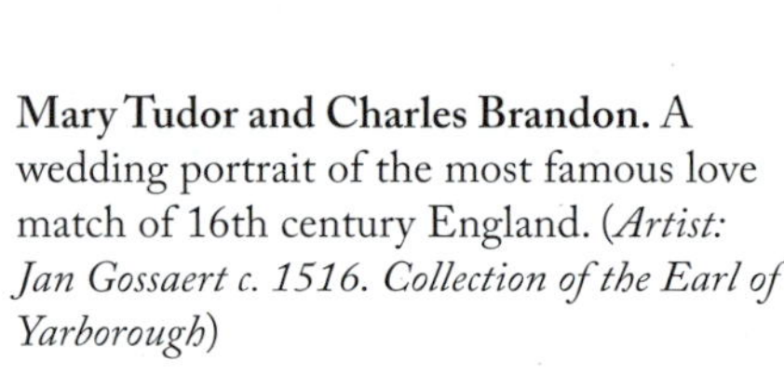

Mary Tudor and Charles Brandon. A wedding portrait of the most famous love match of 16th century England. (*Artist: Jan Gossaert c. 1516. Collection of the Earl of Yarborough*)

Parliament being opened by Henry VIII. The earliest surviving contemporary illustration of the opening of Parliament. To the left of Henry is William Warham and then Thomas Wolsey. Below, on the left, sit rows of bishops and various lords face them on the right. The faded figures at the bottom are members of the Commons. Thomas More, the Speaker of the House, is probably the tallest one in the centre. (*Artist: Sir Thomas Wriothesley, 1523. Royal Collection. Posted to Flickr by Revan Lamishvili*)

Hans Holbein. Arguably, the greatest portrait artist of all time, Holbein accurately captured the people and fashion of Henry VIII's reign. His gaze suggests that he may have been looking into a mirror. (*Self-portrait, c.1542. Uffizi gallery*)

Anne Boleyn. The face that launched a new religion. (*Artist: unknown, late 16th century. Based on a missing contemporary portrait*)

Sir Thomas More. The scholarly martyr whose execution shocked much of Europe. (*Artist: Hans Holbein, 1527. The Frick Collection*)

Thomas Cranmer. The Archbishop of Canterbury who drove the English Reformation forward. (*Artist: unknown, after 1556. Lambeth Palace*)

Thomas Cromwell. The man who engineered one of the greatest political and religious revolutions in England's history. (*Artist: Hans Holbein, 1532/33. The Frick Collection*)

Henry Fitzroy. Henry VIII's heir? A miniature with diameter of 4.4cm. Fitzroy seems to be wearing a night shirt and night cap. (*Artist: Lucas Horenbout, 1533/34. Royal Collection*)

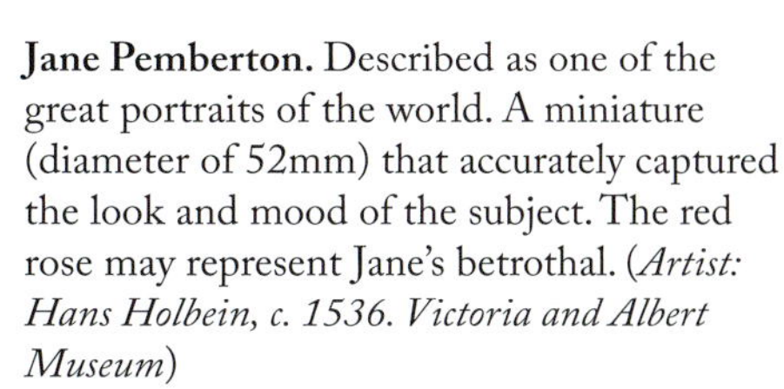

Jane Pemberton. Described as one of the great portraits of the world. A miniature (diameter of 52mm) that accurately captured the look and mood of the subject. The red rose may represent Jane's betrothal. (*Artist: Hans Holbein, c. 1536. Victoria and Albert Museum*)

A victim of the Dissolution of the Monasteries – the ruins of Tintern Abbey. (*Author: Saffron Blaze, 2011*)

Jane Seymour. A portrait that was unfinished possibly due to Jane's sudden death. (*Artist: Hans Holbein, 1536/37. Kunsthistorisches Museum*)

Anne of Cleves. The betrothal portrait that led to embarrassment for Henry VIII and death for Thomas Cromwell. (*Artist: Hans Holbein c.1539. Louvre Musuem*)

Portrait of unknown woman, previously thought to be Catherine Howard. Now believed to be Elizabeth Seymour, sister of Jane Seymour, or even Anne of Cleves. (*Artist: Hans Holbein, c.1535–40. Toledo Museum of Art*)

Mary Rose. The position of gun ports is inaccurate but note the heavy weaponry, high castles at the stern and prow and the anti-boarding netting above the top deck. (*Artist: Anthony Anthony, from the Anthony Rolls c.1546. Pepys Library*)

Family of Henry VIII. From left to right: Jane Fool, Princess Mary, Prince Edward, Henry VIII, Jane Seymour, Princess Elizabeth, Will Somer. An imaginary sitting as Seymour died twelve days after Edward's birth. (*Artist: unknown, c.1545. Royal Collection*)

Henry Howard coat of arms. The coat of arms which cost Henry Howard his life. The offending arms of Edward the Confessor are middle left-most. (*Author: Silver&Gold. Based on a contemporary drawing*)

Edward VI. (*Artist: Workshop of Hans Holbein, c.1545. Metrpolitan Museum of Art*)

Mary I. The much-vilified queen. Or just another victim of Protestant propaganda? (*Artist: unknown, 16th century. In the manner of Anthonis Mor. Private collection*)

Edward Seymour, Duke of Somerset. The 'Good Duke' or was he simply out of his depth? (*Artist: Follower of Francois Clouet, 16th century. Weston Park*)

Thomas Gresham. The portrait probably commemorates Gresham's marriage to Anne Ferneley. Their initials frame the wedding vows in the top-right corner. The skull symbolises mortality and the worthlessness of worldly goods. (*Artist: unknown, 1544 via Wikimedia Commons*)

William Cecil, Lord Burghley. The architect of Elizabethan greatness, Cecil wears his robes of the Knight of the Garter and holds the white wand of office. (*Artist: Unknown. Possibly Marcus Gheeraerts, between 1585 and 1598 via Wikimedia Commons*)

Elizabeth I playing the lute. As well as being adept at playing the lute and virginals, Elizabeth loved to dance, sing, read, watch plays and hunt with a crossbow. She also wrote poetry and translated some classical works into English. Portrait miniature (4.8cm x 3.9 cm) (*Artist: Nicholas Hilliard c.1580. Private collection*)

Elizabeth I. 'Gloriana' in the Armada Portrait, which commemorates the defeat of the Spanish Armada in the background. The 800 pearls represent her wealth and chastity and her fingers resting on America may represent her claim to that part of the world. (*Artist: George Gower, 1588. Woburn Abbey*)

Mary, Queen of Scots. The queen whose life was a 16th century soap opera and, to this day, divides opinion. (*Artist: Francois Clouet, 1558-60. Royal Collection*)

John Hawkins. A trader in slaves and tobacco and yet a key figure in developing England's navy. (*Artist: unknown, 1581. Royal Museums Greenwich*)

Hardwick Hall. 'More glass than wall'. The spectacular, symmetrical renaissance home of Bess of Hardwick was completed in 1597. The increasing heights of the windows draws the eye up to a series of 'ES's (Elizabeth Shrewsbury) upon the rooftops. (*Author: Barry Skeates, 2015. Wikimedia Commons*)

Unknown 21-year old, thought to be Christopher Marlowe. The great man of mystery. Even the circumstances of his death are unclear. (*Artist: unknown, 1585. Corpus Christi College*)

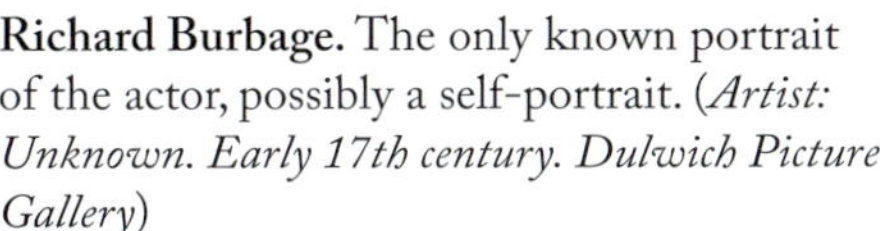

Richard Burbage. The only known portrait of the actor, possibly a self-portrait. (*Artist: Unknown. Early 17th century. Dulwich Picture Gallery*)

Robert Devereux, 2nd Earl of Essex. Essex represents the last attempt by the nobility to dominate the Crown. (*Artist: Studio of Marcus Gheeraerts, 1596-1601. National Gallery of Art*)

Route of the Armada. The Spanish crescent formation is clearly discernible in the North Sea. Prevailing winds are shown next to the compass roses. (*Artist: Augustine Ryther; Robert Adams, 1590. National Maritime Museum, Greenwich*)

Map of Ireland. Heavily-forested Ulster can be seen on the right (north) and Dublin is centre-bottom (east). Kinsale, where Spanish troops landed, can be seen centre-left (south) in Munster where so much of the violence occurred. (*Reproduction of the Map of Ireland by Pieter van den Keere, Linen Hall library, Belfast, 1591*)

Gerard, John (Father Gerard)

(1564–1637)

Jesuit priest and missionary.

Gerard was born in Lancashire to a **Catholic** family. When he was five, his father, Sir Thomas Gerard, was imprisoned for plotting to free **Mary, Queen of Scots** and for three years he had to be looked after by another family until his father was released. At the age of twelve, he was enrolled at Oxford University but only stayed for a year due to the authorities' attempts to enforce attendance at a **Protestant** church.

At fourteen, Gerard entered the **Jesuit** society at Douai and later transferred to a college near Paris. After falling ill in 1584, he decided to return to England but was arrested straightaway for having travelled abroad without a permit. He later likened Marshalsea Prison to 'a school of Christ' due to its large number of Catholic inmates. After a year, he was released after the payment of a bond by Sir Anthony Babington and then fled abroad to Rome. Whilst there, he was given the task of returning to England in order to provide aid to its Catholic citizens.

He and five other priests were secretly landed on the Norfolk coast in 1588 and headed inland. They could not have picked a more dangerous time, however. The **Spanish Armada** had just been defeated and anti-Catholic hysteria was running high. The priests separated and Gerard managed to get to London, sometimes pretending that he was looking for a lost falcon to explain why he was off the road. In London, he was met by a Jesuit Superior who introduced him to known Catholic families, many of whom found it hard to believe he was a priest given his disguise as a young, charismatic gentleman who enjoyed gambling and hunting.

For six years he avoided capture, often having to make last-minute escapes or hide in priest holes. In one such hiding place, he had to stand in ankle deep water in a sewer with nine other priests for four hours. In another house, he had to hide under a fireplace for four days and almost starved to death. At one point, guards had even lit a fire above his head causing burning embers to rain down upon him.

Eventually, a household's servant betrayed him to the authorities and he was arrested and imprisoned for three years. In the **Tower of London**, he was tortured into giving the names of other priests but, despite being hung by chains attached to his manacled hands, Gerard refused to speak. Then, on an October night in 1597, he was rescued by Nicholas Owen, a Catholic carpenter who had previously designed many ingenious priest holes. Owen managed to affix a rope across the castle's moat upon which Campion, another priest and his gaoler (whom he had befriended!) escaped. Gerard then found refuge in more

Catholic households, including that of Robert Catesby – leader of the 1605 Gunpowder Plot.

For eight more years, he continued to work in England, bolstering people's faith and managing to convert some to Catholicism. In 1605, he was accused of being involved in the Gunpowder Plot, which he denied through the distribution of leaflets. However, he had become such a wanted man that even he realised that he would have to flee the country which he did, disguised as a uniformed servant of the Spanish ambassador (1606).

For the remainder of his life, Gerard worked in various Jesuit colleges on the continent and he wrote an autobiography which vividly described his adventures. He eventually died in Rome aged seventy-three.

Gilbert, Sir Humphrey

(c. 1539–83)

Soldier and explorer.

Gilbert was born near Torbay in Devon. His father died when he and his three siblings were minors and his mother then married the father of **Walter Ralegh**. He was educated at Eton then Oxford University and, soon after, he became a protégé of Sir Henry Sidney and served at the siege of Le Havre, where he was wounded.

Between 1566 and 1569 he served under Sidney with courage and brutality in overcoming uprisings in the south-west of **Ireland**. In the process, he advocated the killing of women and the laying down of decapitated heads of his fallen enemies outside his camp in order to terrify the local inhabitants. He also worked, unsuccessfully, to create English Protestant settlements on the island. For his services in crushing the rebellion he was knighted by Sidney.

Upon returning to England in 1570, Gilbert became an MP for Plymouth and married Anne Ager, who bore him seven children. Two years later, he was helping the Dutch in their long war against Spain but, for most of the decade he spent much time studying and writing. He had found his own **education** very dull and wrote plans for a new type of school with a broader curriculum. His ideas were eventually put into effect by **Sir Thomas Gresham**, who founded Gresham College in London. Above all, Gilbert became obsessed with the idea of a north-west passage around North America and wrote a treatise on the subject. He was also interested in alchemy and was fascinated with the black rock that **Martin Frobisher** brought back from Baffin Island.

Gilbert then turned his attention to the colonisation of America. In 1578, **Elizabeth I** granted him permission to settle lands in and around Newfoundland.

Storms, however, scattered his fleet, which had to return to Plymouth. By 1583, he had managed to raise enough funds to make another attempt. One ship though, had to turn around due to inadequate food supplies and his crews, comprising criminals and pirates, were quite lawless. However, Gilbert finally succeeded in reaching St John's – a temporary, multinational fishing settlement – and claimed it for the queen. This was England's first overseas colony but a lack of supplies meant that he could not establish a permanent settlement there.

The perils of sea voyages. (*Artist: Hans Holbein. From The Dance of Death c. 1526. Cleveland Museum of Art*)

Gilbert explored further south, seeking other potential sites for settlement but poor leadership allowed his largest remaining supply ship to run aground on a sandbank. Left with no choice, he ordered a return to England. Against all advice, Gilbert preferred to sail in the smaller of the two remaining ships and a few hundred miles from the Azores it was sunk by a huge storm. Ever the optimist, he was last seen holding up *Utopia* by **Thomas More** and crying out, 'We are as near to Heaven by sea as by land!'

Restless, aspiring, brave and determined, Gilbert was one of a crop of distinguished adventurers from Devon. He had intellectual qualities and a thirst for knowledge too. However, he also displayed a tendency to cruelty, pomposity and violent tempers. His plans were ambitious but he lacked the resources, knowledge and organisational skills to fulfil them. He did, however, sow the seeds of English colonisation of the New World, for it was his half-brother, Walter Ralegh, who took up the mantle and attempted further settlement of America.

Grenville, Sir Richard

(1542–91)

Adventurer and naval commander.

Grenville was born in north Devon and was a cousin of **Walter Ralegh** and **Humphrey Gilbert**. He was only three years old when his father, the captain of the *Mary Rose,* went down with his ship. He later finished his **education** at London's Inns of Court – a sort of finishing school combined with legal studies. Whilst there, he became involved in a brawl on the Strand and ran someone through with his sword but after three months branded as an outlaw, he was pardoned.

In 1565, Grenville married Mary St Leger and they went on to have four sons. A year later, he went to Hungary to fight the Turks and afterwards, he attempted to annex lands in the south-west of **Ireland** but an Irish revolt put paid to these plans. He was elected MP for Cornwall in 1571 and later appointed High Sheriff of the same county. In that role, he zealously hunted down any reported **Catholic** priests who were in hiding.

In 1574, Grenville proposed a plan to sail into the Pacific Ocean, terrorise Spanish shipping and seek a new, shorter route to the Indies. At this time, however, **Elizabeth I** and her chief minister, **William Cecil**, were keen not to antagonise Spain and so his suggestion was turned down. Only three years later, however, **Francis Drake** carried out just the same mission and Grenville was so furious that he refused to sail with Drake thereafter.

In 1585, he was given command of a fleet to carry out Ralegh's plan to colonise North America. Storms initially blew him south into the Caribbean where he raided Spanish ships and settlements then, after sailing north, he landed the English settlers at **Roanoke** Island (in modern-day North Carolina) before returning home to fetch more supplies. He returned the following year only to find that that the starving colonists had been rescued by Drake just a few weeks earlier. He left fifteen men behind to defend the tiny settlement but they were never seen again. He also brought a native American Indian back to north Devon and had him christened Ralegh but he died a few years later from influenza.

When the **Spanish Armada** sailed in 1588, Grenville and Ralegh were put in charge of the land defences of Devon and Cornwall. After Spain's defeat it was decided to go on the counter-attack and destroy the Spanish treasure ships as the they approached the Azores on their way from America. Grenville was appointed second-in-command of the expedition and sailed in the *Revenge*, considered to be one of the most powerful ships around.

The fleet, however, was surprised by a much larger Spanish squadron that had set out to convoy the approaching treasure ships to Spain. The English

Early 20th-century depiction of the last moments of the *Revenge*. (*From* Story of the Greatest Nations, *1913 by E. Ellis and C. Horne. University of California Libraries via Flickr*)

managed to get away but, for reasons that are not clear, Grenville ordered his crew to stay and fight. In an epic battle that lasted fifteen hours the *Revenge* sank two ships, damaged many others and repelled two boarding parties. Cannon and musket fire were exchanged at point-blank range causing terrible casualties until Grenville himself was wounded. He ordered his remaining crew to scuttle the ship but, instead, they surrendered and Grenville accused them of treachery before dying of his wounds. Soon after, the *Revenge* and many Spanish ships were sunk by a storm.

The exploits of Grenville and his crew have gone down in the annals of the Royal Navy's history and have been commemorated in poetry. The Spanish, despite their losses, learned the value of the convoy system and, thereafter, were much more successful in defending their gold and silver supplies.

Gresham, Sir Thomas

(c. 1519–79)

Merchant and financier.

Gresham was born in London, the son of an important cloth merchant. He completed his B.A. at Cambridge at the age of sixteen and went to work for his father and uncle in the Mercers Company in Antwerp in the Netherlands. Antwerp was a major trading and financial centre on the continent with a population twice that of London's. By 1543, he was also working for the Crown as a spy and an arms dealer, smuggling gunpowder and weapons hidden inside other goods across the North Sea to England.

In 1544, he married Anne Ferneley, an aunt of Francis Bacon, and milliner for Queen **Elizabeth** and they had a son who died at the age of nineteen. Gresham bought a large property in London but continued to spend most of his time in Flanders.

Edward VI appointed him as his Royal Agent in Antwerp in 1551 with a view to rescuing the value of the English currency, which had collapsed after the Great Debasement of the 1540s. Through clever insider dealing, he managed to manipulate the exchange rate in the Flemish stock exchange in order to raise the value of English coin. At the same time, he persuaded the government to cease the **debasement** of its currency. He is credited, incorrectly, with the principle of Gresham's Law, which states that bad money drives out good. In other words, inferior, debased coins will always swamp the market as the superior coins will either be hoarded or melted down.

Under **Mary I**, he temporarily fell out of favour possibly due to his **Protestant** leanings but he was soon reinstated when his replacement proved unsuccessful. Soon after **Elizabeth** became queen, he was knighted and set about restoring England's finances. The exchange rate had plummeted again and the country was suffering severe inflation.

Gresham addressed the problem in several ways. First, he arranged for coins to be re-minted to the pre-debasement levels (37/40) of silver. Second, he initiated a trade war with the powerful Hanseatic League by by-passing their ports and granting fewer export licenses to its London-based merchants. The League retaliated but to no avail and the position of English traders was strengthened. Third, he used his own money to found an idea of his father's – the Royal Exchange – which opened in 1571. On the ground floor was The Pawn – England's first shopping centre with 150 stalls. Above, however, were rooms where merchants regularly met to trade and invest. They could also pool resources and lend money to the Crown at much more favourable interest rates than the Antwerp Exchange had.

Warfare in the Netherlands forced Gresham to permanently return to England in 1567 where he continued to work for the queen until ill **health** and a worsening limp (caused by a fall from a horse) made him retire in 1574. Before that, he had had to act as her gaoler when he was asked to take charge of Lady Mary Grey, sister of **Lady Jane Grey** and a potential heir to the throne. Reluctantly, he had to tolerate her presence in his home for three years.

Elizabeth was very grateful for all of his services and even visited his house on a few occasions; she had gained much, financially, from his reforms. Gresham himself had built up a huge fortune from a myriad of financial transactions, sometimes unscrupulously. He died suddenly from a stroke in 1579. In his will, he left instructions for the founding of an idea by **Sir Humphrey Gilbert** – London's first seat of higher **education** – Gresham College; an unusual institution that had no students but offered free lectures in the arts and sciences (in English, not Latin) every day of the week. The powerful Cambridge University objected but the college's doors opened in 1597. Today, it is in a different location but it still offers 140 free lectures to the public every year.

Grey, Lady Jane

(c. 1537–54)

Queen of England, 10 July–19 July 1553.

Jane was the granddaughter of **Mary**, younger sister of **Henry VIII** and therefore, a great-granddaughter of **Henry VII**. Her father, Henry Grey, came from a long line of nobility that had risen to prominence during the reign of Edward IV. Therefore, she and her two younger sisters had reasonably strong claims to the English throne. Indeed, in the Succession Act of 1544, Henry VIII had declared that should none of his three children have heirs then the throne should go to the descendants of his sister, Mary.

At around the age of nine, Jane was sent to live in the household of **Catherine Parr** who, by this time was married to **Thomas Seymour**. Lady **Elizabeth** was living there at the same time but they probably had little to do with each other as the princess was about four years older. More importantly was her relationship with Catherine. They grew very fond of each other and it was Catherine who strengthened her belief in the **Protestant** faith.

In the following year, Catherine died and Seymour was arrested for treason. Jane returned home and, whilst there, she was provided with an excellent **humanist education** by visiting tutors. Jane was a serious and academic student and accounts show that she disliked her parents. She complained that they would beat her for the slightest infringements, showed a lack of piety and were far too interested in material wealth and social advancement.

In May 1553, she was forced into a political **marriage** to Guildford Dudley, a son of **John Dudley**, the Duke of Northumberland. Northumberland was head of King **Edward VI**'s ruling council and the most powerful man in the country. Soon after, the young king became terminally ill and, possibly persuaded by Northumberland, altered Henry VIII's succession act by declaring his sisters **Mary** and Elizabeth illegitimate and proclaiming Jane to be his heir. Edward had probably needed little persuasion: as an ardent Protestant he would have detested the idea of the **Catholic** Mary becoming queen. Elizabeth was Protestant but he could not bastardise one without the other.

Jane was suddenly thrown into the limelight and events moved quickly. On 6 July, Edward died. Four days later, the ruling council was browbeaten by Northumberland into declaring Jane queen of England. Northumberland then moved to isolate Mary but she escaped and raised an army of her own. It appears that the general populace had seen through his schemes and stayed loyal to Mary by refusing to support the duke. At the same time, the Council switched its allegiance and, on 19 July proclaimed Mary as queen and Jane and her husband were thrown into the **Tower of London**.

Northumberland himself was soon captured and executed for treason. It is harder to be clear about Jane's guilt, however. In her pleading letter to Mary, she admitted that she should not have accepted the crown but declared that she had had no knowledge of Northumberland's plans and no desire to take the throne. She stated that she had been bullied by her parents and Northumberland and, in the end, had had no control over events.

Judging by what we know of Jane's character, it would appear that she was telling the truth. Certainly, Mary believed her and, despite her advisors

Execution of Lady Jane Grey. (*19th-century engraving by Paolo Mercuri based on 1833 painting by Paul Delaroche. Wellcome Images*)

suggesting otherwise, she showed clemency and kept her alive in the Tower where she was well treated.

Her fate, however, was sealed by her father's actions a year later. In protest against Mary's plans to marry Prince Philip of Spain, Henry Grey helped to organise **Wyatt's Rebellion**. Mary now believed that she could not keep Jane alive, as a potential figurehead for future revolts. On 12 February 1554, at the age of seventeen, Jane was beheaded, a few hours after seeing the corpse of her decapitated husband go past her window. Her father was then executed eleven days later but her mother was allowed to live at court.

It is easy to feel much sympathy for Jane and it is no wonder that she figured prominently in Foxe's ***Book of Martyrs***. Pushed unwittingly into the whirlwind of politics at a tender age, she was the archetypal pawn and victim of those much greedier than she.

Grindal, Edmund

(c. 1519–83)

Archbishop of Canterbury from 1575 to 1583.

Grindal was born in St Bees, the son of a tenant farmer working in the local priory. He was a childhood friend of Edwin Sandys (ancestor of the author!) who was always one step behind him in his career in the Church.

In 1538, Grindal graduated from Cambridge University, where he met **Nicholas Ridley** whom he impressed with his eloquent arguments against tenets of the **Catholic** faith. When Ridley later became Bishop of London, he appointed Grindal as one of his chaplains. He was then promoted to be one of **Edward VI**'s chaplains and, in 1552, was partly responsible for examining the Forty-Two **Articles** of religion before they became official doctrine. Upon the accession of **Mary I** the following year, however, Grindal fled to the continent along with hundreds of other **Protestant** exiles and, whilst living in Strasbourg, he helped John Foxe produce the ***Book of Martyrs***.

Along with Sandys, he returned to England on the day that **Elizabeth I** was crowned and worked with others to establish the new Elizabethan Church of England. In 1559, he was appointed Bishop of London. In this role, he had the difficult task of enforcing the Church's tenets upon the numerous Catholic and **Puritan** dissenters, a task made harder by his own sympathies with the latter group. He was criticised for not being severe enough and so was appointed Archbishop of York – a see that had far fewer Puritans.

Upon the death of Archbishop **Parker** in 1575, Grindal was recommended by Elizabeth's chief advisor, **William Cecil**, to take up the leadership of the

Church at Canterbury. Cecil believed he had the moderating skills which would enable him to bring the Puritans into the Church of England fold. Soon after, however, he fell foul of the queen's temper when he refused her order to ban Puritan discussion groups. She took away his powers of legal jurisdiction and threatened to dismiss him but he held firm. Eventually, after a long illness and increasing blindness he died in 1583.

Grindal's detractors accused him of being weak and ineffective at a time when the fledgling Elizabethan Church needed strong leadership whilst others, including the Puritans, later praised him for his tact and moderation. His most enduring legacy was the foundation of a free grammar school in his native St Bees.

H

Hatton, Sir Christopher

(1540–91)

Courtier and favourite of Queen **Elizabeth I**.

Hatton was born into a long line of landed gentry in Northamptonshire but very little is known of his youth. After leaving Oxford without a degree he received further **education** at London's Inns of Court. However, he seemed more interested in literature and drama than the law. He came to Queen Elizabeth's attention whilst performing in a play; his tall physique and dancing ability later earned him the nickname, 'The Dancing Chancellor'.

Sir Christopher Hatton. (*From Catalogue of portraits, miniatures, etc in the possession of Cecil George Savile, 4th Earl of Liverpool, 1905 based on a 1589 original painting. Getty Research Institute*)

In 1564, he became one of her gentlemen pensioners – private bodyguard – and she later appointed him her captain of the yeomen of the guard. By 1571, he had become a member of **Parliament** and was rivalling **Robert Dudley** to be the centre of her attention. Whilst Elizabeth called Dudley her 'eyes', she referred to Hatton as her 'lids'. Initially, Dudley was jealous of the attention that the queen gave Hatton but they later became good friends. We cannot be sure of where Elizabeth placed them in her affections but it seems that Dudley was always her true love.

However, she loved Hatton's genuine adoration and devotion to her and, in return, she showered him with many lands and positions. Rumours soon circulated that the pair were lovers. This is unlikely but their relationship may have been the closest to arousing Elizabeth's sexual passion. Unlike her other courtiers, Hatton never married; he believed that this would have been a betrayal of the queen.

Hatton was brought up as a **Catholic** and he always adopted a moderate approach to enforcing their acceptance of the Church of England. His attitude to the **Puritans**, however, was much more stringent. This almost cost him his life when a Puritan fanatic stabbed **John Hawkins** believing him to be Hatton. However, his loyalty to the queen always overcame any private religious views he may have had. He disagreed with **William Cecil**'s cautious policy towards Spain, advised against her marriage to the Catholic Duke of Alençon, was a member of the court that tried Anthony Babington and it was probably he who persuaded Elizabeth's secretary to send off the death warrant of **Mary, Queen of Scots** without the queen's permission.

His most important role, however, was as the queen's representative in Parliament. He defended the monarchy's powers very eloquently and often came to blows with the Puritan MP, **Peter Wentworth**, who argued for Parliament's right to discuss religious matters. More controversial was Hatton's appointment as Lord Chancellor in 1587; members of the legal profession were offended because he had had very little legal training. Possibly, Elizabeth needed someone she could rely on who would work with Archbishop **Whitgift** in suppressing the Puritans. Or possibly, the appointment was due to the political manoeuvrings of his rivals who hoped that it would increase his absences from court and thereby diminish his influence.

Hatton took a great interest in plays and poetry and became a patron of many writers, including **Edmund Spenser**. He also showed much kindness to ordinary people who implored him for help. Despite his income from various sources, he became bankrupt mainly because of the huge three-storeyed property he built at Holdenby, Northamptonshire. As big as Hampton Court palace, it had 123 glass windows (glass was very expensive then), two courts and a state room for the queen. He said that he could never sleep there until she visited but she never did. His debts led him to invest in the voyages of sailors such as **Drake** and **Frobisher**.

In 1591, Elizabeth spoon-fed him as he lay dying of an illness and, afterwards, despite owing her £40,000 (around £7 million in 2024), she ordered a state funeral at St Paul's Cathedral. It is easy to view Hatton as a mere sycophant who simply flattered his way to fame and fortune. However, if he was simply playing the 'game' that so many other Elizabethan courtiers were playing, then he just happened to be very good at it.

Hawkins, Sir John

(1532–95)

Trader, privateer, naval administrator and commander.

Hawkins was born into a prominent ship-building family in Plymouth and his father had been the first Englishman to sail to Brazil. For a time, his second cousin, **Francis Drake**, was brought up in the same household. At the age of twenty, he killed a Plymouth barber but the judge decided that he had acted in self-defence and he received a royal pardon. In the 1550s, he worked in the local shipping industry with his older brother, William. At some point, it seems that he did some service for the Spanish dignitaries travelling to London to arrange Queen **Mary I**'s marriage to Prince Philip. Thereafter, he would jokingly refer to King Philip as 'my old master'.

In the 1560s, Hawkins became involved in the lucrative African slave trade. He would either buy from the Portuguese merchants already trading in Guinea or directly from the tribal kings although, sometimes, he would forcibly seize people. It is estimated that he transported around 1,500 Africans across the Atlantic. The Spanish government had banned its colonists in America from trading with outsiders. However, the settlers were usually happy to provide sugar, hides and pearls in exchange for the slaves. When any local authorities refused to trade, Hawkins had no qualms in using force to steal what he wanted. These voyages became so profitable that **William Cecil** and **Elizabeth I** herself invested in them despite the risk of antagonising Spain. Interestingly, Hawkins was the first to observe American Indians smoking tobacco. He brought tobacco leaves back to England but smoking only started to become popular in the 1580s.

His third slave voyage (1567-69), however, was disastrous and had far-reaching consequences. Hawkins, with Drake, found that the Spanish settlements had become less willing to trade and he had to resort more frequently to force. On the return journey, it was clear that one of his ships needed repairing so he docked at the Spanish port of San Juan de Ulua on the coast of Mexico. The authorities allowed the English to anchor but, a few days later, launched a surprise attack. The battle lasted for six hours. Outnumbered, Hawkins and Drake just managed to escape but they lost four of their ships and many crewmen. The Spanish later claimed that they had simply been dealing with criminal pirates. Although the voyage still made a profit, Hawkins and Drake never forgave the Spanish for their 'treachery' and vowed revenge. The incident proved to be the beginning of a naval conflict between the two countries which led to the **Anglo-Spanish War**.

In 1571, Hawkins became involved as a double-agent in the **Ridolfi Plot**. He managed to persuade the Spanish ambassador that he was an ardent Catholic who wanted to replace Queen Elizabeth with **Mary, Queen of Scots** and that he would lend his ships to help with a Spanish invasion. When the ambassador shared the details of the conspiracy, Hawkins passed them on to Cecil and the plot was foiled.

Later that year, he became MP for Plymouth but in 1573, whilst in London, he was stabbed and nearly killed by a fanatical **Puritan** who mistook him for **Sir Christopher Hatton**.

In 1578, he was appointed Treasurer of the Navy. In this role, Hawkins carried out some important reforms which were based on his past experiences. First, he ordered the creation of more streamlined ships that were easier to manouvre in battle. Second, he initiated a change in naval tactics, which relied more on powerful cannons that could be quickly reloaded. In this way, battles could be won at long range rather than using the unpredictable strategy of boarding the enemy ships. Third, he reduced over-crowdedness on ships which allowed more space in which the crews could operate and enabled fleets to stay longer at sea as there were fewer mouths to feed. He also raised sailors' pay, increased the size of the fleet to twenty-three galleons and dealt with the endemic corruption carried out by contractors in the shipyards. Hawkins was third-in-command when the English fleet battled the **Spanish Armada** in 1588. His reforms were vindicated by the clear superiority of its ships in battle and, subsequently, he was knighted on his ship by **Lord Howard of Effingham**.

In 1591, he proposed an expedition to the Azores in order to capture Spanish treasure ships returning from America. The mission was a failure, though, and resulted in the death of **Sir Richard Grenville** and the capture of his ship, the *Revenge*.

Hawkins and Drake were put in joint command of an expedition to capture Panama in 1595. Nothing was achieved, however, due to storms, the preparedness of the Spanish and damaging quarrels between the two leaders. In November that year, Hawkins fell ill and died off the coast of Puerto Rico.

John Hawkins has been condemned as the man who started the English slave trade. It must be remembered, however, that he lived in a time when it was considered acceptable for one person to own another. Indeed, serfdom still existed in Europe at that time although, admittedly, a big difference was that serfs were leased land which they could farm for themselves. There is no doubt, however, that Hawkins was an incorruptible and loyal servant of the queen. Like Drake, he was a leader who commanded great respect amongst his men. In contrast to his compatriot, though, he was an able administrator who was careful and methodical.

Health and Medicine

The average life expectancy in Tudor England was around thirty-five years (today it is around eighty). This figure, however, is skewed by the very high infant mortality rate. It is estimated that about forty per cent of those who were born did not reach adulthood, compared to 0.37 per cent today. If you could survive childhood, then it was quite possible to reach your sixties or even beyond. For women, this was a little less likely for one of the most dangerous activities was having a baby. Estimates vary considerably but the most conservative figure is that five to seven per cent of women would die giving birth or soon after (0.0089 per cent today) with about half of all pregnancies ending in miscarriage.

People living in Tudor times were, if anything, healthier than people are today as they did far more physical activity and the majority had a good **diet**. Obesity-related illnesses, such as heart disease and strokes, were relatively rare. This was less true of the wealthier classes though and poor harvests would lead to malnutrition for many of the ordinary people.

The biggest killer of people, by far, in the sixteenth century was disease. The most common were:

Tuberculosis (known as consumption). Caused by a bacterial lung infection and highly infectious.
Dysentery (known as the Bloody Flux). Infection caused by food/water contaminated with faecal bacteria.
Typhoid (known as fever). Very similar cause to dysentery.
Smallpox. A lethal viral infection that can cause disfigurement.
Bubonic Plague. A bacterial infection caused by flea bites.
Influenza. A viral infection of the lungs.
Sweating Sickness. A mysterious disease of unknown causes with a very high mortality rate.

Very few of these exist today due to improved sanitation, antibiotics, better medical knowledge and vaccination programmes. The latter, for example, has eradicated smallpox worldwide.

Many diseases would appear in devastating epidemics. The influenza epidemic of 1557, for example, has been described as the worst mortality crisis of early modern England and there were five outbreaks of the sweating sickness between 1485 and 1551. Plague would never go away completely but 1563 and 1593 saw particularly bad outbreaks. Children tended to suffer the most as their bodies were weaker and they had less immunity.

There were some advances in medical knowledge in the sixteenth century as more scientists started to place increased emphasis on evidence and observation. In the Spanish Netherlands, for example, Andreas Vesalius created accurate descriptions of the human anatomy by carrying out dissections, which were to revolutionise medicine. On the whole, however, medical practice had changed little since the Middle Ages. It was not until the 1670s that the microscope was invented and micro-organisms were discovered. Therefore, remedies were still based upon old superstitions.

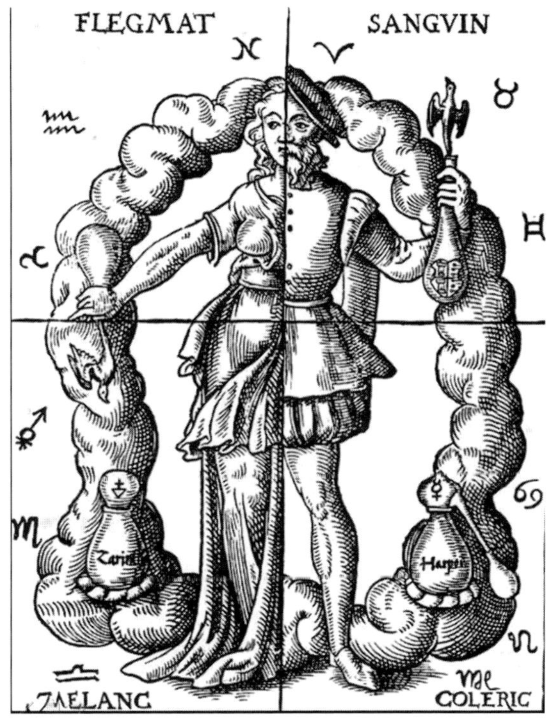

Medical chart displaying the four humours. (*Artist: unknown, 1574. Illustration for* Quinta Essentia *by Leonhard Thurneysser. Private Collection*)

Physicians believed that the human body was comprised of four fluids or 'humours' – blood, phlegm, black bile and yellow bile – and that illnesses were caused by an imbalance of these humours. Treatment would depend on the perceived excess fluid. For example, for too much blood, a doctor would either cut a vein or apply leeches to the skin. Most Tudor doctors also studied astrology, believing that different zodiacal signs ruled different parts of the body. More sensibly, perhaps, the smell, colour and even taste of a patient's urine was used to make a diagnosis.

For most, physicians were too expensive and so herbal remedies, known as 'simples', were very popular. Monks tended to study the effects of different herbs and most women learned how to make them. A mixture of sage, lavender and marjoram, for example, was used to treat a headache. Amputations and tooth extractions were performed by barber-surgeons, who cut people's hair the rest of the time.

Predictably, perhaps, there were many outlandish 'cures' that sometimes did more harm than good. Here are just a few examples:

- **Jaundice:** swallow nine lice mixed with ale each morning for a week.
- **Rheumatism:** wear the skin of a donkey.
- **Baldness:** smear the grease of a fox onto the scalp.

- **Gout:** apply a mixture of worms, herbs, pig's marrow and red-haired dog which have been boiled together.
- **Deafness:** the gall of a hare mixed with the grease of a fox inserted into the ears.

Henry VII

(1457–1509)

King of England from 1485 to 1509 and founder of the Tudor dynasty.

Henry was born in Pembroke Castle, the son of Edmund Tudor, the First Earl of Richmond, and **Margaret Beaufort** and the **Wars of the Roses** had just broken out between the families of York and Lancaster. The Tudors were on the Lancastrian side and his father died in captivity before Henry was born. Henry then went into the care of his uncle, Jasper Tudor, after Margaret remarried. When the Yorkist king, Edward IV, was victorious in 1461, Jasper fled to the continent and both Henry and his mother were kept under close supervision.

Ten years later, after the defeat of a Lancastrian coup, Henry was forced to flee abroad where the Duke of Brittany took him under his wing. Now, at the age of fourteen, he had become the main Lancastrian claimant to the throne as most of the other candidates had been killed. A chance came when Edward IV died in 1483. His brother, Richard, seized the throne and rumours spread that he had murdered his two nephews – the Princes in the Tower. His unpopularity sparked an uprising and Henry set sail with a small invasion force to combine with the rebels. Storms, however, dispersed his fleet, which was fortunate given that the rebellion had already been crushed.

With the Breton government now under considerable pressure to hand him over to King Richard, Henry managed to flee to France. Whilst his mother secretly amassed support for him at home, Henry gathered supplies and troops from the French king to attempt a second invasion. In 1485, with about 3,500 men, he landed near Pembroke and, flying the flag of the Welsh red dragon, he gathered more supporters as he marched through Wales. On 22 August, he met and defeated Richard III's army at the **Battle of Bosworth Field** where Richard was killed and Henry proclaimed king of England.

Securing his throne at home

After Bosworth, Henry VII claimed the English throne by right of conquest. His actual dynastic claim was so weak that discussion of it was never allowed. His paternal grandfather had possibly married the widow of Henry V and their son, Edmund, was only declared legitimate by **Parliament** in 1452. Meanwhile, his maternal great-grandfather was the illegitimate child of a mistress of a son of Edward III (!). The children of this line had been legitimised too but only on the condition that they could never claim the throne.

Henry realised that he needed to employ other methods to strengthen his claim. After his coronation, one of his first acts was to obtain Parliament's recognition of his position and then he issued an edict stating that anyone who swore loyalty to him would be guaranteed their properties. The inverse threat behind this decree was obvious to all. Soon after, in early 1486, he carried out a prior promise to marry **Elizabeth of York**, daughter of Edward IV. This appeased many Yorkists and led to the creation of the Tudor Rose – a red and white symbol that represented the new dynasty as well as the end of the civil war.

Rim lock and key. A portable lock designed by a court locksmith. This one was used for one of Henry VIII's chests. Henry VII had one installed on his bedroom door wherever he travelled. (*Author: unknown via Wikimedia Commons*)

Henry still faced revolts though. In 1487, the Earl of Lincoln, John de la Pole, attempted to put the impostor, **Lambert Simnel** on the throne but was defeated and killed at the Battle of Stoke. Another impostor, **Perkin Warbeck**, caused more trouble by persuading the Scottish king to invade and then attempting to prolong the **Cornish Rebellion** in 1497 but he too was defeated and later executed. Henry had succeeded in staving off the threats but the events fuelled the feeling that his throne was not secure.

Baronial power had enabled the Wars of the Roses and so Henry was determined to crush it. Firstly, he enacted laws against livery and maintenance. Livery was the uniforms of the lords' private armies and the new law stated that you had to buy a licence to have any men in livery and would be fined £5 (£3,000 in 2024) for every man illegally retained. Maintenance was the process of a lord intimidating a local law court if one of his men was on trial and the new law made this practice illegal. Furthermore, Henry used the court of **Star Chamber** to deal with those too powerful to be tried in ordinary courts and employed more justices of the peace to oversee the correct enforcement of law around the country. Finally, when noble families died out, instead of ennobling more, he took control of their lands. This made him wealthier whilst reducing the number of lords and potential enemies.

Securing his throne abroad

Henry knew that foreign powers could destabilise a regime. After all, Brittany and France had enabled his own conquest of England! He therefore set about befriending countries through **marriage** alliances. Consequently, his eldest son, **Arthur**, was married to the Spanish princess, **Catherine of Aragon**. When he died a few months later, Henry acquired papal permission for his other son, Prince **Henry**, to marry his brother's widow. He also wedded his eldest daughter, **Margaret**, to the Scottish king (a marriage that would lead to the union of the English and Scottish crowns in 1603) whilst his youngest child, **Mary**, was betrothed to the son of the Holy Roman Emperor. In each case, guarantees were acquired from each country not to support Yorkist plots.

Henry avoided war as a general rule – it was risky and expensive. He did, however, make an attempt to prevent the French takeover of Brittany and, although this failed, at the Treaty of Etaples (1492) he managed to extract from the French king a generous annual pension and a withdrawal of his support for Warbeck.

Much more preferable were trade deals, which he arranged with many countries, and he subsidised **John Cabot**'s voyages of discovery in the hope of finding new trading opportunities in the Far East. Henry also commissioned Europe's first dry dock at Portsmouth and established the Royal Navy – ships designed for war – to defend the coasts and trade routes.

Securing financial strength

Henry realised the importance of financial security – a poor king was a weak king. So he avoided expensive wars and encouraged trade instead (which meant more customs duties). He also kept a personal eye on Crown income and expenditure in order to cut down on corruption and incompetence and thereby maximise the profits from his lands. As a result, annual income from his Crown lands increased from £29,000 to £42,000 over the course of his reign.

In addition, he heavily fined nobles who broke any laws. In 1505, for instance, the Earl of Northumberland was fined a staggering £10,000 for assuming control of a wardship without royal licence. His use of a device known as **Morton**'s Fork ensured that no one could avoid payment of taxes and even more unpopular was the ruthless exploitation of feudal rights that he resurrected. An example was wardship. When a minor inherited land, Henry imposed his right to take the land and its revenues until the child came of age.

Henry is usually accused of being miserly but, despite his financial caution, evidence shows that he was often very extravagant. He understood the importance of a powerful king needing to look powerful and so lavish court ceremonies with processions, banquets and jousts were almost as common in his reign as his son's. He himself enjoyed hawking, hunting and gambling, would spend generously on gifts for his family and even owned a private zoo.

Death mask of Henry VII. This wax cast would have lain on Henry's funeral casket. (*Artist: unknown, 1509. Westminster Abbey via Wikimedia Commons*)

The later years of Henry's reign were marred by personal tragedy and a general sense of repression caused by his stringent policies. The death of Arthur in 1502 hit him badly. Usually quite a reserved man, his displays of intense grief shocked his courtiers. Even worse was the death of Elizabeth a year later. By all accounts, their marriage had a been a loving one and, even more unusually, he was never known to have a mistress. He, himself, became badly ill for a short time afterwards and her loss made him become more withdrawn and isolated in the last years of his reign. Henry made some half-hearted attempts at remarriage into the Spanish royal family but negotiations came to nothing.

He died from tuberculosis at Richmond Palace in April 1509. It seems that not many people mourned his passing and there was a widespread feeling of optimism that his seventeen-year-old son, Henry VIII, would usher in a happier and more glorious future for the country.

The general belief is that Henry VII was a secretive, grasping and paranoid king who would do anything to ensure his position on the throne. However, his achievements were numerous. By destroying the power of the barons, he took England out of the Middle Ages and into the modern age. He inherited a bankrupt treasury and left his son a small fortune. He delivered a fairer system of justice and his reign was largely peaceful and prosperous. He centralised administration and started the practice of employing lower-born men of ability, such as John Morton and **Richard Foxe**, to run the government. Above all, he transformed a country at civil war into one that allowed the first peaceful accession of a king since 1422. Henry VII might not have been the greatest of England's monarchs but he must be considered as one of its most successful.

Henry VIII

(1491–1547)

King of England from 1509 to 1547.

Born in Greenwich Palace, Henry was the third child and second son of **Henry VII** and **Elizabeth of York**. Before he was four years old, he was appointed an array of prestigious titles such as Constable of Dover Castle, Earl Marshal of England and Lord Lieutenant of Ireland. The reason for these appointments was to enable his father to control these positions rather than giving them to his nobles whom he mistrusted. Not much is known of Henry's early life because he was never expected to become king. In fact, it seems likely that his father planned a career for him in the Church.

It appears that he was brought up in a loving household and was particularly shown affection by his mother. He was eleven when she died and new pictorial evidence shows him weeping beside her deathbed. She had helped to provide him with a first-class **education** in which he excelled – not only could he speak French, Italian, Spanish and Latin he was also an excellent musician, dancer and sportsman and enjoyed intellectual theological discussions.

Henry's accession to the throne in 1509, aged seventeen, could not have been more advantageous: he inherited a peaceful kingdom, submissive nobles and full coffers in the treasury. Moreover, after the gloomy latter years of his father's reign, the energetic and handsome new king was joyously welcomed by his subjects, a mood he positively encouraged by executing the chief tax-collectors of the previous reign – Richard Empson and Edmund Dudley.

The Succession

All of the Tudor monarchs carried concerns about who would succeed them. For Henry VIII, it was vital to have a legitimate male heir. England had never had a ruling queen and that was considered a path to civil war and destruction. In order to provide the male heir, as well as maintain an alliance with Spain, Henry agreed to marry **Catherine of Aragon**. Catherine had been married to Henry's older brother, **Arthur**, but he had died five months after their **marriage**. The Bible stated that a man should not marry his brother's widow but special papal dispensation was provided, which even covered the possibility that Catherine and Arthur had consummated their brief marriage (this was unlikely and both Catherine and her chaperone denied it).

Catherine had between six and ten pregnancies; all bar one were stillborn, died at birth or soon after. The most shocking was the death of little Prince Henry after seven weeks, soon after the king and nation had rejoiced at his birth. Only a girl, Princess **Mary** (born 1516), survived to adulthood. By the mid-1520s,

Catherine was approaching forty and it was becoming clear to many, including the king, that she would not produce another heir. Henry set his chief minister, Cardinal **Wolsey**, the task of solving his 'Great Matter' – acquiring papal permission to annul his marriage based on the grounds that the initial dispensation should never have been granted in the first place. Indeed, it seems that Henry truly believed that Catherine's failure to produce a male heir was divine punishment for flouting Biblical code.

Pope Clement VII. The pope at the centre of the storm during Henry VIII's 'Great Matter'. (*Artist: unknown, 1568 vis Wikimedia Commons*)

Pope Clement VII was in a difficult position. Wolsey combined scholarly arguments with threats from his master that he would by-pass the papacy and weaken its control over the Church in England. At the same, however, the Pope was under pressure from an invading army led by the Holy Roman Emperor, Charles V, who happened to be Catherine's nephew. Clement could ill-afford to upset him and so he simply procrastinated.

Henry considered other options. He tried to persuade Catherine to retire to a nunnery (which would have formally ended the marriage) but she refused to betray her loyalty to the holy concept of matrimony. The king also toyed with the idea of naming his illegitimate son, **Henry Fitzroy**, as his successor but this carried the risk of him not being widely recognised as a true heir.

Matters became more urgent after Henry fell in love with one of Catherine's ladies-in-waiting, **Anne Boleyn**. Anne's sister, Mary, was already one of the king's mistresses but Anne was more ambitious and refused Henry's attentions until he was ready to wed her. By 1529, it was clear that the papal annulment would never come and Wolsey was blamed and discarded under the suspicion that he was too closely attached to the Papacy. Henry replaced him with able men of undoubted loyalty who would be prepared to get their master married to Anne using any means available – **Thomas More** (followed by **Thomas**

A love letter from Henry VIII to Anne Boleyn. Henry wrote 17 love letters, in French, to Anne Boleyn despite his dislike of writing. Her replies have not been discovered. (*Author: Henry VIII c. 1527. Vatican Library*)

Cromwell) and the new Archbishop of Canterbury, **Thomas Cranmer**. Their job was facilitated by a **Parliament** that had largely become anti-clerical due to the evident abuses within the Church. In the mid-1530s, it issued a series of laws that eroded the Church's powers as well as those of the Pope.

Events had to move fast in 1533. Anne had finally succumbed to Henry's desires, had become pregnant and the two secretly wed in January in order to make the heir legitimate. Cromwell drafted the Bill of Restraints in Appeals, which Parliament enacted in April. This made the king the final legal authority in all religious matters and banned appeals to Rome. In May, Cranmer declared Henry's union with Catherine null and void and validated his marriage to Anne Boleyn. Four days later, Anne was crowned queen. The break with Rome was formalised by Parliament's Act of Supremacy (1534) which officially declared Henry as the Supreme Head of the English Church. The speed of events shocked many at home and abroad and resulted in the excommunication of Henry and Cranmer but the result was permanent – England had broken away from the authority of Rome, a tie that had lasted for almost 1,000 years.

In September, a girl was born – **Elizabeth** and, soon after, Parliament passed the Act of Succession which declared Princess Mary illegitimate and made Elizabeth the king's heir. Henry would brook no disagreement over this and even had More and Bishop **Fisher** beheaded for refusing to swear the law's accompanying oath. For the king, the disappointment of a girl, however, must have been enormous and he and some of his inner circle were starting to tire of Anne's overbearing behaviour. Henry still hoped for a boy, though, despite starting an affair with **Jane Seymour** – one of the new queen's attendants.

In late January 1536, Henry was thrown by his horse during a tournament and was badly injured and unconscious for two hours. The news sent Anne, who was pregnant again, into shock and caused a miscarriage and death of a baby boy (on the same day as Catherine of Aragon's funeral). The king felt betrayed and, urged on by the anti-Boleyn faction in court, had Anne arrested in May on trumped-up charges of adultery. She was executed on the 19 May; Henry and Jane were married eleven days later. In October 1537, she gave birth to the son that Henry craved – **Edward**. The boy survived although, tragically, Jane never recovered and died twelve days later. She was the only one of his wives for whom Henry went into mourning.

A second Act of Succession had already declared Elizabeth illegitimate and, therefore, Edward became the king's sole heir. Henry's three remaining marriages (**Anne of Cleves**, **Catherine Howard** and **Catherine Parr**) were more for political and personal reasons and produced no children. Later, in 1543, the king had a change of heart and Parliament passed the Third Act of Succession, which restored Mary and Elizabeth's claims to the throne but only behind those of Edward and any of his offspring. As Henry was approaching death in 1546, Edward was still only nine years old, so he appointed a regency council to rule until the boy came of age – sixteen men with a balance of both **Catholic** and **Protestant** views.

Religion

Henry's religious policy, if it can be called that, was remarkable for its inconsistency. He himself was always a Catholic and after the onset of the **Reformation**, he had even written (possibly aided by More or Fisher) a treatise in 1521 that defended papal supremacy and attacked the new Protestant ideas of Martin Luther. For this, the Pope awarded him the title of Fidei Defensor – Defender of the Faith – the reason why the letters F.D. are still on our coins today.

However, several events allowed Protestantism to creep into the country. First, the break with Rome, in 1533/34, abolished papal authority. This had been preceded in 1532 by the Submission of the Clergy; the Church's leaders were bullied into surrendering their right to make laws independent of Parliament. Second, the **Dissolution of the Monasteries** (1536–40) deprived the Church of much of its wealth and influence and, lastly, reformers such as Cranmer and Cromwell held much sway over the king. Henry was not even averse to marrying Protestants – Anne of Cleves, Catherine Parr and, possibly, Anne Boleyn. Concurrently, the spread of printing presses, both at home and abroad, brought Protestant pamphlets and cheaper versions of the English Bible to broader sections of society.

The apogee of Protestantism in Henry's reign came with the issue of the Ten **Articles** of 1536, which eroded aspects of the Catholic doctrine. This, however, contributed to the **Pilgrimage of Grace**, a rebellion in the north of England, which probably sowed seeds of doubt in Henry's mind that the pace of reform was going too far. Moreover, in 1539, King Francis of France and the Holy Roman Emperor, Charles, looked like they might combine to attack the 'heretical' England. So Henry felt compelled to order the Six Articles of 1539, which reinstated the full Catholic doctrine again.

After Cromwell's fall from power in 1540, his approach to religious policy became even more confused and appeared to depend on how the king was feeling or whoever had his ear. At times, the Protestant faction dominated such as when he ordered **Coverdale**'s English Bible to be placed in churches. On other occasions, conservatives such as Bishop **Gardiner** held sway and managed to reverse any Protestant gains. An increasingly paranoid, erratic and temperamental king saw enemies everywhere and happily executed both Catholics and Protestants in large numbers for supposed treason.

When Henry died in 1547, he left behind a confused Catholic nation that had tasted the Protestant faith and it would take a further twelve years before a permanent settlement was finally reached. His 'Great Matter' had inadvertently opened the door to a religion that Henry personally disliked and, had Catherine of Aragon produced a healthy boy, it is more than possible that England would still be a Catholic country today.

Foreign Affairs

Henry VII had viewed foreign adventures as being risky and expensive. Not so, his son, who saw war as an opportunity to gain glory and land that had been lost at the end of the Hundred Years' War less than sixty years earlier.

In the **First Anglo-French War**, he joined an alliance against France. His forces captured two towns and won a minor battle and, more significantly, an invading Scottish army was destroyed at **Flodden**. However, short of money and let down by his allies, Henry concluded a peace treaty. The war had achieved little and used up all that his father had saved although Henry had announced himself on the world stage as a potentially useful ally in the rivalry between France and the Habsburgs (rulers of Spain and the Holy Roman Empire).

The following eight years were defined by the king's chief minister, Cardinal Wolsey, who sought the role of arbiter of peace. This culminated in Henry's grandiose meeting with King Francis of France at the **Field of the Cloth of Gold** (1520) and two smaller-scale meetings with Charles I of Spain (Charles V of the Holy Roman Empire).

Charles then tempted Henry into the **Second Anglo-French War**. A large English army came within fifty miles of Paris but, again, Henry was deserted by his more powerful ally. This, along with another shortage of funds, forced the king to make peace.

The 1530s were dangerous years for England. After the break from Rome, the country was seen as a heretical state and the Pope encouraged its invasion. In a desperate desire to seek an ally in Germany, Henry agreed to marry Anne of Cleves (1539) but both the marriage and the alliance were short-lived. Fortunately for Henry, conflict and mutual distrust between Francis and Charles meant that both rulers felt they had bigger fish to fry.

By 1542, Henry was ready for another conflict. Buoyed by a rapprochement with Charles and the windfall from the Dissolution of the Monasteries, he initiated the **Third Anglo-French War**. This also sparked the **War of the Rough Wooing** with Scotland in an attempt to marry his son to **Mary, Queen of Scots** and rid England's northern neighbour of French influence. In France, English forces managed to capture Boulogne but, after Charles made a separate peace with Francis, Henry had to retreat. For the remainder of the war, England was on the back foot as French forces landed in Scotland and threatened an invasion of the south. Eventually, both sides recognised the stalemate and made peace.

These wars provided little gain and at a huge cost. Many monastic lands had to be sold off thereby reducing the Crown's annual income and attempts to raise taxes, both with and without Parliament's permission, were deeply unpopular. Even worse was the decision to allow the **debasement** of the coinage: this led to severe inflation that would damage the economy for many years to come. The conflicts also made clear England's junior status as a European power as, time and again, it had been cast aside by its allies and shown itself incapable of achieving any sustained success on the continent.

Henry VIII stands like a colossus staring down at us through the pages of history; his huge figure and beady eyes carry a discernible threat. He is, perhaps, the most famous of all England's monarchs, renowned for his wives and wars, the break from Rome and the Dissolution of the Monasteries. People grew to fear him and his unpredictable nature as he gradually metamorphosed from an athletic, young **Renaissance** prince into a dangerous and obese tyrant. Maybe as many as 57,000 people were executed in his reign out of a total of 80,000 in the entire Tudor period. Even contemporaries were shocked by some of these, such as **Anne Askew** (heresy) and the sixty-eight-year-old Margaret Pole (having royal ancestors).

It is also well known that Henry preferred lavish banquets, sport and hunting to the mundane matters of administration, which he left to men of ability such as Wolsey and Cromwell (the latter's execution was his only act that he publicly regretted). Sometimes, it is hard to tell how much influence Henry had on any particular policy. He was certainly interested in military matters and so probably oversaw the building of naval defences on the south coast and the expansion of the navy to eighty-five warships armed with powerful cannon. On the other hand, the integration of Wales into the English legal and administrative systems (Act of Union, 1536) was probably driven solely by Cromwell.

Possibly no other English monarch had as much power as Henry VIII and yet, when he died, he left behind a divided and bankrupt nation. In the last years of his reign, he deteriorated into a suffering, physical wreck. After his jousting accident he was prone to chronic leg ulcers which reduced his physical activity. At the same time, he continued to feed his immense appetite and so his waistline expanded from thirty-two to fifty-two inches, which necessitated his transportation in a wooden chair by mechanical cranes in the last years of his reign. Plagued by headaches, too, it may have been Type II diabetes, heart disease or liver / kidney failure that killed him. On his deathbed, his last request was to send for Cranmer. When the archbishop asked the king if he trusted in the mercy of Christ, all Henry could do was squeeze his hand before passing away. He was buried at Windsor Castle beside Jane Seymour.

Holbein, Hans

(c. 1497–1543)

Most significant artist of the Tudor period in England.

Sometimes known as Hans Holbein the Younger, his father was Hans Holbein the Elder – a respected artist from the German city of Augsburg. After learning the trade from his father, Holbein moved to Basel in Switzerland where he started to gain a reputation as an excellent painter. He developed a unique style that combined influences from his father (Late Gothic) and **Renaissance** Italy.

Initially, like his father, he focused on religious themes with an eye on realism, detail and the use of perspective. Later, after a visit to Italy, Holbein started to place more emphasis on secular subjects that displayed human nature.

Whilst in Basel, he married a widow and the couple went on to have three children. In the first half of the 1520s he was prolific, creating murals, book illustrations and designs for stained glass windows and woodcuts. Most impressive, perhaps, was his *Dance of Death* (1523–25) – a series of miniature woodcuts that revealed Death visiting thirty-four people from different levels of society, even the Pope. By now, the **Reformation** had come to Switzerland, which provided him with a new, **Protestant** audience. However, in the late 1520s, the more radical ideas of Ulrich Zwingli came to dominate. Consequently, the demand for religious images declined and some of his work was even destroyed.

As a result, the great **humanist**, Desiderius Erasmus, suggested that he find work in England. Holbein had already painted a few portraits of Erasmus, who was so impressed that he recommended him to his friend, **Thomas More**. During this first visit (1526–28), he tended to focus on portraits of those with links to Erasmus, his most famous works being a portrait of More and another of More with his family.

Holbein went back to Basel for four years before returning to England and spending the rest of his life there. By 1532, however, More had fallen from favour and he became patronised by the new powers in the ascendancy – the **Boleyn** family and **Thomas Cromwell**. This was a period of predominantly portrait paintings, when Holbein was commissioned to paint various merchants and courtiers. Cromwell also used him to produce works of reformist propaganda such as anti-clerical woodcuts and the title page to **Coverdale**'s English Bible.

Two of his most well-known paintings are *The Ambassadors* (1533) and *Prince Edward* (1538) but even more famous is his mural at Whitehall Palace. It was partly destroyed by fire in 1698; the surviving left half shows a domineering Henry VIII, standing with arms akimbo, with his father behind him. The missing second half was copied before the fire did its work so we know that it contained **Jane Seymour** standing in front of **Elizabeth of York**. He also painted portraits of a few foreign princesses including **Anne of Cleves** (1539), which led to King Henry's agreement to wed her. When he saw her in the flesh, however, he was hugely disappointed and ordered an embarrassing annulment of the **marriage**. Fortunately for Holbein, it was Cromwell who received the blame. However, he appeared little in court afterwards and he mostly worked on private commissions.

He saw very little of his wife and children in Basel, although he continued to support them, and probably had at least two mistresses and two illegitimate children in London. Remarkably, very little is known about his views or beliefs as no letters of his have survived. His death at his home in Aldgate was either caused by the plague or an infection and his burial site still remains unknown.

The quality of Holbein's work is such that many have described him as the greatest portrait artist of all time. His paintings showed an incredible eye for detail and realism, not just of people's faces but also of their clothes and ornaments. Moreover, he often included features that gave clues about a character's personality or achievements. The sheer scale and variety of his work is astonishing, too, ranging from oil/chalk/charcoal portraits, murals and book illustrations to jewellery and clothing designs and miniature portraits for lockets that became very fashionable at the time. Without a doubt, Holbein has provided us with a very valuable insight into the lives of the Tudors.

Hooper, John

(c. 1495–1555)

Bishop and **Protestant** martyr.

Almost nothing is known of the first forty years of Hooper's life. He took a degree at Oxford University in 1519 and then he may have joined a monastic order. After the **Dissolution of the Monasteries**, he became the chaplain to Sir Thomas Arundell in Wiltshire. Whilst there, he became a convert to the ideas of Huldrych Zwingli, who preached an extreme form of Protestantism. He decided to spread these ideas to Oxford but the Act of Six **Articles** (1539) forced him to flee to the continent. He spent most of the 1540s in Zurich, where he met likeminded Zwinglists and published some doctrinal works.

After the accession of **Edward VI** in 1547, Hooper returned to England and became chaplain to the king and, later, to the **Duke of Northumberland**. His denouncements helped to imprison bishops **Bonner** and **Gardiner**, for which they would later take their revenge. Hooper's sermons, preached twice daily, were very popular. He often argued in favour of the legality of divorce and the concept of predestination: the belief that good works cannot obtain salvation but that God has already decided who shall and shall not go to Heaven.

After preaching to the king in 1550, he was offered the see of Gloucester but he refused to wear vestments, which he believed smacked of **Catholic**ism. He followed this with criticism of the Privy Council for which he was imprisoned in the Fleet. Uncharacteristically for Hooper, he backed down and became Bishop of Gloucester after agreeing to wear vestments. He was a hard-working bishop who argued vehemently for social justice and decried the practice of **enclosures**. He also made great efforts to improve the standard of his see's clergy when he discovered that over half could not repeat all of the Ten Commandments and some could not even recite the Lord's Prayer.

When the king died in 1553, Hooper actually opposed the coup to put **Lady Jane Grey** on the throne instead of the Catholic Princess **Mary**. Nevertheless, his extreme and outspoken form of Protestantism made him one of the first targets of the new regime. He was quickly thrown into prison and denounced by Bonner and Gardiner, who had just been released from theirs. In February 1555, Hooper was one of the first to be condemned for heresy and burned at the stake in his own diocese of Gloucester. By all accounts, he died very bravely and painfully. The wind was blowing the flames away from him and so he pleaded for more wood to be piled up. After an agonising forty-five minutes, he eventually died.

Hooper's death, like those of other martyrs, furthered the Protestant cause. He was one of the most extreme and uncompromising Protestant reformers in England and his views would later have a strong influence on the **Puritans** in **Elizabeth I**'s reign.

Howard, Catherine

(c. 1524–42)

Fifth wife of King **Henry VIII** and Queen of England
from July 1540 to November 1541.

Catherine Howard was a niece of the powerful **Third Duke of Norfolk** and a cousin of **Anne Boleyn**, Henry VIII's second wife. However, she was born into a poor branch of the family and was her parents' tenth child. When she was four, her mother died and she was sent, along with some of her siblings, to be raised in the household of her grandmother, Agnes Howard. This was common practice at the time although Agnes's household was unusually large (up to a hundred people) and unusually lax, with the older girls often stealing food from the kitchen and having male visitors. The girls also slept in dormitories and shared beds – only the wealthiest people had beds to themselves then. A rudimentary **education** was provided, too, but Catherine, who was described as being vivacious, distractible and giggly, was not interested in academic studies.

At around the age of twelve, possibly influenced by the older girls, she had her first relationship, with Henry Mannox, her music teacher. During the later adultery inquisition, both denied that there had been any sexual intercourse but they admitted that he had touched 'secret parts' of her body.

In around 1538, she started seeing Francis Dereham, a secretary of Agnes Howard. Later, they both admitted that they had consummated this relationship and had even called each other 'husband' and 'wife'. What is not clear is whether or not they became engaged, a fact which would have invalidated any future **marriage** to someone else.

In 1539, her uncle found her a position serving the new queen, **Anne of Cleves**. It had quickly become clear that King Henry would soon discard Anne and so it is likely that Norfolk was hoping his beautiful, young niece would attract the king's attention and thereby win the Howard family much influence in court. The plan worked. Henry was besotted by her looks and youthful energy and Catherine, in turn, was dazzled by the lavish lifestyle at court.

In July 1540, the couple were married by Bishop **Bonner** on the same day as **Thomas Cromwell**'s execution. Interestingly enough, we cannot be certain what Catherine looked like. Some art historians now believe that **Holbein**'s supposed portrait of her was actually just another painting of Anne of Cleves. There is certainly a strong resemblance. Also, we can only guess at the teenager's feelings towards her new, overweight forty-nine-year-old husband. However, the marriage seemed to start well enough. Escaping the plague in London, the new couple embarked on a leisurely progress/honeymoon to York and he showered her with expensive gifts.

Upon their return to London, Catherine's past caught up with her. Archbishop **Cranmer** began to receive reports about her previous relationships, including one with Thomas Culpepper, one of the king's favourites. An eyewitness stated that she had seen Culpepper secretly entering the queen's apartments in the spring of 1541 but both he and Catherine later denied that she committed adultery. The reformist Cranmer, only too keen to remove the conservative, **Catholic** Howard influence from court, presented his findings to the king.

Henry was furious and demanded an inquiry. Mannox denied carnal knowledge, Dereham denied a formal engagement and Culpepper denied her adultery. However, it was clear from the various admissions, including Catherine's, that she had not been chaste when she married Henry. The king felt humiliated and executions followed. In December 1541, Dereham was hanged, drawn and quartered. Culpepper, being a former favourite, was spared that fate by being beheaded. Catherine, herself, although weak with fear, apparently died with dignity. After being led past the impaled heads of her former lovers into the **Tower of London**, she asked for the executioner's block to be placed in her room the night before her death so she could practise laying her neck upon it. She was beheaded on 13 February 1542 on the same spot as Anne Boleyn and then buried near her in the same chapel within the Tower.

The whole affair made King Henry increasingly despondent, temperamental and paranoid. He raged at those around him for deceiving him and mourned the loss of his faithful servant, Cromwell. The Howards were banished from court and Norfolk retreated to his duchy, denying all knowledge of his niece's past. As for Catherine, she has widely been accused of being a foolish and promiscuous girl who only sought glamour and wealth. However, she was the least educated of Henry's wives and the least prepared for the intrigues of court. It is probably fairer to say that her only **crime** was being a naïve, fun-loving teenage girl.

Howard, Charles (Lord Howard of Effingham)

(1536–1624)

Lord Admiral of the English fleet.

Charles Howard was a grandson of the **Second Duke of Norfolk** and a cousin of **Anne Boleyn**. His father, William Howard, had loyally served the Crown as a diplomat, soldier and Lord Admiral for many years. In the 1550s, it seems that Howard served at sea with his father and gained some valuable experience for when he himself later became Admiral.

Upon **Elizabeth I**'s accession, he became a prominent courtier and diplomat who helped to negotiate the end of the **Fourth Anglo-French War**. His **marriage** to Catherine Carey in 1563 undoubtedly helped his career. Carey was a close personal attendant and intimate friend of Elizabeth, who attended the wedding herself. In 1569, Howard helped to suppress the **Northern Rebellion** and, when his father died in 1573, he inherited the title of Lord of Effingham along with its Surrey estates.

Lord Howard of Effingham. (*From* The Royal Navy, a History from the Earliest Times to Present *by W. Laird Clowes, 1897. Based on a 1620 portrait by a workshop of Daniël Mijtens*)

In 1585, he was appointed Lord Admiral. With the outbreak of the **Anglo-Spanish War** in the same year, along with the threat of a Spanish invasion, this position carried much responsibility. There were abler and more popular naval commanders, such as **Drake** and **Hawkins**, who might have been appointed instead but Howard carried the authority which went with his rank. Had the position been given to a mere knight, such as Drake, it would have probably led to jealousy and quarrels amongst the other seamen. Moreover, Howard recognised his shortcomings as a sailor and was keen to frequently meet with his commanders and heed their advice. Indeed, it seems that he and Drake worked very well together.

During the **Spanish Armada** campaign of 1588, Howard showed sensible and cautious leadership and maintained a disciplined fleet during its pursuit up the Channel. He also kept up a regular communication with the queen and government, making constant requests for more supplies, food and pay for his men. Howard showed much compassion for his crews and, in 1590, helped to set up a naval charity known as 'The Chest at Chatham'. One fair criticism that can be levelled at him, however, was his lack of tactical decisiveness at the Battle of Gravelines. Instead of joining the other squadrons in attempting to annihilate the Spanish fleet, he preferred to focus his entire squadron on the capture of booty aboard a single galleon that had become stranded.

In 1596, he co-led, with the **Earl of Essex**, a largely successful attack on Cadiz. The two leaders did fall out over the mission's objectives, though, with Essex wanting to maintain a permanent English presence in the city and the more cautious Howard demanding a strict adherence to Elizabeth's instructions by returning to England. Later that year, Howard was made Earl of Nottingham, much to Essex's chagrin because he was now ranked below him given that Howard was also Lord Admiral. Five years later, it was Howard who led the soldiers that put down Essex's rebellion and, afterwards, he interrogated Essex and sat at his trial.

The death of his wife in February 1603 sent Elizabeth into a depression that may have hastened her own death a few weeks later. The ever-loyal Howard was at her bedside before she died and it was apparently to him that she declared James VI of Scotland as her heir.

Under King James, Howard continued to hold high office and was given important tasks such as helping to negotiate the peace treaty with Spain in 1604. However, he retained the position of Lord Admiral for too long as he lacked the energy or vision to battle with the endemic corruption within his offices. He was finally bought out from his position in 1619, at the age of eighty-three and retired on a pension of £1,000/year (equivalent of £130,000 in 2024).

Howard, Henry (Earl of Surrey)

(1517–47)

Soldier and poet.

Henry Howard was the eldest son of the **Third Duke of Norfolk** and Elizabeth Stafford and became Earl of Surrey upon his grandfather's death in 1524. From the age of twelve, he was brought up at Windsor with **Henry Fitzroy**, the illegitimate son of **Henry VIII** and, being a member of England's most powerful noble family, he steadily rose in prominence. In 1530, plans were put forward for his **marriage** to the king's daughter, **Mary**, but these were discarded and he married Frances de Vere instead (1532). In the same year, he accompanied the king and his cousin, **Anne Boleyn**, on a diplomatic mission to France and, four years later, he assisted his father in quashing the **Pilgrimage of Grace**.

Soon after, the **Seymour**s became pre-eminent at court and accused Howard, ironically, of conspiring with the rebels. He was placed under arrest at Windsor but the accusations were patently false and he was soon released. Despite his family's fall from grace following the execution of his cousin, **Catherine Howard**, Howard was given military responsibility during the **Third Anglo-French War**. He fought bravely, was wounded and made commander of the garrison at Boulogne.

It was during this period, however, that he increasingly revealed his reckless and outspoken nature. Twice, he was incarcerated at Fleet Prison. First, for assaulting a courtier and, second, for riotous behaviour and smashing windows in London. Like his father he despised his 'low-born' rivals such as **Thomas Cromwell** and the Seymours but, unlike his father, he could not prevent himself from verbally abusing them in public.

In 1546, he went too far. He openly discussed his opinion that his father was the obvious choice to be Lord Protector for the future **Edward VI** upon the king's death. Discussion of such a topic was dangerous enough but then, out of foolish pride, he started to display the arms of Edward the Confessor, a Howard ancestor, upon his own coat of arms. It did not take much persuasion from the Seymours to convince an increasingly paranoid king that the Howards were plotting treason. Their **Catholic** faith also led to accusations that they planned a return to papal supremacy. Along with his despairing father, he was arrested and imprisoned in the **Tower of London**. During the subsequent investigation, his sister revealed that Howard had asked her to seduce the king in order to gain influence. In January 1547, despite the lack of any clear evidence, he was beheaded for high treason.

Henry Howard, Earl of Surrey. (*Artist: Hans Holbein, c. 1533*)

If that was the end of the story, then Henry Howard would probably have gone down in the history books as a foolish footnote. However, he was also a leading English **renaissance** poet. Along with Sir Thomas Wyatt, he was the first English poet to write in the sonnet form and the first to publish blank verse in iambic pentameter, both of which **Shakespeare** later used. His poetry, written during his various imprisonments, was first published in 1557 and became very popular during the reign of **Elizabeth I**.

Howard, Thomas (Second Duke of Norfolk)

(1443–1524)

Soldier and statesman.

Thomas Howard was born in Suffolk and educated at Thetford Grammar School. During the **Wars of the Roses**, his father, Sir John Howard, was a loyal supporter of the Yorkist king, Edward IV and the young Howard served as a henchman for the king. In 1471, he was badly wounded at the Battle of Barnet but he recovered and was later knighted for his services.

Upon Edward IV's death in 1483, Howard and his father transferred their loyalty to the former king's brother, Richard III, and carried out duties at his coronation. In return, Howard was created Earl of Surrey and his father became the Duke of Norfolk. They both fought on the Yorkist side at the **Battle of Bosworth Field** (1485), where Howard was wounded again and his father was killed. The new, Lancastrian king, **Henry VII**, imprisoned him in the **Tower of London** for the next three years and stripped him of his lands.

During the **Lambert Simnel** rebellion in 1487, Howard was apparently offered a chance to escape but, for some reason, refused to accept. Henry saw this as a sign of his loyalty, released him and restored him to the earldom of Surrey. In the 1490s he served as Lieutenant-General of the North. In this role, he effectively dealt with a Scottish invasion and humanely quelled a revolt in Yorkshire. In 1501, he joined the king's privy council and, along with **William Warham** and **Richard Foxe**, became Henry's chief advisor. He headed some important diplomatic missions too such as the negotiation of a **marriage** treaty between Princess **Mary** and Prince Charles of Castile and was appointed an executor of the king's will.

Howard was already sixty-six when **Henry VIII** acceded to the throne and was automatically the most senior statesman on the new king's privy council. He encouraged the new king to maintain his father's policies of promoting peace abroad and building up strength at home. However, Henry VIII was nothing like his father and he turned to **Thomas Wolsey** to organise a war against France. By 1512, Wolsey had become the king's chief advisor, much to Howard's bitterness; the elder statesman saw him as an upstart who would lead Henry down the wrong path.

During the **First Anglo-French War**, Howard was left behind to guard against an attack by France's ally – Scotland. The Scots duly invaded and Howard won a landmark battle at **Flodden** in 1513 (at the age of seventy!). The king showed his gratitude by creating him **Second Duke of Norfolk** and his son, also called **Thomas Howard**, who had also fought at Flodden, became the new Earl of Surrey. In addition, both received new lands along with their revenues and Howard's coat of arms now included the lion of Scotland pierced through the mouth with an arrow.

Howard continued to loyally serve the king in his old age. It was he, for instance, who led his own men into London to suppress the **Evil May Day** riots in 1517. He even faithfully carried out commands with which he disagreed such as arranging the marriage of the king's sister, Mary, to the king of France. Unbelievably to us, he was asked in 1521 to preside over the treason trial of his oldest friend, the Duke of Buckingham, who was also his daughter-in-law's father. Even more unbelievably, he accepted, especially when you consider that treason trials were a foregone conclusion in those times. It is said that he shed copious tears as he passed a sentence of death.

He retired from his public duties two years later and died at Framlingham castle at the age of eighty. Thomas Howard was a remarkable figure who put duty to the Crown above all else. His descendants include **Anne Boleyn** (granddaughter) and, through her, **Elizabeth I**, and it was in the household of his second wife, Agnes, that another granddaughter, **Catherine Howard**, was raised. Most impressive of all, perhaps, is the fact that he managed to loyally serve four different monarchs and went from henchman to the most widely admired and respected man in the realm.

Howard, Thomas (Third Duke of Norfolk)

(1473–1554)

Soldier and statesman.

Thomas Howard was the eldest son of the **Second Duke of Norfolk** and his first wife, Elizabeth Tilney. His father fought on the losing side at the **Battle of Bosworth Field** and was subsequently imprisoned in the **Tower of London** for three years. During this time, Howard was placed as a page in the household of **Henry VII**, where he was undoubtedly taught subservience to the new dynasty, which may have helped persuade his father to remain loyal.

In 1495, he married Anne of York, daughter of Edward IV and younger sister to **Elizabeth of York**, the king's wife. None of their four children reached adulthood, though, and she died in 1511. Two years later he married Lady

Elizabeth Stafford (despite having five children, this proved to be an unhappy **marriage**. He took a mistress, she claimed he was physically violent and they eventually separated). In the 1490s he showed his loyalty and military ability by assisting in quelling the **Cornish Rebellion** and dealing with Scottish incursions in the north.

Under the new king, **Henry VIII**, Howard was appointed Lord Admiral upon the death of his elder brother and, in 1513, ably assisted his father in defeating a larger Scottish army at **Flodden**. As a result, he was given the earldom of Surrey while his father was promoted to Duke of Norfolk. In 1520, he was appointed Lord Lieutenant of **Ireland** and given the almost impossible task of bringing it under the Crown's authority. He advised a full military conquest but Henry had his eyes set on greater glories on the continent. Later, he was recalled to lead naval operations during the **Second Anglo-French War**. His under-resourced fleet managed to raid the French coast but achieved little else.

Upon the death of his father in 1524, he became Duke of Norfolk. Despite now being the most prominent noble in the realm, he had little influence compared to **Thomas Wolsey**, whom he despised as a low-born upstart. This all changed in the late 1520s when King Henry started his relationship with Howard's niece, **Anne Boleyn**. Along with the **Duke of Suffolk** and the Boleyn family, Howard managed to manufacture Wolsey's downfall.

The early 1530s represent the high-tide mark for Howard's fortunes. He became a chief advisor to the king and, despite quarrels with his combative niece, he was given important diplomatic missions, more titles and a large grant of monastic land in East Anglia. His daughter, Mary, even married **Henry Fitzroy**, the king's illegitimate son. For most of that decade, however, the real power lay with **Thomas Cromwell**, another 'new man' whom Howard despised. He was not helped by the Boleyns' fall from power in 1536 and he may have presided over Anne's trial in order to prove his loyalty to Henry.

Howard represented the head of the conservative, landed, **Catholic** faction at court which disliked the **Protestant** reform party led by Cromwell, Archbishop **Cranmer** and the **Seymours**. Like a pendulum, their fortunes would first swing one way and then the other. The Six **Articles** of 1539 were promoted by Howard and, after the debacle of the king's marriage to **Anne of Cleves**, it was Howard who helped persuade Henry to arrest and execute Cromwell. In 1541, though, he had to flee to Norfolk and apologise for the pre-marital behaviour of his niece, **Catherine Howard**, the king's fifth wife.

His military prowess, though, was required during the **Third Anglo-French War** and he was appointed Lieutenant-General of the army in France. He was, however, severely rebuked by Henry for giving up the siege of a French city and retreating to Calais. At the same time, his influence in court was being eroded by the Seymours.

In 1546, an increasingly erratic and paranoid king was outraged when Howard's son, **Henry Howard**, added the arms of Edward the Confessor upon his own coat of arms. Technically, this was allowed as the Howards were descendants of the eleventh-century king. However, King Henry saw this as an attempt to belittle his own ancestry and suspected the Howards of having plans to usurp the crown from his son, the future **Edward VI**, and reverse the break with Rome. In December, both Howard and his son were arrested and sent to the Tower. Henry was beheaded in January 1547 but Howard, himself, was lucky. On the morning of his execution, the king died and he was granted a reprieve.

He was kept in the Tower for the duration of Edward VI's reign whilst his estates were distributed to supporters of the new regime. Upon the Catholic, **Mary I**'s accession in 1553, he was released, his titles and lands were restored to him and he regained his place on the privy council. The following year, at the age of eighty, Howard provided his last service to the Crown by leading royal forces against **Wyatt's Rebellion**. Several months later, after a prolonged illness, he died in Norfolk and was interred in the family church in Framlingham beside his first wife.

Howard, Thomas (Fourth Duke of Norfolk)

(1536–72)

Nobleman and politician.

Thomas Howard was the son of **Henry Howard**, Earl of Surrey and Lady Frances de Vere and grandson of **Thomas Howard, the Third Duke of Norfolk**. When he was ten, his father was executed for high treason by **Henry VIII** and he and his siblings were sent to Reigate Castle to be raised by his aunt, Mary Howard. Along with his cousin once removed, **Charles Howard**, they were tutored by John Foxe who later became famous for writing the ***Book of Martyrs***. Although Foxe was a **Protestant**, Howard, like the rest of his family, remained a **Catholic** but astutely learned to be discreet about his religious views during the tumultuous years of the English **Reformation**.

When **Mary I** became queen in 1553, his grandfather was released from captivity and soon replaced Foxe with a Catholic tutor. Howard was one of those who escorted Mary to her coronation and, in the following year, was appointed as a gentleman of the Chamber of Prince Philip of Spain, the queen's new husband.

Soon after, his grandfather died and Howard inherited the dukedom of Norfolk along with its vast estates and income and, in 1555, he married Mary

Fitzalan but she died soon after giving birth at the age of seventeen. In total, Howard was to marry three times with each union bringing him more lands and power.

Being the most senior peer in the realm, he organised the coronation of **Elizabeth I** in 1559. His position was further enhanced by the fact that he and the new queen were second cousins who both shared the same great-grandfather – **Thomas Howard, Second Duke of Norfolk**. Like his ancestors, he bore the Howard superiority complex: he looked down on the 'new men' such as **William Cecil** and was jealous of Elizabeth's favourite, **Robert Dudley**, who came from an 'inferior' Protestant family. On one occasion, they quarrelled in front of the queen, who ordered them to make amends.

In 1568, Howard's fortunes were irrevocably altered by the arrival of **Mary, Queen of Scots**. Mary had fled from Scotland after an uprising largely caused by her **marriage** to the suspected murderer of her second husband. This was a major problem for Queen Elizabeth – Mary was a Catholic and her cousin once removed and, as such, could be a figurehead for any attempt to remove her from the throne. Indeed, in the following year, the **Northern Rebellion** attempted exactly this but was crushed.

Howard now came under extreme suspicion. Although nominally a Protestant, he came from a Catholic family and it became known that he had been offered the chance to marry Mary. The idea appealed to his vanity. In addition, he felt it would provide the solution to the question of who would succeed Elizabeth, who was looking increasingly likely not to marry, let alone have children. He backed out at the last moment though and appealed to the northern lords to end the revolt. This, however, did not prevent him from being locked up in the **Tower of London**. He pleaded his innocence and, without sufficient evidence, he was released the following year but ordered to remain at his London home.

Nevertheless, he continued to correspond with Mary who, it seems, was still keen to marry him. It appears certain that, to some degree at least, he was involved in the **Ridolfi Plot** of 1571, which aimed to remove Elizabeth. Again, he was imprisoned. This time, the evidence convinced a court that he was guilty and he was sentenced to death for high treason. Elizabeth, however, was very reluctant to execute a relative and her highest-ranking noble, despite the mounting pressure from Dudley, Cecil and her other advisors. Eventually, she bowed to pressure from **Parliament**, which petitioned for the deaths of both Mary and Howard; in order to save Mary, the queen finally signed Howard's death warrant.

A new scaffold had to be built on Tower Hill as the old one had not been used for sixteen years. In his final speech, he admitted his guilt but declared himself a loyal subject and denied that he was a Catholic. After an hour passed, he was ordered to finish speaking and lay his neck upon the block. Howard's head was severed with a single blow and he was buried in the Tower's chapel.

His lands and titles were forfeit and the great dukedom was not restored until four generations later when another Thomas Howard became the Fifth Duke of Norfolk in 1660.

Humanism

A philosophy that dominated modern thinkers in the sixteenth century.

Humanism was an intellectual movement founded in Italy in the late fourteenth century and brought about by a renewed interest in the scholars of Ancient Greece and Rome. The movement received a boost in the mid-fifteenth century when the Turks captured Constantinople, causing many Byzantine scholars to flee west, bringing with them many ancient Greek manuscripts from their libraries. Soon after, the development of the printing press allowed humanist ideas to spread to northern Europe more easily.

Whilst the medieval Church focused on theological dogma and its control of all knowledge, humanists believed that it was more important to study what it meant to be human. The ancients, such as Cicero, had not been controlled by an all-powerful Church. Instead, they had discussed wide-ranging concepts such human virtue, rhetoric, moral philosophy, history, poetry and grammar. These subjects were known as 'humanities', which led to the term humanism. Humanists believed that, by studying the humanities, people could lead better lives and make a more positive contribution to society. For this purpose, **education** needed to be provided for all and include the study of Latin so that people could read the works of ancient Romans for themselves.

Most humanists were Christians who believed that God had given humans free will and should make the most of it instead of blindly following a religious doctrine. They believed in papal authority, too, but saw an urgent need for the Roman **Catholic** Church to be reformed. Ironically, they therefore contributed to the outbreak of the **Reformation** early in the sixteenth century.

The 'father' of humanism in northern Europe was Desiderius Erasmus from the Netherlands. At first, he and Martin Luther, whose actions sparked the Reformation, had much to agree on. For example, Erasmus defended Luther's attack on indulgences – the Church's practice of selling people pardons for their sins. Later, however, they fell out. Erasmus disagreed with Luther's belief that faith alone, rather than good deeds, would bring salvation and he did not want to see a schism within the Church. Luther, in turn, called Erasmus a traitor whose beliefs in reform were too shallow.

Erasmus published many books including the hugely popular *On Copia* (1512), which taught students how to argue and revise texts, and produced

Desiderius Erasmus. (*Artist: Franz Huys, after a design by Hans Holbein, 1601. Rijksmuseum*)

guides on how to establish schools along with appropriate syllabuses. Erasmian thought became very popular with many scholars in England, both Catholic and **Protestant**, such as **Thomas More, John Colet, Thomas Cranmer** and **John**

Fisher. Henry VIII was an intellectual who was attracted to humanism but that did not stop him executing some humanists. **Elizabeth I** received an excellent humanist education and it was chiefly during her reign that its ideas flourished.

Humanism had a profound effect on England, just as it did elsewhere. As it trickled down from the educated elite, it instilled a belief in individuality, a questioning of received wisdom and a thirst for knowledge. It allowed for the future blossoming of the arts, literature and science and, ultimately, it led to the founding of a more democratic society.

I

Ireland

In the latter half of the twelfth century, the island of Ireland had been conquered, firstly by Norman lords and then by the English king, Henry II. The conquest had been sanctioned by the Pope, in order to bring the island under full papal control, and the lords and Irish chiefs had sworn fealty to the English king.

The descendants of the Norman lords (the Anglo-Irish) had gradually intermarried with the Irish and adopted many Gaelic laws and customs so that, by 1485, the area of direct English control had shrunk to a small area around Dublin called the Pale, which was protected by a ditch and earthworks. 'Beyond the Pale' were considered dangerous lands full of barbarous, wild natives where internecine border wars and cattle rustling predominated. Even within the Pale, English control was nominal as it was administered by the Anglo-Irish Earl of Kildare, who was theoretically the English king's representative in Ireland.

Matters may well have continued in this vein for many more decades. However, the arrival of the Tudors in 1485 was to have a dramatic effect on the island. The Irish lords had generally favoured the Yorkists during the **Wars of the Roses**. They therefore supported **Lambert Simnel**'s rebellion, crowned him 'Edward VI' in Dublin and even minted coins in the new king's name. The arrival of the even more dangerous pretender, **Perkin Warbeck**, in the 1490s forced **Henry VII** into action and he sent Sir Edward Poynings to replace Kildare and enforce direct control. He implemented 'Poynings Laws', which stated that the Dublin parliament could only issue laws with permission from London and that all laws from England's **parliament** were valid in Ireland. After a few years, the administrative costs of implementing direct control were considered too expensive by Henry and Kildare was reinstated.

Matters became more serious after England's break with Rome. **Henry VIII** wanted to extend royal supremacy to Ireland and avoid it being used by enemy powers such as France and Spain. Therefore, in the 1540s, the policy of 'surrender and regrant' was implemented in order to bring Ireland firmly within England's orbit. Henry was made King of Ireland and the Gaelic chiefs and Anglo-Irish lords were offered English titles, royal protection and seats in the Dublin Parliament if they surrendered their lands to the king who would then regrant them back if they swore loyalty to the English Crown. They were also expected to follow English laws and customs, speak English, wear English costume and accept royal supremacy over the Church. Several Irish chiefs and lords saw political advantage to be gained over hostile neighbours and signed up to this. If the English plan was to sow more discord within Ireland, then it worked.

Eventually, this policy might have succeeded as more and more chiefs may have seen the need for royal protection. However, two more elements were added to the intricate mix, which resulted in the slaughter and destruction that was to follow.

One was religion. Henry VIII's **dissolution of the** Irish **monasteries** was not popular although many Irish lords who accepted 'surrender and regrant' benefitted from the sale of monastic land. In addition, attempts to enforce a **Protestant** Church upon a **Catholic** people in the reigns of **Edward VI** and

Iryshe.	Latten.	Englishe,
Cones ta tu.	Quomodo habes.	How doe you.
Taim go maih.	Bene sum.	I am well,
Go ro maih agad.	Habeo gratias.	I thancke you.
In eol duit gealag do labairt.	Possis ne hibernice loqui.	Cann you speake Iryshe
Abair laidean.	Dic latine.	Speake Latten
Dia le Banriogan Sasana	Deus adiuuat Reginā Angliæ	God saue the Queene off Englande:

Elizabeth I's primer on Irish. Presented to the queen as an aid for understanding Irish. (*Author: Sir Christopher Nugent, c. 1564. Wikimedia Commons*)

Elizabeth I caused much resentment. The second element was the policy of plantations whereby areas of land were colonised by English settlers. This was another attempt to pacify the island but it only led to more chiefs uniting against the hated English.

Inevitably, rebellions broke out – the Desmond uprisings of 1569–73 and 1579–83 in Munster were provoked by plantations and attempts to implement English laws and customs. English commanders, such as **Humphrey Gilbert** and **Walter Ralegh**, were brutal in their suppression of the revolts. A scorched earth policy was adopted and many Irish non-combatants were murdered. The resulting famine was estimated to have killed 30,000 people in six months of 1582 alone.

English incursions into Ulster created a far more serious conflict – **Tyrone's Rebellion** (1594–1603) – when the Earl of Tyrone attempted to unify the whole island and drive out the English. Due to the on-going **Anglo-Spanish War**, Queen Elizabeth could ill-afford to allow Ireland to become a base for Spanish forces and so immense resources were expended in attempts to crush the revolt. Eventually, it was **Lord Mountjoy**'s successful military strategy and defeat of a Spanish landing that led to Tyrone's surrender.

Afterwards, plantations could spread more easily throughout the island, with Ulster particularly targeted by Scottish settlers. For the first time, the whole of Ireland was under centralised government control but at what cost? Despite the majority clinging on to their Catholic faith, the Irish were to have most of their laws, customs and language replaced and the victims of the violence could probably be numbered in the hundreds of thousands. Even harder to measure was the simmering resentment that would flare up into more violence over the following centuries.

J

Jesuits

Jesuits were members of the Society of Jesus, a religious order that was established by the Spaniard, Ignatius of Loyola. Ignatius had been a soldier who experienced a spiritual conversion whilst recovering from a wound. He compiled his insights into a prayer manual, known as 'Spiritual Exercises', which intended to help people seek the will of God. Ignatius founded the order with the aim of serving the Roman **Catholic** Church wherever it needed the most help and it was given the Pope's blessing in 1540.

Ignatius also saw the need to modernise the Church and so he banned many medieval practices from the order, such as regular penance and fasting, and introduced a highly centralised and hierarchical organisation. Its membership increased rapidly as it devoted itself to the education of priests and missionary work around the world. In Ignatius's own lifetime, Jesuits were working in India, China, South America and the Holy Land. The order also established charities to help the poor, sick, prisoners and former prostitutes.

Jesuit priests spearheaded the Counter-**Reformation** in an attempt to reverse the spread of **Protestant**ism and they played an important part in winning back several areas of Europe, such as Poland, Lithuania and southern Germany. It was England, however, that proved to be the most difficult and dangerous assignment for them. In 1570, the Pope excommunicated the Protestant queen, **Elizabeth I** which, in effect, gave English Catholics permission to disobey her. The vast majority remained loyal but, following the **Northern Rebellion** (1569), the government became more alert and Elizabeth's principal secretary, **Francis Walsingham**, created a spy network to seek out any threats. Catholics became increasingly persecuted – non-attendance of church services was fined and even the ownership of rosary beads and crucifixes was banned. In 1584, **Parliament** passed the Jesuits Act, which ordered Jesuits to leave the country or face the penalties of high treason. Nearly a hundred Jesuits were to be executed in England over the next century.

The dangers, however, did not prevent many brave priests from attempting to help their fellow Catholics in England. After being trained at the college at Douai (founded by **William Allen**), they were smuggled onto the English coast where they would be met and led to the house of a sympathiser. Under disguise, they would then go from one safe house to another providing spiritual succour to their hosts and always trying to keep one step ahead of the authorities. There is even some evidence that **William Byrd** and **William Shakespeare** may have sheltered Jesuits. Some of the larger Catholic homes created secretive priest holes where a Jesuit could hide in case Walsingham's agents received a tip-off and raided the property.

Many were caught, however, such as **Edmund Campion**. Usually tortured, in order to recant their faith or reveal the locations of other priests, they were then hanged, drawn and quartered. Some survived though. The most famous example was **Father Gerard**, who not only undertook two missions to England but also managed to survive imprisonment and torture in the **Tower of London**.

There is no doubting the courage and faith of these Jesuit priests. The Tudor propaganda machine painted them as dangerous spies who wanted to topple the government but the vast majority of them merely sought to support Catholics living in a Protestant realm.

K

Kett's Rebellion

(July–August 1549)

A serious uprising in the reign of **Edward VI**.

The disturbances started at Wymondham, ten miles south-west of Norwich on 8 July 1549, when several people started to tear down fences and hedges which had recently been put up to enclose land for sheep grazing. **Enclosures** had become increasingly popular with landowners due to the higher demand for English wool on the continent, which meant higher prices. Unfortunately, the land they enclosed was formerly common land and so the 'commoners' now had very little of their own for farming. On top of this, there had been a poor harvest and prices were rising, partly due to the **debasement** of the coinage.

One of their first targets was Robert Kett, a wealthy landowner about fifty-seven years of age. Kett actually agreed with their demands, helped to tear down his own fences and led them off to Norwich. It is quite possible that he believed he was working for the government as the Lord Protector, the **Duke of Somerset**, had sympathised with the plight of the rural poor and had ordered an investigation into illegal enclosures.

Many local villagers joined Kett and proceeded to set up camp on Mousehold Heath, an area of land overlooking Norwich. They were soon joined by many labourers from the city itself until the throng numbered around 16,000, which made it bigger than Norwich (**population**, 12,000). The camp became well organised: Kett set up a representative council which heard cases, dealt out justice and sent out warrants to obtain food supplies and weapons. The council then created a list of twenty-nine grievances and sent it to Somerset. The grievances were largely economic and concerned enclosures and price increases. However, they also included complaints about corrupt local government and priests who could not do their jobs properly.

The government was in a difficult position. Many of its best troops were tied down in Devon in response to the **Prayer Book Rebellion** so its response was to offer a general pardon if the rebels dispersed. Kett rejected the offer on the grounds that they were not rebels and therefore could not be pardoned. Then, on 22 July, his men stormed Norwich and captured it. Soon after, they defeated a small royal force and now controlled England's second largest city (due to the buoyant cloth trade) and the area around it. News of this success sparked off further disturbances and riots throughout East Anglia. For the government, the situation was starting to get seriously out of control.

A larger force of 14,000 men was sent led by the experienced **John Dudley**, the Earl of Warwick. After entering the city, there followed some vicious street battles and it was only after the arrival of 1,400 German mercenaries that Dudley managed to eject the rebels and gain full control of Norwich. Fearing encirclement and starvation, Kett then led his men off Mousehold Heath on 27 August but, out in the open and without cavalry, they were routed and about 3,000 were slaughtered. Kett was captured the following night and, after being found guilty of treason, was hanged in chains from the walls of Norwich castle and allowed to starve to death.

Kett's rebellion is significant for several reasons. It added to the growing feeling that Somerset was too weak and hastened his downfall. It showed how much the new **Protestant** faith had developed in East Anglia (some demands were anti-Catholic in nature). It slowed the growth of enclosures – when Dudley became Lord Protector he prosecuted illegal enclosures. It was also the first major class struggle since the Peasants' Revolt of 1381. Around Norfolk today, Kett is seen as a champion of social freedom and justice for the poor.

L

Latimer, Hugh

(c. 1485–1555)

Bishop and martyr.

Latimer was brought up on a small farm in Leicestershire. Not much is known of his early life other than he began learning Latin at the age of four. At fourteen, he was sent to Cambridge University, studied divinity and was ordained a priest in 1515.

In the early 1520s he railed against the **Protestant** ideas that were emerging and he later described himself as 'an obstinate papist'. However, it was whilst he was arguing against a group of reformists that he experienced a conversion and became a Protestant himself. He and like-minded theologians such as **Ridley**, **Parker** and **Tyndale** would often meet at the White Horse tavern in Cambridge to discuss the ideas of Martin Luther. They called it 'Little Germany' and referred to themselves as the 'Germans'. During this time, he began to harbour doubts about transubstantiation, started to argue that the Bible should be translated into English and that images should be removed from churches.

These were dangerous ideas at the time and Latimer began to arouse the interest of the authorities who tried to ban him from preaching. Cardinal

Wolsey, himself, rebuked him and gave him an official warning and later, **Thomas More** called him a heretic. His arguments in favour of annulling **Henry VIII**'s marriage to **Catherine of Aragon** gave him royal protection, however, and in 1535 he was given the bishopric of Worcester.

Hugh Latimer. (*Artist: unknown, c. 1530. New Catholic Encyclopaedia Vol. VI*)

His sermons became increasingly popular – he had an eloquent and witty, yet coarse, style of speaking and, in his tirades against clerical abuses, he was not afraid of mocking those in high office. Latimer also called for much greater support for the poor and he once said, 'wherever you observe persecution, there is more than a possibility that truth lies on the persecuted side'. Denying the presence of purgatory, he argued that the Church should spend more time giving alms than praying for the dead. Such speeches would cause such joyous uproars that church pews sometimes became damaged.

By 1536, he had become so prominent that, during the **Pilgrimage of Grace**, it was the removal of him and Archbishop **Cranmer** that the rebels demanded. However, King Henry decided that reform had gone too far and, when Latimer refused to accept the Six **Articles** of 1539, he fell from favour and resigned his see. He remained in disgrace for the remainder of the king's reign and even ended up in the **Tower** in 1546.

Upon **Edward VI**'s accession the following year, he was released and soon began working with Cranmer to fully reform the Church. His sermons became ever more aggressive against the conservative clergy, supportive of the downtrodden and he denounced **enclosures** as being immoral. He also demanded the bastardisation of the **Catholic** Princess **Mary** in order to prevent her from becoming queen.

In 1550, he retired and went back to live in the village of his birth. However, when a vindictive Mary became queen three years later, Latimer was one of the first to be arrested and charged with heresy. At his trial in Oxford, he refused to recant but violently attacked the Catholic Church instead. On 16 October 1555, he and Nicholas Ridley were led to a stake to be burned alive. As the flames started to rise, Latimer heard his friend groaning in pain and reportedly uttered the famous words, 'Be of good comfort, Master Ridley, and play the man. We shall this day light such a candle by God's grace, in England, that I trust shall never be put out.' Latimer's death was relatively quick as he was asphyxiated by the smoke.

Hugh Latimer was one of the driving forces of the English **Reformation**. Full of vitality and fervour, he was able to convince many that religious change would improve their well-being. In effect, he brought Protestantism to the masses. Possibly, his uncompromising views could partly be blamed for increasing the bitter religious divide within the country and maybe he could have served his convictions better by working with, rather than against, those whom he opposed. However, there is no doubt, that the manner of his death and its subsequent publicity in the ***Book of Martyrs*** was a huge boost to the Protestant cause.

M

Margaret, Queen of Scots

(1489–1541)

Sister of **Henry VIII** and wife of James IV of Scotland.

Margaret was the eldest daughter of **Henry VII** and **Elizabeth of York** and named after her paternal grandmother, **Margaret Beaufort**. She was largely brought up, with her siblings, at Eltham Palace but would often travel to Westminster and Windsor to see her parents. From a young age, she showed little interest in academic studies but started her lifelong passion for beautiful clothes, dancing and music. Like her younger brother, Henry, she had an energetic and sociable nature combined with a tendency to stubbornness.

Before she was six, she was placed on the European **marriage** market. It was Scotland, however, that particularly interested her father. The pretender, **Perkin Warbeck**, was stirring up England's northern neighbour and so, in 1502, Henry eventually managed to arrange a marriage treaty with the Scots' king, James IV, known as the Treaty of Perpetual Peace – the first peace deal between the two countries for 170 years. The following year, the thriteen-year-old Margaret was married by proxy to the twenty-nine-year-old James and henceforth became known as Margaret, Queen of Scots.

From 1507, Margaret became pregnant six times in six years but only one child survived infancy – the future James V. Her circumstances were to change dramatically after her brother became Henry VIII of England. Far more bellicose than his father, Henry soon went to war against France and James IV, already angry about not receiving the full dowry since his marriage, decided to invoke the Auld Alliance with France and invade England. Margaret tried to dissuade him but it was in vain. The resulting **Battle of Flodden** (1513) was a disaster for Scotland and the king was killed.

In his will, James had declared that Margaret should be regent of Scotland until his son came of age, so long as she remained unmarried. The Scottish court was now divided into pro-English and pro-French factions. Margaret was the sister of Scotland's enemy and she made her position completely untenable when she secretly married the powerful Earl of Angus in 1514. This alienated most of the other nobles and lost her the position of regent, which now went to the pro-French Duke of Albany. After being forced to surrender her son to Albany's care, Margaret absconded to England in 1515 where she gave birth to her only child by Angus – Margaret. Much later, this Margaret was to become the mother of Lord Darnley, who would marry his cousin, the daughter of James V – **Mary, Queen of Scots**.

After another Anglo-Scottish peace agreement, Margaret returned to Scotland and was reunited with her son. The following years were chaotic: Margaret discovered her husband's infidelities and a power struggle between the two ensued (Albany had returned to France). In 1527, she managed to get a papal annulment of their marriage much to her brother's disapproval (ironically!). Margaret wanted to draw England and Scotland closer together but she was not helped by her brother's support for the unpopular Angus or her own decision to marry Henry Stewart and raise him to a position of power.

When James became king in his own right in 1528, Margaret and Stewart were his principal advisors. Margaret tried to arrange a grand meeting between James and Henry and hoped for a marriage between her son and Henry's daughter, **Mary**, but internal opposition thwarted these plans. In fact, her influence seriously waned when James accused her of giving away secrets to the English. Worse still, she discovered her third husband's infidelities and demanded another annulment but this was blocked by her own son. Even an attempt to flee the country failed and she was brought back to court with her remaining authority much diminished.

Margaret stated that she was tired of Scotland but there was little she could do. In her later years, however, she did reconcile with Stewart and became friends with her daughter-in-law, Mary of Guise. In 1541, she died at Methven Castle after suffering a massive stroke.

One cannot help but feel sympathy for Margaret and there are some uncanny parallels between her and her granddaughter, Mary. Both were queens in a distrusting, foreign land. Both had to fight for their positions in a male chauvinistic court. Both suffered three unhappy marriages that created further problems.

Marlowe, Christopher

(1564–93)

Playwright and poet.

The life of Christopher Marlowe is shrouded in mystery and the only available evidence lies in a few official documents and legal records. Trying to separate fact from fiction is no easy task.

Firstly, here are the facts as we know them. Marlowe was born in Canterbury, two months before **William Shakespeare**, and his father was a well-to-do shoemaker. At sixteen he attended Cambridge University with the expectation that he would join the clergy. However, he turned to writing and it was as a poet that he first made his name. His controversial translation of Ovid's *Amores* was considered too salacious and led to Archbishop **Whitgift** ordering its copies to be burned. However, the epic *Hero and Leander* became very popular.

After moving to London in 1587, Marlowe began to write the plays that made him famous. Most notable were: *Dido, Queen of Carthage, Tamburlaine the Great, The Famous Tragedy of the Rich Jew of Malta, The Troublesome Reign of Edward II* and most famous of all, perhaps, *The Tragical History of Dr. Faustus* – based on a German legend about a doctor-turned-wizard who sold his soul to the Devil in exchange for knowledge and power. *Tamburlaine* was significant as it was the first play that used blank verse (not rhyming and usually in iambic pentameter; first used by **Henry Howard** in his poetry). Marlowe's plays became a hit: they were freshly edgy, exciting, violent, energetic and employed jaw-dropping special effects. In one production of *Tamburlaine*, a pregnant woman and her child were accidentally killed by a gunshot from the stage. He also hired Edward Alleyn as his lead actor – a large man with a dominating stage presence.

Marlowe seems to have had a volatile temper which often got him into trouble. In 1589, he was involved in the fatal death of a poet, Thomas Watson, and imprisoned for two weeks. In 1592, he was arrested for street brawling.

Everything else about Marlowe is based on various degrees of conjecture. The most likely of the stories that surround him is that he was a government spy working for **Francis Walsingham, Elizabeth I**'s principal secretary. It appears that, in 1587, whilst he was at university, he visited the **Jesuit** college in Rheims. The university, fearing that he was going to train as a **Catholic** priest refused to issue him with his degree. The Privy Council, no less, intervened and provided assurances of his 'good service' and the minutes of one of its meetings state that he was 'in matters touching the benefit of this country'. At the same time, he started to spend far more on food and drink than he could afford. Was he benefiting from a secondary income?

During his life, Marlowe was accused of being an atheist who was helping Catholics in the Netherlands. It was more likely, though, that this was merely a cover he used in his work for the government. He was also accused of being a homosexual – a capital offence in Tudor times. Other than portraying the gay king in *Edward II* in a sympathetic way, there is no evidence of this.

The biggest mystery of all, perhaps, surrounds his death. In May 1593, Marlowe had been accused of creating leaflets in order to stir up hatred against **Protestant** Dutch immigrants. Then, on 30 May, he was killed after feasting with colleagues in a tavern in Deptford. The official enquiry stated that he had got into an argument over the payment of the bill and had wounded Ingram Frizer with his knife. Frizer had retaliated and inadvertently killed Marlowe with a stab wound to the head. However, this was based on the eyewitness accounts provided by Frizer and his associates – all consummate liars and low-level criminals who had recently carried out dirty work for the government. This has led to many questions. Was he murdered on the orders of **Walter Ralegh**, who feared he was going to reveal his supposed atheism? Was he murdered on the orders of the government because he had become too much of a loose cannon who knew too many official secrets? Was he murdered on the orders of his patron's wife, jealous of her husband's supposed homosexual relationship with Marlowe? And the most outlandish – did he fake his death and continue working under the pseudonym 'William Shakespeare'? The truth is unlikely to ever be known.

Whatever his private life, Marlowe achieved a great deal in a very short career and transformed English theatre. Shakespeare was inspired by much of his work and refined it to create some of his greatest plays. Marlowe's work can be seen in *The Merchant of Venice* (Jew of Malta), *Anthony and Cleopatra* (Dido) and *Macbeth* (Dr. Faustus). Perhaps Shakespeare's greatest tribute appears in *As You Like It* when he quoted a line from *Hero and Leander* and alluded to Marlowe's death as 'a great reckoning in a little room'.

Marriage

In Tudor times, marriage was only allowed between people of different genders. The 1533 Act for the Punishment of the Vice of Buggery made homosexuality a criminal offence for the first time (beforehand, it had been a matter for the Church courts). Those convicted were usually hanged and their property was confiscated by the state. Accusations of homosexuality were often used to undermine a person's social status, such as the playwright, **Christopher Marlowe**. Gay relationships still occurred in private, though, often between master and servant or within the Church, armed services and the theatrical community.

The process of getting married was much simpler than it is today. A couple merely had to make a verbal agreement by saying, 'I marry you' or 'Thomas is my husband'. Or the words, 'Joan, I will marry you' followed by consummation. It was preferable to have a witness for this (and for the consummation!) to avoid later disputes. It was just such a marriage that landed **Catherine Howard** in trouble prior to being wedded to **Henry VIII**.

In the sixteenth century, the Church increasingly encouraged weddings to formally occur in churches and a reading out of the banns in the three services before the marriage. This was designed to discourage children marrying against their parents' wishes and to make sure that the rules of consanguinity were followed. This meant that you could not marry a close blood relative (cousin once removed was acceptable but not cousin).

The minimum age for getting married was twelve for girls and fourteen for boys. However, it was generally considered inappropriate for girls to start child-bearing until their mid-teens (**Margaret Beaufort**, giving birth at thirteen, was considered unusual). For this reason, **Henry Fitzroy** and Lady Mary Howard, both fourteen, were not allowed to live together after their marriage. Women were basically treated as second-class citizens and this continued after marriage. A wife was expected to be an obedient child-bearer and she relied heavily upon her husband for economic support. Any assets owned by a widow would immediately become the property of her new husband. Some widows were wealthy enough to stay single if they wanted. Margaret Pole, the Countess of Salisbury, for example, remained a widow for thirty-six years and, by 1538, was the fifth richest peer in the realm.

With the infant mortality rate as high as forty per cent it was necessary for couples to have many children in order to carry on the family business or estate. For this reason only, certainly not for pleasure, the Church encouraged sex and discouraged contraception. Various contraceptive advice was given, however, such as for the woman to carry the testicles of a castrated weasel between her breasts. Far more effective was the use of a condom made of lambskin known as a 'Venus Glove' whilst women might insert beeswax to cover the entrance to the cervix. The Church also had strict rules about when you could have sex. It was forbidden on Wednesdays, Fridays and Sundays, holy days, in the daytime or when the woman was breast-feeding and couples had to be clothed and use the missionary position! It can safely be assumed that, given the lack of monitoring, these rules were largely ignored.

The reasons for and the circumstances around marriage varied according to one's class. For the wealthiest, marriage was all about producing alliances and maintaining one's social and financial status. Marriage negotiations could start straight after a child's birth and would include the sizes of the dowry (payment by the bride's father) and the jointure (provision for the bride should she become a widow, paid for by the groom's father). Prince **Arthur** and **Catherine of Aragon** were only two and three, respectively, when they were betrothed. The question of love did not come into the equation and it was considered a bonus if a couple did love each other. A notable exception was the marriage of **Mary Tudor** and **Charles Brandon**.

Battle for domination in marriage. (*Artist: unknown, 1540s. Wikimedia Commons. Rijksmuseum*)

For the growing middle classes, similar considerations were followed. The values of the dowries and jointures would be less and children would have more say in their choice of spouse. However, planned marriages by the parents were still prevalent with the intention of preserving a family's wealth and status.

Amongst the poorer masses, people had a far greater say in their choice of spouse and, on average, would also get married much later, usually in their mid- to late-twenties. The reason for this was that children would usually leave home between the ages of seven and fourteen to seek work and it would take many years to accumulate enough money to maintain a family. A wife was expected to help run her husband's business, usually, as well as look after the children and household. The custom of providing dowries and jointures did not apply due to the lack of money.

Multiple marriages were very common in Tudor times due to the low life expectancy and the dangers of childbirth. Most people married at least twice and, for the wealthiest class, three or four times was quite normal as they first got married at a younger age (**Catherine Parr** married four times). The record-holder for the number of marriages in the period was not Henry VIII but a certain Sir Gervaise Clifton, who totalled seven spouses. For the lower classes, a quick remarriage was vital for financial and practical reasons. It was quite common, for instance, for a tradesman's widow to marry his apprentice in order to keep the business going.

Unhappy marriages must have been very common but matrimony was considered a lifelong commitment (it was one of the seven sacraments of the **Catholic** Church) and adultery by a woman was considered petty treason for which she could be burned. The concept of divorce did not exist but it could be possible to acquire an annulment, which stated that the couple were never truly married in the first place. Certain conditions had to be met, though, to persuade the Church to annul a marriage. These included insanity of a spouse, a pre-existing marriage contract, non-consummation of marriage, being too closely related and impotence of the husband. All required proof, of course! Alternatively, you could remarry if your spouse joined a convent or monastery – an option Henry VIII tried to foist onto Catherine of Aragon. Alternatively, one could try to persuade a bishop to agree to separation (allowed to live apart but not remarry).

Mary Tudor

(1496–1533)

Sister of **Henry VIII** and Queen of France.

Mary was the youngest surviving child of King **Henry VII** and **Elizabeth of York**. Her **education** focused on French, Latin, music, dance and embroidery and she had a particularly close friendship with her brother, Henry, who would name his eldest daughter after her. At the age of ten, she was betrothed to the future Holy Roman Emperor, Charles V, who was four years her junior. Despite a fragile health, she became well known for her liveliness, beauty and grace.

In 1514, the betrothal fell through but Mary's brother, now Henry VIII, saw an opportunity. He had wanted to end the **First Anglo-French War** and sweetened the peace deal by offering his sister's hand in **marriage** to the fifty-two-year-old King Louis XII. Mary was naturally horrified and only agreed if she was allowed to marry anyone of her choice if she outlived the French king. In October, she and Louis were married in Abbeville and Mary was now Queen of France. It did not last long though. Desperate to have a male heir, Louis apparently over-exerted himself in the bed chamber and died of a heart attack (it was probably complications arising from severe gout though).

Mary was kept in isolation for several weeks in case she was bearing an heir. At the same time, various French suitors, each keen to increase their own power, made advances on her. Mary was rescued, however, by the love of her life – **Charles Brandon**, the Duke of Suffolk and great friend of the English king. Henry had ordered Brandon to bring Mary back from France and not to propose to her. A strange decision, perhaps, assuming that Henry must have known how the two felt about each other. Possibly, given his prior promise to Mary, he had accepted their future marriage but wanted it to be on his terms. Unsurprisingly perhaps, Mary and Charles soon wed at a secret ceremony in Paris in front of just ten witnesses.

Henry was furious. Marrying into the royal family without the king's permission was a treasonable offence and he had just lost a very useful bargaining chip for other potential marriage treaties. However, Cardinal **Wolsey** smoothed things over and Henry could not stay angry with his beloved sister and friend for long. After being ordered to pay a huge fine in annual installments, they were allowed to return home where they had a formal wedding, in Henry's presence, in Greenwich Palace. The fine would have impoverished Brandon but, in fact, only a small amount was ever repaid and the remainder was never chased up.

Mary was now the Duchess of Suffolk but she was always referred to as 'the French Queen'. Her marriage to Brandon was a happy one and they had four children. Two girls survived, including Frances, who would become the mother of **Lady Jane Grey**. She spent most of her time at the family manor in Suffolk. Little more is known about her apart from a private quarrel she had with her brother in the late 1520s concerning his 'Great Matter'. Mary argued against the annulment of his marriage to **Catherine of Aragon** probably because she had a personal dislike of **Anne Boleyn**. Anne had been one of her maids of honour once and it would have been galling to see her elevated to queen.

Mary was often ill and further weakened by a dose of the **sweating sickness** that she caught in 1528. She eventually died from an unknown illness aged thrity-seven.

Mary I

(1516–58)

Queen of England from 1553 to 1558.

Mary was the only surviving child of King **Henry VIII** and **Catherine of Aragon**. Her childhood seems to have been a very happy one – her parents doted on her and Henry called her 'the greatest pearl in the kingdom'. She received an excellent **education**, excelling at music and languages, and was heavily influenced by her mother's deep **Catholic**ism. From a very early age, she became a pawn on the chess board of international **marriage** as potential unions with the royal families of France, Scotland and the Holy Roman Empire were considered. In 1526, Mary was made Princess of Wales and went to live in Ludlow Castle under the care of Margaret Pole, the Countess of Salisbury, and **John Dudley** (her future nemesis!) before returning to London.

However, in the late 1520s, her life changed dramatically for the worse. It became clear that Henry wanted to annul his marriage to Catherine in order to marry **Anne Boleyn**. Clearly, this jeopardised Mary's legitimacy. Not only was she no longer considered marriage material but her own father did not want to see her anymore. In 1531, she was banned from seeing her mother again and she started to suffer from depression and irregular menstruation. During one serious illness, Henry did send his own physician, **William Butts**, but would not even allow her to attend her mother's funeral in 1536.

In 1533, the king married Anne Boleyn and Mary was bastardised by act of **Parliament**. Subsequently, her servants were dismissed, she received little income and was appointed as lady-in-waiting to the newborn Princes **Elizabeth** at Hatfield House, Hertfordshire. At this point, Mary showed defiance and great character. Although now simply called 'Lady Mary' she still referred to herself as 'Princess', refused to acknowledge Anne as the queen and refused to enter a convent, all of which infuriated her father. She even refused to swear the oath of supremacy which declared Henry as Head of the English Church instead of the Pope. This was a treasonable act, which could have led to her execution but Henry could not do that to his former 'pearl'. It was rumoured, though, that Anne did consider having Mary poisoned.

In 1536, Anne fell from power and Mary's position improved. Her father's new wife, **Jane Seymour**, encouraged a rapprochement between the two. Henry offered to bring Mary back into the royal fold if she accepted him as Head of the English Church and acknowledged her own bastardy. With great reluctance, she accepted. For the remainder of her father's reign, she was given a household befitting her position and further marriage projects were considered. She was made godmother to her new half-brother, **Edward**, and, despite her illegitimacy, she was even restored to the succession (after her brother, Edward, but before Elizabeth) by the 1543 Act of Succession. She was much saddened, however, by the brutal execution of her own godmother, and former governess, Margaret Pole, on trumped-up charges of treason.

After Henry VIII's death in 1547, Mary inherited several estates in East Anglia. Her half-brother, now Edward VI, made repeated requests for her to give up her Catholic faith but she refused and continued to celebrate Mass in her private chapel. She was actually very fond of Edward; it was his advisors that she detested and their efforts to enforce the **Protestant** religion upon the country.

As he lay dying, in 1553, Edward made a last-minute alteration to the Act of Succession by naming his Protestant cousin once removed, **Lady Jane Grey**, as his heir. Possibly, he was persuaded by the Lord Protector – the **Duke of Northumberland** – who just happened to be Jane's father-in-law. The country saw through the scam, however, and Northumberland's coup failed. To much rejoicing, Mary was proclaimed queen on 10 July. This was soon followed by Northumberland's execution but, other than that, she showed remarkable clemency towards those involved in the coup.

The Succession

Mary was now thirty-seven years old and saw the importance of producing an heir quickly. Otherwise, the throne would go to her Protestant sister, Elizabeth. Parliament and her advisors preferred her to marry an English nobleman such as Edward Courtney, the great-grandson of Edward IV, but Mary was swayed more by the advice of her cousin – the Holy Roman Emperor, Charles V. He persuaded her to marry his son, Prince Philip of Spain. In some respects, this made sense: an alliance with France's enemy should strengthen England abroad and it represented a return to her Spanish Catholic roots. Many English, however, felt differently and feared foreign domination. Given the dangers of childbirth along with the fact that she was eleven years older than Philip, there was a real possibility that Mary would die first and England would be absorbed into the Spanish empire. Consequently, in early 1554, **Wyatt's Rebellion** broke out in order to prevent the marriage and put Elizabeth on the throne. The revolt was crushed and its leaders, along with Lady Jane Grey, were executed. Again, though, Mary showed clemency by imprisoning her sister and ignoring calls to have her executed. As for the marriage, it went ahead in July in Winchester – London had become a hotbed of anti-Spanish feeling.

The terms of the marriage treaty were quite advantageous for England. Philip was known as 'King of England' and all official documents needed his signature. However, this was only for Mary's lifetime. Moreover, he could not act without Mary's consent or appoint foreigners to office and any child of theirs would inherit the Spanish Netherlands along with England. Philip was not happy with these terms but for him (and Charles) it was a marriage of political convenience that would help to keep both France and English Protestantism in check.

It also seems clear that Philip was not physically attracted to his new wife – he was known for his mistresses and he would have found Mary too pale and sombre for his liking – although Mary seemed very fond of him. He only paid two visits to England but, nevertheless, in early 1555, rumours spread that the queen was pregnant and thanksgiving services were held throughout London. However, it turned out to be a false pregnancy, which can be caused by trauma, various medical conditions or simply the deep psychological desire to have a baby. Today, around 5 in 22,000 pregnancies are false. For Mary, the experience was deeply humiliating and it merely represented her desperate desire for an heir.

Religion

Mary was keen to restore Catholicism to her realm and so her first Parliament repealed the Protestant laws of her brother's reign and the Church of England was restored to the orthodoxy of the 1539 Six **Articles**. Any priests who had married were forced to resign. This was well received by the majority of people and so she pressed ahead with further reform. Her second Parliament reinstated

Catherine Willoughby going into exile. The fourth wife of Charles Brandon flees the Marian persecutions (seen on left) with her second husband, daughter and wet nurse.(*Artist: unknown, 17th century*)

the Pope as the Head of the English Church and enacted heresy laws, which made it illegal to speak out against Catholicism. Her chief advisor, Bishop **Gardiner**, and even the Pope, however, warned her not to go too far for fear of upsetting Protestant sections of society and Mary did relent from enforcing a return of monastic lands lost during the **Dissolution of the Monasteries**. Besides, most of these lands were now owned by nobles sitting in Parliament and so a restoration would have been very unlikely anyway. Mary was now aided by Cardinal **Reginald Pole**, son of Margaret Pole and a former exile who had returned to England.

The heresy laws prompted around 800 leading Protestants to flee abroad but those that remained now suffered persecution. From February 1555 to the end of the reign, 283 Protestants were executed, mostly by being burned alive (it was believed that only flames could cleanse a heretic's spirit). Of these, around 100 were clergymen; the majority were ordinary people – tradesmen, women, elderly, blind and even a baby. Most notable amongst the victims were bishops **Hooper**, **Latimer** and **Ridley** and Archbishop **Cranmer**. The latter was burned despite his recantation due to his involvement in the annulment of the marriage of the queen's mother. Most of the executions occurred in the south-east where Protestantism was strongest. In Bishop **Bonner**'s diocese of London, 120 were executed in public places like Smithfield market; this averaged around three per month. These figures actually pale in comparison to what was happening on the continent but England had never seen anything like it. Even Philip advised Mary to desist because he saw what was happening – the burnings were creating Protestant martyrs and an increasing hatred of Catholicism.

Foreign Affairs

In **Ireland**, the policy of plantations began in order to pacify the island after some local uprisings. They failed due to local resistance but it is interesting to note that it was a Catholic monarch that initiated the policy although plantations would become associated with Protestantism.

In 1556, Charles V abdicated and Philip became king of Spain. He soon began trying to persuade Mary to aid him in his war against France although, by the terms of their marriage treaty, England was under no obligation to do so. However, tensions between England and France had been rising: an abortive conspiracy to depose Mary had included a planned invasion from France and, in 1557, French troops had assisted an attack on Scarborough. So, despite the disruption to trade and a lack of necessary provisions and money, Mary initiated the **Fourth Anglo-French War** in August 1557. English forces acquitted themselves well at the Battle of St Quentin (Anglo-Spanish victory) but, in January 1558, the French captured Calais, England's last possession on the continent. England had owned parts of France for hundreds of years and so the loss was a great blow to her prestige despite being a financial drain. Mary was so upset that she apparently said, 'when I am dead and opened, you shall find Calais lying on my heart.'

The much-hoped-for increase in trade with the Spanish empire did not materialise as the Spanish continued to monopolise their trade routes. Mary therefore encouraged exploration to discover new routes for England and granted a charter to the Muscovy Company, governed by **Sebastian Cabot**. Her reign also saw useful regulation of customs revenue and plans to reverse the damaging currency **debasement**, which her father had started.

Mary suffered another phantom pregnancy after Philip's brief visit in 1557 and became seriously ill in May the following year. She died in November, probably from ovarian cancer. Philip, who was in the Netherlands at the time, later wrote, 'I felt a reasonable regret for her death.' In her will, Mary had asked to be interred next to her mother but, instead, she was buried in Westminster Abbey in a tomb that she would later share with her sister.

Queen Mary I received a very bad press from later historians. Protestant propaganda, such as Foxe's *Book of Martyrs* was largely responsible along with her unpopular marriage and the loss of Calais. Some efforts were made in the late twentieth century to improve her reputation though. These focus on the overall popularity of her initial religious reforms and the brevity of her reign. What might she have achieved had she lived longer? It is hard, however, to get away from the revulsion caused by the burnings and Mary's uncompromising nature when it came to religion. At the same time, one cannot help but feel sympathy for a person who suffered so much personally and had to charter the unknown waters of being England's first ruling queen. It is quite likely that her successor, Elizabeth I, learned important lessons from her sister's reign.

Mary, Queen of Scots

(1542–87)

Queen of Scotland from 1542 to 1567.

Mary was the only surviving child of King James V of Scotland and the French noblewoman, Marie of Guise. She is also known as Mary Stewart, a descendant of Robert II, who founded the Stewart dynasty in 1371. When she was only six days old, her father died, supposedly of grief, after the Scots' defeat at the **Battle of Solway Moss** in late 1542. He had been ill for a while so it is more likely that he died from cholera or dysentery.

King **Henry VIII** of England was keen to secure his northern border and break the Franco-Scottish Auld Alliance. So, at the Treaty of Greenwich (1543) the Earl of Arran, regent of Scotland, agreed to the future **marriage** of Mary to the English king's five-year-old son, **Edward**. However, the pro-French faction in the Scottish government blocked this so Henry decided to force the issue by launching the **War of the Rough Wooing**. In 1548, it was decided to keep Mary away from the invading English forces by moving her to the safety of France, where she was to live for the next thirteen years. It was agreed that Mary would marry the French Dauphin in return for French influence in Scotland. In the meantime, regents (including her mother, from 1554) would rule Scotland in her name.

In France

As she grew up in France, she became exposed to all the latest ideas of the **Renaissance** and received a top-class **education**. She became fluent in French, could speak Latin and Spanish and excelled at music, singing, dancing and outdoor sports. Vivacious and beautiful, Mary became very popular in court and, by the age of fifteen, she stood at an imposing height of almost six feet. In contrast, her fiancé, Francis, was short, had a stutter and was often ill. In 1558, they married each other at Notre-Dame Cathedral. The following year, the French king died in a jousting accident and the sixteen-year-old Mary was now Queen of France as well as Scotland.

Soon after, following the accession of **Elizabeth I**, she claimed the throne of England too. Mary, being a **Catholic**, did not recognise Elizabeth's right to the English throne because the Pope had never annulled Henry VIII's marriage to **Catherine of Aragon**. This meant that she regarded **Anne Boleyn** (Elizabeth's mother) as merely being one of Henry's mistresses. Moreover, Mary herself had a good claim to the English throne as she was the granddaughter of **Margaret, Queen of Scots**, a sister of Henry VIII. This, naturally, infuriated Elizabeth, especially after Mary displayed the French royal coat of arms quartered with those of England.

From late 1560, however, her life became a long series of misfortunes. Late in that year, her husband, King Francis II, died from an abscess in his brain. Her mother-in-law, the formidable Catherine de Medici, became regent and saw Mary as a focal point for any opposition to her second son becoming king. She made it very clear that Mary was not welcome anymore and so, nine months later, she returned to Scotland to claim her inheritance.

In Scotland

This was quite a bold move by Mary. Maybe she felt that she had no choice but she would have known that Scotland was far more austere than anything she was used to and that, in her absence, the **Reformation** had started to take a grip there and **Protestant** nobles now dominated the government. When she arrived on a gloomy, foggy day in August 1561, nothing would have prepared her, however, for the factionalism that had riven Scottish politics during her absence. Somehow, she had to tread a path between groups with radically opposing views and maintain her authority at the same time.

For the first few years, she practised religious tolerance and the general populace received their graceful, beautiful new queen with great joy during her progress around the country. However, she found herself under constant attack by the firebrand Protestant reformer, John Knox, who decried her religion and flamboyant lifestyle. At the same time, she upset potential Catholic supporters by packing her privy council with Protestant lords and crushing a Catholic rebellion in the Highlands. It would seem that Mary had one eye on the English throne and wanted to prove that she was no threat to the new Church of England. After all, in 1562, Elizabeth almost died from smallpox so she must have felt close to achieving her ambition.

Mary knew that she needed to marry in order to create an heir. A potential match with the king of Spain's mentally unstable son came to nothing but she considered Elizabeth's suggestion of marrying the **Earl of Leicester**. Leicester was the English queen's favourite and Elizabeth probably thought he would control Mary but he refused to consider the idea. In the end, she went for her cousin – the handsome and athletic nineteen-year-old, Lord Darnley. It may have been love or, again, it may have been with another eye on the English throne for Darnley had a claim to England himself.

The marriage went ahead in 1565 without the Pope's permission (needed for marrying a first cousin) but Mary had made a terrible choice. Not only did this upset other, jealous lords but Darnley was an arrogant and vicious character who resented Mary for not allowing him equal powers as a king. He also grew jealous of her friendship with her Italian secretary, David Riccio, and rumours circulated that the Italian was the father of Mary's unborn child. In March 1566, Darnley and some friends burst into Mary's room and murdered Riccio in front of the six-month-pregnant queen. Mary could never forgive him and suspected him of trying to kill her by causing a miscarriage.

In June, Mary gave birth to a son and heir, James, and then formed a strong attachment to the Earl of Bothwell. Many suspected that they were lovers and were plotting to get rid of Darnley. In February 1567, Darnley fell ill – possibly syphilis or smallpox – and Mary sent him to the former abbey of Kirk o' Field, just inside Edinburgh's city walls, to recuperate. She visited him on 9 February and then in the early hours of 10 February the house was blown up and Darnley's body was found in the gardens. He had apparently been asphyxiated. Darnley had acquired many enemies but Bothwell was the chief suspect. In April, Mary was abducted (possibly with her consent) by Bothwell and taken to Dunbar Castle. He was later accused of raping her and bullying her into marrying him. Certainly, some element of scheming went on because, soon after, she showered favours upon Bothwell and, in June, married him in a Protestant ceremony only twelve days after he had divorced his wife on the grounds of his adultery with her servant.

Most European rulers, let alone the Scottish lords, were scandalised by this sequence of events. The fact that the queen had quickly married the suspected murderer of her husband appeared to show that she lacked any moral compass. In June 1567, twenty-six Scottish lords raised an army in open rebellion. Mary and Bothwell's small force met them at Carberry Hill but they soon surrendered after suffering mass desertions. Bothwell managed to escape abroad, where he eventually died in a Danish prison, and Mary was imprisoned in a castle on an island in Loch Leven. Whilst there, she miscarried twins and was forced to abdicate the throne in favour of her one-year-old son. A year later, the brother of the castle's owner rescued her and she raised another army. This was defeated by the lords at Langside, near Glasgow, from where she fled by sea to England.

In England

Mary had chosen England, despite advice to the contrary, in the hope that her cousin would help her to reclaim her throne. Elizabeth, for her part, was initially pleased to have her rival in her clutches and kept her in captivity in various country houses and castles. She went through some sham negotiations with the Scots about Mary's return but, not surprisingly, the Scottish lords were not interested. A show trial ensued at York to decide if Mary had been guilty of conspiracy in Darnley's murder but the lack of evidence led to a not guilty verdict.

In 1569, the **Northern Rebellion** made it very clear to Elizabeth that, despite being a prisoner, Mary was a threat simply by being a figurehead for Catholic opposition. Various northern lords had plotted to rescue Mary, marry her to the

Fourth Duke of Norfolk and topple the queen. The rebellion was crushed but Mary was kept under closer supervision even though she had probably had little to do with the uprising. Elizabeth's Principal Secretary, **Sir Francis Walsingham**, now used his network of spies to closely monitor Mary's communications with the outside world. Although confined, Mary led a very comfortable existence. Permitted to have many of her own domestic staff, thirty carts were required to transport her belongings from one home to another. She was sometimes allowed outside under very close supervision but she spent most her time indoors doing embroidery.

In 1571, Mary gave her blessing to the **Ridolfi Plot**, which aimed to replace Elizabeth with Mary and Norfolk by way of another rebellion aided by a Spanish invasion force. Walsingham's agents uncovered the plot, however, and Norfolk was executed. **Parliament** and the queen's advisors called for Mary's execution too but Elizabeth refused to condone the killing of a relative and fellow-monarch. What kind of example would it set?

Mary later became involved in the abortive **Throckmorton Plot** (1583) but it was the **Babington Plot** of 1586 that finally brought about her demise. Walsingham could finally produce evidence which proved that Mary had given permission for an attempt to assassinate Elizabeth. In August, Mary was arrested, taken to Fotheringhay Castle and put on trial for treason. She protested that she had not been shown the evidence against her and had not been allowed any legal counsel. Moreover, as she was not an English subject, how could she have committed treason? On 25 October, however, she was found guilty and sentenced to death.

Elizabeth still procrastinated, though, and even enquired about the possibility of making Mary's death look natural. Under great pressure from Parliament and her advisors, she finally signed the death warrant on February 1, 1587 and entrusted it to William Paulet, a member of the Privy Council. The Council then secretly met and decided to send the warrant to Fotheringhay immediately without the queen's permission. On February 8, Mary knelt on the scaffold and, as was customary, forgave the executioner, saying, 'I forgive you with all my heart, for now, I hope, you shall make an end of all my troubles.' It took three blows of the axe to finally decapitate her. According to witnesses, her auburn wig fell off, revealing short, grey hair, her lips kept moving for another fifteen minutes and a small dog appeared from under her skirts.

Straight afterwards, her clothes, the block and anything touched by her blood were burned in order to deter relic hunters. Mary had asked to be buried in France but, instead, she was interred in Peterborough Cathedral. Later, when her son, James, became king of England, he reburied his mother at Westminster Abbey in a chapel opposite Elizabeth's tomb. Elizabeth, herself, was furious when she found out and sent Paulet to the **Tower** for nineteen months. She even

Execution of Mary, Queen of Scots. (*Artist: Robert Beale, 1587. British Library*)

wrote a letter to King James revealing her outrage about what had happened. It is entirely possible, however, that this was all a facade and it was just her way of making herself look innocent in the whole matter. James's own reaction was muted. He did not want to prejudice his own chances of succeeding Elizabeth and, besides, he had last seen his mother when he was only ten months old.

Historians' views about Mary, Queen of Scots have wildly differed. Her detractors have accused her of being a foolish, unprincipled woman who brought about her own downfall, a queen who lacked the ability to govern her lords but wanted nothing more than to govern England. The opposite view, however, states that she was a courageous woman who was thrown into an impossible situation when she returned to Scotland, a queen who became the pawn of quarrelling nobles and there being no hard evidence of her part in Darnley's murder. The truth probably lies somewhere in between. There is no doubt, though, that her life story is a tragedy that continues to fascinate us even today.

Mary Rose

Flagship of **Henry VIII**'s navy.

Constructed between 1509 and 1511, the *Mary Rose* was one of the first warships built in the reign of Henry VIII. Weighing around 500 tons and measuring thirty-two metres long and twelve metres wide (a modern warship is around ten times longer and 100 times heavier), it was the sister ship of the *Peter Pomegranate*. Possibly, it was named after Henry's sister, **Mary**, and the Tudor rose but the habit of the time was to give ships Christian names so 'Mary' probably referred to the Virgin Mary. The pomegranate was **Catherine of Aragon**'s badge and so the ships were probably named in honour of Henry and his first wife. These vessels marked the beginning of Henry's plans to establish a larger navy, which would aid England in its foreign wars.

Building the *Mary Rose* would have required around 600 large oak trees from about forty acres of woodland. It was of a carrack design, meaning that it had high 'castles' at the stern and bow, a narrow waist and four decks (including the hold at the base of the ship). In 1536, it was modernised by inserting larger beams so that it could carry extra weight and had more gun ports cut into the hull. This was a reflection of the new style of warfare that was developing. Before the sixteenth century, the main strategy was to board an enemy vessel and then conduct a 'land battle' but advances in armaments technology now enabled the construction of longer-range cannons. This meant that the *Mary Rose* was one of the first ships that could fire broadsides from a safe distance in order to try and sink or cripple its opponents. These cannons were heavier, though, and so needed to be installed below the top deck, hence the cutting out of gun ports.

The cannons themselves, reflected the latest developments in weaponry. The *Mary Rose* had a combination of the older style iron cannons and the more modern bronze ones. The iron variety were cheaper to make and quicker to reload but had a shorter range and only fired stone balls, which tended to shatter on impact and so it was more of an anti-personnel weapon. The bronze cannons could fire iron balls at a longer range with a flatter trajectory, thus doing far more damage to the hull of a ship and it would take a cannon crew about three to four minutes to reload them. On the upper deck and the 'castles' there was also a variety of lighter, short-range, anti-personnel guns.

The *Mary Rose* first saw action in the **First Anglo-French War**, when it distinguished itself at the Battle of St Mathieu (1512) off the coast of Brittany. It was the first time that ships went into battle without attempting to board each other. The following year, it won a sailing race before being sent to Brest, where its commander, Edward Howard, was killed in action. In 1520, it escorted Henry across the Channel to the **Field of the Cloth of Gold** and, soon after, escorted troops during the **Second Anglo-French War**.

The *Mary Rose*'s final appearance was during the **Third Anglo-French War** at the Battle of the Solent (19 July 1545). Early in the battle, she sailed to engage the enemy when disaster struck. She suddenly leaned over on her starboard side and started taking in water through her open gun ports. Supplies, ammunition, cannons and the brick oven came loose, rolled to starboard and thereby accelerated the influx of water. Many of those who were not crushed by the falling objects became trapped at the upper deck's hatches, which acted as fatal bottlenecks. Those already on the upper deck fared no better as anti-boarding netting prevented the sailors from leaping into the water. It is not known how many were on board but probably between 450 and 700 sailors drowned, including the admiral of the fleet, Sir George Carew, whilst only thirty-four survived, most of whom had been on the masts when the ship keeled over. The *Mary Rose* sank in a matter of minutes and the king, himself, witnessed the disaster from the shore. Hearing the screams from the ship, he was heard to say, 'Oh, my gentlemen. Oh, my gallant, gallant men.'

The causes of the disaster have been long debated. It appears that, after firing a starboard broadside, the *Mary Rose* was completing a sharp turn in order to fire its port guns when a gust of wind accentuated the ship's lean and allowed water to start pouring through the gun ports. It also seems certain that the ship was overloaded with men and had too many cannons after its 1536 refit, making it a sailing death-trap. In addition, Carew was heard complaining about his disobedient crew and this may explain why they did not close the starboard gun ports before turning. There was also an outbreak of dysentery in Portsmouth at the time – maybe many of the men were too ill to follow orders quickly. The final possibility is that the French had holed the *Mary Rose* in the hull during her first broadside thus enabling water to enter.

Days afterwards, attempts were made to salvage the ship as it had only sunk in twelve metres of water but it was stuck too deep into the clay seabed and only a few cannons were rescued. Apparently, the ship could still be seen at low tide in **Elizabeth I**'s reign. In 1836, the wreck was rediscovered by fishermen and this was followed by another, more destructive salvage attempt, which also failed. It was not until October 1982, that the *Mary Rose* was finally raised. Today, its remains can be seen at a museum in Portsmouth, along with a host of fascinating artefacts that reveal what life had been like aboard a Tudor warship.

More, Sir Thomas

(1478–1535)

Scholar, lawyer, Lord Chancellor and martyr.

More was born in the City of London, the second of six children and his father was a successful lawyer and judge. Between the ages of twelve and fourteen he served as a page boy in the household of **John Morton** – Lord Chancellor and Archbishop of Canterbury. Morton enjoyed his intelligence and lively wit and predicted that he would become 'a marvellous man'. More, in turn, was introduced to an early form of **humanism** and later portrayed Morton as the wise and flexible statesman in *Utopia.*

More spent two years at Oxford University before studying law in London. After qualifying, he seriously considered becoming a monk instead and lived for two years in a monastery. Eventually, he decided that he could better serve God as a layman although, for the rest of his life, he secretly wore a rough sack cloth under his clothes, occasionally committed self-flagellation and shied away from ostentatiousness.

In 1504, More became a member of **Parliament** and dared to agitate against levying a tax to pay for the marriage of **Henry VII**'s daughter, **Margaret**, considering it to be an unfair burden on the people. From 1510, he became one of the two under-sheriffs of London – an important position that oversaw law and order, revenue collection and the courts. In this role, More acquired a reputation for honesty and efficiency and he also demonstrated courage, when he confronted the rioters on **Evil May Day** (1517). For twenty years, More's reputation earned him a rapid stream of promotions and increasing influence. He joined **Henry VIII**'s Privy Council (1514), became a trusted associate of Cardinal **Wolsey**, was knighted in 1521, was elected as Speaker of the House of Commons (1523), became High Steward of Oxford and Cambridge universities and Chancellor of the Duchy of Lancaster (1525), which basically put much of northern England under his control. This stellar rise was set to continue.

More's private life only added to his reputation. In 1505, he married Joanna 'Jane' Colt and they had three daughters and a son. As a humanist, More believed in the importance of **education** for all. He taught his poorly educated wife himself whilst ensuring that his daughters received the same humanist education as his son. This was unusual at the time but became an example to others. His eldest daughter, Margaret or 'Meg', became one of the most learned women in sixteenth-century England and was the first non-royal to write a translation (a book by Erasmus from Latin into English). When Jane died in 1511, More quickly remarried a widow and raised her daughter as if she were his own. He also took on the guardianship of two other girls and provided for

Island of Utopia. (*Artist: unknown. From Thomas More's* Utopia, *1517*)

their education. More liked to entertain guests in his London home too and these included the great Dutch humanist thinker, Desiderius Erasmus. The two became close friends and Erasmus even offered him as a model for the intelligentsia of Europe.

More also became known as a scholar. He assisted Henry VIII in writing his attack on the **Protestant** reformer, Martin Luther, and wrote a *History of King*

Richard III, which became well known for its dramatic literary style. Its bias against the former Tudor enemy is obvious, though, and it became the basis for **Shakespeare**'s play, *Richard III*. Most famous of all, however, was *Utopia*, published in 1516 (1551 in England). Utopia was an imaginary island on which there existed an ideal society in which there were no wars, private property or lawyers and education and religious tolerance existed for all. Most saw it as a thinly veiled criticism of sixteenth-century governments and society.

By the late 1520s, More had become the unofficial secretary of the king and the two of them had become friends. Henry would even pay unannounced visits to More's house in Chelsea, eat with the family and walk around the garden with his arm around his host. More never fully trusted him though, saying, 'If my head should win him a castle in France, it should not fail to go.' Despite this, after Wolsey's fall in 1529, More accepted the post of Lord Chancellor, a position in which he oversaw the legal system. In this role, More ensured the rapid dispensing of justice and revealed just how devout a **Catholic** he was by persecuting Protestants and censoring the press; he was particularly vigorous in ordering burnings of **Tyndale**'s English Bible.

However, he became increasingly at odds with Henry's position regarding the king's 'Great Matter'. He could not condone Henry's attempts to annul his marriage to **Catherine of Aragon** in order to marry **Anne Boleyn**. Neither could he accept the king's attacks on the independence of the Church. In 1532, after the clergy were forced to surrender their right to make laws, More resigned. He was astute enough to realise that he was probably safe as long as he kept his views private. However, he did offend Henry when he refused to attend Anne Boleyn's coronation in 1533 and efforts were made, in vain, to find him guilty of treason by conspiring with the 'Nun of Kent', **Elizabeth Barton**.

It was More's refusal to swear the oaths of Supremacy and Succession, though, that brought about more determined efforts to make him conform. More could not accept either oaths because that would have betrayed his belief in papal supremacy. As a result, he was thrown into the **Tower of London** along with his 'co-conspirator', Bishop **John Fisher**. More was careful, however, never to explain his position because, by law, silence had to be accepted as consent. The Solicitor-General, Sir **Richard Rich**, then claimed that, during an interview, More actually stated his position. More denied this and cast aspersions on Rich's honesty. This was enough for the court, though, which found him guilty of treason. On 6 July 1535, More was beheaded on Tower Hill but not before declaring that he was 'the king's good servant, but God's first'. His body was buried in the Tower's chapel and his head put on a pike on London Bridge for a month, as was customary. It was later rescued by his daughter, Meg, and it possibly ended up in her family's tomb in Canterbury.

The execution of Sir Thomas More shocked many people, both in England and abroad for he had gained an international reputation. Since then, he has been described as one of the greatest people in English history and a person of the greatest virtue that this country has ever seen. There is certainly little doubt that he was a man of great integrity, wit and intelligence, whose views, as expressed in *Utopia*, were far ahead of his time. In the end his devout Catholic faith, possibly too rigid, made him a martyr and, in 1935, he was canonised. His feast day in the Catholic calendar is 22 June (shared with Fisher).

Morton, John

(c. 1420–1500)

Statesman, cardinal, Lord Chancellor and Archbishop of Canterbury.

Morton was born into minor gentry in Dorset and later went to Oxford University where he studied both civil and canon law. In the reign of Henry VI, he received numerous ecclesiastical posts and so owed his allegiance to the Lancastrian side when the **Wars of the Roses** broke out in 1455.

Morton was present (though not as a combatant) at the brutal Battle of Towton in 1461 at which the Yorkists were victorious. Straight afterwards, he fled to France, to the court of Margaret of Anjou, wife of Henry VI. He was with the Lancastrian forces when they briefly reclaimed the throne in 1470–71 but, after their defeat at Tewkesbury, he remained in England and made his peace with the Yorkist king, Edward IV. Edward probably saw Morton as a useful ally and servant and gave him various diplomatic posts and appointed him Bishop of Ely.

In 1483, he fell out with the new king, Richard III, who briefly imprisoned him in the **Tower of London**. The following year, Morton helped to organise a rebellion against Richard but, when this failed, he fled to France. Whilst there, he worked on coordinating support for the Lancastrian claimant, the future **Henry VII**.

After Henry's victory at the **Battle of Bosworth Field** (1485), Morton became a key administrator in the new Tudor regime. As a long-standing supporter of the Lancastrian cause, Henry trusted him implicitly and made him one of his first privy councillors. In 1486, he became his Lord Chancellor as well as the Archbishop of Canterbury and, in 1493, he was appointed a cardinal by the Pope. Up until his death, in 1500, he was the king's right-hand man in all judicial, financial, administrative and diplomatic affairs. He even had time to address abuses within the clergy and supervise building projects such as alterations to Lambeth Palace and Canterbury Cathedral.

Morton is probably most famous for 'Morton's Fork'. This was a taxation method designed to maximise Crown revenues: if a person looked rich, they could afford to pay taxes; if someone looked poor, they had clearly saved enough to pay taxes. Morton had certainly become unpopular as someone who represented Henry VII's stringent fiscal measures but the 'Fork' had little to do with him as it already had been used in Edward IV's reign. If anything, it seems that he actually attempted to restrain the king from further financial exactions.

In his will, Morton left much money to the poor but his lasting legacy was perhaps more subtle. Many years later, **William Shakespeare** wrote his famous play, *Richard III*, which vilified the former king, accusing him, amongst other things, of murdering the Princes in the Tower and being deformed. Shakespeare based his play on the writings of **Sir Thomas More**, who had once been a page boy in the household of Morton from whom he obtained his information. Morton, himself, had hated Richard, had been imprisoned by him and did not like facts to get in the way of a good story. It is, therefore, from Morton's pen that much Tudor propaganda flowed.

Mountjoy, Lord

(see Blount, Charles)

N

Norfolk, Second Duke of

(See Howard, Thomas. Second Duke of Norfolk)

Norfolk, Third Duke of

(See Howard, Thomas. Third Duke of Norfolk)

Norfolk, Fourth Duke of

(See Howard, Thomas. Fourth Duke of Norfolk)

Northern Rebellion

(1569)

An uprising in support of **Mary, Queen of Scots**.

The causes of this rebellion were mainly religious. The north of England was still largely **Catholic** and many people were unhappy with **Elizabeth I**'s Church settlement of 1559, which had established England as a **Protestant** country with the queen as the Governor of the English Church. The settlement attempted to sweeten the pill by including elements of compromise but Catholics were still banned from celebrating Mass and had to attend services using the English Prayer Book and a communion table instead of an altar. The situation was further exacerbated by Elizabeth's decision to continue her father's policy of centralising power and taking authority away from local lords.

What tipped the balance, however, was the sudden appearance of the Catholic Mary, Queen of Scots, who was forced to flee south in 1568 after being deposed by her Scottish nobles. In many Catholics' eyes, including her own, Mary was the true queen of England because the Pope had never annulled the **marriage** of **Henry VIII** and **Catherine of Aragon**. Therefore, they did not recognise Henry's subsequent marriage to **Anne Boleyn**, which meant that her daughter, Elizabeth, was illegitimate.

A plan was put together by the two most powerful northern lords – the earls of Northumberland and Westmoreland. An army would be raised and gather support as it marched south and a landing of Spanish troops would lend assistance. After releasing Mary from her captivity, she would marry the **Fourth Duke of Norfolk** – the most powerful noble in the realm. Mary and Norfolk had already agreed to this although it is unlikely that either were involved in other parts of the scheme.

In November, 1569, Northumberland and Westmoreland raised a force of around 6,000 men and captured Durham. In the city's cathedral, Mass was performed, the English prayer books were burned and the communion table destroyed. The rebels then moved south as far as Wetherby but the support of local leaders did not materialise and neither did the Spanish soldiers (not surprising, given the recent outbreak of violence in the Spanish Netherlands). Worse still, Norfolk begged for Elizabeth's forgiveness and urged the rebels to return home and even Mary offered no support. When news arrived of much larger, royalist forces approaching, the rebels split up and returned to their homes. Northumberland and Westmoreland fled to Scotland. The former was captured, returned to England and later executed; the latter fled to the Netherlands where he lived the rest of his life in poverty.

Elizabeth wanted to send a clear message and so her reprisals were quite brutal. Martial law was imposed on the north, lands were taken off some suspected local lords and around 700 people were hanged in their towns and villages. This was harsh, given that most of them had not supported the poorly planned uprising. Further consequences were a tightening up of anti-treason laws and greater surveillance by the state as the queen and her advisors became more paranoid about further plots.

Northumberland, Duke of

(See Dudley, John)

P

Parker, Matthew

(1504–75)

Archbishop of Canterbury.

Parker was born in Norwich and his father was a weaver. He went to Cambridge University at the age of sixteen and, whilst there, he became familiar with the new **Protestant** ideas coming from abroad. He was a regular visitor to the White Horse Inn or 'Little Germany' and mixed with the likes of **Hugh Latimer** and **William Tyndale**. Unlike his colleagues, though, he was less interested in people's religious views and public debate but more concerned about researching historical facts in order to discover how religion should be practised.

He was ordained a priest in 1527, despite his doubts about the **Catholic** faith, and became a popular preacher in the Cambridge area. With some reluctance, Parker became the chaplain to **Anne Boleyn** and, just before her fall from power in 1536, she made him promise to be responsible for the spiritual care of her baby daughter, **Elizabeth**. Faithfully, he was to adhere to this vow. Afterwards he became chaplain to King **Henry VIII** himself, who aided his election as Master of Corpus Christi College, Cambridge. Parker had previously argued against the Catholic concepts of transubstantiation and purgatory, which led to accusations of heresy. However, his reputation and closeness to the king protected him. In 1545, he became Vice-Chancellor of Cambridge University, where he fell out with the Chancellor, **Stephen Gardiner**, over a play the students produced which derided the Church.

Straight after **Edward VI**'s accession to the throne in 1547, he wedded Margaret Harlestone. They had been waiting to become married since 1540 but only now was it legal for clergy to wed. It was a happy **marriage** and they had five children. Parker was in Norwich when **Kett's Rebellion** (1549) broke out and he preached to the rebels advising them to surrender in order to avoid bloodshed and destruction but this was ignored.

When the Catholic **Mary I** came to the throne in 1553, Parker lost all of his positions and was forced to go into retirement – a punishment that allowed him more time to study the history of the English Church. However, new laws forced Margaret and him to live apart for the duration of Mary's reign. Unlike many other Protestants, Parker was not arrested as he had never been publicly outspoken against the Catholic Church or the Papacy. However, the fact that he survived when so many others were martyred at the stake did not endear him to the Protestant exiles when they returned after Mary's death in 1558.

The new queen, Elizabeth I, needed an Archbishop of Canterbury who could enforce her Church Settlement in a firm yet conciliatory way, a man of deep learning who could show balanced judgement and navigate her new Church of England through the anticipated religious disputes of her reign. Her chief advisor, **William Cecil**, requested Parker take on the post. He did so with great reluctance, perhaps realising how difficult and time-consuming the role would be, but agreed on account of his promise to the queen's mother.

Parker was largely responsible for drawing up the 39 **Articles** in 1563, which were to become the basis of today's Church of England. The articles confirmed that England would follow a Protestant path but also acknowledged some basic Catholic beliefs. This, however, led to increasing clashes with the growing number of **Puritans** who hankered for a purer form of Protestantism and refused to wear vestments or even have organs in their churches. At the same time, with the perceived threats from France and **Mary, Queen of Scots**, he had to clamp down on any Catholic non-conformist practices.

What made Parker's situation even more difficult was his testy relationship with Elizabeth. She complained that he was failing to enforce the rules of the new Church but refused to give his initiatives royal sanction. This, in turn, made it harder for Parker to acquire approval for his plans from **Parliament**, which had an increasingly Puritan outlook. This all left him in a very isolated position in which he received all the blame. His relationship with the queen was difficult on a personal level too. She had made it clear her disapproval of married clergy, disliked his wife and once suggested that she was Parker's mistress.

When Parker died in 1575, the Church of England was still very much a work in progress but he can be considered one of its founding fathers. He was not an inspirational leader – Parker was far too modest and private for that – but he was exactly the non-confrontational type of character that was needed to smooth the way for England's new religion. A reluctant leader, he was far more at home carrying out scholarly research. Typical of a man who believed in compromise, he worked hard to try and demonstrate that the Church of England was, in fact, the old Catholic Church before it had been altered during the Middle Ages. For instance, he proved that the ban on clergy marriage was a medieval innovation. Much of our knowledge of Anglo-Saxon history stems from Parker's valuable research.

Parliament

Parliament, in the form of Lords and an elected Commons, had existed in England since 1265 and had been two separate chambers since the reign of Edward III. By the time of King **Henry VII**'s accession, the Lords sat in Westminster Palace and the Commons met in the dining hall of nearby Westminster Abbey. It was only in 1547 that the Commons joined the Lords in the Palace when they moved to St Stephen's Chapel.

The Lords was considered the most important chamber and was comprised of about sixty senior clergy and peers. After the **Reformation** and the subsequent removal of the abbots, the non-ecclesiastical 'lords' became the majority for the first time. The number of members in the Commons rose from around 290 to 400, an increase that was partly due to the 1536 Act of Union, which allowed for MPs from Wales for the first time.

Members of the Commons tended to be important, local, middle-class men such as landed gentry, merchants and lawyers. Some were also important national figures such as **Thomas Cromwell** and **William Cecil** and had seats on the Privy Council – the monarch's advisory committee. Around one quarter of the Commons came from the shires or counties. The others were from city boroughs; most boroughs had two representatives whilst London had four.

Parliaments were summoned and dismissed by the monarch, who would signal the need for a new session by issuing orders to local sheriffs to hold elections. Elections for the Commons would hardly be recognisable today. A shire MP, known as a Knight of the Shire, was usually picked by the local noble or, sometimes, the position was hereditary! Some boroughs were controlled by the Crown and so their candidates were hand-picked. In other boroughs there was a relatively broad electorate of all the 'freemen' but they were usually not called upon to vote. A representative was usually chosen after informal negotiations amongst the city's leaders. Occasionally, the Crown would try to nominate its preferred candidate but these attempts were usually rebuffed by the local authorities, which took pride in their civic independence.

The nature of Parliament and its relationship with the Crown changed significantly during the Tudor period. In the reign of Henry VII, Parliament was completely subservient to the king. The nobility had been decimated by the **Wars of the Roses** and the remnants were forced, by a combination of threats and rewards, to enact laws that prevented future baronial resistance. Henry did recognise the importance of Parliament, however, and used it as a rubber stamp to legitimise his claim to the throne and strengthen his position. Once he had achieved this, he only summoned Parliament once after 1496, a fact made possible by his avoidance of war and the need to raise extra revenue.

If his son had been just as financially prudent, then matters may have turned out very differently. However, **Henry VIII**'s wars with France and Scotland were only made possible by grants of money voted for in Parliament. Wealth generated from the **Dissolution of the Monasteries** and **debasement** of the currency certainly helped in the **Third Anglo-French War** but even this was not enough.

In his reign, religion and the royal succession became important elements that were added to the mix. Henry needed to show the Pope and other foreign powers that he was acting with the will of the English people when he decided to break from Rome, annul his marriage to **Catherine of Aragon** and alter the succession. To do this, he summoned the longest Parliament that had ever sat – the Reformation Parliament (1529–36). This body enacted a series of important laws, probably unaware of their profound impact on the country's future. The members were also just as likely unaware of the power shift that was starting to happen. Parliament was no longer just the rubber stamp that passed laws and raised taxes; it had now become a vital instrument in matters of religion and even the succession.

The Crown was still the ultimate authority though. Indeed, the Statute of Proclamations (1539) marked the zenith of Henry's despotic rule by allowing the king to make laws without Parliament's approval. His chief minister, Cromwell, had pushed it through to allow Henry to make quick decisions but the law was repealed in 1547. Henry and Cromwell were also very good at manipulating Parliament – they would 'pack' it by ensuring their men won by-elections and, during key votes, the king would intimidate MPs by making himself present and even order his opponents to stay at home. On the whole, though, Henry's parliaments were very anti-clerical, which made it a lot easier for him but even he recognised the need to compromise whenever Parliament objected.

The shift in power must have become more noticeable in **Mary I**'s reign. Her attempts to 'pack' Parliament with **Catholic** MPs were largely in vain and she was not able to push through several religious reforms. Parliament even enforced restrictions on the powers of her husband, Prince Philip of Spain.

By **Elizabeth I**'s reign, the Lords was still the senior chamber but its members continued to be compliant as they directly owed their titles and lands to the

Crown. The **Northern Rebellion** (1569) represented the final fling of nobility attempting to reimpose itself but its failure only served to emphasise their submissiveness. The Commons, on the other hand, was becoming more vocal and assertive. This was partly due to the Crown's greater reliance on Parliament to push through its agenda but also the sixteenth century saw the growth of England's middle class. Increased prosperity though greater trading opportunities, more authority given to middle-class officials, such as justices of the peace, due to centralisation of the state and the distribution of land and wealth caused by the Dissolution of the Monasteries were just some of the reasons for this.

So, of all the Tudors, it was Elizabeth who had the unhappiest relationship with Parliament, even though it often expressed its 'love for her'. Amongst the Commons' demands were that she married in order to provide an heir, the execution of **Mary, Queen of Scots**, the inclusion of **Puritan** principles in the Church of England and freedom of speech within the chamber. In response, the queen ordered Parliament to only discuss issues that she proposed and tried to bully the Commons into submission and create 'packed' parliaments. She even imprisoned her most vocal critic, **Peter Wentworth**, in the **Tower of London** on three occasions. Towards the end of her reign, however, it was Elizabeth who blinked first. Desperate for money to fund the **Anglo-Spanish War** and suppress **Tyrone's Rebellion**, she increasingly gave way to Parliament's demands. The 1597–98 Parliament was the first to pass laws that *it* had initiated, not the Crown.

After Elizabeth's death, there was little affection for her successor, James I, and the Commons made more strident attempts to flex its new muscles. It is a great irony that it was Henry VIII's use of Parliament to increase royal power that eventually led to Parliament's destruction of the Crown's authority in the English Civil Wars one hundred years later.

Parr, Catherine

(1512–48)

Sixth wife of King **Henry VIII** and Queen of England from 1543 to 1547.

Catherine was the daughter of Sir Thomas Parr, an important northern landowner and a friend and courtier of Henry VIII. Her mother, Maud Green, was a lady-in-waiting to **Catherine of Aragon**, after whom Catherine was probably named. After her husband's death in 1517, Maud ensured that her daughter received a sound, **humanist education** like that being encouraged by **Sir Thomas More**. As well as becoming fluent in French, Latin and Italian, Catherine learned **etiquette** and could sing, dance and play music.

Catherine is the most married queen in English history. At seventeen, she was wedded to Sir Edward Borough but, after four years of ill-health, he died. In the following year, she married Lord Latimer, who already had two children from his previous **marriage**. In 1536, Catherine and her step-children were held hostage by rebels during the **Pilgrimage of Grace** and threatened with death and it is quite possible that this experience started her conversion to the **Protestant** faith.

Soon after moving to London, Latimer died (1543) and Catherine found a place in Princess **Mary**'s household. At the same time, she fell in love with **Thomas Seymour**, the brother of King Henry's third wife and it seems that they would have quickly married had she not caught the king's attention. He made his own proposal and sent Seymour to Brussels to keep him out of the way. Out of a sense of duty, Catherine agreed to marry Henry despite his decrepit state and the recent execution of his fifth wife, **Catherine Howard**. The wedding took place in July 1543 and they honeymooned at the king's favourite hunting lodges in Surrey whilst avoiding an outbreak of plague in London.

Catherine was a caring stepmother to Mary, **Elizabeth** and **Edward** and ensured that the latter two received an excellent humanist education from scholars such as **John Cheke** and Roger Ascham. She was also partly responsible for reconciling Mary and Elizabeth with Henry and having them included in the succession in 1543. It seems that Henry was very pleased with his new wife too. Apparently the marriage was consummated, despite his growing impotence, and he enjoyed having her sit on his lap and watching her dance.

However, the Catholic faction at court, led by Bishop **Gardiner** and the Lord Chancellor, Thomas Wriothesley, were concerned that Catherine was a reformist whose influence was dangerous. Their concerns were magnified by the Protestant friends she kept and by Henry appointing her regent whilst he was in France in 1544. At first, they tried to prove her connection to the Protestant preacher, **Anne Askew**. After that failed, charges of heresy were brought against her on the basis of expressing non-conformist views to her friends. Forewarned of her arrest warrant, Catherine rushed to the king. She explained that she just enjoyed theological debates, like she did with Henry, and begged for his forgiveness. This was granted and when Wriothesley arrived with soldiers the next day to arrest her, he received a verbal tirade from the king and told to leave.

After Henry VIII's death (1547), Catherine retired to her manor in Chelsea on a very generous pension and when Thomas Seymour returned, he and Catherine renewed their courtship and secretly married. This caused a scandal as a dowager queen was supposed to seek royal permission to remarry and Edward VI and Princess Mary showed their displeasure. At the same time, a row broke out between Catherine and Anne Seymour, the wife of the Lord Protector (**Edward Seymour**), over should be allowed to wear the queen's jewels.

This also led to bad blood between the Seymour brothers.

Much to Catherine's surprise, she became pregnant at the age of thirty-five in late 1547, having failed to conceive in her previous three marriages. Her husband, however, was taking an unhealthy interest in the fourteen-year-old, Princess Elizabeth, who was staying in their household and allegedly had plans to marry her. After catching the pair in an embrace, Catherine sent Elizabeth away to another household. In August 1548, she gave birth to a daughter, Mary, but died six days later from 'childbed fever' – a common cause of death due to the lack of hygiene during childbirth. Hers was the first Protestant funeral, held in English, that was performed in Britain.

Catherine Parr. (*Artist and date: unknown. Based on a miniature by Hans Holbein. Wellcome Images*)

There is much to admire about Catherine Parr. She had an independent spirit combined with a great sense of loyalty and was, possibly, the most educated of Henry VIII's wives. She was the first woman to have work published, under her own name, in English, and wrote three small religious books. Her third, *The Lamentation of a Sinner*, published after Henry's death, clearly showed her Protestant beliefs.

Pilgrimage of Grace

(1536)

A major uprising in northern England.

The prelude to this revolt was an uprising that occurred in Lincolnshire in October, 1536. The threat of armed suppression was enough to make the rebels disperse within a few days and most of the ringleaders were executed. It did, however, inspire a more serious uprising in Yorkshire, in which the participants referred to themselves as 'pilgrims' on a religious journey, rather than rebels.

There was a combination of religious, economic and political causes although it was religion that provided the spark. The 'pilgrims' wanted papal supremacy to be restored after **Henry VIII**'s break from Rome and were unhappy with the closure of the smaller religious houses at the start of the **Dissolution of the**

Monasteries. There was a higher concentration of monasteries in the north and they played an integral part in people's lives such as providing alms for the poor, care for the sick and employment on their estates. Also, in the previous year, the king had sharply raised taxes and there were rumours of further taxes to come. On top of this, an increasing **population**, a series of bad harvests and the spread of **enclosures** had caused great economic hardship. Politically, they demanded the removal of Henry's advisors – **Thomas Cromwell**, Archbishop **Cranmer** and Bishop **Latimer**, in particular, and the restoration of Princess **Mary** to the royal succession. Finally, centralisation of the state left many in the north feeling that they no longer had any political representation.

A lawyer called Robert Aske, was chosen as leader and the rebels took control of Hull, York and Pontefract. A few noble families joined the revolt and, within a few weeks, the rebels numbered around 35,000 men. The **Third Duke of Norfolk** was despatched with troops but was hopelessly outnumbered. He also knew that many of those who opposed him were experienced soldiers who had frequently fought with Scottish border raiders. So he decided to play for time and parley on the king's behalf near Doncaster. He promised to submit their demands to Henry, offered a general pardon and a promise to cease the closures of monasteries until at least **Parliament** had met in York to discuss the matter.

With these assurances, the rebels dispersed and returned home. Aske was invited to London to discuss the grievances in more detail and, in so doing, revealed the names of all the other ringleaders. By the time Aske returned home, many rebels were suspicious that they had been betrayed by the king and maybe by their own leaders too. No general pardon had been issued and Norfolk's forces were still in the vicinity. Possibly, there would have been no repercussions but Henry was unlikely to forgive rebels who had dared to question his authority and judgement. In any case, the perfect excuse was provided in February 1537 when Sir Francis Bigod led a further uprising in Cumberland.

This was crushed and, despite, the leaders of the 'Pilgrimage' condemning the new revolt, fifteen of them were rounded up for treason. After some sham trials, most were executed in London and Aske was hanged at York. At least 200 others were executed too; these victims representing the cross-section of society that had protested – several lords and knights, seven abbots, thirty-eight monks, sixteen priests and the rest, commoners.

The Pilgrimage of Grace might have succeeded if the leadership had been more united and decisive and shown less trust in the king. If they had marched south, they may well have attracted more support and had the Pope denounced Henry and urged a foreign power to attack then matters may have turned out very differently. All of the monasteries were dissolved by 1540 but the uprising cannot be deemed a complete failure though – the pace of religious reform was halted by the Six **Articles** of 1539, more political representation was provided in the Council of the North, illegal enclosures were reduced and a few taxes were postponed or reduced.

Pinkie Cleugh, Battle of
(1547)

A significant battle, militarily, in the **War of the Rough Wooing**.

In 1543, King **Henry VIII** had initiated the **Third Anglo-French War**, which, in turn, had brought France's ally, Scotland, into the conflict. At the same time, Henry had been keen to betroth his son, **Edward**, to the baby **Mary, Queen of Scots** in order to bring the two kingdoms closer together and nullify Scotland as a threat to his northern border. The dominant pro-French faction in the Scottish government, however, refused to comply and requested French military aid. Henry had, therefore, launched the War of the Rough Wooing in order to force the issue. Henry died in early 1547 but Edward VI's Lord Protector, the **Duke of Somerset**, had decided to continue the war and inflict a decisive defeat upon the Scots.

In September, English forces, numbering around 17,000, crossed into Scotland and marched up the east coast, accompanied and supplied by a fleet of thirty warships. The Scottish regent, the Earl of Arran, drew up his army of about 26,000 men five miles east of Edinburgh. He took up a defensive stance along a north–south ridge with the River Esk in front of him and, with the Firth of Forth protecting his left flank and a large marsh guarding his right, this was a formidable position for his English opponents to storm.

The sixteenth century was, militarily, a period of transition and both armies were still some way behind their continental counterparts in terms of tactics and weaponry. However, changes were underway as both sides were beginning to embrace the gunpowder revolution by employing more artillery and arquebusiers. An arquebus was an early matchlock musket which fired lead balls that could penetrate armour at an effective range of up to twenty-five metres. The Scots' army had both but it still relied upon its echelons of pikemen, which were

Nineteenth-century depiction of sixteenth-century knight and arquebusier. (*From* Military and religious life in the Middle Ages and at the period of the Renaissance *by PL Jacob, 1870. Getty Research Institute*)

very effective against cavalry and could even be an excellent offensive force when well-coordinated. The Scottish forces also included more mobile Highlanders, armed with longbows, swords and small axes and around 1,500 cavalry.

The English army, too, looked largely medieval with the majority of its troops armed with longbows and bills (shorter than a pike but lighter and had a cutting edge). However, Somerset had also hired 800 musketmen, including a troop of Spanish mounted arquebusiers who could shoot, wheel away to reload and return to fire again. His forces also included significantly more artillery and around 5,000 mounted troops.

The day before the battle, Somerset sent his fastest mounted lancers to clear an overlooking hill of enemy cavalry. The Scottish horsemen were so badly mauled that they could play no future significant role. After this, Arran sent a request for the battle to be decided by two champions in single combat and, later, by twenty hand-picked men but Somerset refused.

On the next day, 10 September, Arran was faced with a dilemma. If he stayed where he was, English cannons would eventually reach the hill he had just lost and pour fire upon his troops. Equally bad, a retreat would leave his men horribly exposed to the enemy cavalry. That morning, however, an unexpected opportunity arose. The English forces were spotted heading north, either to embark on their ships or occupy another hill overlooking the Scots' positions. Seeing the exposed enemy flank, he ordered his infantry to attack at great speed before the English ranged units could be brought to bear.

The speed of the Scots' advance caught the English by surprise. With his infantry at risk of being overwhelmed, Somerset had no choice but to throw in his cavalry. Against rows of massed pikes, English casualties were high and the commander himself, Lord Grey, received a pike thrust into his mouth. The attack, however, did slow the Scots down and give the English artillery and arquebusiers time to deploy. At the same time, Somerset's warships opened fire on the Scottish left flank where swathes of Highlanders were mown down by murderous cannon fire. This caused them to move inland and become entangled with Arran's centre, thereby slowing the pace of the Scottish attack even further.

The Scots' pikemen, well trained by French officers, maintained their discipline, though, and drove off another cavalry attack. At one point, the English standard was nearly captured and the Scots cheered, holding up its snapped-off staff, as the cavalry retreated. By now, however, they had lost all momentum and their fate was sealed. English cannons, arquebuses and longbows now unleashed a hail of projectiles at close range. Inevitably, the Scottish lines broke as they flung aside their weapons and fled west, pursued by a vengeful English cavalry right up to the gates of Edinburgh.

The Scots suffered most of their fatalities during these final stages but the number of overall casualties for both sides is not clear. Conservative estimates

19th-century depiction of the fight for the standard at Pinkie. (*From* British Battles on Land and Sea, *volume 1 by James Grant, 1873. British Library via Flickr*)

suggest around 6,000 Scots and about 500 English. The Scots called this defeat 'Black Saturday' but they refused to surrender. French reinforcements beefed up their defences and the young Mary was spirited away to safety in France. In addition, Somerset's garrisons in southern Scotland were forced to withdraw over the next couple of years. The battle, therefore, had negligible political effect.

Pinkie Cleugh was the last pitched battle fought between England and Scotland (future clashes, such as Culloden, were fought against Scottish rebels). From a military point of view, it also had much significance and has been described as Britain's first modern battle. It was the first time, in the British Isles, that all three wings of an army – infantry, cavalry and artillery – combined in a coordinated fashion and the first time a naval bombardment supported a land battle.

Pole, Reginald

(1500–58)

Cardinal and Archbishop of Canterbury.

Pole was born at Stourton Castle, Staffordshire, the son of Richard and Margaret Pole. Richard was a cousin of **Henry VII** and Margaret was a niece of the Yorkist king, Edward IV so **Henry VIII** took a great interest in his second cousin, generously financing his **education** at Oxford and Padua universities and giving him a deanery in Dorset in order to acquire an income. Whilst at Padua, Pole came into contact with many of Europe's leading scholars and corresponded with the great humanist, Desiderius Erasmus.

After returning from Italy in 1527, Pole was given a series of posts in the Church, despite not even being ordained, and, two years later, the king sent him to Paris in order to obtain the views of its university regarding a possible annulment of his **marriage** to **Catherine of Aragon**. He returned a year later and Henry, keen to have his eminent kinsman on his side, offered him the archbishopric of York. Pole, however, was feeling increasingly at odds with the king's plans to annul his marriage and weaken the Pope's power and so politely declined.

In 1532, he went into a self-imposed exile from which he would not return for another twenty-two years. Henry sent several messages imploring him to return but, in 1536, their friendship became irrevocably broken. Pole, now in Italy again, had heard about the executions of Bishop **Fisher**, **Thomas More** and several abbots who refused to acknowledge the king as the Head of the English Church. When the **Dissolution of the Monasteries** began, he could no longer remain loyal and wrote a book condemning Henry's actions. Furthermore, he urged foreign rulers to invade England to support the **Pilgrimage of Grace** and recover the realm for the Pope. Henry was incensed and sanctioned assassination attempts on Pole. When this failed, he took his revenge on Pole's brothers and mother by imprisoning them and taking their lands. Most shocking of all was the ill-treatment of the frail, old Margaret in the **Tower of London** before being beheaded in 1541. After her death, Pole was one of the last surviving Yorkist claimants to the throne and there were discussions about marrying him to the **Catholic** Princess **Mary**. This would have maintained the Tudor-Yorkist union and brought England back to the papal fold but he was never really interested.

Pole was now persuaded to accept the position of cardinal and papal legate to England by the Pope, which only served to further infuriate Henry. In 1549, he was nearly elected Pope (there has only ever been one English pope) but the French and Italian cardinals did not like his closeness to Charles V, the Holy Roman Emperor and they considered him too liberal in his views. He had previously succeeded in brokering a deal with German **Protestants** by compromising with them. This, in turn, led to accusations that he was a Protestant himself.

After Mary I's accession to the English throne in 1553, the Pope and Charles V delayed Pole's journey to England for fear that an immediate return of a papal legate might stir up English public opinion and wreck Mary's plan to marry Charles's son, Prince Philip of Spain. Moreover, it was rumoured that he disapproved of the marriage himself. The Pope, instead, asked him to attempt to broker a peace deal between the warring Charles and Henry II of France.

Pole eventually returned to the country of his birth in November, 1554 and was finally ordained a priest before being appointed Archbishop of Canterbury. He officially restored papal authority to England and, along with Bishop **Gardiner**, reinstalled Catholic practices to the English Church. After Gardiner's death in 1555, Pole was Mary's chief minister. He has been accused of helping to organise the persecution of Protestants but there is no evidence of this. He had always hated extremism and, in fact, issued pardons to three condemned heretics in order to save them from the stake.

He dared not speak out against the burnings, however, as he had fallen out with the new Pope who detested the mild, Catholic **humanism** that Pole favoured. The Pope's dislike of Pole was exacerbated by Mary's decision to help her husband and attack his ally, France. Although Pole had implored Mary not to join the war, the Pope accused him of heresy and demanded his presence in Rome. The queen refused to let him go, however.

Reginald Pole had been quite frail for a number of years and it was an influenza epidemic that took his life in November 1558, twelve hours after Mary's death. He was a man of deep convictions although he was never ambitious for himself and always believed in moderation and this applied to his private life too. He must have died with a great sense of disappointment, not only with the actions of the Pope but also knowing that Princess **Elizabeth**'s accession to the throne would undo all that he had striven for.

Poor Laws

Between 1440 and 1519 the price of wheat had stayed consistently low. This was largely due to stagnant population growth and therefore the low demand for bread. During the sixteenth century, however, England experienced a rapid **population** growth, which led to greater demand and higher prices and was not matched by increased work opportunities. This naturally led to a great increase in the numbers of those in poverty.

Other factors also came into play which exacerbated the problem in the Tudor period. First and foremost was the **Dissolution of the Monasteries** (1536–40). Previously, religious houses had provided alms relief for the poor and employment on their estates and, after their closures, nothing replaced them on the same scale. In the mid-sixteenth century, **debasement** of the coinage increased inflation and the spread of **enclosures** by landowners led to people being forced off their lands and an increase in the price of wheat as more land was being given over to sheep. The effects of warfare should not be forgotten either. During the **Wars of the Roses**, fighting had been intermittent and limited to just a few months at a time. However, England was at war for over a quarter of the entire Tudor period. This led to increases in poverty-inducing taxes, widows who could not provide for their children and returning soldiers unable to work due to their injuries. On top of all these were the intermittent poor harvests that led to price increases in food.

As a result, it has been estimated that about one third of the population was in poverty. For successive Tudor governments, the idea of thousands of people wandering around the country to beg or find work was anathema – it was important that people stayed with their masters and not upset the social order. Therefore, attempts were made to deal with the effects, not so much the causes, of poverty and a carrot-and-stick approach was generally adopted.

The 1494 Vagabonds and Beggars Act of **Parliament** stipulated that anyone wandering around without a job should be put in the stocks for three days and nights then returned to wherever they had come from. The 1530 Vagabonds Act raised the punishment level to whipping but it was the first law to provide some relief for the needy – those unable to work due to sickness, age or disability were able to acquire a licence to beg by their local justices of the peace. These 'impotent poor' were further aided by a 1536 law, which, for the first time, put the onus of responsibility onto parishes which were supposed to organise weekly, voluntary collections. The 1547 Vagabonds Act was possibly the harshest of all the 'sticks' and stated that all non-impotent vagabonds should be enslaved for two years or sent back to the town of their birth and be a slave in its community.

The 1550s saw the beginning of more serious efforts to help the poor. For those who could not find jobs, each parish had to build a workhouse, where they would work in return for food and shelter. Everyone in the parish was

Vagrant being punished in the streets. (*Artist: unknown, c. 1536. Wikimedia Commons*)

supposed to donate money and those who refused would be reported to the local bishop. The parishes also had to create a register of their poor and provide those registered with a badge, which allowed them to beg.

By **Elizabeth I**'s reign, the issue of poverty and the associated rise in **crime** rates had become much more serious. It is estimated that about ten per cent of the population were wondering around looking for work. So in the 1560s and 1570s, laws were enacted that provided the first comprehensive attempt to tackle the problem. For the first time, the poor were officially categorised into two groups: deserving poor (who were unable to work or were looking for work) and undeserving poor or sturdy beggars (those who chose not to work). It was made compulsory for all people to pay to help those unable to work and raw materials, such as wool, hemp, flax and iron had to be provided for those looking for work. A long list was produced to show the types of undeserving poor, which included fraudsters, travelling entertainers and university students!

The 1601 Poor Relief Act formalised previous poor laws and tidied them up into one piece of legislation. This included the provision of apprenticeships for poor children and putting undeserving poor into 'houses of correction', where they had to carry out unpaid, hard labour. For its time, it was considered to be very compassionate in its approach to poverty. It had its flaws, of course. For example, levels of provision varied wildly from parish to parish and poor people tended to gravitate towards the more generous parishes which would often try to send them back. This final Tudor statute became the basis of all future poor-related legislation right up to 1834.

Population

The estimated population of England in 1400 was 2 million people. By 1500, it had crept up to 2.2 million; by 1600, it had exploded to 4.1 million. The higher fertility rate in Tudor England may have been due to increased immunity to diseases such as the plague that had first arrived in the mid-fourteenth century. Also, the higher mortality rate caused by the plague in the fifteenth century had probably weakened the patriarchal system, which allowed women to have more control over their pregnancies. During the Tudor period, the patriarchal system was reasserted and it was the fathers who determined the number of children, which they tended to regard more as economic assets. The fertility rate in England in 1580 is estimated to have been 34.5 live births per 1,000 people (compared to 1.6 today) although the very high infant mortality rate in Tudor times must be taken into account.

In 1600, Scotland's and Ireland's populations were around 850,000 and 500,000 respectively. Compared to most continental countries, however,

Earliest known map of London. The Tower is clearly visible on the right with the city wall snaking around anti-clockwise from its north side. London Bridge, in the foreground, leads to the open fields, theatres, brothels and bear-baiting pits on the south side. The amount of river traffic shows the importance of the Thames as a transport artery. West of the city, Fleet Street and the Strand pass by the Temple law courts and orchards before reaching the centre of government at Westminster in the bottom-left corner. The slums north of the city are starting to appear. (*Artist: Ralph Agas. Civitas Londinium, 1570–1605. From* Maps of old London *by G Mitton, 1908*)

England's population was dwarfed. France had 16 million people, the Holy Roman Empire had 20 million and Spain and Portugal combined had about 9 million. Looking at these figures, it is easy to see why lack of numbers and less taxation revenue made England a small-time player when it tried to compete in continental wars. Conversely, Scotland and Ireland were always at a military disadvantage compared to England.

The supply of basic foodstuffs was not able to keep up with the increased demand caused by population growth, which led to high inflation. It has been estimated that the price of staple food increased six fold in the sixteenth century with half of that growth occurring after 1570. Simultaneously, a larger number of people on the labour market meant that landowners could charge higher rents and pay lower wages. Measured against inflation, the value of people's wages roughly halved between 1500 and 1600. All of this inevitably led to a much greater degree of poverty amongst the masses and food riots in the 1580s and 1590s became commonplace.

For some, however, population growth provided an opportunity. Lower wages and higher rents led to bigger profit margins for landowners. Their extra wealth allowed them to beautify their homes and buy extra political influence and the greater possibility of entering **Parliament**. In the towns, merchants and traders could reinvest their extra profits to grow their businesses or invest in new opportunities. This contributed to the development of a larger and more vocal middle class.

Seventy-five per cent of England's population lived in rural communities (twenty-one per cent today). The largest town, by far, was London. Between 1550 and 1600, its population rose from 120,000 to 200,000 (population of Rochdale or Milton Keynes in 2024). Nearly all of this rise was fuelled by migration with an estimated 12,000 fleeing rural poverty every year. This led to the growth of slums north of the city and the associated endemic diseases within them. The next largest towns were Norwich and Bristol (around 20,000 each) and York (12,000). Most towns had between 2,500 and 4,000 inhabitants.

Although growing, the population of Tudor England was roughly four per cent of what it is today. It is easy not to realise the impact of living in a society with much smaller communities. The effect of any single event would be hugely magnified: a public hanging in the market place, the conversion of a prominent family to a new faith, knowledge of who was deserving poor and who was not, an eminent citizen with a new item of fashion, a handful of men killed in a war, an influenza epidemic, a royal progress passing through, an adulterous affair. Even in a century without the internet and social media, nothing could remain hidden and influencers made a greater impact.

Prayer Book Rebellion

(1549)

An uprising in Cornwall and Devon in the reign of **Edward VI**.

Resentment had been simmering in the far south-west of the country for quite a while. **Population** growth, currency **debasement** and **enclosures** had caused much economic hardship, which was exacerbated by a poor harvest in 1548 and a recent poll tax on sheep that had been imposed to fund a war in Scotland. Being a peripheral part of the country, its people were generally more conservative, superstitious and resistant to change. For these reasons, the **Dissolution of the Monasteries** (1536–40) had been deeply unpopular, notwithstanding the fact that the monks had provided alms for the poor.

After Edward VI's accession to the throne, attempts were made to create a **Protestant** Church of England. Churches were the centres of rural communities and now, these too were under attack. Religious processions were banned and all symbols of the **Catholic** faith, such as candlesticks, paintings and altars, began to be removed from churches. The final straw came in May 1549, when priests were ordered to use the new English Prayer Book, devised by Archbishop **Cranmer**. Western Cornwall, where few could speak English, particularly resented this further encroachment on their native language.

The uprising began in the small town of Sampford Courtenay, mid-Devon, where the priest was forced to perform the traditional Catholic Mass and not use the new prayer book. A mob of demonstrators then marched to Exeter in order to demand an end to the changes and a return to the Six **Articles** of 1539, which had asserted the Catholic religion in **Henry VIII**'s reign. At the same time, a force of Cornishmen, led by Sir Humphrey Arundell, had gathered at Bodmin and, by the end of June, had joined the Devon rebels outside Exeter. It was hoped that the city would open its gates and then be used as a fortified base but, despite messages of support from inside the walls, the city managed to withstand a five-week siege.

The Lord Protector, the **Duke of Somerset**, sent an army, led by Lord Russell, Lord Grey and Sir **Peter Carew**, which now approached from the east. It numbered around 8,500 troops, some of whom were well-trained German pikemen and Italian arquebusier mercenaries. Arundell, with 7,000 men, now had to split his forces, with some maintaining the siege of Exeter and the majority blocking the king's forces to the east. After a couple of indecisive engagements, the rebels were finally forced back near the village of Clyst St Mary. Russell now had 900 prisoners but, fearing they would break out, ordered their throats cut, an act that was carried out in just ten minutes. News of the slaughter caused Arundell to launch a fierce assault. The ensuing Battle of Clyst Heath (6 August) lasted all day and even Lord Grey, a veteran of **Pinkie Cleugh**, had never seen such ferocious fighting.

The rebels were decisively beaten, though, and many were killed as they retreated west. Russell triumphantly entered Exeter but then heard that Arundell had regrouped his forces at Sampford Courtenay, where the revolt had begun. There, the hopelessly outnumbered rebels fought bravely but were routed. Their leaders, including Arundell, were captured and later executed in London. During the fighting and its subsequent brutal aftermath, an estimated 5,500 men were killed (about three per cent of the combined counties' population).

Prayer Book Rebellion. The commemorative plaque at Sampford Courtenay. (*Author: Michael Garlick, 2016*)

Had Exeter opened its gates, had the rebels marched east earlier and gained more support and had they managed to coordinate their actions with those involved in **Kett's Rebellion** in Norfolk (unlikely, given the distance between them) things may have turned out differently. As it was, it took many years for the far south-west to recover and the decline of Cornish culture and its language was accelerated. It was not until 2007 that the Bishop of Truro apologised, on behalf of the Church of England, for the massacre and repression.

Protestant

A follower of Protestantism, a form of Christianity that appeared in the sixteenth century.

The word 'Protestant' first appeared in the 1520s to describe someone who protested against the Roman **Catholic** Church. Initially, Protestants did not aim to start a new religion but merely wanted to reform the Catholic Church and their views had become known as early as the late-fourteenth-century. John Wycliffe in England and Jan Huss in Bohemia had started movements that demanded change but they and their followers were declared heretics and had been persecuted.

Protestantism resurfaced in 1517 when the monk and theologian, Martin Luther, nailed ninety-five arguments against indulgences to a church door in Wittenberg, Germany. An indulgence was a forgiveness for one's sins that could be purchased from the Church. Luther also declared that the Catholic

Church had become corrupt and offered some profound beliefs that seriously challenged its authority:

1. Salvation could only be achieved through one's faith in God and purgatory did not exist. Good works, such as pilgrimages and charity, were unnecessary. Catholics believed in both faith and good works as well as purgatory.
2. Christians only needed to look to the Bible as the source of all truth. Many traditions of the Catholic Church were false and the Pope and his bishops were not infallible. Catholics believed that the Bible and their Church had equal authority and their leaders should not be questioned.
3. Following on from this, the Bible should be translated into national languages so that more people could understand it for themselves. Catholics believed that Latin was the holy language and only priests could interpret the Bible's teachings.
4. The worship of saints and idols, such as statues and stained-glass windows, was unnecessary. These were merely distractions and barriers between people and God. The use of idols in churches had been a Catholic tradition for centuries and represented God's glory, according to Catholics, and saints should be worshipped.
5. As faith was a private affair, it did not matter if priests married. Catholics believed that celibacy for priests was vital if they were to devote themselves wholly to God's work.
6. God is merely present during the Eucharist; the bread and wine are only symbols of Christ's body and blood. Catholics believed in transubstantiation – that the bread and wine actually turn into Jesus's body and blood.

Luther's views sparked the **Reformation** in Europe. His belief in religion having a more individual focus, with less dependence on the established Church was a serious challenge to the Pope's authority. He was excommunicated but local German princes protected him because his rapidly growing popularity strengthened their push for greater independence within the Holy Roman Empire.

Protestantism quickly spread throughout much of northern Europe and became a tool of nationalism as many countries declared it to be their national faith and split away from Rome. As it spread, it splintered into various forms such as Zwinglism, Calvinism and Presbyterianism (Scotland). In England, Protestantism only became established in **Elizabeth I**'s reign, after three decades of religious turmoil. Its form, known as Anglicanism, was a watered-down version that tried to appeal to England's Catholic **population**.

Luther himself had never wanted a schism within the Church. He had started something that had spiralled out of control and would have shuddered at all the subsequent persecutions and wars of religion that were to engulf Europe for over a hundred years.

Puritan

A follower of Puritanism, a religious movement that arose in the reign of **Elizabeth I**.

Puritanism in England coalesced around those who had fled the persecutions under **Mary I** and become exposed to a more ardent form of **Protestant**ism abroad. They returned to England after Elizabeth became queen and, in the 1560s, started to campaign for a Church of England that was completely purified of all traces of **Catholic**ism. Basically, they thought that the queen's Church Settlement of 1559 did not go far enough. Their main beliefs were:

1. Predestination. God had already decided who was going to Heaven and Hell. As no one knew who had been 'elected' for Heaven, it was important to live a simple life, like Jesus had, and which was based on the teachings in the Bible, in case God changed his mind.
2. There should be no church hierarchy, especially bishops. Churches should be run by their congregations.
3. Churches should be plain, with no organs, candlesticks, clerical vestments, etc.
4. Nothing should be done to excess, such as drinking, dancing, attending the theatre, reading for pleasure or dressing extravagantly.
5. Only religious study should be allowed on Sundays.

Puritanism took root especially in the south-east of the country and amongst members of the growing middle class, such as lawyers and merchants. Even members of Elizabeth's Privy Council, such as **Cecil**, **Walsingham** and **Leicester** had Puritan sympathies although their loyalty to the queen always came first.

During her reign, Elizabeth faced a series of challenges from the Puritans. In **Parliament**, their members in the Commons became vocal and made demands that concerned the queen's marriage, freedom of speech, changes to the Church of England and the execution of **Mary, Queen of Scots**. These angered Elizabeth, who ordered Parliament not to discuss these matters and imprisoned those who went too far.

She also clamped-down on printing presses that distributed Puritan pamphlets and banned 'prophesying' groups (religious training meetings for Puritans). The largest protest was by Puritan priests who refused to wear vestments as they believed that the wearing of special clothes suggested that one person was superior to others. Archbishop **Parker** simply removed them from their posts and many parishes had no priests for a while.

By the 1590s, the challenge from Puritanism had died down. Elizabeth had been determined to defend the Church of England and her repression of the dissenters had largely succeeded as well as the fact that most of the older Puritan leaders had died. However, it was left to her Stuart successors to deal with resurgent Puritanism that was to contribute to the outbreak of the English Civil Wars in the mid-seventeenth century.

R

Ralegh, Sir Walter

(1552/54–1618)

Courtier, explorer and writer.

Ralegh was born into a wealthy, Protestant landowning family in east Devon and he was a younger half-brother of **Humphrey Gilbert** and a cousin of **Richard Grenville**. His father had once hidden in a church to avoid an angry mob during the **Prayer Book Rebellion** and, during **Mary I**'s reign, he had had to hide in a church again to escape execution.

As a result, Ralegh grew up with a hatred of **Catholicism**, which explains why he fought on the Protestant side in the French Civil War (1569) and helped to brutally suppress a rebellion in south-west **Ireland** (1579–80). Afterwards, he was granted land there, introduced English and Scots settlers and built a family home in Youghal. He was also much influenced by Gilbert, with whom he voyaged in the Atlantic, and by the mathematician, **John Dee**, who shared his vision of a Tudor empire in North America.

He came to Queen **Elizabeth I**'s attention soon after his return from Ireland in the early 1580s. The story goes that he laid his expensive cloak on the ground so that she could walk across a puddle. True or not, it does reflect Ralegh's gallant and self-confident nature, which, along with his wit, charm and tall physique, would have endeared him to the queen. During the 1580s they spent much time together, playing cards or riding horses, and she enjoyed listening to his poetry. He, in turn, received many favours and positions, was knighted in 1585 and she granted him lucrative monopolies in wine licenses, tin and playing cards. Ralegh's wealth, closeness to the queen and flamboyant dress sense tended to arouse much envy and disdain from his peers, such as **Leicester** and **Essex**. However, he was never admitted to the Privy Council as Elizabeth did not trust him with any position of real authority.

Walter Ralegh. (*Artist: Robert Vaughan, 1650. Copy of an engraving by Simon van de Passe. British Museum*)

In 1584, the queen issued Ralegh with a charter to colonise new lands in North America, a project he had long dreamed about. In his first attempt, he landed soldiers on **Roanoke** Island in an area he called Virginia, in honour of his 'Virgin Queen'. They were too dependent on the native Indians for food, however, and had to be rescued by **Francis Drake**. His second attempt (1587) was better planned and included whole families who were more able to look after themselves. However, a mission to resupply them was delayed by three years, partly because of the threat from the **Spanish Armada**. When the supply ship finally arrived, the colonists had all mysteriously disappeared.

Ralegh made no more similar ventures but his settlements, albeit temporary, were the first English colonies in America. One returning ship is thought to have brought the first potatoes to England. At first, they were regarded with suspicion and only given to livestock before being considered worthy of the poor. Tobacco had already been introduced by **John Hawkins** in the 1560s but Ralegh did popularise the habit of smoking, stating that it was a good cure for coughs! It became a craze in court in the 1590s and eventually spread to the rest of the country.

Ralegh fell from favour in 1592 when it was discovered that he had secretly married Bess Throckmorton, one of the queen's ladies-in-waiting. Elizabeth was furious as the queen's servants were expected to ask for permission to marry and so both were imprisoned in the **Tower**. After a few months, Ralegh was released in order to divide the spoils of a Spanish treasure carrack that one of his ships had captured. Bess followed soon after, only to find that her baby son had died of the plague in her absence. Now banned from court, Ralegh busied himself as a member of **Parliament** but had to defend himself from accusations of atheism, of which there was no proof.

Upon hearing rumours of El Dorado – a city of gold – in the middle of South America, Ralegh organised an expedition, which sailed up the Orinoco River in 1595. In the process, he raided some Spanish settlements but never succeeded in his main objective.

In 1596, he was involved in the successful capture of Cadiz despite being wounded in the leg and having bitter arguments with his commanders – Essex and **Lord Howard of Effingham**. The following year, Ralegh was wounded a second time and unfairly accused of insubordination by Essex during an abortive attempt to capture Spanish treasure ships in the Azores. Out of favour with the queen again, he returned to his Irish plantation only to find that he had been embezzled by his steward and so had to sell his lands there.

After Elizabeth's death in 1603, Ralegh led the Royal Guard at her funeral. However, the new king, James I, immediately showed his dislike of a man whose previous actions ran counter to his desire for peace with Spain. He also received a letter, probably written on **Robert Cecil**'s orders, in which Ralegh was accused of atheism and being hostile to James's accession. It was, after all, in Cecil's interests to remove a rival for the position of First Minister to the new king. Ralegh was stripped of his monopolies, titles and lands and then accused of being involved in a plot to remove James from the throne. The subsequent trial was a complete farce as no evidence was produced and Ralegh was sentenced to death. James then issued him with a pardon but he was to remain in the Tower of London for the next thirteen years.

He led a comfortable existence, however. His family often stayed with him and a son was conceived and born there! Whilst in captivity, Ralegh put much energy into writing poetry and prose, which was well received. His *History of the World* (he got as far as the second century BC) sold more copies than all the works of **Shakespeare** for a while and his *Report of the Truth of the Fight about the Isles of Azores* gave a dramatic account of the last moments of Richard Grenville's life. He also found time to experiment with herbs and alchemy.

Short of money, King James decided to release him in 1616 in order to find the gold mines which Ralegh had assured him were further up the Orinoco. He was under strict instructions, however, not to attack any Spanish settlements. Ralegh sold all that he had left to finance the voyage and set off across the Atlantic in March 1617. Contrary winds and an ill-disciplined crew made progress so slow that many died of disease. At the mouth of the Orinoco, Ralegh was too unwell to go any further and sent a reconnaissance party up the river led by his son, Wat. Wat was an energetic and rash young man who, at the dinner table a year previously, had boasted about sleeping with a local whore. When Ralegh found out that he had slept with the same woman just an hour previously, he had boxed his son's ears!

Unfortunately, Wat made one mistake too many and decided to lead an attack against a small Spanish fort. Not only did he lose his life in the process but he also condemned his father to death. Unable to find any gold, Ralegh returned to England where an outraged Spanish ambassador demanded his execution. James was embarrassed as he was in the middle of negotiating a marriage deal between his son and the Spanish infanta and so he invoked the original death sentence of 1603. In October 1618, Ralegh bravely laid his head on a block outside Westminster Palace. Detecting the executioner's hesitation, he cried, 'What dost thou fear? Strike man! Strike!' His embalmed head was presented to his wife who kept it in a velvet bag in a cupboard so it could be presented to his admirers. After her death, it was reunited with its body in St Margaret's Church, Westminster.

Sir Walter Ralegh was a flamboyant character whose airs and graces had never made him popular in court. There was, however, much sympathy for him at the end of his life for being a victim of injustice. He was one of those great dreamers who tended to put action before careful planning but, above all, he was the last of the great Elizabethans.

Reformation

The Reformation was the religious revolution that split the Christian Church in Europe into two camps – **Catholic** and **Protestant**. The Roman Catholic Church, led by the Pope in Rome, had dominated European Christianity for many centuries. Criticism of the Church had started as early as the late fourteenth century but 1517 is usually regarded as the beginning of the Reformation. In that year, a religious academic called Martin Luther nailed ninety-five arguments against indulgences to a church door in Wittenberg, Germany. Luther was also a monk who had become increasingly disenchanted with the Church but the selling of indulgences (pardons for sins) to fund the rebuilding of St Peter's Basilica in Rome was the last straw.

Martin Luther as an Augustinian monk. (*Artist: Lucas Cranach the Elder, 1520. Metropolitan Museum of Art*)

Luther went on to demand that the Church be purged of all the corruption that had built up over the centuries. He stated that the Bible should be the chief authority, not the Pope, and that salvation was through faith alone, not good works. He also argued that the Bible should be translated out of Latin and into languages that people could understand. Through the use of the recently introduced printing press, his ideas spread rapidly and fed into the anti-clerical mood at the time. Those who agreed with Luther became known as Protestants and a few, notably, Jean Calvin and Huldrych Zwingli, became leaders of splinter groups which advocated different strands of Protestantism.

Several leaders of northern countries adopted this new faith to foster a national identity by breaking away from the Pope's authority. In England, which already had a strong national identity, Protestantism slipped in accidentally, being a by-product of **Henry VIII**'s 'Great Matter' and his attempts to annul his marriage to **Catherine of Aragon**. Luther had never wanted to create a schism within the Christian Church but that is exactly what happened.

In response to the growing threat, the Catholic Church began the Counter-Reformation in the 1540s. This involved tackling the abuses within its own organisation, initiating an inquisition against heretics in Catholic territories, sending **Jesuit** priests to convert Protestants and using military power to counter Protestant forces. The Counter-Reformation achieved much success over the next hundred years by reversing the Protestant advances in France, southern Germany, Poland, Italy and the Spanish Netherlands but countless lives were lost in the persecutions and wars of religion that ensued.

Renaissance

The Renaissance was the revival of European culture that promoted the 'rebirth' of ancient classical literature, art, architecture and philosophy. It began in Italy in the late fourteenth century but did not reach England and northern Europe until the sixteenth century. Its causes were varied and complex. The discovery of Ancient Greek and Roman texts, interaction with the Arab world and its Muslim culture, the growth of a middle class that could invest more in luxuries, the increased patronage of rulers and technological innovations such as the printing press and improved ship design are to name but a few.

In England, the Renaissance started to become evident in the reign of **Henry VIII** but did not really flourish until the Elizabethan age. It was very much tied in with the growth of **humanism**, a philosophy that focused on individuality and how to improve society. Some of the earliest humanist scholars were **John Colet** and **Sir Thomas More**.

The English Renaissance was most noticeable in literature and music. The **Reformation** was key to the growth of literature as it ushered in works written

A sixteenth-century printing press in Germany. (*From Johann Ludwig Gottfried's Historical Chronicle, 1631. 1908 edition vis Wikimedia Commons*)

in English rather than Latin, which fewer people could understand. The spread of printing presses could then disperse these works to a far greater audience. The poems of Thomas Wyatt, **Henry Howard, Philip Sydney** and **Edmund Spenser**, for example, became much sought after and playwrights such as **William Shakespeare** and **Christopher Marlowe** contributed to the huge increase in popularity of theatres in **Elizabeth I**'s reign.

In music, **William Byrd** was the dominant composer. The quality and sheer quantity of work he produced was so revolutionary, especially for keyboards, that he had a major influence on continental composers. The Renaissance had much less effect on visual arts in England although there was a change in architectural style. Hampton Court Palace (finished in 1525) shows signs of this but it became more obvious in Queen Elizabeth's reign. She herself built no new palaces but encouraged her courtiers to modernise their grand mansions so they could house her on her summer progresses around the country. **Christopher Hatton**'s Holdenby House (1583), **William Cecil**'s Burghley House (1587) and **Bess of Hardwick**'s Hardwick Hall (1597) are fine examples of the English Renaissance style.

The greatest scientific figures in the realm were **John Dee** and Francis Bacon. Dee's efforts to push the boundaries in astronomy, mathematics, alchemy and geography impressed many foreign courts whilst Bacon's belief that deductions could only be made through careful observation and using measurable evidence were a great step forward from medieval thought.

Rich, Sir Richard

(1496–1567)

Politician and Lord Chancellor.

Richard Rich. (*Artist: Hans Holbein, 1532–43. Royal Collection*)

Rich's father was a cloth merchant from Hampshire but little is known of his early life. He probably studied law at Cambridge University and went to the Middle Temple in London to complete his **education**. After seeking backers to advance his career, he succeeded in being nominated as a member of the **Reformation** Parliament for Essex in 1529.

His career took off in 1533 when he was knighted and appointed Solicitor-General. In this position, he worked under **Thomas Cromwell** by drafting anti-clerical bills for **Parliament** and prosecuting those who refused to swear the oath of succession, which bastardised Princess **Mary**. His two most eminent victims were **Sir Thomas More** and Bishop **John Fisher** and, through his own deceit, brought about their executions despite More having been a friend of his at the Middle Temple.

In 1536, despite nominally being a **Catholic** himself, Rich was appointed Chancellor of the Court of Augmentations, which disposed of the proceeds of the **Dissolution of the Monasteries**. He carried out this role with great zeal and profited by acquiring a vast estate in Essex. During the **Pilgrimage of Grace**, he was one of the king's advisors that the rebels demanded be sacked.

After 1539, Rich became more associated with the anti-reform party in government and, in the following year, he was one of the chief witnesses in the trial that led to the execution of his former benefactor, Cromwell. By now, he was in the Privy Council and had enormous influence. It was Rich who examined and supervised the torture of Thomas Culpeper and Francis Dereham during the investigations against **Catherine Howard, Henry VIII**'s fifth wife. It was also Rich who personally tortured **Anne Askew** in the **Tower** in an attempt to remove Henry's last wife, **Catherine Parr**.

Before the king's death, he ingratiated himself with the Seymour family as it was clear that they were to dominate the regency council that was to rule in

Edward VI's name. In the old king's will, he was apparently offered a peerage and so he was made Baron Rich of Leez (in Essex) and, soon after, he contrived to have Thomas Wriothesley removed from the post of Lord Chancellor and was given the position himself. He supported Lord Protector **Somerset**'s **Protestant** reforms but, in 1549, saw that the tide was turning and threw his lot in with **John Dudley** during the coup against Somerset.

Rich was involved in the prosecutions of the Catholic bishops, **Bonner** and **Gardiner**, and signed the document declaring **Lady Jane Grey** to be queen when King Edward was ill. After the king died (1553), he soon switched sides, though, by refusing to raise the troops he had promised Dudley and, instead, entertaining Queen Mary at his home in Essex. Apart from being forced to return some monastic lands on his estate, the new queen did not punish Rich but he was no longer a central figure at court. He did, however, vigorously oversee the hunting of Protestant heretics in Essex and witnessed several of their burnings in Smithfield market himself. After 1558, the new queen, **Elizabeth I**, kept her distance from him and he spent his last years working as a justice of the peace in Essex. He did, however, finally show his true religious colours by refusing to accept the new Church of England – the only time he showed disagreement with a reigning monarch.

Richard Rich was efficient at whatever he put his mind to and displayed astounding skills in surviving the reigns of four Tudor monarchs. Other than that, there is very little praise he can be offered. A BBC poll in 2005 rated him one of the 'Ten Worst Britons' of the last 1,000 years and the historian, Hugh Trevor-Roper, described Rich as a man 'of whom nobody has ever spoken a good word'. It is hard to argue with these assertions. Perfectly willing to use deceit and torture in order to betray his colleagues and faith for his own gain, Rich epitomises the hard and cold realities of Tudor politics.

Ridley, Nicholas

(c. 1500–55)

Bishop and martyr.

Ridley was born in Northumberland, the son of a wealthy landowner. Educated at Cambridge University, he studied Latin, Greek, Philosophy and Divinity. An outstanding scholar, who displayed great powers of argument, he became private chaplain to Archbishop **Cranmer** in 1537. By now, he had converted to **Protestant**ism although it took many years of research and debate before he finally decided against the belief in transubstantiation.

In 1543, he was accused of heresy but he skilfully argued against his prosecutors and, thereafter, he assisted Cranmer in advancing the reformist agenda in his diocese. After King **Henry VIII**'s death in 1547, he was appointed Bishop of Rochester and probably assisted Cranmer in writing the new English Prayer Book. Ridley was involved in the dismissal of the **Catholic** bishops, **Edmund Bonner** and **Stephen Gardiner**, and, in 1549, replaced Bonner as Bishop of London. In this role, he assisted in advancing the Protestant **Reformation** by enforcing the new prayer book, removing images from churches and replacing altars with plain wooden tables. He showed much kindness to Bonner's family, however, insisting that they live with him at his palace and that Bonner's mother should always sit at the head of the dining table. His most serious opponents, though, were the extreme Protestants. They were quite numerous in London and wanted a greater pace of reform. Nevertheless, Ridley always insisted on enforcement of the rules and, in one long-running argument with Bishop **Hooper** concerning the wearing of vestments, he finally won.

As King **Edward VI** lay dying, he supported plans to enthrone **Lady Jane Grey** and publicly preached in favour of the bastardisation of the Catholic,

Burning of Latimer and Ridley. Thomas Cranmer (top right) is being forced to watch the deaths of his friends. (*Author: John Foxe, 1563, from the* Book of Martyrs. (The Horizon Book of the Elizabethan World [*which credits the Folger Shakespeare Library*], *American Heritage / Houghton Mifflin, 1967*)

Princess **Mary**. These acts only guaranteed his fate when Mary acceded to the throne in 1553. She immediately threw him into the **Tower of London** along with Cranmer and his friend, Bishop **Latimer**. In the following March, all three were sent to Oxford to await trial. Mary wanted, more than anything, for these three leading Protestants to publicly recant their faith but Ridley and Latimer refused. From his prison, Ridley wrote a defence of Protestantism which was smuggled to Europe, where it was printed and then redistributed in England.

In October 1555, he and Latimer were found guilty of heresy and burned together at the stake. Latimer died quickly but a poor arrangement of greenish, wooden faggots meant that the fire on Ridley's side merely smouldered and burnt the lower half of his body. After crying out, 'I cannot burn! For God's sake, let the fire come to me!' a bystander rearranged the faggots so that the flames rose higher. Ridley then leaned into the flames so that the pouch of gunpowder around his neck was ignited and hastened his death.

Nicholas Ridley was one of the more likeable, scholarly and gentle figures of the English Reformation although he was always firm when enforcing the rules. He did much to bring Protestantism to the country but, as one of the Oxford Martyrs, it was his death that helped to ensure its survival.

Ridolfi Plot

(1571)

A plot to replace **Elizabeth I** with **Mary, Queen of Scots**.

The arrival of Mary, Queen of Scots in England in 1568 provided a figurehead for those English **Catholics** who regarded Queen Elizabeth as illegitimate and wanted to restore the Catholic faith to the realm by removing Elizabeth from the throne. The **Northern Rebellion** (1569) failed in its attempts to accomplish this and, due to their involvement, led to a closer observation of both Mary and the **Fourth Duke of Norfolk** (both under house confinement).

Roberto di Ridolfi was an Italian banker who had settled in England in the 1550s. He acquired a large network of powerful clients throughout Europe and, in 1567, became the Pope's secret envoy. Ridolfi was keen to restore Catholicism to England and was convinced that the majority of the **population** desired this too. With his widespread connections, he was in an ideal position to stitch together a plot to remove Elizabeth. As a banker, he had a good excuse for travelling between each of the involved parties and one of his clients was even the Secretary of State, **William Cecil**, and so he had gained the government's trust. Before the Northern Rebellion, Ridolfi had distributed funds to the northern lords. Afterwards, government officials questioned him about this but he convinced them that he had merely been acting as their banker.

Ridolfi was certain that the uprising would have succeeded if it had been backed by a foreign invasion so he devised a new plan. A Spanish army of 10,000 troops from the Netherlands, led by the Duke of Alva, would land in south-east England and support a mass rebellion by all the Catholic lords. Elizabeth would be assassinated, Mary would marry the Duke of Norfolk (second cousin to the queen and supposed Catholic) and take the throne. Using the Spanish ambassador in London and the Bishop of Ross (Mary's agent and go-between) Ridolfi communicated his idea to all the relevant parties. The Pope agreed; he had, after all, only excommunicated Elizabeth the year before. Mary gave her approval as it was now clear that she was not going to be released. Norfolk dragged his feet before consenting. King Philip of Spain disapproved but English piracy and the theft of Spanish gold changed his mind. However, Alva had serious doubts about the plot, did not think Ridolfi could keep it a secret and would only commit his troops after the uprising began, not before.

Alva was right. Too many people were told about the conspiracy and Elizabeth was warned. The Spanish ambassador, himself, revealed it to the seaman, **John Hawkins**, who was acting as double agent. Hawkins then passed on the information to Cecil, who activated his agents in an attempt to seek evidence. At Dover, Ridolfi's agent was found with coded letters for Norfolk and Ross. Two of Norfolk's men were discovered sending gold to Mary's Scottish supporters. Under torture, they revealed the location of more coded letters and their cypher at one of Norfolk's homes.

The evidence was incriminating: Norfolk was arrested and executed, Mary was kept under closer confinement and the Spanish ambassador was expelled. Ridolfi was in Italy at the time, where he eventually died of old age. He gave his name to a plot that, in retrospect, was never going to succeed. It had been based more on optimism than detailed plans and, in the end, too many people had known about it.

Roanoke

England's first attempt to create a colony outside Europe.

Elizabeth I's courtier, **Walter Ralegh**, had long been interested in establishing an English colony in North America so he sent an exploratory expedition to its east coast in 1584. Encouraged by its reports of verdant forest, plentiful game and friendly Indians, Elizabeth granted Ralegh a charter to colonise and govern lands which he named 'Virginia', in honour of his virgin queen. The intention was to create a base from which English privateers could harass Spanish shipping and it was also hoped that precious metals could be found and that the local Indians would be converted to Christianity.

He 1585, he financed a second expedition, led by Sir **Richard Grenville**, carrying soldiers and tradesmen. After the loss of a supply ship on the shallow banks, there was only enough food to leave behind a small colony of 108 men on Roanoke Island under the command of Ralph Lane. This was much fewer than had been originally planned. Lane made contact with several surrounding native villages but many Indians starting dying of imported European diseases, probably influenza or smallpox. Some of the tribes now saw the Englishmen as a threat and resented their demands to supply them with food. In March 1586, **Sir Francis Drake** was passing by on his return from the West Indies and, faced with starvation and hostile tribes, Lane accepted his offer to rescue the colony and return home. This was unbeknownst to Grenville, who arrived with supplies two weeks later but he left behind fifteen men to guard against Spanish claims.

Undeterred, Ralegh organised another expedition in 1587. This time, the 115 settlers included no soldiers but consisted of families, including the pregnant daughter of the colony's leader, John White. These people were middle-class Londoners hoping to become landed gentry and some may have been **Puritan**s seeking religious freedom. Upon landing on Roanoke in July, nothing was found of Grenville's men save for the remains of a skeleton. Soon after, White's granddaughter, Virginia Dare, was born but there were also some violent incidents involving the local Indians. According to White, the colonists beseeched him to board the returning ships so that he could explain their situation to Ralegh.

He endeavoured to return with supplies as quickly as possible but war with Spain had broken out and all ships were ordered to defend against the threat of the **Spanish Armada** (1588). White finally disembarked on Roanoke for the second time in 1590 only to find that the camp had been abandoned. All possessions had been removed but there were no signs of violence, just the word 'CROATOAN' carved onto a post. It had earlier been agreed that, if the settlers had to move location, they would carve the new destination onto a post and would also carve a cross if they were under duress. To White's relief, no cross was found and so he assumed they had simply relocated to Croatoan Island. Storms, however, wrecked his attempts to find them and he had to return home.

Ralegh never made any serious attempt to solve the mystery of the 'Lost Colony of Roanoke' and nothing was ever seen of the settlers again. After England's first permanent colony was established in Jamestown in 1607, rumours were heard of people living to the south wearing European clothes. They could not be traced, however, and it is unlikely that the clothes would have been wearable after twenty years. No amount of archaeological or genetic research

19th-century depiction of John White's return to Roanoke. (*From* A popular history of the United States *by W Bryant and S Gay, 1876. Lincoln Financial Foundation Collection*)

has solved the mystery and the most likely outcome is that, either the settlers were massacred or were assimilated (either under compulsion or voluntarily) into the local Indian villages.

S

Seymour, Edward (Duke of Somerset)

(1500/6–52)

Soldier and statesman.

Seymour was born in Wiltshire, the son of Sir John Seymour who was knighted for his part in putting down the **Cornish Rebellion** in 1497. In 1514, he was a page in **Mary Tudor**'s wedding party in France and in 1523 fought with the English army during the **Second Anglo-French War**. For his services during the conflict, he was knighted by the **Duke of Suffolk**.

Seymour's star continued to rise. He became an esquire in **Henry VIII**'s household in 1524, a justice of the peace and Master of the Horse for Henry's illegitimate son, **Henry Fitzroy**, the following year and the king's personal attendant in 1531. His career really took off, however, after his sister, **Jane Seymour**, married the king in 1536. The following year, he was made Earl of Hertford and joined the Privy Council and, after Jane gave birth to Prince **Edward**, he had the honour of carrying the young Princess **Elizabeth** at the new baby's christening ceremony.

After his sister's death, Seymour remained a royal favourite and was given more responsibilities. In 1544, he was made Lieutenant-General of the North and captured Edinburgh during the **War of the Rough Wooing**. Afterwards, he fought in France and, after organising a brilliant defence of Boulogne, he helped to negotiate the peace treaty that ended the **Third Anglo-French War**.

It is not known how much jockeying for power went on in the last few months of Henry's reign but Seymour was certainly helped by the downfall of his main rival, the **Third Duke of Norfolk**, caused by the unwise behaviour of Norfolk's son. In the old king's will, Henry stated that he wanted a regency council of sixteen lords and bishops to rule the country until Edward came of age. A controversial last-second addition to the will allowed for the council members to receive new lands and honours. Seymour made himself the Duke of Somerset and the majority of the Council accepted him as Lord Protector. This was probably due to the absence of any rival with similar prestige and the fact that he was the king's nearest living relative. By March 1547, he had been granted absolute authority and was king in all but name.

Seymour had two dominant polices. First, he wanted to finish the war in Scotland and force the betrothal of the young **Mary, Queen of Scots** to King Edward. He personally led an army north and won an emphatic victory at **Pinkie Cleugh**, a few miles east of Edinburgh. However, the French sent reinforcements, Scottish resistance stiffened and Mary was spirited away to safety in France. The cost of keeping garrisons in southern Scotland and the hiring of foreign mercenaries eventually forced the English government to cease hostilities in 1550.

Seymour's second main policy was to bring uniformity to the Church of England based on the new **Protestant** religion but which included compromise with the old **Catholic** faith. So Archbishop **Cranmer**'s English Book of Common Prayer was introduced, priests were allowed to marry and images within churches started to be removed. At the same time, he repealed Henry VIII's heresy laws, which had banned disagreement with the Crown's religious policies, and another law required two witnesses instead of one for someone to be convicted of treason.

Events of 1549, however, brought about Seymour's downfall. Minor uprisings throughout the country were followed by two major revolts – The **Prayer Book Rebellion** in Cornwall and Devon and **Kett's Rebellion** in Norfolk. The former was primarily caused by the religious changes, the latter mainly by the spread of **enclosures**. Seymour was blamed for the troubles, especially as, previously, he had publically sympathised with the rebels' stance on enclosures. He was further undermined by the actions of his brother, **Thomas Seymour**. Thomas had secretly married Henry VIII's widow, **Catherine Parr**, and after she died he schemed to marry Princess Elizabeth and control the king. Seymour had no choice but to execute his brother but the damage was done.

The Council, already unhappy with his arrogance and refusal to consult them, staged a coup. In October, 1549, Seymour was removed from office and imprisoned in the **Tower** but early the following year he was released by the new Lord Protector, **John Dudley**, the Earl of Warwick, was readmitted to the Council and had his lands restored. Somerset's daughter even married Dudley's son. Later that year, though, growing dissatisfaction with Dudley combined with rumours that Seymour was planning a comeback, forced the Lord Protector to imprison his rival again. This time, Seymour was found guilty of trumped-up charges of treason and was beheaded in January 1552. Such was his popularity that people were ordered to stay at home on the morning of his execution, a decree that was backed up by 1,000 soldiers patrolling the streets.

Traditionally, Seymour has been considered the 'Good Duke', an intelligent liberal who showed compassion and compromise. More recently, though, he has been criticised for being a weak, yet arrogant, idealist who was unsuited to dealing with the problems he faced. A good soldier but his expensive war forced him to order another **debasement** of the coinage, which led to further misery for the mass of people.

Seymour, Jane

(c. 1508–37)

Third wife of **Henry VIII** and Queen of England
from May 1536 to October 1537.

The eldest daughter of Sir John Seymour, Jane was probably born in Wiltshire but very little is known of the first twenty years of her life. At some point, she became a lady-in-waiting, first to **Catherine of Aragon** and then **Anne Boleyn**, Henry VIII's first two wives. Henry may have first noticed her in that capacity or when he paid the Seymour family a great honour by visiting their Wiltshire home in 1535.

It was only in February 1536 that his interest in her was first noted. In contrast to Anne's outspoken and temperamental character, Jane's gentle and meek demeanour must have greatly appealed to the king. One cannot be sure how willing she was to replace Anne or how much she was a pawn of her brothers' (**Edward** and **Thomas Seymour**) ambitions. It is also possible that she was manipulated by Henry's chief minister, **Thomas Cromwell**. His son had married Jane's sister and a close family union with the king would have only strengthened his own position.

Anne's fury at the king's new love interest made no difference and, in May 1536, she was executed for supposed infidelities. The news of her death was signalled by the boom of a cannon whilst Henry was out hunting. He immediately raced to the Seymour home and, in a nearby church, he and Jane became engaged. Ten days later, the couple were married at Whitehall by Archbishop **Cranmer** and Jane was declared queen. Her wedding gift from the king included 104 manors in four different counties and a number of forests! Soon after, **Parliament** passed a new act of succession, which stated that Jane's children would inherit the throne and made Anne's child, **Elizabeth**, illegitimate.

It appears that Jane was a **Catholic** in her beliefs and Martin Luther called her, 'an enemy of the Gospel'. She once asked Henry to pardon the rebels in the **Pilgrimage of Grace** but was warned not to meddle in affairs of state like his previous wife had. Jane also played a key part in reconciling the king with his eldest child, **Mary**. It seems that her compassionate and obedient nature made her popular in court but it was vital that she produced a male heir if she was to maintain her position.

In early 1537, Jane became pregnant. This, combined with the outbreak of plague in London, delayed plans for her coronation (as a result, she was never crowned) but every attention was lavished upon her. Even a sudden craving for quail was satisfied by Henry ordering a special delivery from Flanders. On 12 October, after a long and difficult labour, Jane gave birth to a boy, **Edward**, at Hampton Court Palace. Bonfires were lit and celebrations held throughout England but, tragically, she died from a post-natal infection twelve days later. Jane was the only wife for whom Henry went into mourning. For three months he wore black and little was seen of him. Ten years later, he was buried beside her in St George's Chapel at Windsor Castle.

Seymour, Sir Thomas

(c. 1508–49)

Politician

Thomas Seymour was the fourth son of Sir John Seymour, younger brother of **Edward Seymour** and elder brother of **Jane Seymour**. In the early 1530s, he was a messenger for the English ambassador in France but it was only when his sister married King **Henry VIII** in 1536 that his career started to take off. In the following year, he was knighted and, soon after, received some land brought about by the **Dissolution of the Monasteries**. Having a charming, bold and garrulous nature, combined with grace, humour and a handsome physique, Thomas was considered suitable to go on various diplomatic missions and receive several military appointments. During the **Third Anglo-French War**, he was made second-in-command of forces fighting near Boulogne.

Plans were put forward for Seymour to marry Lady Mary Howard, daughter of the **Third Duke of Norfolk** and widow of the king's illegitimate son, **Henry Fitzroy**. This would have been a very advantageous match for Seymour but it seems that the plans were blocked by Mary's brother, **Henry Howard**. In around 1542, he began to charm **Catherine Parr** but their **marriage** plans were scuppered when the king sought her for himself and appointed Seymour his ambassador to Brussels.

Seymour must have felt the window of opportunity opening for him in 1547, when the king died. His brother, Edward, became head of the regency council that governed for the boy-king, **Edward VI**, and Seymour, now back in England, renewed his courtship with Catherine. Edward (now the Duke of Somerset) appointed his younger brother Baron of Sudeley and Lord High Admiral but it was not enough. Perhaps it was pure jealousy borne out of sibling rivalry or maybe a false sense of security brought about by being the new king's uncle, but Seymour's actions became increasingly rash as he sought to undermine his brother.

First, he secretly married Catherine without the king's or Somerset's permission. He was forgiven for this but he now shared the same household as Lady **Elizabeth**, the king's older sister. After Catherine became pregnant, Seymour started to flirt with the fourteen-year-old princess. Coming into her bedroom, he liked to tickle her and slap her on her behind. We cannot be sure how Elizabeth felt about all this but, after Catherine caught them in an embrace, she sent her away to another household. When Catherine died after giving birth in 1548, he renewed his interest in Elizabeth and proposed marriage but she tactfully kept her distance.

Seymour now started to try poisoning the king's mind against Somerset. Telling him that his brother was unlawfully acting as king, he gave him extra pocket money and said that he did not need a Lord Protector anymore. After the autumn of 1548, his plans became more daring. He made a deal with pirates on the west coast to support his navy in the event of an uprising and arranged for the mint at Bristol to be defrauded in order to raise a rebel army. The regency council heard of these developments and demanded that Seymour explain himself.

Instead, however, for reasons only known to him, he attempted to break into King Edward's bedchamber on the night of 16 January 1549. Finding the door locked, he shot dead the king's barking spaniel and fled. The next day, he was arrested for trying to kidnap Edward and sent to the **Tower of London**. Accused of thirty-three charges of treason, backed up with plentiful evidence, even Somerset realised that he could not save his brother. On 20 March, Seymour was beheaded on Tower Hill after two blows of the axe.

It is hard to sympathise with Thomas Seymour. Possibly the most foolish of all Tudor statesmen, his violent end seemed inevitable. At the time, Bishop **Latimer** said, 'surely he was a wicked man, and the realm is well rid of him,' and, after hearing of his death, Elizabeth herself commented, 'This day died a man of much wit and very little judgment.'

Shakespeare, William

(1564–1616)

Poet, Actor and Playwright

Shakespeare was born in Stratford-upon-Avon on around 23 April 1564. His father, John, was a glove maker and important town official and his mother, Mary Arden, was the daughter of a local landowner. Shakespeare received a normal **education** at his local grammar school and probably left at the usual age of fourteen. At eighteen, he hastily married Anne Hathaway, the daughter of a wealthy farmer, as she was already pregnant. Six months later, Susanna was born and, two years after that, she gave birth to twins – Hamnet and Judith. Hamnet, his only son, was to die eleven years later.

1585–92 are known as the 'Lost Years' because nothing is known about Shakespeare in this period. He reappears in the records in London in 1592, by which time it seems that he had already acquired a literary reputation. In 1594, he became a founding member, actor and playwright for a stage company called The Lord Chamberlain's Men. His leading actor was the hugely popular **Richard Burbage** who, no doubt, contributed to Shakespeare's success. Another factor was their popularity with Queen **Elizabeth** for whom the company performed several private plays at court. She particularly loved the character of Falstaff in *Henry IV* and asked for more of him, which explains why he reappeared in *The Merry Wives of Windsor*.

Shakespeare may have started working at the Swan Theatre in Southwark but, by 1599, he, Burbage and others had built the Globe Theatre nearby and it was here where most of his productions were performed. The huge demand to watch his plays made him very wealthy and he was able to buy the second-largest house in Stratford for his wife and daughters (New Place), along with other properties.

Shakespeare's literary output was impressive. He wrote thirty-eight plays, 154 sonnets and two narrative poems as well as other poetry. He was equally skilled at writing histories, such as *Richard III, Henry V* and *Julius Caesar*, tragedies such as *Romeo and Juliet, Hamlet* and *Macbeth* and comedies, including *A Midsummer Night's Dream, Taming of the Shrew* and *The Comedy of Errors*. There are several reasons why his plays were so popular. For instance, he touched on universal themes – love, grief, lust, anguish, desire for revenge – that everyone could identify with. Second, as a poet, Shakespeare understood the power of language. His use of iambic pentameter in blank (non-rhyming) verse – first used by **Henry Howard** in the 1540s – and rhyming couplets were very pleasing on the ear. Audiences also enjoyed his ability to create imagery and atmosphere through words as well as his characters' witty insults. Lastly, his plots were enthralling, ranging from despairing love stories and outrageous comedies to tales of evil greed and barbarism.

We do not know if Shakespeare ever met his great contemporary, **Christopher Marlowe**, but it is likely and quite probable that he was influenced by his work in the late 1580s. They may even have worked together and, such was Shakespeare's respect for Marlowe, that the play, *As You Like It*, is considered a tribute to him. Oddly enough, though, it was Shakespeare's poetry, not his plays, that mostly accounted for his contemporary fame. His narrative poem, *Venus and Adonis* (1593), was hugely charming and erotic and made him an overnight success.

Shakespeare continued to write plays right up until the last years of his life. His final production (possibly co-written) was *Henry VIII* in 1613. Tradition has it that he, himself, spoke the Prologue at The Globe and was present when the theatre was destroyed by fire. He spent an increasing amount of time with his family in Stratford, where he died on the same day as his given birthday, 23 April.

Given Shakespeare's fame, it is surprising how little is known of him. None of his letters have survived, the spelling of his surname is inconsistent (even by himself in his surviving signatures!), he was apparently sweet and gentle although he once got into trouble for a violent argument with a **Puritan**, and we cannot even be certain of what he looked like or how he died. None of his original play scripts have

William Shakespeare. An engraving, possibly based on an unknown portrait. The nearest we have to a contemporary image of Shakespeare, Ben Jonson implied that it was a good likeness. (*Artist: Martin Droeshout, 1623. Bodlean Library*)

survived because they were just considered to be working documents for the actors. The printing of them was simply not allowed – plays were to be seen, not read.

By the time of his death, Shakespeare had acquired a huge degree of fame and popularity. His contemporary and fellow playwright, Ben Jonson, described him as 'the star of poets' and that he was, 'not for an age, but for all time'. His plays continued to be performed after his death although they tended to suffer some brutal amendments during the Restoration period. In the Victorian age, he received a 'reboot' and was given his idol status and today, he remains the most famous playwright in the world with his work being translated into over one hundred languages. Such is Shakespeare's influence that we still use phrases he wrote in our everyday speech. 'We have seen better days', 'I have not slept one wink', 'Too much of a good thing', 'cruel to be kind', 'wear my heart upon my sleeve' and 'break the ice' are to name just a few.

Sidney, Sir Philip

(1554–86)

Poet, courtier and soldier.

Sidney was born in Penshurst Place, Kent, the son of Sir Henry Sidney and Mary Dudley – lady-in-waiting to Queen **Elizabeth**. He was also a grandson of **John Dudley** (Duke of Northumberland), nephew of **Robert Dudley** (Earl of Leicester) and named after his godfather, Philip of Spain, who attended his birth. Despite such an auspicious start, Sidney came from a relatively poor noble family and was never a central figure in the Tudor government.

After excelling in his studies – especially drama, oratory and horsemanship – at Shrewsbury Grammar School and Oxford University, the queen granted him permission to travel throughout Europe. In this period (1572–75), he impressed and befriended a good number of scholars and politicians throughout France, Italy and Germany with his intellect, charm and wit. The king of France, himself, was so dazzled by his charisma that he created him 'Baron de Sidenay'. Sidney was in Paris to witness the Saint Bartholomew Day's Massacre of French **Protestant**s in 1572. The gruesome events may have instilled a hatred of **Catholic**s within him and influenced his later writings, which included several violent scenes. As for himself, he was considered as **marriage** material for **Lord Burghley**'s daughter, Anne Cecil, and **Robert Devereux**'s sister, Penelope but he eventually wedded **Francis Walsingham**'s daughter, Frances, in 1583.

After his return to England, Elizabeth appointed him the prestigious position of Cupbearer but he sought more political service for the Crown. This led to a serious argument with the Earl of Oxford, who recommended the queen's marriage to the French Catholic, Duc D'Alencon. The two almost fought a duel but Elizabeth forbade this and Sidney fell out of favour after protesting vehemently against the marriage proposal.

No longer wanted at court, Sidney had more time on his hands and so turned to writing. There were three works, in particular, that were to make him famous. *Astrophel and Stella* was a sequence of 108 sonnets and eleven songs written about Penelope but later dedicated to Frances. Focusing on the sorrows of love, it used an innovative rhyme scheme and is considered to be the best cycle of sonnets after **Shakespeare**'s. Indeed, it is likely that Shakespeare was much influenced by Sidney. His unfinished *Arcadia* claims to be the first novel written in English. A hugely influential piece of prose, it was essentially a romance that combined various styles, included complicated sub-plots and explored new themes such as kidnapping, crowd scenes and escape from drowning. He also portrayed female characters with great skill and sensitivity. Sidney's third major work, *A Defence of Poetry*, is regarded as one of the greatest pieces of critical writing of the **Renaissance** era. In it, he argues that poetry is the path to virtue and should be used to influence society. Unshackled from the realities of life, poetry explored the dreams to which people should aspire.

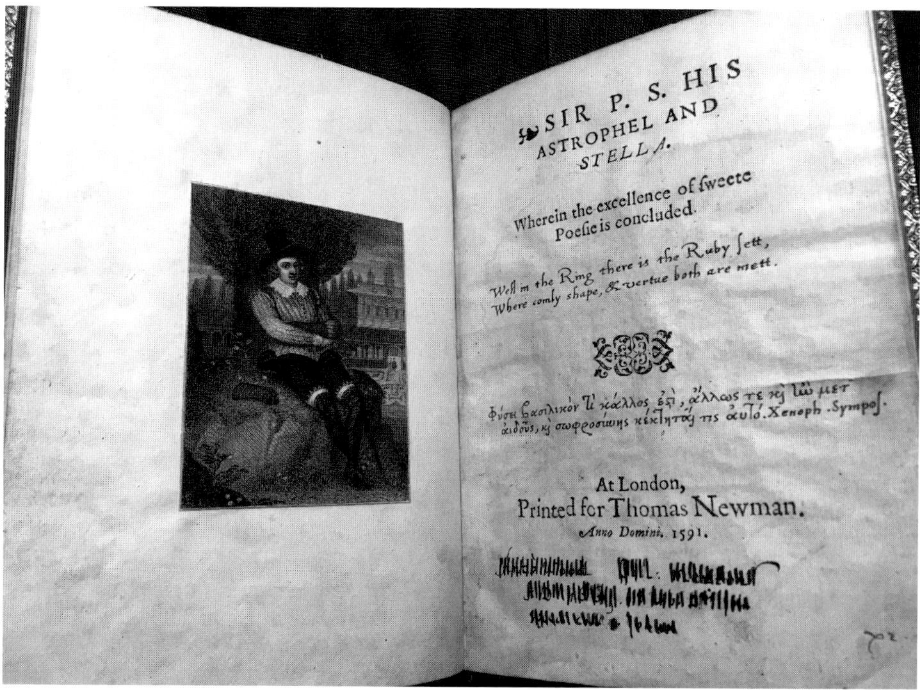

Second edition of *Astrophel and Stella*. (*Author: Sir Philip Sidney, 1580s. This edition 1591. British Library. David P Kendal*)

Sidney never saw himself as a writer and banned the publication of his work until after his death. After returning to the queen's favour, he advocated a more aggressive policy against Spain. He was knighted in 1583 and, two years later, was appointed Governor of Flushing in the Netherlands in order to help the Dutch in their war of independence. Always demanding bold and decisive action, he led an attack against the Spanish at the Battle of Zutphen (1586), was wounded in the thigh and later died from a gangrenous infection. The story goes that he had previously removed his thigh armour because he thought it wrong to be better-armed than his men. Also, as he lay wounded, he apparently gave his water to another soldier, saying, 'Thy necessity is yet greater than mine.'

True or not, these accounts reflect the reputation that Sidney had acquired. He had become the epitome of the perfect English nobleman – intelligent, brave, chivalrous, charming and romantic. Widely mourned, he was given one of the most expensive funeral processions ever seen, buried at St Paul's Cathedral and later memorialised by the poet, **Edmund Spenser**, in his elegy, *Astrophel.*

Simnel, Lambert

(c. 1476–?)

Pretender to the English throne.

After **Henry VII**'s victory over Richard III at the **Battle of Bosworth Field**, there were still Yorkist elements who regarded him as a Lancastrian usurper who had no proper dynastic right to the English crown. One of these was an Oxford priest called Richard Symonds who, in 1487, saw an opportunity to foment a rebellion against a king who was not yet secure on his throne. He spotted a boy of around ten years of age, Lambert Simnel, who bore a resemblance to Edward, Earl of Warwick, nephew of the Yorkist king, Edward IV. Warwick had been imprisoned in the **Tower** after Bosworth and many believed that he was dead. As Simnel was merely the son of an Oxford craftsman, Symonds had to train him in courtly manners and **etiquette** before announcing that he was the Earl of Warwick who had escaped from the Tower.

Simnel was whisked off to **Ireland**, where there had always been strong support for the Yorkist kings. The Earl of Kildare, Lord Deputy of Ireland, was willing to play along and had Simnel crowned 'King Edward VI' in Dublin and coins were minted in his name. King Henry scoffed when he heard this, declaring that the Irish would 'crown an ape' if it gained them power, and proceeded to parade the real Earl of Warwick (very much alive!) around London.

However, it was not from London that the threat came. The heir apparent to Richard III had been his nephew – John de la Pole, the Earl of Lincoln.

Despite being reconciled to Henry after Bosworth, Lincoln saw an opportunity. Fleeing abroad to the court of his aunt, Margaret, the Duchess of Burgundy, he persuaded her to provide money and troops to support a rebellion. With 2,000 German mercenaries, led by the renowned Martin Schwarz, he then proceeded to Ireland. There, they were joined by several thousand Irish soldiers led by Kildare's younger brother, Thomas Fitzgerald. Whether or not Lincoln, Kildare or Margaret really believed that Simnel was the true Earl of Warwick is not known but it seems likely that they considered him to be a mere puppet who could enable Lincoln's bid for the throne.

The Yorkist army landed on the Cumberland coast, hoping to pick up support as it marched south. However, Henry's 'carrot-and-stick' approach to dealing with his barons deterred them from lending their help. Also, people generally wanted stability after the long **Wars of the Roses** and did not particularly want to fight for a foreign-looking army.

Outside the village of East Stoke in Nottinghamshire, on 16 June 1487, Lincoln's 8,000 met Henry's 12,000 in what is regarded as the final battle of the Wars of the Roses – the Battle of Stoke. After a vicious, three-hour engagement, the Yorkists were defeated with half their number killed. Amongst the dead were Lincoln, Fitzgerald and Schwarz. Simnel was captured and treated with remarkable leniency. Henry appointed him turnspit in the royal kitchens and, when Kildare visited a few years later, it was Simnel who waited upon him at the royal banquet. Years later, he was promoted to falconer but, after that, he disappears from view. As for Henry, the failure of the rebellion served to cement his position as the new king of England.

Solway Moss, Battle of

(1542)

A border engagement between England and Scotland.

Anglo-Scottish relations had generally been peaceful since the **Battle of Flodden** (1513) but there had been a gradual deterioration since the mid-1530s. The Scots' king, James V, had renewed the Auld Alliance by marrying into the French royal family and he had also given support to rebels in **Ireland** as a counter to King **Henry VIII**'s support for his opponents in Scotland. By 1541, Henry was planning war with France and wanted a friendly neighbour on his northern border. So he invited James to a meeting in York to discuss the idea of Scotland breaking away from the Roman Church, just like England had done several years previously. James, a devout **Catholic**, refused to attend so the English king authorised border raids into Scotland.

These raids caused much damage although one was defeated by a smaller Scottish force at Haddon Rig. Eager to follow up this success, James, although too ill to lead, ordered a large counter-raid of around 16,000 men into Cumberland. Opposing them was a force of 3,200 troops led by Lord Wharton, the Deputy Warden of the Western Marches. The Scots crossed the River Esk on 24 November 1542, spotted Wharton's men on higher ground and assumed they were just the vanguard of a larger English army. Hesitation and uncertainty ensued, compounded by political infighting amongst the Scottish leaders over who should be in charge. Wharton quickly ordered a cavalry charge. Panic and the lack of an effective command structure caused a rout, with many Scots being trapped between the local marshes and the Esk, where hundreds drowned.

Casualties were quite low but the English captured 1,200 men, several important lords and ten cannon at the cost of seven dead. Although a relatively minor battle compared to Flodden or **Pinkie Cleugh**, the defeat was a humiliation for Scotland and was said to have caused James V's death, although he was probably already dying from cholera or dysentery. It forced the Scots to accept the Treaty of Greenwich (1543) which stated that James's baby daughter, **Mary, Queen of Scots**, would later marry Henry's son, **Edward**. However, the Scottish **Parliament**'s refusal to ratify the treaty would lead to the **War of the Rough Wooing**.

Somer, Will

(c. 1514–60)

Court fool.

Nothing is known of Somer's early life and in around 1535 he was introduced to **Henry VIII** by a merchant from Calais. Somer probably had a hunchback and was what was known as a 'natural fool', rather than a professional court jester, which meant that he had some mental disability. It was common for the aristocracy to keep such fools – not only were they amusing but their tendency to speak the truth meant that many believed them to be closer to God than most other humans.

Somer was certainly far more honest and forward than any of Henry's courtiers dared to be. He called the king, 'Harry', 'Hal' or 'Uncle' and could wittily include important messages in his poetry or songs. Advisers, such as **Thomas Cromwell**, probably preferred to give the king brutally honest advice through Somer. Once, in 1535, though, he went too far and referred to **Anne Boleyn** as a whore and Princess **Elizabeth** as a bastard. Henry almost killed him on the spot and Somer had to flee court.

He soon returned though and Henry developed such a soft spot for him that he even included him in some family portraits. As the pain in the king's leg increased, he would often turn to Somer to provide light relief and probably confided his innermost thoughts in him. In his will, Henry ensured that Somer was cared for during his son's reign and he later became Queen **Mary**'s fool. Mary took great care of him as he was reportedly the only person who could make her laugh. His last public appearance before his death was at Elizabeth's coronation in 1559.

Other court fools worth mentioning are Sexton, or 'Patch', and Jane Fool. Patch had been **Thomas Wolsey**'s fool and, during the cardinal's downfall, was given to Henry as a conciliatory gift. So terrified was Patch about leaving Hampton Court that it took six guards to remove him. Jane was the fool of Anne Boleyn, **Catherine Parr** and Queen Mary. She sometimes performed with Somer but rumours that the two were married cannot be verified. The famous portrait of Henry VIII with his family has two figures on the sides. Under the right arch is Somer; under the left is, possibly, Jane.

Somerset, Duke of

(See Seymour, Edward)

Spanish Armada

(1588)

A naval campaign in the **Anglo-Spanish War**.

King Philip II of Spain had every good reason to attempt a conquest of England. As the head of the most powerful **Catholic** nation on Earth, he saw it as his God-given duty to protect England's Catholics by removing its **Protestant** regime. For this, he also had the backing of the Pope, who regarded war with heretical England as a crusade and offered to bear one third of the costs. Also, if Philip could add England to his empire, his traditional French enemies would be completely surrounded and the Dutch rebels fighting for independence in the Spanish Netherlands would become more isolated. His annexation of the Portuguese empire in 1580 had boosted his ambitions as well as his resources and supply of ships. Another motive was to deal with the English privateers who had been waging an unofficial war against Spanish settlements and treasure ships in the Caribbean throughout the 1570s. The final outrage had occurred in 1585 when Queen **Elizabeth I** actually sent troops to assist the Dutch in their revolt.

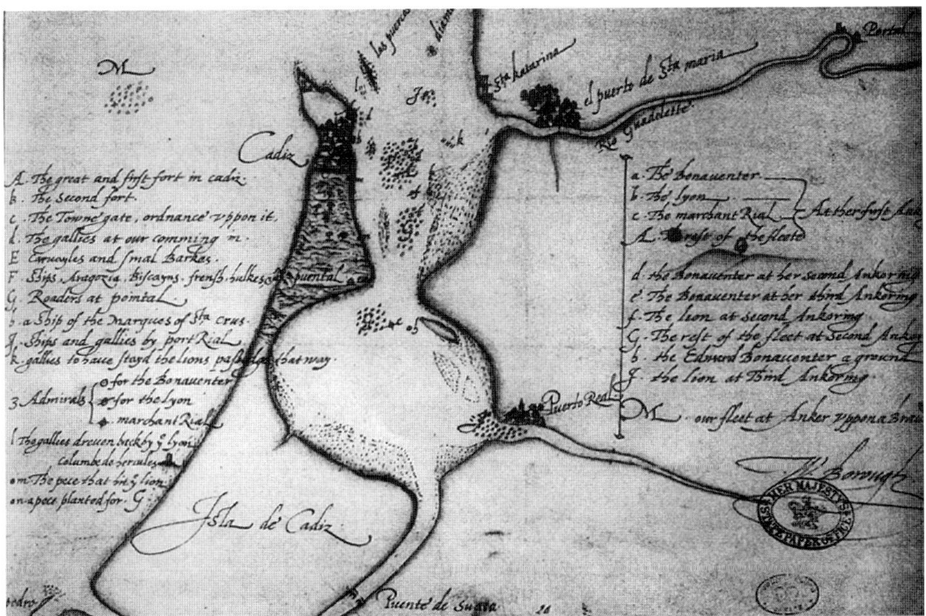

Singeing of the King of Spain's Beard. A plan of Cadiz, its harbor, fortifications and positions of the Spanish ships. The English fleet, under the ornate letter M in the top left corner, is about to launch its successful 1587 assault. (*Artist: William Borough, 1587. Lopez Martin Collection*)

Philip probably initiated his plans in 1585 after hearing reports about the English privateer, **Francis Drake**, ransacking properties and churches in northwest Spain. The enterprise required huge numbers of men, ships and supplies; Spain had to purchase many resources on the open market and acquire Italian galleys. Such activities, however, could not be kept a secret from England's spies and so Elizabeth countenanced a pre-emptive attack. Drake's raid of 1587 became known as 'The Singeing of the King of Spain's Beard'. In it, he destroyed and captured over 100 Spanish ships in Cadiz and along the Portuguese coast. The losses included valuable supplies such as staves for barrels needed for drinking water. Drake's subsequent departure for the Azores in order to pillage treasure ships arriving from America forced many Spanish warships in that direction and so delayed the sailing of the invasion fleet for another year.

On 28 May 1588, the Spanish Armada, or *Grande y Felićisima Armada* (Great and Fortunate Fleet), started sailing from Lisbon with around 130 ships. Only about a quarter were purpose-built warships. The rest were supply and transport vessels and it took two days for the whole fleet to leave port. On board, were roughly 10,000 sailors, 20,000 soldiers and 180 priests to provide spiritual support. Following the death of the experienced admiral, Santa Cruz, the man in charge was the Duke of Medina Sidonia, who, like his English counterpart – **Lord Howard of Effingham** – was a high-ranking nobleman who could maintain authority over his captains. Medina Sidonia had little naval experience but was an excellent administrator who carried out his instructions to the best of his ability. These orders were disarmingly simple: maintain a crescent formation with the warships on the 'horns' and sides protecting the weaker ships, sail to the coast of Flanders and escort a Spanish army, led by the Duke of Parma, over to south-east England.

The Armada was spotted off the Lizard on 29 July and warning beacons were lit to relay the news around the country. The English fleet, initially hemmed in by the wind, eventually sailed out of Plymouth to engage. A sort of running battle up the English Channel ensued, with the nimbler English ships, aided by Dutch vessels, firing from range and avoiding the grappling irons of their opponents. Despite having a numerical superiority in warships, however, the English attacks had little effect and, on 7 August, the Armada anchored off Calais, still in its packed crescent and only twenty-seven miles from Parma's waiting army. In England, a small force of 5,000 men, led by the **Earl of Leicester**, gathered at Tilbury, in Essex, to await the invasion.

Lord Howard now consulted with his subordinate commanders – Drake, **John Hawkins** and **Martin Frobisher** – about the best course of action. It was agreed to use an old tactic of sending in fire ships in order to break up the enemy formation before attacking. On the night of 7 August, eight warships were sacrificed by being filled with tar and brimstone, set alight and allowed to drift towards the Spanish fleet. Prepared Spanish patrol boats managed to tow three of these away but the remaining 'hellburners' caused panic and many ships cut their anchor cables in order to make a quick escape. The formation was now broken and the English went on the attack.

The subsequent Battle of Gravelines highlighted the differences in ships and tactics between the two sides. The Spanish still used the old style of naval warfare. This involved firing a broadside before closing in, firing anti-personnel cannon (known as 'murderers') and boarding the enemy vessel with their superior number of soldiers. The English, however, under the direction of Hawkins, had developed ships that were lower in the water, more manoeuvrable and relied on damaging ships with their long-range cannon. At Gravelines, therefore, the English avoided close quarters. More essentially, however, they were able to inflict far greater damage because their superior gun carriages and greater space on deck allowed for a far greater rate of fire. Some Spanish ships may have run out of ammunition but, ultimately, Spanish gun crews lacked the training and the ability to fire multiple broadsides.

By 4pm, the English had run out of ammunition and withdrew. Only one Spanish ship had been sunk and several had become grounded on the nearby sandbanks. Medina Sidonia then skilfully gathered his fleet together but had to decide whether to complete his rendezvous with Parma. However, a strong breeze appeared from the south and he decided that his battered ships, many with missing sails and injured crews, were in no fit state to tack southwards. He decided to return to Spain by heading into the North Sea and, from there, sail around Scotland and **Ireland**. Howard ordered a pursuit as far as the Firth of Forth in Scotland before deciding that the threat had been neutralised. After rounding Scotland, the Armada's hungry crews and damaged ships, some held together by cables, ran into fierce storms off Ireland. Without their anchors, many were shipwrecked or beached. A few intrepid survivors eventually got home but thousands were drowned or slaughtered then robbed by the local inhabitants or English troops.

The first ships, including Medina Sidonia's *San Martin*, limped home on 21 September. Over the next few weeks only about half of the Armada returned. An estimated 12,000 lives were lost plus many who died from their wounds and disease after disembarking. Initial rumours had mentioned that Parma's army was marching on London and that Drake and Howard had been captured. So as the news of the disaster spread, a shocked nation went into mourning and it was said that every noble family had lost a son or husband. Philip shut himself away for days although he, unlike others, refused to blame Medina Sidonia. For him, the weather had caused the defeat.

In England, predictably, the news was received with joyous celebrations and thanksgiving services. The victory fostered a greater sense of English nationalism and was celebrated in literary works such as **Spenser**'s *The Faerie Queene*. Elizabeth, herself, was raised to a god-like status, helped by a famously inspiring speech to the waiting troops at Tilbury. However, the government's poor treatment of its sailors should be noted. The English navy had lost no ships and only a few hundred men but thousands died from diseases and the crews were sent home without pay. Many had to rely on the charity of officers such as Hawkins and Howard.

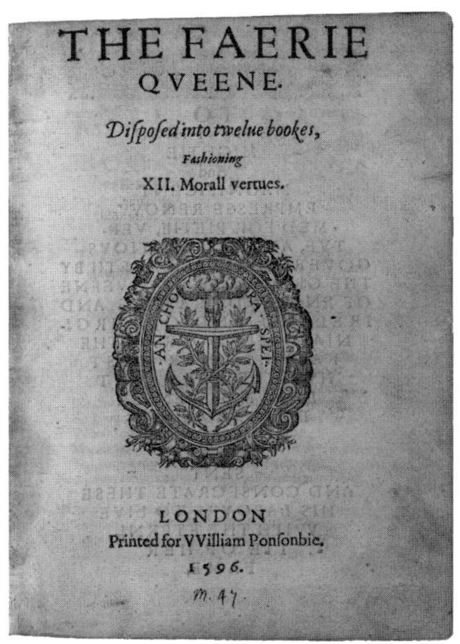
THE FAERIE QVEENE.

Diſpoſed into twelue bookes, Faſhioning XII. Morall vertues.

LONDON
Printed for VVilliam Ponſonbie.
1596.

Title page of *The Faerie Queene*. (*Author: Edmund Spenser, 1596. Folger Shakespeare Library*)

Both sides believed that the weather had affected the outcome and they were right. It is also true that superior English ships and gunnery had played an important part. The general feeling amongst historians, though, is that the Armada was doomed from the start. The vital part of the Spanish plan – the joining of the fleet with Parma's army – seemed to be based on hope rather than detail. Parma was waiting near Dunkirk with many flat-bottomed transports ready to rush his troops out to sea. Patrolling Dutch ships were waiting to ambush these vessels so Parma refused to move until the Armada had cleared the way. Medina Sidonia, meanwhile, waited near Calais and asked for Parma's assistance. Was he aware of Parma's predicament? Messages were sent, attempting to coordinate their movements, but events travelled at a far greater speed. By the time Parma realised where Medina Sidonia was, it was too late and the Armada was being mauled off Gravelines.

One could argue that the speculation is merely academic and that the events of 1588 made no difference. England attempted to follow up its victory with its own counter-armada the following year but it was a ruinously expensive fiasco. Philip, determined to succeed, sent further armadas in the 1590s but none came close to success and the war dragged on until 1604. On the other hand, had the Armada of 1588 succeeded, it would have dealt a huge body blow to the Protestant **Reformation** and probably have dashed Dutch hopes for independence.

Spenser, Edmund

(c. 1552–99)

Poet.

Spenser was the son of a London cloth-maker and went to Merchant Taylors' School. From 1569, he attended Cambridge University as a sizar – one of the poorer students who had to carry out various menial tasks to help pay their way. Whilst acquiring his BA and MA, he was introduced to the forms of poetry and classical literature that would later influence his own work.

In 1579, Spenser was introduced to **Philip Sidney** and the **Earl of Leicester** and it was these connections that helped to launch his artistic and political careers. In the same year, he published his first major work, *The Shepherd's Calendar*, which he dedicated to Sidney. This was a poem comprised of twelve philosophical conversations (one for each month) amongst shepherds. With each conversation written in different meters (rhythmic patterns) it idealised rural, pastoral life. The following year, he was sent to **Ireland** as a secretary to the new Lord Deputy, Arthur Grey. In this role, he witnessed the second Desmond Rebellion and subsequently acquired lands in the Munster plantation. One of his new neighbours there was **Walter Ralegh**, who would later help promote his literary work.

It was whilst he worked as a civil servant in Ireland that Spenser produced most of his work. One such piece was *A View Of The Present State Of Ireland*, a pamphlet containing a conversation between two Englishmen, which advocated extremely harsh measures in order to subjugate the Irish. His most famous work, however, was *The Faerie Queene*, published in two parts, in 1590 and 1596. Each part contained three books; Spenser originally intended to write twelve and so it is probably incomplete. *The Faerie Queene* is an allegory set in a land called 'Faerie' (England) ruled by 'Gloriana' (Queen **Elizabeth**) and each book follows the adventures of one of her knights, who represent different virtues. Despite being incomplete, it remains one of the longest poems in the English language. Using innovative nine-line stanzas, the work carries a patriotic, anti-Catholic agenda and alludes to several people and events of the time such as **Mary, Queen of Scots** and the **Spanish Armada**.

The Faerie Queene became widely popular and earned Spenser an annual pension of £50 (£9,000 in 2024). He may have hoped for an official court position but such ambitions were curtailed by his next publication, the satirical *Mother Hubberd's Tale*, which was considered a veiled criticism of the Lord Treasurer, **Lord Burghley**. Back in Ireland, Spenser had time to write other pieces of work but the destruction of his home during **Tyrone's Rebellion** forced him to flee to London in 1598.

He died of unknown causes the following year, by which time he had assumed the mantle of England's most famous poet from Sir Philip Sidney. His coffin was carried by other writers and laid to rest near Chaucer's tomb, in 'Poets Corner', in Westminster Abbey. Edmund Spenser had been inspired by the classical writers such as Virgil and Homer but he created a unique style that was much admired by later writers such as Milton, Wordsworth, Byron and Tennyson. The epitaph on his tomb describes him as 'the prince of poets'.

Sport and Leisure

The Tudors participated a wide variety of entertainments, which were enjoyed by all classes. Generally, though, the wealthy had more time to indulge in leisure activities, which were often only open to men. The following is a non-exhaustive selection:

<u>Jousting</u>. The most prestigious of all the sports and only available to the male aristocracy. Attempting to knock your opponent off his horse, with a lance, at full speed was clearly a dangerous activity! It killed King Henry II of France in 1559 and, in 1536, injured **Henry VIII** badly enough to adversely affect his health for the rest of his life.

<u>Real Tennis</u>. Again, only a sport for the wealthy as it required a large hall in which to play. One of the oldest racquet sports, the ball could be hit off the

A game of tennis. (*Artist: Johan Christoph Neyffer, 1606. Stadtmuseum Tubingen*)

walls upon which were three goals that players could aim for. Henry VIII loved the game and had a special court built at Hampton Court Palace.

Hunting. All the forests in England were owned by the monarch and only they and their nobles could hunt the deer and wild boar within them, using longbow and dogs (mastiffs and spaniels, for instance). Women, too, could hunt and both **Elizabeth I** and **Mary, Queen of Scots** took much pleasure from it. The poor were not allowed into the royal forests but could hunt rabbits and game birds on common land to supplement their **diet**. Another form of hunting was hawking. Goshawks were used most often, with herons being the most popular prey.

Bear-baiting. A very popular gambling sport for both rich and poor, bear-baiting involved a pack of dogs attempting to kill a chained bear. 'Bear gardens' proliferated on the south side of the Thames and both Henry VIII and Elizabeth I enjoyed watching. The former even had a bear pit constructed in the grounds of Whitehall Palace for ease of viewing. In 1583, a 'bear garden' stand collapsed, killing seven people and **Puritan**s saw this as divine retribution for watching sport on a Sunday. **Parliament** passed a law banning bear-baiting on Sundays (the only day when people had time to watch) but Queen Elizabeth over-ruled.

Football. A very popular sport with the lower classes, football was usually played between villages several miles apart. The ball, made from a bloated pig's stomach, could be kicked, thrown or carried and the aim was to get it to the centre of the opponents' village. With no limits on the number of players, and no ban on punching, biting, spitting or kicking, football had more fatalities than any other sport. Henry VIII tried to ban it in 1540 in order to encourage archery practice but to little avail.

Card games and dice. These games usually involved gambling and, despite his reputation, **Henry VII** loved to risk his money on cards and dice. Playing cards were relatively new and the most popular game was Primero, a forerunner of poker. Henry VIII was awful at the game whilst Elizabeth I would cheat mercilessly! In 1512, the government tried to forbid the masses from playing such games as it believed they should be spending more time working.

Board games. The Tudors referred to tables as 'boards' as they were simply loose wooden boards resting on legs. On some of these boards, they would scratch or chalk markings for games. Fox and Geese, Nine Men's Morris and Backgammon were all very popular in the sixteenth century and, of course, gambling added to the fun. Between 1529 and 1532, Henry VIII lost £3,243 on gambling (equivalent to £1.5 million in 2024).

Music and dance. All social classes loved to sing and dance and the lute was the most popular instrument at the time. Taverns would even keep some for customers to play. For the upper classes, playing a variety of instruments,

16th-century lawn bowling. (*Artist: unknown. From* English Life in Tudor Times *by Roger Hart, 1972*)

as well as composing music, was a sign of good breeding. **Anne Boleyn** was proficient at playing the harp, flute and fiddle whilst **Edward VI** was adept at playing the virginals (a keyboard instrument). Church music was widespread but more secular ballads became increasingly popular with time. Dances were more elaborate the further up the social scale one went, from a simple dance around the maypole on May Day holidays to the energetic 'galliard' and 'la volta' in the royal court.

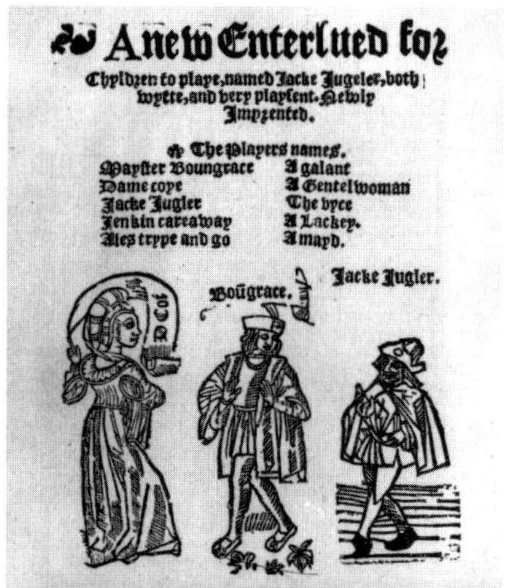

Jack Juggler **title page.** One of the earliest examples of a comedy in English. Probably performed by child actors at court during the Christmas season. (*Artist: unknown. 1562 via Wikimedia Commons*)

Theatre. Mumming plays were performed by troupes of amateur male actors who would visit houses on holidays and perform mummer plays. These traditionally revolved around St George killing an evil knight who was then brought back to life by a doctor. In London, the construction of theatres began in the 1570s and watching plays, written by the likes of **Shakespeare** and **Marlowe** and performed by the likes of **Burbage**, became very popular. Women were not allowed to act and so their parts were played by young boys. Different social classes would attend, with the poorest paying a penny to stand in the pit, where they could raucously shout at the actors. For those outside London, troupes of actors, hired by local lords, would travel around the country and perform in different mansions.

Literature. Reading was a luxury for those who were literate and so the English Bible and the works of those such as **More**, **Vergil**, **Sidney** and **Spenser** were only available for the educated upper and middle classes. The spread of printing presses, growth of the middle class and improved **education**, however, did enable the spread of reading as a leisure activity.

Star Chamber

Court of law.

The Star Chamber was named after the star-studded ceiling of a room in Westminster Palace where its members met. Its origins as a law court are not altogether clear but it seemed to be acting as part of the King's Council during the medieval period.

The Star Chamber Act of **Parliament** in 1487 made the Star Chamber a separate entity although its members were still Privy Councillors along with some judges. After the chaos of the **Wars of the Roses, Henry VII** wanted a powerful law court that could mete out justice to those too powerful to be punished by the common law courts. In effect, it was one of his weapons used to control his barons. Ordinary people could also use it as a court of appeal in cases which they felt had been unfairly influenced by those more powerful than they. The Star Chamber was allowed to hand out fines, torture and imprisonment but never the death penalty. The speed and fairness of its dealings gave it a very good reputation for much of the Tudor period.

However, it did have certain, inherent features which would later bring about its demise. To enable the quick dispensation of justice, the Star Chamber was not bound by the rules that applied to other law courts. For instance, no jury was required and no appeal was allowed against its decisions. It could also punish people for moral offences that it considered illegal although, at that time, were lawful. Such cases included perjury, libel, slander, forgery, conspiracy and unsuccessful attempt to commit a crime.

Under the leadership of Cardinal **Wolsey**, its activities increased tenfold as he encouraged people to bring cases directly to the Star Chamber – by-passing the common law courts – and he widened the scope of its cases. These now included any offences against the king's proclamations and any acts that were considered a breach of the peace. In the latter half of the sixteenth century, less of the court's business was civil as the Star Chamber became increasingly used for criminal cases and cases involving sedition.

The very features which had originally made the court popular caused it to become a hated symbol of royal authority in the early Stuart period. Not bound by normal rules and procedures and with the ability to decide what was legal or not, the Star Chamber became seen as a tool of oppression as it was increasingly used as a weapon against political opponents.

Suffolk, Duke of

(see Brandon, Charles)

Surrey, Earl of

(see Howard, Thomas. Third Duke of Norfolk)

Sweating Sickness

A mysterious and deadly illness.

Also known as 'The English Sweat', the first recorded outbreak of this illness took place in August 1485. There were four more epidemics in England – 1508, 1517, 1528 and 1551 after which, it never reappeared. Only once, did it spread to the continent (1528–29) where it killed thousands in northern and eastern Europe. Italy, Spain and France (except English-owned Calais) were unaffected.

Contemporaries recorded the following symptoms: shivers, headache, exhaustion and pains around the body. After a few hours, there was the onset

— 131 —

The ‚Ars medendi' deals with general therapeutics (dietetic prescriptions, instructions concerning purgation, cure of dyspepsia, etc.), and also contains one or two chapters upon the preparation of drugs.» (Neuburger.)

Unusually tall copy. A few pp. slightly foxed.

Copho. See also No. 481.

Corbeil, Gilles de. See No. 8.

398. **CORDUS,** Euricius. **Für die newe, hievor vnerhörte vnd erschröcklich tödtliche kranckheyt vnd schnellen todt, die Englisch schweyssucht geannt,** also das ein mensch inn 24 stunden gesundt vnd todt ist. So yetz in Engellandt, Sachsen, Meichsen (!), Westphalen etc. vnd zu

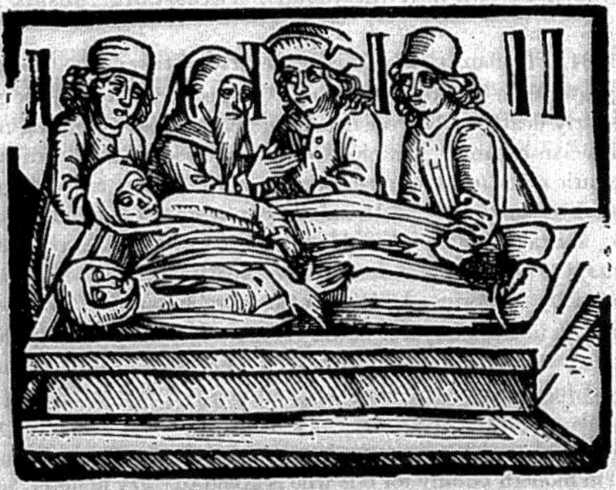

398. Cordus. Für die newe kranckheyt.
Strassburg, 1529.

Cöln grausamlich regiert. Ein trostlich artznei vnd Regiment. Black letter. 6 leaves. *With curious woodcut* on the title-leaf. 4to. Wrappers. Strassburg, Christian Egenolph, 1529.

See reproduction above. Fr. 250. —

Extremely rare tract on sweating sickness (compare Nos. 268 and 306). «One of the most gifted and scholarly men among all who figured in German botany in the early sixteenth century is E. Cordus (1486—1535). He was a genius.» (Greene.) He was the father and the educator of Valerius Cordus. At Ferrara, in 1522, E. Cordus received the Doctorate in Medicine at the hands of the venerable Leonicenus then 94 years of age. In 1527, he accepted an appointment to the chair of medicine in the newly founded Protestant university at Marburg. (The present tract is dedicated to the municipal council of this city.) Later, he served as city physician at Bremen.

399. **CORDUS,** Euricius. **Ein nützlich büchly,** darinn allerley gewüsse vnnd bewärte stuck vnd artzny **für die grusam̄e plag dess Steinwees** begriffen: durch den wytberümpten Doctor der artzny Euricium Cordum beschriben, mit einer vorred Joannis *Dryandri* Medici. M. D. XLII. 12 leaves, last blank. 8vo. Vellum. (Marburg ?), 1542. Fr. 120. —

Rare tract on calculi, with numerous receipts. Concerning Dryander, who wrote the preface, see No. 481.

Victims of the sweating sickness. The German text, in bold, reads: 'For the new, previously unheard of and frighteningly fatal disease and quick death, the English sweating sickness'. (*Artist: Euricius Cordus, 1529. Wellcome Images*) of a high temperature, thirst, heart pain and a drenching sweat. The mortality rate was high (30–50 per cent) and death would come within twenty-four hours. In some areas, half of the **population** was wiped out and survival did not guarantee immunity either. Sweating sickness also only appeared in the summer and early autumn months, largely affected young, healthy men and took a heavy toll on the wealthy, thereby earning the nickname, 'Stoop Gallant'.

The disease appears to have been infectious or contagious or it may have been spread by insects, such as ticks, that appeared in the summer. The causes are unknown. Poor sanitation and infected drinking water have been blamed but that would not explain why the disease would disappear from a region within a few weeks. There is also speculation that it was brought over with **Henry VII**'s invading army, possibly mercenaries who had caught it in Rhodes, and some contemporaries started to believe that it was divine punishment for supporting the Tudor invasion. However, there is some evidence that it was already around earlier that year.

Scientists today are still puzzled by a disease which was clearly not plague, influenza or any other illness that was common at the time. The best guess is a mutation of the hantavirus, which has similar characteristics. However, hantaviruses can also affect individuals, not whole communities, and did not simply disappear as rapidly as the sweating sickness did.

Notable victims included Prince **Arthur**, **John Colet**, the two sons of **Charles Brandon** and the wife and two daughters of **Thomas Cromwell**. Reputed survivors include **Catherine of Aragon**, **Anne Boleyn** and **Cardinal Wolsey**. It is impossible to accurately estimate the number of deaths caused by 'The English Sweat' but, in London alone, over a six-week period in 1485, it accounted for 15,000 deaths (30 per cent of the inhabitants).

T

Throckmorton Plot

(1583)

An attempt to depose **Elizabeth I**.

The Throckmortons were a notable, **Catholic** family who lived in the west Midlands. Francis Throckmorton was the son of John Throckmorton, who had been knighted by Queen Elizabeth in 1565. After the failure of the **Ridolfi Plot** (1571), however, his family, like many others, felt the effects of stricter anti-Catholic repression. In 1578, Throckmorton's mother got into trouble for attending a Catholic Mass and Francis, himself, was briefly punished for his Catholic practices. In the following year, his father was sacked as chief justice for Chester, accused of lacking impartiality, and he died a broken man in 1580.

The combination of his family's treatment along with his faith led Throckmorton, along with his brother, Thomas, to go abroad and seek service with those who could destroy the English **Protestant** regime. Falling in with Catholic exiles in Paris, they heard of a plan by the Duke of Guise (head of the Catholic faction within France) to invade England and, with the support of English Catholics, replace Elizabeth with the imprisoned **Mary, Queen of Scots** and restore the Catholic faith. The whole operation would be financed by the Pope and King Philip of Spain.

Elizabeth's First Secretary, **Francis Walsingham**, soon got wind of the plot through his extensive spy network. In November 1583, Throckmorton was arrested whilst writing a coded letter to Mary. Sent to the **Tower of London**, he was ordered to provide the details of the plot but he refused. After being tortured on the rack twice, he finally confessed and gave all the information he knew. This included his contacts and the exact location of where Guise would land his forces on the south coast (Arundel). His brother managed to escape abroad but the Spanish ambassador, who had been heavily involved, was expelled. Francis, who had merely been the plot's go-between, was beheaded at Tyburn. Before his death, he stubbornly refused to ask for the queen's forgiveness, as was customary.

The Throckmorton Plot, like others, had been a hopelessly under-planned and over-ambitious affair and yet it led to further repression of English Catholics, the vast majority of whom were loyal to the Crown. Mary, herself, was kept under closer scrutiny as Elizabeth refused to countenance her execution. Walsingham did, however, succeed in drawing up the Bond of Association (1584), a document that obliged all signatories to execute anyone who usurped or attempted to usurp the queen. Mary, herself, was made to sign it and it provided the basis of her execution after the failure of the **Babington Plot** two years later.

Tower of London

A castle on the north bank of the River Thames in the city of London.

The Tower of London – or the 'Tower' – was the first stone castle built in England and completed in the late eleventh century to demonstrate royal authority. Over the following centuries it was, first and foremost, the chief royal residence and several kings added extensions and strengthened it.

The nature of the Tower's role, however, changed during the Tudor period. In 1503, **Henry VII**'s beloved wife, **Elizabeth of York**, died after giving birth in the Tower's royal apartments. From that point on, he hardly visited it and the Tower's main purpose became that of a giant armoury, including the nation's supply of gunpowder, as well as the country's main mint. To guard these important supplies, Henry VII created the Yeomen Warders. They were later nicknamed 'Beefeaters' as they were allowed to eat as much beef as they liked from the king's table. **Henry VIII** and his children likewise preferred other royal residences, most notably Westminster Palace, Hampton Court Palace, Whitehall Palace and Windsor Castle. The Tower remained a symbol of royal power though and, in 1517, its cannons fired on the mob during the **Evil May Day** riots.

In 1483, Edward IV's sons had been sent to the Tower by their uncle, Richard, in order to prepare for Edward V's coronation. It seems likely that they were murdered there but the Tower's sinister reputation as a prison where people were tortured and executed did not really become established until the 1530s. Henry VIII's determination to assert his authority after the break with Rome and to crack down on any dissent led to a large increase in the Tower's inmates. In his reign alone, thirty-one prisoners were executed there. The majority met their fate just outside the Tower, on Tower Hill. These included Empson and Dudley, Bishop **Fisher**, **Sir Thomas More**, **Thomas Cromwell** and **Henry Howard**. More private and secure executions were carried out within the Tower's walls, on Tower Green. These included **Anne Boleyn**, Margaret Pole and **Catherine Howard**.

Tower of London. The Thames is in the foreground with Traitor's Gate to the right. A scaffold can be seen on Tower Hill, centre left. (*Artist: Nathaniel Whittock, 1849. Copy and alteration of a 1540s drawing by Antony van den Wyngaerde. Bodlean Library*)

Spates of executions occurred in 1552 (after **Northumberland**'s coup against **Somerset**) and 1554 (after **Wyatt's Rebellion**) but only eight were killed at the Tower in the whole of **Elizabeth I**'s reign, most notably the **Fourth Duke of Norfolk** and the **Earl of Essex**. In total, during the Tudor period, sixty-four people were executed there.

Only a fraction of the Tower's prisoners were ever tortured. Technically, torture was illegal under English law and the Lieutenant of the Tower could only authorise it with permission from the monarch or Privy Council. The three main methods were to stretch the body (the rack or Duke of Exeter's Daughter), compress the body (the Scavenger's Daughter) or hang the body (manacles). Between 1540 and 1640, forty-eight cases of torture were recorded. **Father Gerard**, for instance, was manacled but, most infamous of all, was the racking of **Anne Askew**.

Many prisoners had to endure entering the Tower via its riverside access – Traitor's Gate – after being rowed under the impaled heads of recently executed inmates on London Bridge. This happened to Princess Elizabeth in 1554. Terrified of meeting the same fate as her mother, she sat outside the Gate in the pouring rain, refusing to enter. The conditions of imprisonment tended to depend on your wealth and status. The poorest could expect little in the way of food and comfort but the rich could pay for most of life's luxuries (with a cut going to their warders!). **Sir Walter Ralegh**, for example, lived his thirteen years in the Tower in great comfort. His apartment was altered so that his family could live with him and he even had a son born there!

Tyndale, William

(c. 1494–1536)

Scholar, linguist and martyr.

Tyndale was born into a wealthy family in Gloucestershire. He later gained his BA and MA at Oxford University and was ordained as a priest. In around 1517, he went to Cambridge University, possibly attracted by its more reform-minded religious views and associations with the **humanist**, Desiderius Erasmus. Whilst there, he developed his linguistic talents and started to become fluent in Greek, Hebrew, Latin and several modern languages. He also became involved with the budding group of reformers who met at the White Horse Inn or 'Little Germany', men like **Miles Coverdale** and **Hugh Latimer**.

By the early 1520s, Tyndale was becoming increasingly disillusioned with the **Catholic** Church. He complained about priests who simply memorised the Church's teachings without actually knowing anything of the Bible. He became influenced by Martin Luther's **Protestant** views and proclaimed that the Bible should be translated into English so that it could be understood by all. Tyndale travelled to London to seek the patronage of its bishop, Cuthbert Tunstall, but he was warned against any heretical translations. Instead, he received support from reformist merchants who persuaded him to start his work in Germany.

In 1524, Tyndale moved to Wittenberg where he met Luther, whose earlier translation of the Bible into German had inspired him. Under the pseudonym of Gulielmus Daltin (his surname's syllables reversed), he started to translate the Bible, not from the Church's authorised Latin version but from its original language – Greek. Interrupted by the Catholic authorities, Tyndale then moved to the more Protestant city of Worms. He was now able to complete the New Testament, copies of which were printed and smuggled into England, where Tunstall and Cardinal **Wolsey** ordered them to be burned.

Tyndale then fell into a war of words with the Catholic scholar, **Thomas More**, with both sides descending into personal abuse. Upon becoming Lord Chancellor in 1529, More spent much energy persecuting Tyndale's followers. King **Henry VIII**'s position was more ambivalent though. Tyndale's *Obedience of a Christian Man* (1528) was the first book in English to advocate the divine right of kings and he argued that monarchs should run the Church, not the Pope. Apparently, this work greatly influenced Henry's later decision to break with Rome. However, his *Practice of Prelates* (1530) not only attacked the papacy but also undermined Henry's theological reasons for wanting to annul his first **marriage**. An infuriated king demanded Tyndale's extradition but Charles V, the Holy Roman Emperor, cited a lack of evidence and refused. After a failed kidnapping attempt, Tyndale kept on the move – Worms, Hamburg, Antwerp. At the same time, he managed to start work on a translation of the Old Testament.

The death of William Tyndale. (*1907 edition of John Foxe's* Book of Martyrs. *Image altered from the original. The Library of Congress*)

Although relatively safe from his English enemies, it was a far greater authority that Tyndale needed to fear. Pieces of his translations had greatly upset the papacy. For instance, he used the word 'overseer' instead of 'bishop' or 'priest' but far more subversive was the translation of the Greek word '*ekklesia*', a word Jesus had used that had been interpreted as 'The Church', i.e. the Catholic Church. Tyndale, however, believed it meant 'congregation' – a translation that hugely undermined the Church's authority. In 1535, he was betrayed by an English 'friend' who was possibly working for conservative members of the English clergy. Lured out of the safety of the English merchant quarter in Antwerp, Tyndale was arrested by the local authorities. After an eighteen-month imprisonment, a court found him guilty of heresy and sentenced him to death. **Thomas Cromwell** intervened, asking for leniency, but to no avail and, in October 1536, in Vilvoorde (near Brussels), Tyndale was strangled before his body was burned. At the stake, he was said to have called out, 'Lord, open the King of England's eyes.'

Indeed, three years later, King Henry did allow the first English Bible to be read in all churches. It was prepared by Coverdale, who completed the translation of the Old Testament, but it was largely Tyndale's work. This Bible then became the basis of the celebrated King James Version of 1611. According to the historian, Brian Moynahan, 84 per cent of the New Testament's and 76 per cent of the Old Testament's words are Tyndale's and it became the most influential and best-selling book of all time. Tyndale translated into a clear, modern English, almost poetic in places, and in the process, standardised the language and created words and phrases that have come into everyday usage such as, 'a moment in time', 'a law unto themselves', 'let there be light', 'the powers that be' and 'salt of the Earth'. Even the famous atheist, Richard Dawkins, described the King James Version as being, 'a giant step in the maturing of English literature' so it should be no surprise that Tyndale was voted twenty-sixth in the BBC's poll of 'Hundred Greatest Britons' conducted in 2002.

Tyrone's Rebellion

(1594–1603)

An Irish uprising, also known as the Nine Years' War.

In the early 1590s, the English administration in **Ireland** started to encroach on the northern clans. Attempts to enforce English officials and **Protestant**ism upon the **Catholic**, Gaelic communities were met with strong resistance and militarily repulsed under the leadership of Hugh Roe O'Donnell of Tyrconnell (in Donegal). The most powerful Gaelic lord in the north was Hugh O'Neill, the Earl of Tyrone. After the murder of his father, Tyrone had been looked after by the English in Dublin until he had come of age and was granted his earldom in 1587. Tyrone, at first, aided the English in the hope that Queen **Elizabeth I** would make him Lord of Ulster. When it became clear that this position would go to an English official instead, Tyrone realised that attack was the best form of defence and, in 1595, openly joined the revolt.

Tyrone started with some initial advantages. The English forces in Ireland were under-strength – most financial and military resources were being directed to the **Anglo-Spanish War**. Second, Ulster was a difficult part of the island to attack; it had not been properly mapped and its mountains, marshes and dense woodland provided excellent natural defences. Last, Tyrone had a sizeable force (6,000 men by 1601), which was supplied with pikes and arquebuses from abroad, reinforced by Scottish mercenaries and later trained by Spanish veterans.

He wrote to King Philip of Spain, requesting assistance for the Catholic cause and in return he offered Ireland as his vassal state. At first, there was no response and so Tyrone accepted a truce but any chance of a permanent peace was wrecked by Spanish promises of support in 1596. Philip was only too pleased to open up a second front against England and so, in the same year, an armada set sail from Lisbon but was decimated by storms and returned to port.

Meanwhile, in Ireland, Tyrone's superior forces were scoring military victories as successive English offensives were driven back. Most notable was the Irish success at the Battle of the Yellow Ford (1598) when 2,000 English troops were killed – England's heaviest defeat in Ireland. The victory inspired island-wide revolts, which Tyrone assisted with his own troops. In Munster, in the south-west, the hated English plantations were overrun and landowners, such as **Edmund Spenser**, had to flee for their lives.

With English forces now confined to only the largest towns and the Pale around Dublin, Elizabeth sent her favourite, the **Earl of Essex**, to restore order. His mission, however, was poorly led, under-funded and under-resourced. Cutting his losses, he decided to make a truce with Tyrone and return to London in 1599. Later that year, Tyrone sent Elizabeth his peace proposals: a self-governing Ireland with its restored lands and Catholic religion under English overlordship.

This was ignored and the English government, now realising the full extent of the crisis, sent a larger force, better resourced and with able commanders, under the leadership of **Lord Mountjoy**. A divide and conquer strategy worked in retaking the south whilst, in the north, a seaborne landing and scorched earth tactics weakened Tyrone's position considerably. In late 1601, hope came in the form of 3,500 Spanish troops landing at Kinsale in Derry. These soldiers soon became trapped though as Mountjoy quickly laid siege to the town. Tyrone and Tyrconnell, realising that no more foreign support would come if they did nothing, left their hideouts and quickly marched their troops 300 miles south to relieve the Spanish. Outside the town, at the Battle of Kinsale (January 1602),

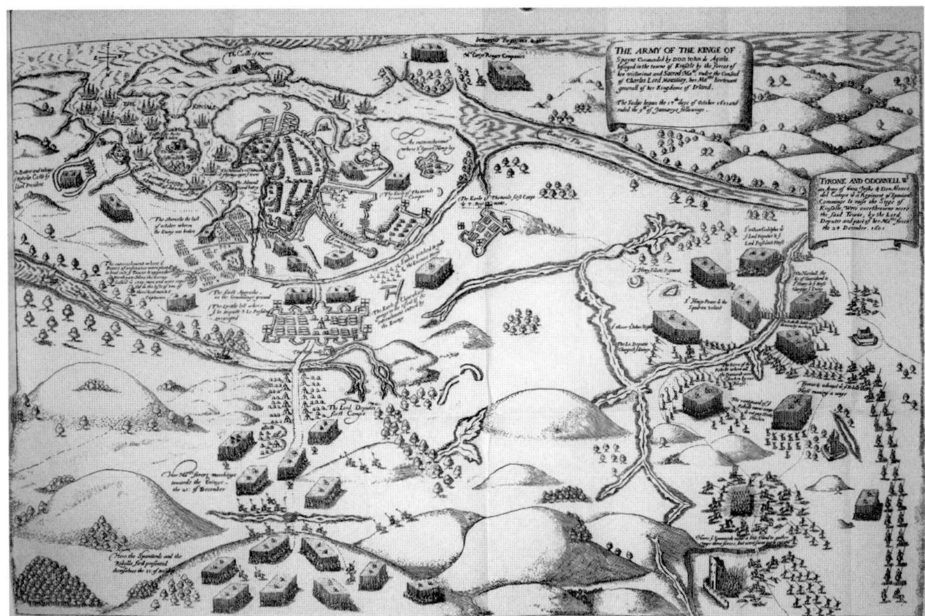

Siege of Kinsale. Top left – Kinsale is besieged by English ships. Centre left – Mountjoy's base. Right – Tyrone and O'Donnell's forces. (*From a 1907 edition of Fynes Moryson's* An Itinerary: Containing His Ten Years Travel, *1617. University of California Libraries*)

the English cavalry demonstrated its superiority and the Irish their unsuitability for a conventional battle. Tyrone's forces were routed and many froze or starved to death during their northward retreat. The Spanish in Kinsale meanwhile surrendered and were allowed to sail home.

After this, Tyrone continued to hold out in the forests of Ulster. Meanwhile, the cost of maintaining an English army of 20,000 – far larger than the force in the Netherlands – amounted to 75 per cent of annual revenue and Elizabeth was persuaded to allow a conditional surrender. This led to the Treaty of Mellifont on 30 March 1603, six days after the queen's death. Under the terms of the treaty, Tyrone was pardoned and retained the core of his territory. In return, he swore loyalty to the English Crown, accepted English law and English as the official language and agreed that no Catholic churches would be built on his lands. Further persecution after the Gunpowder Plot (1605) forced Tyrone and other lords to flee abroad to seek Spanish help (Tyrconnell had already died in Spain in 1602). This was known as the 'Flight of the Earls', after which their lands were confiscated and became plantations for Protestant Scottish and English settlers. Tyrone, himself, died an exile in Rome in 1616.

For a while, the rebellion/war had taken the form of Ireland's first national uprising and had been a major drain on English resources. The cost in lives, though, had been far worse. Around 100,000 Irish died – ten per cent of the

population – largely through famine caused by crop and livestock destruction and 30,000 English soldiers were killed, mainly from disease. Ultimately, though, it led to the island's complete subjugation although, remarkably, the Catholic religion managed to survive and prosper.

V

Vergil, Polydore

(c. 1470–1555)

Historian.

Polidoro Vergilio was born in the Duchy of Urbino, in Italy, and came from a wealthy and educated family. After attending Padua University, he was ordained as a priest in 1499. He travelled to England in 1502 to assist in the collection of 'Peter's Pence' – an annual tax given to the Pope and later abolished by **Parliament** in 1534. Whilst there, Vergil (his anglicised name) was granted several clerical positions and England became his adopted country. In 1510, he was naturalised English. He made several short visits to Italy during his life, until he made a permanent return to the country of his birth in 1550.

By 1502, Vergil was already gathering a reputation as a writer. In 1498, his *Adagia* (a list of Latin proverbs) was printed. This led to a friendly rivalry with the great humanist, Desiderius Erasmus, who claimed that his *Adagia* had come out first. Vergil's greatest work, however, was *De Inventoribus Rerum* (1499), an incredibly popular and ambitious series of books that attempted to explain the origins of all inventions and Christian practices.

A renowned scholar and advocate of the latest ideas in **humanism**, Vergil was welcomed to the royal court where **Henry VII** asked him to write a history of England. The original manuscript of *Anglica Historia* appeared in 1513, which was followed by several printed versions, the last edition being in 1555. The work is divided into twenty-five books. The first seven deal with events before 1066, Book VIII focuses on the reigns of William I and William II and each of the remaining books is dedicated to subsequent monarchs. The final edition concludes the narrative in 1537.

Anglica Historia became the basis for future historians' work and provided much material for **Shakespeare**'s history plays. However, it has been accused of containing too much pro-Tudor bias. Vergil was, after all, in the pay of the Tudors so there is next to no criticism of Henry VII and **Henry VIII** but much vilification of Richard III. He also has harsh words for **Thomas Wolsey**; in a previous spat, Wolsey had accused him of undermining his attempts to become a cardinal and had him briefly imprisoned in the Tower in 1515.

However, Vergil drew upon a huge amount of resources, including foreign ones, and used rational analysis to try to uncover the plain facts no matter how unpopular it made him. For example, he controversially doubted the existence of King Arthur and stated that Cambridge had the oldest university, not Oxford. Due to his ability to interview witnesses, however, it is the period after 1450 that is most valuable today and can be considered as primary evidence. His work is flawed but, for some, Vergil's attempts to discover the truth have earned him the title 'The Father of English History'.

W

Walsingham, Sir Francis

(1530/32–90)

Statesman and 'spymaster'.

Walsingham was born in Kent, the only son of William, a successful London lawyer, and Joyce Denny, who had connections in the royal court. From his mother's side of the family, he probably inherited his **Protestant** views which were reinforced during his attendance at Cambridge University. As was fashionable at the time, he went abroad to continue his **education** in 1550. He returned two years later and started his legal training but the accession of the **Catholic**, **Mary I** to the throne forced him to flee abroad. He continued his training in Italy and Switzerland, became fluent in Italian and French and began to make the first of his many contacts abroad.

Walsingham returned to England soon after **Elizabeth** came to the throne and, through the support of influential friends, became a member of **Parliament** in 1559. He married twice and it was his second wife who bore a daughter, Frances, who would later marry **Philip Sidney** and the **Earl of Essex**. Due to recommendations and his knowledge of foreign languages, he came into the employment of **William Cecil**, Elizabeth's First Minister, in 1568. Soon after, he started to make contact with French and Italian exiles in London in order to discover any hostile intentions from abroad. In the aftermath of the **Northern Rebellion**, Cecil asked him to interrogate the Italian banker, Roberto di Ridolfi, but it seems that Walsingham was entirely hood-winked and believed Ridolfi to be innocent of any involvement.

In 1570, he was appointed ambassador to France and asked to support the French Protestants in their negotiations with King Charles IX. He negotiated a defensive Anglo-French treaty in 1572 but, later in the same year, he witnessed the brutality of the St Bartholomew Day's Massacre. Several Protestants sought refuge in his house including his future son-in-law, Philip Sidney, and the events served to sharpen his anti-Catholic views.

After his return to England in 1573, Walsingham was appointed Privy Councillor and became one of the queen's principal secretaries. He was given several other posts throughout the 1570s and was knighted in 1577.

Francis Walsingham. (*Artist: Jacobus Houbraken, 1738. Engraving based on a 1585 portrait. Yale Center for British Art*)

Walsingham wielded much power and influence in the Elizabethan government, being second only to Cecil as the queen's chief advisor. His constant demands for a more aggressive, proactive, anti-Catholic approach included increased military aid for the French and Dutch Protestant rebels and the execution of 'that devilish woman', **Mary, Queen of Scots**. This ran counter, however, to Cecil's more cautious pragmatism, which Elizabeth usually backed. Sometimes, out of frustration, Walsingham would become quite outspoken in his opposition to the queen's views and this, in turn, would provoke her furious responses. His angry denouncement of her **marriage** negotiations with the French Catholic, Duc D'Alencon, for instance, led to his dismissal from court for a few months in 1579 but, at the end of the day, she knew she could trust him to do whatever she asked. This included sending him on various diplomatic missions to achieve policies that she knew he disagreed with.

Walsingham's reputation as Elizabeth's 'spymaster' is well founded. Using his contacts abroad, he built up a large and successful spy network that stretched from Constantinople and Algiers to Rome, Madrid and Paris. It was said that he knew of policy decisions in Rome before they reached the Spanish king. Out of his own pocket, he paid for fifty-three agents in foreign courts and eighteen other, more dubious, employees for the rougher kind of work that was required. One of his agents, in all likelihood, was the playwright, **Christopher Marlowe**. In his London office, he also employed experts in codes and cyphers

St Bartholomew Day's Massacre. The massacre of many thousands of French Protestants in Paris had a profound effect on Protestant Europe. (*Artist: Frans Hogenberg, c. 1572. Wikimedia Commons*)

and those who could break open letters and reseal them. Walsingham's ability to penetrate Catholic circles, including the **Jesuit** training colleges, helped to uncover plots to usurp the queen. Most famous of all was his exposure of the **Babington Plot** (1586), which finally led to the execution of Mary, Queen of Scots. In the following year, he successfully masked **Drake**'s raid on Cadiz by feeding false information to the English ambassador in France who he had correctly guessed was in the pay of the Spanish.

Walsingham was a great supporter of all sea voyages that could increase trade or disrupt Spain's monopoly in the Americas. For this reason, he helped to fund Drake's expedition to the Pacific and **Frobisher**'s and **Davis**'s attempts to discover a north-west passage to Asia. He also toyed with the idea of encouraging a colony for Catholics in America as a way of removing them from England. Walsingham gave much support to men of learning, too, such as **John Dee** and **Edmund Spenser**, and founded a lectureship in divinity at Oxford.

Since 1571, Walsingham had complained of pains around his body, especially when passing urine. He probably suffered from kidney stones or a urinary infection but it seems that it was testicular cancer that killed him in April 1590. His simple funeral ceremony in St Paul's Cathedral was appropriate for a man who disliked ostentation but it probably reflected his huge debts caused by acquiring the debts of his son-in-law, Sidney, after his early death in 1585.

His detractors have accused him of being over-zealous and cruel but he was none more so than his contemporaries in other countries. In fact, he only resorted to torture on a few occasions and objected to its use as it could create Catholic martyrs. Little is known of Walsingham's character as his private papers were lost but it seems that Elizabeth had little love for him, calling him 'my Moor' due to his dark complexion and deriding him as a 'rank **Puritan**' because of his sombre appearance and demeanour. However, she also realised that she needed him – the perfect foil to the cautious Cecil and ever alert to any threats to her throne. Without a doubt, he can be considered a pioneer in the subtle art of espionage who used different methods, since copied, to gather intelligence. His maxim was, 'Knowledge is never too dear'. Ironically, Walsingham's greatest tribute came from King Philip II of Spain. Upon reading a letter from England informing him of Walsingham's death and the sorrow it had caused, he wrote in the margin, 'There, yes! But it is good news here.'

Warbeck, Perkin

(c. 1474–99)

Pretender to the English throne.

The tale of Perkin Warbeck reads like a fictitious adventure story in which the main protagonist is swept along by outside events as he stumbles from one setback to another. This, however, is a true story even though some of the facts may be a bit hazy.

Perkin Warbeck. (*Artist: unknown, 15th century. Wikimedia Commons*)

In the Netherlands, in 1490, Warbeck announced that he was Richard of York – the younger son of Edward IV and one of the Princes in the Tower who had disappeared in 1483. He claimed that his older brother, Edward V, had been murdered whilst the gaolers had shown him sympathy and allowed him to escape. Only when he came of age, at sixteen, did he decide to reveal himself and claim his inheritance – the English throne.

According to Warbeck's later confession (probably acquired under duress), however, he was the son of a minor customs official from Tournai in the Holy Roman Empire. He was later employed as a model for a cloth merchant who, in 1491, took him to Cork in southern **Ireland**. Cork was a hotbed of Yorkist sympathisers who saw the new king, **Henry VII**, as a Tudor upstart. When the inhabitants saw this tall, elegant boy dressed up in the merchant's fine clothes, they persuaded him to pretend to be Richard of York. At seventeen, he would have been about the right age and, as the real Richard had disappeared, Henry could not prove that Warbeck was a fake. Support from the Lord Deputy of Ireland, the Earl of Kildare, was not forthcoming, though, as he had learned his lesson a few years earlier when supporting another Yorkist pretender, **Lambert Simnel**.

Between 1491 and 1495, Warbeck caused much trouble for Henry as he sought support and recognition in other foreign courts. Both King Charles VIII of France and Emperor Maximilian I saw him as a useful political bargaining chip and recognised him as 'Richard IV'. Henry had to resort to an invasion of France and a trade war with the Empire in order to remove their support but Warbeck spent most of this time in the court of Margaret of Burgundy, Edward IV's sister. She had never met her nephews and we cannot be sure if she believed his claims. She did, however, want to bring about Henry's downfall and so had him trained to act as a member of the Yorkist royal family and supplied him with money, troops and fourteen ships.

Within England, meanwhile, Henry uncovered a plot that supported Warbeck. One of the conspirators was the man who had helped him win the **Battle of Bosworth Field**, William Stanley. He and several others were executed but later that year (1495), Warbeck attempted an invasion at Deal in Kent where his small force was driven off the steep sloping beach by the local militia. From Kent, he sailed to Ireland and received support from the Earl of Desmond but after failing to capture Waterford, he decided his best chances now lay in Scotland.

There, he was well received by King James IV, who probably saw him as a tool for gaining leverage in negotiations with other countries. Nevertheless, he feted Warbeck at his court and arranged a **marriage** to one of his cousins, Lady Catherine Gordon. In 1496, James and Warbeck led an invasion force into northern England, accompanied by *Mons Meg*, the largest cannon of the time. It was little more than a show of force, though, possibly aimed at obtaining a favourable peace with England, and he soon withdrew after Henry's army approached. In the ensuing treaty, James agreed not to harbour England's enemies and, in mid-1497, Warbeck was requested to leave.

He returned to Ireland and was again repulsed at Waterford. Now, numbering only 120 men in two ships, he was chased away by English vessels and disembarked on the coast of Cornwall in September. Had he been more proactive and landed there a few months earlier, things might have turned out differently. Triggered by taxes raised to fight Henry's war against Scotland, a **Cornish Rebellion** had threatened London itself in July. By the time Warbeck arrived, however, the uprising had been crushed. He managed to gather 6,000 supporters and have himself crowned 'Richard IV' on Bodmin Moor but his forces quickly dispersed when a royal army approached. Warbeck fled and was captured in Beaulieu Abbey in Hampshire before being brought to London.

There, he was paraded through jeering crowds and forced to make a confession regarding his 'true identity'. Henry treated him very leniently and allowed him to live at his court even though dealing with Warbeck during the last six years had cost him over £13,000 (equivalent of about £9 million). After trying to escape, however, he joined his 'cousin', the Earl of Warwick, in the **Tower of London** but after making another escape attempt in 1499, Henry decided to be rid of him and hanged him as a commoner at Tyburn. Soon after, he had Warwick beheaded, possibly to appease the king and queen of Spain during the negotiations for a marriage between their daughter, **Catherine of Aragon**, and Henry's son, **Arthur**. Apparently, years afterwards, Catherine felt much guilt about this and said it was the cause of her later misfortunes. As for Lady Gordon, she became a favourite maid to Henry's wife, **Elizabeth of York**.

The weight of evidence suggests that Warbeck was indeed a fraud but this cannot currently be proved. Certainly, he was said to bear a strong resemblance to Edward IV and it seems odd that he was never introduced to his 'sister', Elizabeth of York, who could easily have proved him to be a fake. Whatever the truth, Warbeck was clearly a tool of late-fifteenth-century international politics and it is difficult to know just how willing a participant he was. One can either sympathise with this political pawn or mock his hopeless persistence.

Warham, William

(c. 1450–1532)

Archbishop of Canterbury.

Warham was born in Hampshire and had lowly origins; his father may have been a tenant farmer and carpenter. He attended Winchester College and then went to Oxford University to study civil law. After being ordained he was appointed Master of the Rolls in 1494 – the most senior clerk in the Chancery law court. King **Henry VII** then employed Warham on various diplomatic missions, including one to Burgundy where he attempted, unsuccessfully, to persuade its duchess to drop her support for the royal pretender, **Perkin Warbeck**. He also helped to arrange the **marriage** between Prince **Arthur** and **Catherine of Aragon**.

Warham now experienced a rapid rise to power. He became Bishop of London in 1502 and then, two years later, Archbishop of Canterbury and Lord Chancellor. The latter two roles meant that he was now both the spiritual and legal guardian of the country. The apogee of his influence came in 1509 when he crowned **Henry VIII** and Catherine of Aragon, despite his misgivings about the legality of Henry's marriage to his brother's widow.

William Warham. (*Artist: Feliks Stanisław Jasiński, 1887. Copy of Hans Holbein portrait, 1527. National Museum in Warsaw*)

Thereafter, his prominence waned. Like a new, young, energetic head teacher, Henry VIII had inherited a staid, old deputy head whom he could not remove. Likewise, Warham disapproved of his new master's actions but remained in his post out of a sense of duty. Within a few years, he had been eclipsed by the king's new, 'go to' man, **Thomas Wolsey**, who, unlike Warham, approved of Henry's continental ambitions. Increasingly side-lined, Warham was replaced by Wolsey as Lord Chancellor in 1515. Maybe he was ousted but, more than likely, he was happy to resign so that he could focus on his spiritual duties.

He next came into the limelight during the king's 'Great Matter'. He himself revealed no opinion on whether Henry could annul his **marriage** to Catherine but, even though he was appointed the queen's counsel, he did little to support her. Perhaps he was held back by his motto – 'the king's anger is death'.

Warham became increasingly cornered after 1529 when the Reformation **Parliament** started to erode the independence and power of the Church. At first, he, like most of the clergy, submitted to the king's demands, seeking only weak compromises. Only in 1532, at the age of eighty-two, did he finally decide to show any meaningful resistance. In the House of Lords, he reproached the king and announced his intention to try and repeal all anti-clerical laws enacted since 1529. For this, he was charged with treason but nevertheless, perhaps emboldened by his approaching death, he planned another defiant speech which he never lived long enough to deliver.

Warham was a very generous man who disliked ostentation and avoided the simple pleasures in life such as wine and playing dice. He donated much money to educational institutions, appreciated the new ideas of **humanism** and supported its great guru, Erasmus. Whatever his personal qualities, though, Warham was not a **Fisher** or a **More** and he lacked the ability or willpower to resist the onset of the **Reformation**.

War of the Rough Wooing

(1543–50)

An Anglo-Scottish conflict, also known as the Eight Years' War.

Following the **Battle of Solway Moss** in November 1542 and the death of their king, James V, soon after, the Scots agreed to the Treaty of Greenwich in mid-1543. King **Henry VIII** of England now saw an opportunity. If he could marry his son, Prince **Edward**, to James's daughter, **Mary, Queen of Scots**, then he could unite the two kingdoms, destroy Scotland's Auld Alliance with France and enable him to wage another war with the French without having to worry about his northern border. Mary was still a baby and Edward was only six years old but it was agreed that when Mary reached the age of ten, she would marry Edward by proxy and then move to England.

The leader of the Scottish party at Greenwich was the regent, the Earl of Arran. Upon his return, however, the news of the agreement only served to sharpen the dividing lines in Scottish politics. A low-level civil war ensued between the **Protestant**, pro-English faction (led by Arran) and the **Catholic**, pro-French party. Arran, however, switched sides and, in late 1543, a large majority in the Scottish **Parliament** refused to ratify the treaty.

Angered by this, Henry duly declared war and sent an army north by sea led by **Edward Seymour**. Seymour then captured Edinburgh, razed it to the ground (May 1544) and marched his forces back to England, pillaging and burning towns en route. More minor English raids followed, including one that was badly beaten at **Ancrum Moor** (February 1545). In mid-1546, the end of the **Third Anglo-French War** brought a temporary truce to the conflict, which was extended by Henry's death in early 1547.

Seymour, now the Duke of Somerset, became the regent of England and decided to continue with England's attempt to force the Scots into a union. He led another army north and, this time, won a major engagement at the **Battle of Pinkie Cleugh** in September, 1547. He then garrisoned troops across southern Scotland in order to force the Scots to accept the treaty terms of Greenwich. They refused, however, and, bolstered by thousands of French reinforcements, they successfully resisted and then began to eject the English from their lands. In August 1548, the five-year-old Mary was spirited away to the safety of France and betrothed to the French king's son.

As Somerset's Scottish policy unravelled and his grip on power loosened, he was removed in a coup and replaced by **John Dudley** in 1549. Dudley was less keen on expensive wars and ended the conflict at the Treaty of Boulogne (March 1550). It is hard to see how Henry's and Somerset's bullying tactics were ever going to work and, in fact, they drove all wavering Scots into the French camp. A more conciliatory strategy may well have achieved success although Edward's premature death in 1553 meant that a union of the two crowns was not to happen for another fifty years. On the plus side, however, the conflict was the last war ever fought between the independent kingdoms of England and Scotland.

Wars of the Roses

(1455–87)

A series of civil wars that ushered in the Tudor Age.

In the mid-fifteenth century, England was ripe for a civil war. Its king, Henry VI, was a weak and shy ruler who lacked authority and any military ambitions that may have united his overbearing lords. Conversely, over the past hundred years, these barons had acquired much land and power and their feudal ties to the monarchy had been weakened by 'bastard feudalism' whereby military service had been replaced by financial payments. This had allowed the lords to build up their own private armies, loyal directly to them, and emasculated the monarchy by depriving it of its own loyal supporters.

Matters came to a head in 1453 when two events happened: the English army suffered its final defeat in the Hundred Years' War against France and King Henry suffered a mental breakdown that rendered him completely incapable of ruling. The former allowed for the return to England of many soldiers ready to fight for their lords. The latter kick-started a struggle to fill the power vacuum, led by the two most powerful branches of the royal family – Lancaster and York. The Yorkists adopted the white rose as their badge. The red rose of Lancaster only came about after the **Battle of Bosworth Field** (1485). At the time and for many years later, the conflict was simply known as 'The Civil Wars'.

Periods of fighting tended to be fairly brief with sustained moments of peace in between. The battles were generally small-scale affairs in which the death or capture of a key protagonist would be hugely decisive. One notable exception was the Battle of Towton (1461), considered to be the largest, longest and bloodiest battle on English soil. Some barons, out for their own gain, would switch sides and the crown exchanged hands a few times. It was the Yorkist, Edward IV, who finally came out on top in 1471.

That might have been the end of it except Edward died unexpectedly in 1483 and left behind two young sons and several daughters. The two boys, Edward V and Richard of York, were sent to the **Tower of London** by their uncle and never seen again. Their uncle was crowned Richard III and was immediately suspected of murdering the Princes in the Tower. His subsequent unpopularity opened

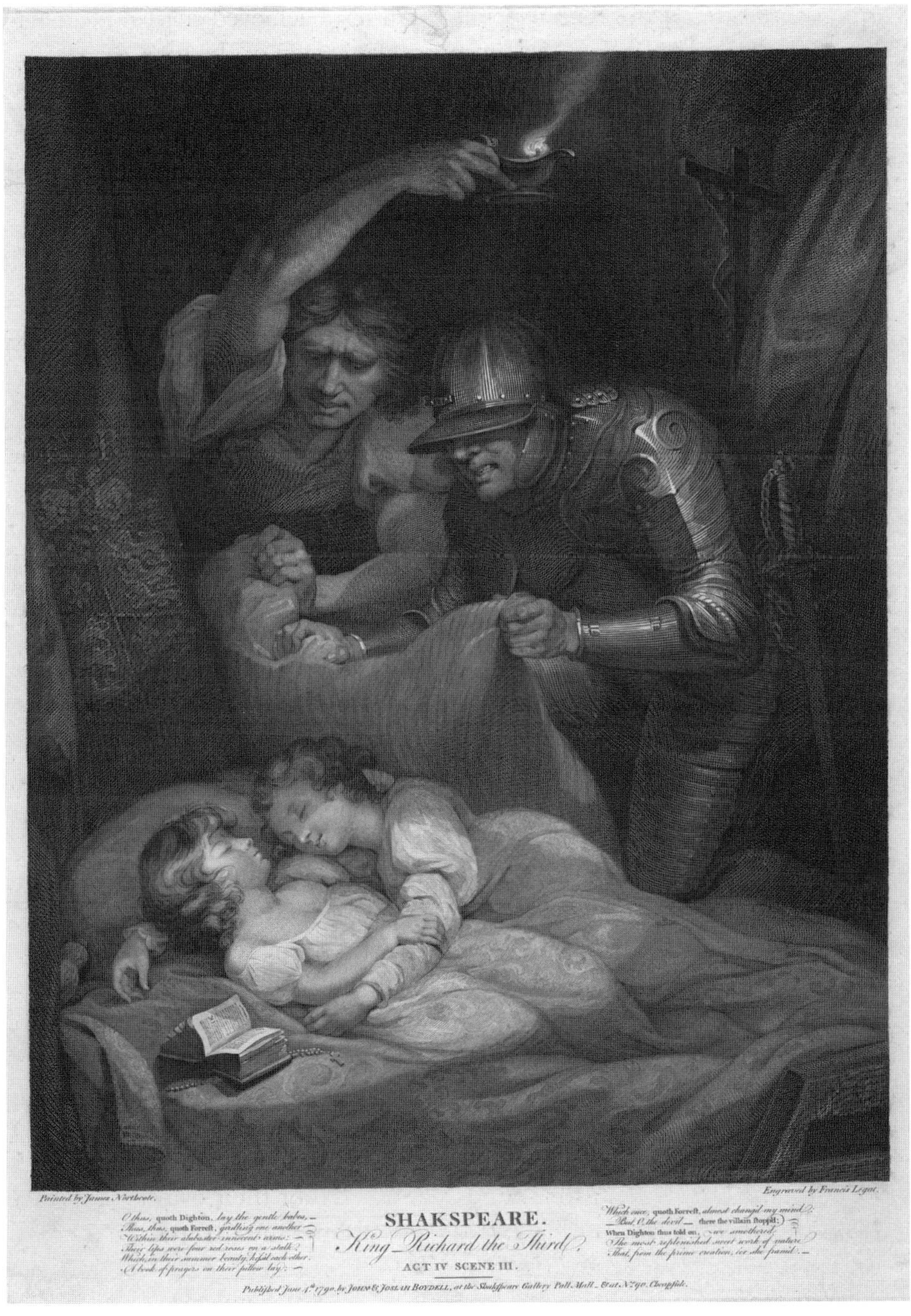

18th-century depiction of the murder of the Princes in the Tower. (*Artist: Francis Legat, 1790. Yale Center for British Art*)

the door for the Lancastrian, Henry Tudor, who invaded in 1485 and defeated Richard at Bosworth Field. To put an end to the civil war, Henry (now **Henry VII**) united the two warring families by marrying Edward's eldest daughter, **Elizabeth of York**. The final death throes of the conflict came two years later when Henry quelled a Yorkist rebellion at the Battle of Stoke.

The Wars of the Roses mark both the end of the Middle Ages and the end of a feudal system that was no longer sustainable. The governance of the country required a complete overhaul and so it was the Tudors who brought England into the Early Modern Age.

Wentworth, Peter

(c. 1524–96)

Parliamentarian.

Little is known of Wentworth's early life other than he came from a wealthy family that owned land in Oxfordshire and Buckinghamshire and he married twice. His first wife, Letitia, was a cousin once removed of **Catherine Parr** and his second wife, Elizabeth, was a sister of **Francis Walsingham**. These connections and his wealth undoubtedly helped him enter **Parliament** but this did not happen until 1571.

Wentworth made a strong impact in each of the six parliaments in which he sat. He was a **Puritan** and accused Archbishop **Parker** of acting like a pope in trying to force **articles** of the Church of England through Parliament. After the **Ridolfi Plot**, he led parliamentary demands for the executions of the **Fourth Duke of Norfolk** and **Mary, Queen of Scots** whom he called, 'the most notorious whore in all the world'.

In 1576, he caused an uproar in the Commons with a speech that attacked the subservience of Parliament to the Crown. He accused Queen **Elizabeth I** of 'great faults' by forcing Parliament to only discuss what she wanted and demanded that the House should have freedom of speech, without any fear of reprisals. So outraged were the majority of his peers that he was interrupted before he could finish, arrested and sent to the **Tower** for a month. Copies of his speech, however, were widely circulated both in England and abroad.

In the 1586–87 Parliament, Wentworth led requests for Puritan changes to the Church. When Elizabeth forbade this, he made more demands for parliamentary freedom of speech. For this, he was sent to the Tower again along with four others.

After his release, Wentworth focused on the question of the royal succession and wrote an essay in which he urged the queen to nominate her successor. His language, as usual, was frank, as he warned her of the terrible fate that would await her soul if she did nothing. At first, he tried to persuade **Lord Burghley** and the **Earl of Essex** to discuss the subject with the queen. However, they knew better than to risk such a venture and, when news of his essay was leaked to the Privy Council, Wentworth was sent to the Tower for a third time in 1593. There he remained for the rest of his life.

His captivity was a comfortable one and his wife was allowed to stay with him (she died in the Tower, too, a few months before her husband). On several occasions, Wentworth was offered his freedom if he repented and promised his future silence but he stubbornly refused. By this time, he had pronounced that James VI of Scotland should be the queen's heir which, ironically, was Elizabeth's dying wish too.

Before Elizabeth's reign, Parliament's role had generally been to rubber stamp the monarch's wishes. From the 1560s, people took more interest in parliamentary discussions and MPs started to keep notes and diaries recording the sessions. It was Wentworth, however, a man who was way ahead of his time, who lit the fires of parliamentary liberty and freedom of speech. Today, we accept his views as being vitally necessary but, less than fifty years after his death, Parliament had to fight for them. Literally.

Whitgift, John

(c. 1532–1604)

Archbishop of Canterbury.

The son of a wealthy Lincolnshire merchant, Whitgift was sent to Cambridge University in 1549. He impressed with his studies and displayed a leaning toward extreme **Protestant**ism. Later, he became a lecturer and was appointed to various college positions but, during the reign of Queen **Mary I**, he kept a low profile and avoided persecution from the authorities.

Soon after the accession of **Elizabeth I**, Whitgift was ordained a priest and started to lecture in theology. His administrative skills and public support for the queen's Church Settlement brought him to the attention of the court and, after hearing him preach, the queen appointed him as a royal chaplain. No doubt, his refusal to marry must have pleased her too although this led to a few, unfounded, accusations of homosexuality. In 1577, he was given the bishopric of Worcester.

In 1583, he was appointed Archbishop of Canterbury after the unsuccessful tenure of **Edmund Grindal** who had been considered too lenient with dissident **Puritans**. Elizabeth had now found an ally who, despite having Calvinist views, was strongly in favour of the English Prayer Book and retaining a hierarchy of bishops. He rigorously enforced conformity to the Church of England by encapsulating its main tenets in three **articles** of faith (1583) and any clergyman who disagreed with any of these articles was removed from his post. Those who continued to work 'underground' could face imprisonment or worse. In 1593, three Puritans – Henry Barrow, John Greenwood and John Penry – were hanged for their continued refusal to cease their dissident activities. During his prior interrogation, Greenwood had described Whitgift as, 'a monster, a miserable compound'. He did become more lenient in his last ten years as the Puritans lost most of their leaders but he remained a figure of hate for them.

Whitgift was a reformer as well as an enforcer. He speeded up the work of the church courts, ensured that bishops enforced the new **poor laws**, encouraged better **education** of the clergy and established the Whitgift Foundation to provide care for the elderly and education for the young. The foundation and three Whitgift schools still exist in Croydon today. Elizabeth, herself, greatly admired and trusted this hard-working defender of her Church and referred to him as her, 'little black husband' due to his dark complexion. She called for him as she lay dying in 1603 and asked him to provide her with spiritual comfort. Her last archbishop had undoubtedly been her favourite.

Wolsey, Thomas

(c. 1473–1530)

Statesman, cardinal and Lord Chancellor.

Wolsey came from famously humble origins. His father was supposedly a butcher, cattle-dealer and innkeeper from Ipswich but he soon recognised his son's intelligence and ensured a good **education**. At the mere age of eleven, he was sent to Oxford University where he earned his degree four years later. After ordaining as a priest in 1498, he worked as a chaplain to some important families including the governor of Calais, who introduced him to **Henry VII**. Henry employed him as his chaplain too (1507) and sent him on various diplomatic missions. He once ordered Wolsey to send a message to the Emperor Maximilian in Flanders. The round trip would normally take ten days so when Henry saw him three days later he started to scold him for being so slow but was astonished to see Maximilian's reply in his hand. Wolsey's reputation for energy and efficiency had begun.

After 1509, the new king, **Henry VIII**, showed little interest in the mundane tasks of running government but he quickly recognised Wolsey's ability to manage detail and allowed him a place on the Privy Council. Wolsey was initially against any foreign ventures but he was good at bending with the wind and supported Henry's enthusiasm for war with France. It was during this **First Anglo-French War** that Wolsey demonstrated great skill at organising and supplying an army on campaign.

Wolsey's rise now became meteoric – Bishop of Tournai (1513), Archbishop of York (1514), appointed a cardinal by the Pope (1515), Lord Chancellor (1515), Pope's papal legate (1518), Abbot of St Albans (1518), Bishop of Bath (1518), Bishop of Durham (1523). Only the incumbency of **William Warham** prevented him from acquiring the archdiocese of Canterbury but this mattered little because, as papal legate, Wolsey could outrank him. With these positions came enormous wealth. At one point, they were bringing in £35,000 per year (about £18 million in 2024); his disposable income was even greater than the king's. From 1515 to 1529, Wolsey ran the country but this is not to say that Henry was no longer in charge. He kept an eye on the broad picture but had complete confidence in Wolsey to master the details. It was left to Wolsey to decide how to implement a policy, which officials to appoint and what information could flow in and out of court.

With such responsibility, he also felt it necessary to impress. Red was the most expensive dye and, by law, only the most important people were allowed to display it. Wolsey not only proudly wore the crimson robes and cap of a cardinal but also dressed his multitude of servants in crimson velvet (the most expensive material). Wherever he went, his ushers would clear the way and demand bystanders make room for their lord. Amongst fifty acres of woodland near the Thames, he had the magnificent Hampton Court Palace built and entertained guests there with the most lavish banquets. This, he later renovated to include aspects of the latest **renaissance** architecture and he did the same to his London home, York Palace (later known as Whitehall). Such ostentation was bound to draw envious criticism from Henry's courtiers but, as long as he had Henry's confidence, Wolsey was untouchable.

Much of Wolsey's time was spent in conducting foreign affairs probably because this was also the king's main theatre of interest, and it was this aspect of his work that caused him the most trouble. This was partly due to the fact that he was a servant of the Pope as well as the king and partly because England was often sought after as a military ally and then, being a junior power, just as easily discarded. The two main rivals on the continent were King Francis I of France and the Charles V of the Holy Roman Empire and Wolsey was often negotiating alliances with either in order to promote England's and Henry's prestige and power.

The zenith of his achievements in this sphere came in 1518–20. In response to the Pope's call for a unified Christendom against the Turks, Wolsey organised the 1518 Treaty of London – a huge peace summit in which forty nations agreed to avoid war with each other. Two years later, he arranged the **Field of the Cloth**

of Gold – an immensely extravagant, two-week, peace summit between England and France. It seems quite possible that Wolsey genuinely was a pacifist who disliked the risks associated with war. More cynical, perhaps, is the view that he hoped that, by raising his international prestige, he would have more chance of becoming Pope. He was certainly disappointed to lose out in the papal election of 1521, despite Henry spending much on bribing the other cardinals.

In domestic affairs, Wolsey was equally hard-working. In his role as Lord Chancellor, he widened the remit of the **Star Chamber** and encouraged people to bring their cases to this court and so by-pass the common law courts. As a result, more wealthy defendants were prosecuted and the work in the common law courts was speeded up. He gave the Court of Requests a permanent place at York Palace, too, and encouraged it, at very cheap rates, to examine poor people's cases. Wolsey also used the law courts to try and stop the spread of **enclosures** although this had limited success.

In order to finance Henry's wars, Wolsey ordered a review of the country's wealth so that he could collect more taxes which were based on people's ability to pay. In order to finance the **Second Anglo-French War**, the wealthy found themselves subject to 'forced loans' (never repaid in full) and 'voluntary' gifts to the king, neither of which required parliamentary approval. In 1525, he tried to collect a new raft of taxes known as the Amicable Grant. Even the poor were affected as their employers had to lay many off in order to pay. There was widespread tax evasion as discontent spread across the country and Suffolk even experienced an armed uprising. Henry ordered a quick U-turn and Wolsey took the brunt of the blame – a humiliation that his growing number of enemies relished.

It was from a different quarter, however, that his downfall came about. From 1527, Henry ordered him to seek a solution to his 'Great Matter' – annulment of his marriage to **Catherine of Aragon** so that he could marry **Anne Boleyn**, who could supply him with the male heir he desperately needed. Wolsey made many eloquent appeals to the Pope to grant this annulment on the basis that Henry should never have been allowed to marry his brother's widow (as stated in *Leviticus* in the Bible). His efforts were futile though, as the Pope was a prisoner of Catherine's nephew, Charles V, who would never agree to an annulment. By 1529, Henry's patience was wearing thin and Wolsey's enemies, polarising around the Boleyn faction at court, persuaded him that Wolsey was actually working against him and with the Pope. This was not true but, previously, Wolsey had privately pleaded with the king not to seek the annulment.

His fall was as spectacular as his rise. In October, 1529, he was accused of treason and stripped of his titles. Wolsey begged for mercy and gave the king Hampton Court and York palaces (the latter, Henry gave to Anne). After Wolsey fell ill in December, Henry was placated and allowed him to retain the archdiocese of York. As he slowly progressed northwards, his enemies led one more attack and produced 'evidence' that he was in secret correspondence with Francis, Charles and the Pope, the latter he apparently asked to excommunicate Henry. An outraged king ordered Wolsey to be arrested and brought back to London. The shock, his ill-health and the journey combined to kill him at Leicester where he was buried at the abbey (the glorious tomb that he had constructed for himself in the crypt of St Paul's Cathedral is now the resting place of Lord Nelson).

Thomas Wolsey has largely received a negative press, partly because much of it was based on evidence written by his contemporaries, who loathed him. It is true that he over-taxed his wealthiest subjects but that was due to his master's military aims. He was guilty of self-aggrandisement, too, although he was partly a medieval man who believed that pomp and extravagance had to go hand in hand with power. He can also be accused of epitomising abuses within the Church – pluralism (holding more than one office at the same time), absenteeism (he never visited York, for example) and, despite being ordained, having a mistress who bore him two children. He was already unpopular with **Parliament** but such abuses only served to increase its determination to destroy the Church's power after it was summoned in 1529. It could also be argued that his failure to reform the monasteries contributed to their demise in the 1530s.

Wolsey was far more popular with the poor than the rich, however, and his ability and loyalty to the king cannot be questioned. He knew he was hated by those around the king who viewed him as a pompous upstart but he was safe as long as his loyalty was reciprocated. However, such a trait did not exist in Henry so, when he failed to achieve the impossible, his doom was assured. Wolsey had had more power than any other royal servant in the country's history and represented the crossover from old to new. He was the last churchman to wield great political power and yet he was also one of the 'new men' – a man of humble birth who earned his way to high office.

Wyatt's Rebellion

(1554)

An attempt to prevent **Mary I's marriage** to Philip of Spain.

In October 1553, Queen Mary announced her intention to marry Prince Philip of Spain. This caused much discomfort even amongst members of her Privy Council. The fear was that England could become another satellite state of the huge Spanish empire to be used in its wars against France. Even with restrictions placed on Philip's power, what if the couple had a child? Would

England then become a mere Spanish province, like the Netherlands? Religious motives behind the uprising cannot be discounted either although these were not proclaimed for fear of alienating **Catholic** sections of the **population**. The uprising's leaders certainly leaned towards **Protestant**ism, however.

By late November 1553, a plan had evolved which centred around a few ringleaders – the Duke of Suffolk (father of the imprisoned **Lady Jane Grey**), Sir **Peter Carew** (brother of the vice-admiral who had drowned on the *Mary Rose*), Sir James Croft (former Lord Deputy of **Ireland**) and Sir Thomas Wyatt (an important landowner in Kent). There was also the possible involvement of Sir Edward Courtenay, the Earl of Devon and last remaining direct descendant of Edward IV. The plan involved four coordinated uprisings that would converge on London, replace Mary with her younger sister, **Elizabeth**, and marry her to Courtenay. A French fleet would also help by preventing the arrival of any Spanish reinforcements. All of the leaders had supported Mary during **Northumberland**'s attempted coup earlier in the year but it was her determination to marry Philip that made them turn to Elizabeth.

The revolt, however, was hampered before it had even begun as news leaked to the Spanish ambassador who forewarned Mary. The conspirators quickly tried to bring the rebellion forward but both Suffolk, in the Midlands, and Croft, in the Welsh Marches, could not raise enough support in time and were captured. Meanwhile, Carew had to flee abroad after encountering similar problems in Devon, which were compounded by the fact that he had helped to brutally suppress the **Prayer Book Rebellion** there less than five years previously. Only in strongly Protestant Kent was there a serious uprising.

Wyatt was the son of Sir Thomas Wyatt (the Elder) – a diplomat and poet who, along with **Henry Howard**, was the first to write in the sonnet form. Wyatt (the Younger) had been raised a Catholic but seems to have become more secular in his views as he grew older. As a headstrong and impulsive youth, he had once been imprisoned for rampaging through London, with Howard, and smashing windows. Soon after, he had fought with much courage and distinction in the **Third Anglo-French War**. By 1554, he was a respected local landowner and member of **Parliament** for Kent and he soon managed to raise 3,000 men.

The **Third Duke of Norfolk** was sent to nip the trouble in the bud but, after several hundred of his own men deserted to the rebels, he had to withdraw to London. After taking Rochester and Dartford, Wyatt led his forces, now numbering 4,000, to Blackheath. Mary, meanwhile, bravely stood her ground and, at Guildhall, on 1 February, made an impassioned speech to the Londoners. She reminded them that she was her father's daughter, claimed that she was married to her country and denounced Wyatt as a traitor. It worked and, despite the majority being Protestant, they remained loyal and flocked to her side for the capital's defence. By the time Wyatt reached London Bridge he found the gate closed and the drawbridge destroyed. Skirting around the south he found the next bridge, at Kingston, also broken. This his men repaired so that they could approach the city from the west. After a brief skirmish in Hyde Park with royalist troops, they arrived at Ludgate where, again, the gates were locked. By now, many of Wyatt's men had deserted. With the remainder cornered and outnumbered in the narrow streets between the City and Westminster, Wyatt decided to surrender.

Mary showed a remarkable degree of leniency afterwards despite pressure for the opposite from her future father-in-law and Holy Roman Emperor, Charles V. Of the 3,000 rebels who surrendered only around a hundred were executed. Croft was pardoned as was later Carew. She sent Elizabeth to the **Tower** but no evidence could be found of her involvement and she was later released. No proof could be provided against Courtenay either so he was exiled to Italy. Suffolk, however, showed no remorse at his trial and was beheaded. Much less fair were the executions of his daughter and son-in-law who had taken no part but Mary saw them as potential figureheads for future trouble. Wyatt, himself, was eventually beheaded and quartered in April but, later, many were to regard him as a nationalist martyr who was just trying to protect his country from foreign domination. Perhaps, had Mary announced her **marriage** plans a year later, after her persecution of Protestants had begun, Wyatt may have encountered Londoners who were far more welcoming and the course of history would have been dramatically altered.

London Bridge from the south. The closure of this bridge was a fatal blow to Wyatt's Rebellion. Note the heads on spikes above the southern gatehouse. (*Artist: Robert Martin c. 1830. From an engraving by John Vischer, 1616. British Museum*)

Sources

activehistory.co.uk
adhs.co.uk
aqa.org,uk
aspectsofhistory.com
azquotes.com
battlefieldstrust.com
bbc.co.uk
biographi.ca
biography.com
bishopmike.com
bl.uk
bluffkingkal.wordpress.com
britainexpress.com
britain-magazine.com
britannica.com
britishbattles.com
britishheritage.com
britnumsoc.org
cambridge.org
capitalpunishmentuk.org
catholicworldreport.com
citymayors.com
clan-forbes.org
classical-music.com
cliffsnotes.com
cs.mgill.ca
ctstatelibrary.org
discovermagazine.com
dkfindout.com
douglashistory.co.uk
eh.net
elizabethan-era.co.uk
elizabethi.org
encyclopedia.com
encyclopediavirginia.org
english-heritage.org.uk
englishhistoryauthors.blogspot.com
englishhistory.net
englishmonarchs.co.uk
explorethearchive.com
famous-explorers.com
findagrave.com
gale.com
gcschools.net
greatestbritons.com
gresham.ac.uk
goconqr.com
henryviiithereign.co.uk
hertford.ox.ac.uk
hetwebsite.net
hevercastle.co.uk
historic-cornwall.org.uk
historicengland.org.uk
historic-uk.com
history.co.uk
history.com
historyextra.com
historyhit.com
historylearningsite.co.uk
history-magazine.com
historyofparliament.org
historyofparliamentonline.org
historyonthenet.com
historytoday.com
historywithhenry.com
historywithouthenry.com
hoddereducation.co.uk
hrp.org.uk
interestingliterature.com
internetshakespeare.uvic.ca
irishtimes.com
jesuit.org.uk

johnwhitgiftfoundation.org
jstor.org
legalhistorymiscellany.com
libbyjanecharleston.medium.com
link.springer.com
localhistories.org
lookandlearn.com
lumenlearning.com
luminarium.org
mainelli.org
mathshistory.st-andrews.ac.uk
medievalists.net
medium.com
museumoflondon.org.uk
marie-stuart.co.uk
matthew.co.uk
nationalarchives.gov.uk
newadvent.org
nih.gov
nms.ac.uk
nosweatshakespeare.com
npg.org.uk
ourmigrationstory.org.uk
ourpastimes.com
ourworldindata.org
ox.ac.uk
oxforddnb.com
parliament.uk
philippagregory.com
planbee.com
plato.stanford.edu
playshakespeare.com
poetryfoundation.org
publicdomainreview.org
readingmuseum.org.uk
rct.uk
reivers.info
rmg.co.uk
royal.uk
royalarmouries.org
rsc.org.uk
sayitstraight.co.uk
scholarship.richmond.edu
schoolshistory.org.uk
sellymanormuseum.org.uk
shakespeare-online.com
shakespeare.org.uk
sixwives.info
spartacus-educational.com
springer.com
stbees.org.uk
stjohnfisherchurch.com
studysmarter.co.uk
tandfonline.com
tastesofhistory.co.uk
tcd.ie
theanneboleynfiles.com
thecanadianencyclopedia.ca
thecollector.com
theconversation.com
thefreelancehistorywriter.com
theguardian.com
thehistoriansapprentice.com
thehistoryjar.com
thehistoryofengland.co.uk
thehistoryofparliament.wordpress.com
thehistorypress.co.uk
thehistoryvault.co.uk
thenational.scot
thetudorchronicles.wordpress.com
thetudorenthusiast.weebly.com
thetudorials.com
thetudortravelguide.com
thinkingfaith.org
thoughtco.com
timesoftudors.blogspot.com
townandcountrymag.com
townof1000trails.co.uk
tudordynasty.com
tudorhistory.org
tudornation.com
tudorplace.com.ar
tudorsociety.com
tudortimes.co.uk
under-these-restless-skies.blogspot.com
undiscoveredscotland.co.uk
uregina.ca
warsoftheroses.com

westminster-abbey.org
Who's who in Tudor England (CRN Routh)
wikipedia.org
wikisummaries.org
wikitree.com
worcestercathedral.co.uk
wordpress.miracosta
worldhistory.org